THE OFFICIAL ® GUIDE TO

The Money

Records

FIRST EDITION

JERRY OSBORNE

HOUSE OF COLLECTIBLES

THE BALLANTINE PUBLISHING GROUP • NEW YORK

Important Notice. All of the information, including valuations, in this book has been compiled from the most reliable sources, and every effort has been made to eliminate errors and questionable data. Nevertheless, the possibility of error, in a work of such immense scope, always exists. The publisher will not be held responsible for losses which may occur in the purchase, sale, or other transaction of items because of information contained herein. Readers who feel they have discovered errors are invited to *write* and inform us, so they may be corrected in subsequent editions. Those seeking further information on the topics covered in this book are advised to refer to the complete line of *Official Price Guides* published by the House of Collectibles.

CONTENTS

Acknowledgments v

Introduction 3

    Sorting Experimental Pressings 4

    Other Criteria for Inclusion 4

    How the Prices Are Determined 4

    Unsolved Musical Mysteries 5

    Tracks and Members 5

    Not All Photos Are Created Equal 5

    Record Grading and the Price Range 6

    Bootlegs and Counterfeits 6

    How You Can Help 7

    What to Expect When Selling Your Records to a Dealer 7

Concluding Thoughts 7

Sample Listing 8

Top 1,000 Most Valuable Records Ranked By Price 9

Top 1,000 Most Valuable Records Alphabetically By Artist 193

    Late Addition Photos 256

    More Late Addition Photos 310

Qualifying Titles That Didn't Make the Cut 311

Valuable Experimental Pressings 315

Directory of Buyers and Sellers 321

ACKNOWLEDGMENTS

The single most important element in updating and revising any price and reference guide is input from as many experts as possible. This is especially true when compiling a first edition listing of the most valuable records in the land.

Some of the people listed below reviewed the first and second draft pages of the book, allowing us to present the most accurate pricing possible. Others we thank for such contributions as sending photocopies of labels and helping with assorted production tasks. Especially deserving in this regard is our faithful research and editorial associate of over 10 years, Judith M. Ihnken Ebner.

Special appreciation is extended to Lou Silvani and Times Square Records for providing the records and location for the photo that graces the cover of this edition.

Also, a few names are included whose publications, catalogs, essays and articles provided additional reference material for this project.

To all we extend a colossal *thank you!*

Here then is an alphabetical listing of the contributors to this edition:

Robert Alaniz	Jeff Kreiter
James Amato	Jim Lavell
Steven W. Banas	Joe Lindsay
Dale Blount	Dale Little
Chris G. Bowman	René Lucas
Susan Kim Bowman	Ron McElroy
Denise M. Brown	Craig Moerer
Pat Brown	Mike Murray
Frank Castillo	Charlie Neu
Bob Clere	Linda Ann Osborne
Perry Cox	Roger Osborne
Robert J. Dalley	George Parrish
Judy Davis	Bruno Pause
Charles Dawson	Victor Pearlin
Devon Dawson	Jef Michael Piehler
William Deibert	Chester Prudhomme
John Diesso	Robert Ritter
Judith M. Ihnken Ebner	Bob Ruggieri
Erik Engelke	Ernie Ruggieri
Frank Fazio	Joel Scherzer
Arnie Ganem	Phil Schwartz
Jean-Marc Gargiulo	Michael Sharritt
Jim Gibbons	Val Shivley
Ray Gora	Lou Silvani
Dennis Hartman	Ed Smith
Todd Hutchinson	Tom Tourville
Al Janoulis	Joel Whitburn
Vernon Joynson	Danny A. White
Tony Kolodziej	Don Wilson
Tracy Kolodziej	Gordon Wrubel

The
Money
Records

INTRODUCTION

What exactly are the money records?

In the early 1960s, few singles sold for more than one dollar, with bargain bins galore filled with unplayed oldies priced from 10¢ to 30¢. Then, money records were mostly rhythm and blues obscurities from the early '50s that sold for four or five dollars.

Inconceivable as it sounds today, one could then buy original, unplayed Sun, Flip and Meteor label 45s and 78s at three-for-a-buck, and Sun albums for $1.50 each – direct from the Sun warehouse. Many of these discs now rank high in our Top 1,000 list.

Then, the retail price for most long-play albums ranged from three to four dollars. A handful of out-of-print LPs from the early-to-mid-'50s sold for five to 10 dollars, qualifying them as the money record albums at the time.

A decade later – about the time we were preparing our very first record price guide – the money record singles were ones valued at $25 and up.

In the mid-'70s, the singles at the top of the most valuable list carried prices of around $500. One rarity in this group was the commercial release of *My Bonnie/The Saints,* by Tony Sheridan & the Beat Brothers.

Now, 20 years later, this disc is still among the most valuable; however, the near-mint price has skyrocketed to $15,000 – a thirty-fold increase.

Singles were still the dominant format then, as evidenced by an auction held by yours truly in October 1975. Among the items in that sale was the (then) only known, still-sealed copy of *The Beatles ... Yesterday and Today.* The winning bid for this pristine monaural copy was $456 – at the time the most paid for any record album, to our knowledge.

The current price for this album is $3,000.

With what most rate as fairly common records now selling for a few hundred dollars, a case can be made that today's money records are those valued at $500 or more. If so, every one of the top 1,000 is clearly a money record, since item number 1,000 on our list carries a price of $650.

With each new year, prices will shift for many of the money records; however, one thing will not change: once a money record always a money record. The items on this list will always be among the world's most valuable ones.

More often than not, it is the money records that offer the best investment opportunities. Higher prices initially notwithstanding, most of the singles and albums seeing the greatest percentage of gain are the money records.

One example of this trend is very fresh in this writer's mind. A single with picture sleeve sold in a set sale in 1996 for $14,000 – approximately $4,000 above the value in the then-current Osborne price guide.

Did the buyer overpay? I think not. Consider the following:

One month later, the seller approached the buyer offering $20,000 to buy the same item back. Despite the temptation of a $7,000 profit in just four weeks, the new owner refused, opting to keep the disc. He later declined a $22,000 offer.

A case can be made that practically any record on this Top 1,000 list is a sound investment, even if purchased at the high end of the price range indicated here. To those willing and able to pay such prices, it is surprising how many of these rarities can be found for sale. During the 12 months before press time, at least one-third of our Top 1,000 have been on the market at one time or another.

SORTING EXPERIMENTAL PRESSINGS

It is our intention that the listings in the Top 1,000 be either commercial or promotional releases. We did not want to immerse the main list with countless experimental and test pressings, even though, pricewise, many easily qualify.

We decided that records made specifically on an experimental basis, intended to sample or tinker with a specific process, deserved a separate section. Most notably in this category are those made during the mid-to-late '70s picture disc craze.

Still, there are several production oddities on the main list, the exact purpose of which we have yet to determine. If a plant employee makes, as a souvenir perhaps, one colored vinyl copy of a disc that is being manufactured with black vinyl, that item can hardly be termed experimental, meaning such eccentric pressings are included in the Top 1,000.

OTHER CRITERIA FOR INCLUSION

Though our review team's primary area of concern is North American issues, our conceptual discussions of this book entertained the idea of including records from anywhere in the world.

Knowing that, collectors and dealers in two or three countries submitted a number of qualifying titles. However, those were the *only* countries represented. To include just those random overseas selections would have left us far short of our "world's" most valuable records goal.

Accepting that adequate worldwide reviewers could not be recruited by our publication date, we narrowed the scope to North American releases only – U.S. and Canadian.

We have also opted to omit fringe recordings that are not really *releases,* such as acetates, test pressings, film props, and discs containing radio spots, radio shows, or commercials. This takes nothing away from the thousands of discs of this ilk that exist – many possessing money record values.

HOW THE PRICES ARE DETERMINED

Beginning six months before our production deadline, we ran quarter-page ads in every issue of *Discoveries* magazine, inviting anyone interested in the project to join our review team. From assorted geographic regions, many of the top people in the field came forth to share their expertise.

Once we narrowed the main list down to approximately 1,200, records, we sent a first-draft to each reviewer, soliciting price updates, additions and corrections.

From those pages we revised the file, making the final cuts to trim down to 1,000 items. A second draft then went to senior reviewers to scrutinize.

As with the values shown in any price guide, the estimates shown here are just that: estimates. That they have been viewed and reviewed by such a knowledgeable board of experts does, however, ensure a considerable degree of accuracy.

UNSOLVED MUSICAL MYSTERIES

A number of pesky questions still remain, and they are appropriately indicated in the text with question marks.

The two most common musical mysteries are:

1. Missing flip sides for singles. If, after exhausting all of our reference sources, we still don't know a flip side title, a question mark appears in its place.

2. Year of release not yet known. For some releases, for which an exact year of issue isn't yet known, we have at least been able to provide the correct decade. Still, the years of release for a few perplexing listings are such mysteries that our only solution is to put question marks in their year column. This is especially common when it is not yet known whether something came out in 1959 or '60. With these we can't even indicate either decade with confidence.

If you have any information that allows us to replace any of these question marks with something more useful, such as factual data, we would be grateful to receive it.

TRACKS AND MEMBERS

When known, we list the exact track listings for EPs and LPs. In most cases, the information comes directly from a copy of the record. If, as sometimes happens, the cover and record label are not in agreement, we have let the label be our guide.

Likewise, when known, individual group members are identified. Though those named were certainly members of the group in question, the possibility exists that not all of them appear on *every* recording in this edition.

For groups with numerous money record entries, such as the Orioles or Castelles, we can't guarantee that their personnel didn't shift somewhat from one recording session to another.

NOT ALL PHOTOS ARE CREATED EQUAL

Most of the photos and photocopies of record labels and covers reproduced in this edition were supplied by members of our review team. Some have never appeared in any previous publication.

With our various contributors having diverse degrees of photographic and photocopying equipment and skills, the printed results are, of course, equally as varied.

In an effort to illustrate as many of the Top 1,000 as possible, we accepted a few of substandard quality. In such cases, what you see here is in fact the best reproduction available to us at the time.

📷 This camera symbol next to a Top 1,000 listing indicates that item is pictured, either in the black-and-white pages, in the eight-page color section, or on the front cover.

The black-and-white illustrations may not be on or near the pages where their corresponding listings appear; however, the photos are in the exact same order by value.

RECORD GRADING AND THE PRICE RANGE

The pricing shown in this edition represents values for NEAR-MINT condition copies. For ranking purposes, only the high end of the price range is used, meaning an item that books for $800 to $1,000 is listed for $1,000.

Within the supplemental notes and other information provided for each recording is the complete near-mint condition price range.

A standardized system of record grading, used and endorsed by buyers and sellers worldwide is as follows:

MINT: A *mint* item must be absolutely perfect. Nothing less can be honestly described as mint. Even brand new purchases can easily be flawed in some manner and not qualify as mint.

To allow for tiny blemishes, the highest grade used in our publications is *near-mint.* An absolutely pristine mint, or still sealed, item may carry a slight premium above the near-mint range shown in this guide.

VERY GOOD: Records in *very good* condition should have a minimum of visual or audible imperfections, which should not detract much from your enjoyment of owning them. This grade is halfway between good and near-mint.

For *very good* condition, figure about 40% to 60% of the near-mint price range.

GOOD: Practically speaking, the grade of *good* means that the item is good enough to fill a gap in your collection until a better copy becomes available. Good condition merchandise will show definite signs of wear and tear, probably evidencing that no protective care was given the item. Even so, records in good condition should play all the way through without skipping.

For *good* condition, figure about 10% to 20% of the near-mint price range.

BOOTLEGS AND COUNTERFEITS

Bootleg and counterfeit records are not intentionally priced in this guide, and we trust that none slipped past our review team.

For the record, a bootleg recording is one illegally manufactured, usually containing material not previously available in a legitimate form. Often, with the serious collector in mind, a boot will offer previously-issued tracks that have achieved some degree of value or scarcity. If the material is easily available, legally, then there would be no gain for the bootlegger.

The counterfeit record is one manufactured as close as possible in sound and appearance to the source disc from which it was inspired. Not all counterfeits were created to fool an unsuspecting buyer into thinking he or she is buying an authentic issue, but some were. Many are designated in some way, such as a slight marking or variance, so as not to allow them to be confused with originals. Such a fake record primarily exists to fill a gap in the collector's file.

Very few of us own an original RCA Victor copy of *The Caine Mutiny,* however many are content to have one of the boots – until the real thing comes along.

Since most of the money records have been counterfeited, it is always a good idea to consult with an expert when there is any doubt. The trained eye can usually spot a fake.

A recommended reference source to assist with counterfeit identification is Lou Silvani's *Collecting Rare Records – Do You Have Originals?* This book is available from Times Square Records. For more information, see their page in this edition's Buyers-Sellers Directory.

HOW YOU CAN HELP

We can never get too much input or have too many reviewers. We wholeheartedly encourage you to submit anything and everything you feel would be useful in building a better record guide. The quantity of data is not a factor — no amount is too little or too much.

Send all additions, corrections, comments and suggestions to:

Jerry Osborne
Box 255
Port Townsend, WA 98368
Fax: (360) 385-6572
e-mail: jpo@mail.com
web site: www.jerryosborne.com

WHAT TO EXPECT WHEN SELLING RECORDS TO A DEALER

As most know, there is a noteworthy difference between the values reported in any price guide and what one can expect a dealer to pay who's buying records for resale.

Unless a dealer is buying for personal use (without thoughts of resale), he or she is simply not in a position to pay full price. Dealers work on a percentage basis, largely determined by the total dollar investment, quality, and quantity of material offered as well as the general financial condition and inventory of the dealer at the time.

Another very important consideration is the length of time it will take the dealer to recover at least the amount of the original investment. The greater the demand for the stock and the better the condition, the quicker the return and therefore the greater the percentage that can be paid.

Most dealers will pay from 25% to 50% of *guide* prices. And that's assuming they are planning to resell at guide prices. If they traditionally sell below-guide, that will be reflected in what they can pay for stock.

If you have records to sell, it would be wise to check with several shops. In doing so you will begin to get a good idea of the value of your collection to a dealer.

Also, consult the Directory of Buyers and Sellers in this edition for the names of many dealers who not only might be interested in buying, but from whom many collectible records are available for purchase.

Whether you wish to sell the records you have, or add out-of-print discs to your collection, consider *DISCoveries* magazine. Each issue is packed with ads, features, discographies, collecting tips and more. For more information, contact: Trader Publications, PO Box 1050, Dubuque, Iowa 52003. A sample issue is available upon request.

CONCLUDING THOUGHTS

All the price guides and reporting of previous sales in the world will not change the fundamental fact that true value is nothing more than what one person is willing to accept and what another is prepared to pay. Actual value is based on scarcity and demand. It has always been that way and always will.

A recording — or anything for that matter — can be 50 or 100 years old, but if no one wants it, the actual value will certainly be minimal.

Just because something is old does not necessarily make it valuable. Someone has to want it!

On the other hand, a recent release, perhaps just weeks old, can have exceptionally high value if it has already become scarce and is by an artist whose following has created a demand.

A record does not have to be old to be valuable.

The purpose of this book is to report as accurately as possible the most recent prices asked and paid for records within the area of its coverage. There are two key words here that deserve emphasis: **Guide** and **Report**.

This book is only a guide. There always have been and always will be instances of records selling well above and below the prices shown within these pages.

Remember too, the true spirit of record collecting lies far less in its investment potential than in the profit found within the gooves of those recordings.

SAMPLE LISTING

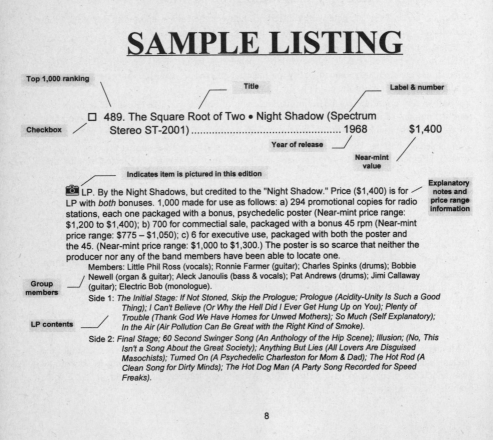

Top 1,000 ranking

Title

Label & number

Checkbox

☐ 489. The Square Root of Two • Night Shadow (Spectrum Stereo ST-2001) 1968 $1,400

Year of release

Near-mint value

Indicates item is pictured in this edition

Explanatory notes and price range information

📷 LP. By the Night Shadows, but credited to the "Night Shadow." Price ($1,400) is for LP with *both* bonuses. 1,000 made for use as follows: a) 294 promotional copies for radio stations, each one packaged with a bonus, psychedelic poster (Near-mint price range: $1,200 to $1,400); b) 700 for commercial sale, packaged with a bonus 45 rpm (Near-mint price range: $775 – $1,050); c) 6 for executive use, packaged with both the poster and the 45. (Near-mint price range: $1,000 to $1,300.) The poster is so scarce that neither the producer nor any of the band members have been able to locate one.

Group members

Members: Little Phil Ross (vocals); Ronnie Farmer (guitar); Charles Spinks (drums); Bobbie Newell (organ & guitar); Aleck Janoulis (bass & vocals); Pat Andrews (drums); Jimi Callaway (guitar); Electric Bob (monologue).

LP contents

Side 1: *The Initial Stage: If Not Stoned, Skip the Prologue; Prologue (Acidity-Unity Is Such a Good Thing); I Can't Believe (Or Why the Hell Did I Ever Get Hung Up on You); Plenty of Trouble (Thank God We Have Homes for Unwed Mothers); So Much (Self Explanatory); In the Air (Air Pollution Can Be Great with the Right Kind of Smoke).*

Side 2: *Final Stage; 60 Second Swinger Song (An Anthology of the Hip Scene); Illusion; (No, This Isn't a Song About the Great Society); Anything But Lies (All Lovers Are Disguised Masochists); Turned On (A Psychedelic Charleston for Mom & Dad); The Hot Rod (A Clean Song for Dirty Minds); The Hot Dog Man (A Party Song Recorded for Speed Freaks).*

TOP 1,000 MOST VALUABLE RECORDS
RANKED BY PRICE

☐ 1. Yesterday and Today • Beatles (Capitol ST-2553)............................. 1966 $25,000

📷 Stereo LP. The words "New Improved Full Dimensional Stereo" appear in a gray banner at the top of the front cover. Cover pictures group wearing butcher smocks and garnished with cuts of meat and pieces of toy dolls. Commonly referred to as the "Butcher Cover." After distributing copies to the media, Capitol sent recipients a recall letter, requesting they return their albums. Aware they had a valuable collectible in their possession, many kept them. Capitol pasted new covers – picturing the Beatles and a trunk – over the Butcher Covers. Original issues, without any modifications, are known as "First State" copies. Cover shows title as *Yesterday And Today*, whereas label reads: *"Yesterday" ... And Today*. Price range of $24,000 to $25,000 is for copies still in original plastic shrink wrap, primarily copies from the Alan Livingston collection. As of press time, three still-sealed "Livingston" copies have each sold for exactly $25,000.

The following essay, prepared by Mitch McGeary and Perry Cox, provides additional background on the "Livingston" Butcher copies:

Though there have been many great discoveries of Beatles records, the most significant is a 1986 unearthing of 24 first state Butcher Cover albums – all still sealed!

Before this event, there were only two sealed stereo, and perhaps six monaural, copies known to exist.

It happened on Thanksgiving weekend at a Los Angeles Beatlefest convention. Peter Livingston, son of former Capitol Records president Alan Livingston (who signed the Beatles to Capitol), walked in carrying four first state Butcher Cover albums – two stereos and two monos.

Since, to most there, Peter's story seemed too good to be true, he finally offered to call his father at his home in Beverly Hills, to verify the source and authenticity of these albums.

One collector present, Beatles price guide author Perry Cox, did not doubt Livingston's story and quickly forked over $2,500 for one of the stereo copies – even before Peter had a chance to call his father.

As word quickly spread of that first sale, crowds gathered around the younger Livingston. Within minutes both mono copies sold for $1,000 each. Peter decided to keep the remaining stereo copy. However, stored at his fathers house, were 18 more monos and three stereos.

One week later, the asking prices jumped to $2,000 for monos and a then-amazing $10,000 for the stereos.

We later learned that, in 1966, at the time of the recall, Alan Livingston took home a full box of the albums – approximately four stereo and 20 monaural copies. Every copy was sealed, and nearly all were in near-perfect condition, with flawless corners, pristine shrink-wrap, and pure white covers.

Stored in a closet under ideal conditions, Alan's stash did not see the light of day for 20 years, when he gave them to Peter.

For authentication, Peter had several notarized letters from his famous father that accompanied each LP sold.

In the months ahead, under pressure and relentless demand from collectors, Peter slowly sold the remaining mono copies. By then the price had risen to $3,000. During the next few years, as word of the "Livingston Copies" spread, the price for monos climbed to $5000.

None of the stereo copies traded until the early '90s when the finest of the sealed ones sold to a Washington collector for $20,000 cash – then the highest price paid for any record. This particular copy, still rated as the best stereo Butcher in existence, resold in 1994 for $25,000.

Around the same time, word that Peter had become seriously ill prompted one collector to contact Alan, to inquire about Peter. Alan informed him that Peter had recently passed away. Later, this same collector asked about the remaining Butcher Covers. Alan said he had two stereo copies left, and offered to sell both. One of these was the opened copy (with seam split), which sold for $2,500, the other a sealed one that went for $7,500. The buyer later resold the sealed one for $25,000.

Alan and Peter's widow each kept a mono copy, which, to our knowledge, they still have.

1.

Capitol RECORDS

EXECUTIVE AND GENERAL OFFICES

CAPITOL RECORDS DISTRIBUTING CORP.

HOLLYWOOD AND VINE • HOLLYWOOD, CALIFORNIA 90028 • TELEPHONE (213) 462-6252

June 14, 1966

Dear Reviewer:

In the past few days, you may have received an advance promotional copy of The Beatles' new album, "The Beatles Yesterday And Today," in accordance with the following statement from Alan W. Livingston, President, Capitol Records, Inc., the original album cover is being discarded and a new jacket is being prepared:

"The original cover, created in England, was intended as 'pop art' satire. However, a sampling of public opinion in the United States indicates that the cover design is subject to misinterpretation. For this reason, and to avoid any possible controversy or undeserved harm to The Beatles' image or reputation, Capitol has chosen to withdraw the LP and substitute a more generally acceptable design."

All consumer copies of The Beatles' album will be packaged in the new cover, which will be available within the next week to 10 days. As soon as they are, we will forward you a copy. In the meantime, we would appreciate your disregarding the promotional album and, if at all possible, returning it, C.O.D., to Capitol Records, 1750 N. Vine Street, Hollywood, Calif. 90028.

Thank you in advance for your cooperation.

Sincerely,

Ron Tepper
Manager
Press & Information Services

RT:s

ALAN W. LIVINGSTON

January 15, 1987

To Whom It May Concern:

I was President and Chief Executive Officer of Capitol Records from 1960 to 1968, and personally signed the Beatles to the Capitol label.

When "The Beatles Yesterday And Today" album was recalled, I kept some copies for my personal collection, and have given a few to my son, Peter Livingston, to dispose of as he wishes.

Please be assured that any album that Peter shows you is from my private collection, and is in its original shrink wrapped condition. You should, therefore, feel absolutely confident of its authenticity. I am confident that these albums are among the few, if not the only, genuine remaining editions, in mint condition, and hope that you will treat and respect them accordingly.

Sincerely,

AWL:jah

State of: California
County of: Los Angeles

On January 15, 1987, before me, the undersigned, a Notary Public personally appeared Alan Livingston, known to me to be the person whose name subscribed to the within instrument and acknowledged to me that he executed the same.

OFFICIAL SEAL
NOTARY PUBLIC - CALIFORNIA
LOS ANGELES COUNTY

Notary Public

Very few of the Livingston copies have changed hands in the '90s, since most collectors consider these the ultimate Beatles record collectible and want to keep them. These LPs are considered pedigree copies, significant for their incredible condition as well as their source and his history and position at Capitol.

The last sale known to us of a mono copy came in 1996 when one sold for $7,000. Compare this to the first sealed Butcher cover album offered for sale, in 1975, when Mitch McGeary paid $456. (See the "Introduction" for more on this sale.)

A 98% mint sealed mono Butcher – not from the Livingston batch – turned up in August 1997 and sold for $5,500.

As of press time, in early 1998, roughly 10 years later, the market value for all 24 of the Butchers from the Livingston find would likely sell for $200,000!.

(For on-line information on rare Beatles records, including *Yesterday ... And Today*, visit Mitch McGeary's web site: http://www.rarebeatles.com.)
Variations of this release in the Top 1,000 can be found at Numbers 21; 175; 495; 967.
Members: John Lennon; Paul McCartney, George Harrison; Ringo Starr.
Side 1: Drive My Car; I'm Only Sleeping; Nowhere Man; Dr. Robert; Yesterday; Act Naturally.
Side 2: *And Your Bird Can Sing; If I Needed Someone; We Can Work It Out; What Goes On; Day Tripper.*

☐ 2. Good Luck Charm/Anything That's Part of You • Elvis Presley
(RCA Victor 37-7992) 1962 $24,000

📷 Compact 33 Single with picture sleeve. Fifth of five mono singles in this somewhat experimental and ultimately failed series. Compact 33s are seven-inch discs with a quarter-inch, LP-size, hole. Price reflects an actual sale and subsequent offers of what is thus far the only known copy. Picture sleeve alone is $8,000 to $12,000. Price range for both: $16,000 to $24,000.

☐ 3. Elvis' Christmas Album • Elvis Presley (RCA Victor LOC-1035) 1957 $18,000

📷 Monaural LP. Red vinyl. Black label, "Long Play" at bottom. Value is based on the one known sale (Nov. 1997). Stories have circulated of a second copy but we have yet to conrfim its existence. (Just hours before press time – and too late to affect its price and ranking in this edition – the current owner of this LP reports he has turned down a $25,000 offer.) Near-mint price range: $15,000 to $18,000.
Side 1: *Santa Claus Is Back in Town; White Christmas; Here Comes Santa Claus; I'll Be Home for Christmas; Blue Christmas; Santa Bring My Baby Back (To Me).*
Side 2: *Oh Little Town of Bethlehem; Silent Night; (There'll Be) Peace in the Valley (For Me); I Believe; Take My Hand, Precious Lord; It Is No Secret (What God Can Do).*

☐ 4. Can't Help Falling in Love/Rock-A-Hula Baby • Elvis Presley (With
Jordanaires) (RCA Victor 37-7968) 1961 $16,000

📷 Compact 33 single with picture sleeve. Fourth of five mono singles in this somewhat experimental and ultimately failed series. Compact 33s are seven-inch discs with a quarter-inch, LP-size, hole. Picture sleeve alone is $5,000 to $8,000. Price range for both: $10,000 to $16,000.

☐ 5. My Bonnie/The Saints • Tony Sheridan & Beat Brothers
(Decca 31382) 1962 $15,000

📷 45 rpm. Price is for commercial issues only. Has Decca's black label with silver print and a multi-color stripe across the center of the label. Selection number is printed in the color bar area or black area of the label. Black and silver Decca labels without the other colors are counterfeits. This is the first appearance of the Beatles – then billed as the Beat Brothers – on a record in the U.S. Since Decca quickly lost interest in promoting this release, commercial discs are much rarer than promos. Near-mint price range: $12,000 to $15,000.
A variation of this release can be found at No. 201 on the Top 1,000.
Members: John Lennon; Paul McCartney, George Harrison; Pete Best.

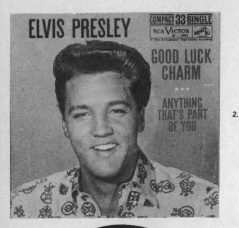

2.

4.

5.

☐ 6. The Freewheelin' Bob Dylan • Bob Dylan (Columbia CL-1986)............ 1963 $15,000

📷 Monaural LP – Commercial or promotional. Has *Let Me Die in My Footsteps, Talkin' John Birch Society Blues, Gamblin' Willie's Dead Man's Hand* and *Rocks and Gravel* (which may also be shown as *Solid Gravel*). We have seen promotional (white label – monaural) copies that do have the correct titles on the labels; however, we know of no copies that have them on the cover. We have yet to see commercial (red label) copies that list the four controversial tracks. Therefore, we suggest verification of the tracks by listening to the LP, rather than accepting the printed information. Some copies of the disc with the rare tracks even have reissue labels. Identification numbers of this press are XLP-58717-1A and XLP-58718-1A.) Near-mint price range: $10,000 to $15,000.
range: $10,000 to $15,000.
Side: 1: *Blowin' in the Wind; Rocks and Gravel; Let Me Die in My Footsteps; Down the Highway; Bob Dylan's Blues; A Hard Rain's A-Gonna Fall.*
Side 2: *Don't Think Twice, It's All Right; Gamblin' Willie's Dead Man's Hand; Oxford Town; Corrina Corrina; Talkin' John Birch Society Blues; Honey, Just Allow Me One More; Chance; I Shall Be Free.*

☐ 7. Introducing the Beatles • Beatles (Vee-Jay SR-1062)......................... 1964 $15,000

📷 Stereo LP. With *Love Me Do* and *P.S. I Love You*. Back cover lists contents. Oval style label logo. Near-mint price range: $10,000 to $15,000.
Variations of this release in the Top 1,000 can be found at Numbers 27; 65; 93; 169; 202; 218; 543; 559; 760; 789.
Members: John Lennon; Paul McCartney, George Harrison; Ringo Starr.
Side 1: *I Saw Her Standing There; Misery; Anna; Chains; Boys; Love Me Do.*
Side 2: *P.S. I Love You; Baby It's You; Do You Want to Know a Secret; A Taste of Honey; There's a Place; Twist and Shout.*

☐ 8. Anna/Ask Me Why • Beatles (Vee-Jay 8)... 1964 $15,000

📷 45 rpm. Promotional issue only. White and blue label. Promotes the Vee-Jay EP *Souvenir of Their Visit to America*. Used as part of a failed attempt to lower EP prices to that of singles (cover reads: "an EP that is selling like a single ... at single record prices"). Near-mint price range: $10,000 to $15,000.
Members: John Lennon; Paul McCartney, George Harrison; Ringo Starr.

☐ 9. River Deep – Mountain High • Ike & Tina Turner (Philles 4011)........... 1966 $15,000

📷 Monaural LP. Covers for a U.S. pressing on Philles are not known to exist. British pressings [London/Philles SHU-8298] do exist with covers. Near-mint price range: $10,000 to $15,000.
Side 1: *River Deep – Mountain High; I Idolize You; A Love Like Yours (Don't Come Knocking Every Day); A Fool in Love; Make 'Em Wait; Hold on Baby.*
Side 2: *Save the Last Dance for Me; Oh Baby (Things Ain't What They Used to Be); Every Day I Have to Cry; Such a Fool for You; It's Gonna Work Out Fine; You're So Fine.*

☐ 10. Elvis/Jaye P. Morgan • Elvis Presley / Jaye P. Morgan (RCA Victor EPA-992 and EPA-689)... 1956 $12,000

📷 Two-EP, promotional sampler, though the discs were standard commercial pressings. This package was made to encourage retail stores to establish themselves in the music/record business. The idea of the Elvis/Jaye P. Morgan coupling was both to emphasize that the Elvis EP (EPA-992) sold 1,000 times better than the Jaye P. Morgan EP (EPA-689) and that record and phonograph sales were on the rise. Cover: Double pocket jacket. Front: Titles are not printed anywhere. RCA Victor logo at upper right, numbers (for both EPs) at lower right. Color Elvis photo. Back: Color slick from Jaye P. Morgan EP. Both inside panels have the promotional pitch; however, at least two variations exist. One is imprinted for "Mr. L.F. Koranda, Associated Merchandising Corp, 1440 Broadway, New York, New York." and another for "Mr. Walter H. Awe, Mutual Buying Syndicate, 11 West 42st Street, New York 36, New York." Other than the representative's imprint, all text is identical. Counterfeits exist but can easily be identified by their poor quality appearance. Since the discs were standard pressings, at least 95% of the value here is represented by the custom EP cover. Near-mint price range: $8,000 to $12,000.

COLUMBIA

THE FREEWHEELIN' BOB DYLAN

RADIO STATION COPY - NOT FOR RESALE

1. DON'T THINK TWICE, IT'S ALL RIGHT 3:37
2. GAMBLIN' WILLIE'S DEAD MAN'S HAND 4:11

CL 1986   Side 2
           (x"Lp" 58718)

3. OXFORD TOWN 1:47
4. CORRINA CORRINA 2:42
5. TALKIN' JOHN BIRCH BLUES 3:45
6. HONEY, JUST ALLOW ME ONE MORE CHANCE 1:57
7. I SHALL BE FREE 4:46

'COLUMBIA' MARCAS REG. PRINTED IN U.S.A.

6.

STEREO
Vee Jay

INTRODUCING THE BEATLES
THE BEATLES

VJLP 1062
63-3402   Side 1
Long Playing   Microgroove

1. I SAW HER STANDING THERE
(McCartney-Lennon)
2. MISERY
(McCartney-Lennon)
3. ANNA
(Alexander)
4. CHAINS
(Goffin-King)
5. BOYS
(Dixon-Farrell)
6. LOVE ME DO
(McCartney-Lennon)

7.

ANNA
(Alexander)

THE BEATLES

Spec. DJ No. 8

45   45

VJ VEE-JAY RECORDS   **VJ** VEE-JAY RECORDS

PROMOTIONAL COPY   PROMOTIONAL COPY

45   45

63-3165 - Vocal

8.

IKE & TINA TURNER
"RIVER DEEP - MOUNTAIN HIGH"

1. RIVER DEEP - MOUNTAIN HIGH
(Mother Bertha Mus.-Trio Music-BMI)
2. I IDOLIZE YOU (Saturn Mus.c-BMI)
(Ike Turner)

SIDE 1
LP-4011
33⅓ RPM

3. A LOVE LIKE YOURS
(Don't Come Knocking Every Day)
(Jobete Mus.c Co. Inc.-BMI)
(Eddie Holland, Lamont Dozier & Brian Holland)
4. A FOOL IN LOVE (Saturn Music-BMI)
(Ike Turner)
5. MAKE 'EM WAIT (Placid Music-BMI)
(Ike Turner)
6. HOLD ON BABY
(Mother Bertha Music-Trio Music-BMI)
(P. Spector, J. Barry & E. Greenwich)

9.

JAYE P. MORGAN

ELVIS

10.

RCA VICTOR COMPACT SINGLE 33

"NEW ORTHOPHONIC" HIGH FIDELITY

37-7908
Elvis Presley
Music Inc., BMI
M2WI-2965
2:06

Marie's the Name
HIS LATEST FLAME
(Doc Pomus-Mort Shuman)

ELVIS PRESLEY

TMGO REGISTERED • MARCA(s) REGISTRADA(s) • RADIO CORPORATION OF AMERICA—MADE IN U.S.A.

11.

Elvis Presley EP
Side 1: *Rip It Up; Love Me.*
Side 2: *When My Blue Moon Turns to Gold Again; Paralyzed.*
Jaye P. Morgan EP
Side 1: *You Turned the Tables on Me; I Fall in Love with You Everyday.*
Side 2: *I Guess I'll Have to Change My Plan; Can't We Be Friends.*

☐ 11. (Marie's the Name) His Latest Flame/Little Sister • Elvis Presley
(RCA Victor 37-7908) 1961 $12,000

📷 Compact 33 single with picture sleeve. Third of five mono singles in this somewhat experimental and ultimately failed series. Compact 33s are seven-inch discs with a quarter-inch, LP-size, hole. Picture sleeve alone is $4,000 to $6,000. Price range for both: $8,000 to $12,000.

☐ 12. A Hard Day's Night • Beatles (United Artists UAS-6366) 1964 $12,000

Stereo LP. Pink vinyl. Original black label with silver print. Purpose of this disc is not yet known. Near-mint price range: $10,000 to $12,000.
Variations of this release in the Top 1,000 can be found at Numbers 206; 724.
Members: John Lennon; Paul McCartney; George Harrison; Ringo Starr.
Side 1: *A Hard Day's Night; Tell Me Why; I Should Have Known Better; I'm Happy Just to Dance with You; And I Love Her (Instrumental).*
Side 2: *I Should Have Known Better; And I Love Her (Vocal); Ringo's Theme; Can't Buy Me Love; A Hard Day's Night.*

☐ 13. I Can't Believe/Lonesome Baby • Hornets & Orchestra (States 127) . 1953 $10,000

📷 45 rpm. Red vinyl. The price range here reflects both one known sale of, and one offer which was declined for the red vinyl pressing. Near-mint price range: $7,500 to $10,000.
Members: James "Sonny" Long; Johnny Moore; Ben Iverson; Gus Miller.
Variations of this release in the Top 1,000 can be found at Numbers 33; 252.

☐ 14. Estelle/Promise Love • Belltones (Grand 102) 1954 $10,000

45 rpm. Red vinyl. One known copy. Near-mint price range: $7,500 to $10,000.
A variation of this release in the Top 1,000 can be found at Number 75.
Members: Fred Walker; Estelle Natson; Irvin Natson; Harry Paschall; Donald Burnett.

☐ 15. The Sensational Harptones • Harptones (Bruce 201) 1954 $10,000

📷 EP. Approximately two known. Near-mint price range: $7,500 to $10,000.
Members: Willie Winfield; Nicky Clark; Bill Brown; Jimmy Beckum; William James.
Side 1: *A Sunday Kind of Love; I Almost Lost My Mind.*
Side 2: *Forever Mine; Ou Wee Baby.*

☐ 16. Their Greatest Hits • Midnighters (Federal 295-90) 1954 $10,000

10-inch LP. Near-mint price range: $7,500 to $10,000.
Side 1: *Get It; Moonrise; Sexy Ways; She's the One.*
Side 2: *Crazy Loving; Annie Had a Baby; Annie's Aunt Fannie; Work with Me Annie.*
Members: Hank Ballard; Henry Booth; Charles Sutton; Sonny Woods; Lawson Smith.
A variation of this release in the Top 1,000 can be found at Number 639.

☐ 17. Caine Mutiny • Various Artists (RCA Victor 1013) 1954 $10,000

📷 Monaural LP. Soundtrack. Recalled immediately after being made, with very few copies making their way into circulation. Has original music and dialogue from the film, including the entire court martial scene. Near-mint price range: $7,500 to $10,000.

As to why this LP is so scarce, several explanations and suppositions have surfaced over the years; however, one of the most believable comes directly from playwright Herman Wouk. In a personal letter, first published in one of our 1981 guides, Wouk writes:

"Here's the approximate story on [RCA Victor] LOC-1013 seen from a memory perspective of a quarter of a century:

13.

15.

15.

17.

16

My play *The Caine Mutiny Courtmartial* made a great hit on Broadway while the film was still being completed. Columbia Pictures hastily rushed out this record to cash in on the play's success. I never saw the record or its slipcover, but I was warned that they intended to feature the "courtmartial scene" from the picture soundtrack; the shoddiest possible piggyback ride on my play.

I am a man of peace, but this annoyed me. I telephoned the brutal, crafty, able head of Columbia Pictures, Harry Cohn, and warned him that the issue of this record meant that Columbia Pictures would never again have an opportunity to bid on one of my novels for filming. Cohn looked into the matter, called me back, and said in his tough gravelly voice, "I've got you beat on the legalities, but I've listened to the record and it's no goddamn good, so I'm yanking it."

Thus was born your collector's item.

Cordially,
Herman Wouk (signed)

Side 1: *The Bright Young Men; I Can't Believe That You're in Love with Me; The Junkyard Navy; The Tow; Yellowstain Blues; Mental Disorders; Heavy Weather Ahead; The Typhoon.*
Side 2: Side 2: *The Court Martial* [original film dialogue of the court martial scene and the final celebration]

☐ **18. Billy Ward and His Dominoes • Billy Ward & Dominoes (Federal 295-94)** 1954 **$10,000**

📷 10-inch LP. Near-mint price range: $7,500 to $10,000.
Members: Billy Ward; Clyde McPhatter; Charlie White; William Lamont; Bill Brown; Dave McNeil; James Van Loan.
Side 1: *Sixty Minute Man; Do Something for Me;Have Mercy Baby; Don't Leave Me This Way.*
Side 2: *These Foolish Things Remind Me of You; When the Swallows Come Back to Capistrano; The Bells; I'd Be Satisfied.*

☐ **19. Cool Off Baby/Almost • Billy Barrix (Shreveport)** 1957 **$10,000**

45 rpm. Selection number not yet known. Near-mint price range: $7,500 to $10,000.
Variations of this release in the Top 1,000 can be found at Numbers 60; 636.

☐ **20. Hear the Beatles Tell All • Beatles (Vee-Jay PRO-202)** 1964 **$10,000**

📷 Monaural LP. Promotional issue. White label with blue print. Label reads "Promotional" on left and "Not For Sale" on right. Contains interviews with the group. Only two known copies verified. Near-mint price range: $8,000 to $10,000.
Members: John Lennon; Paul McCartney, George Harrison; Ringo Starr.

☐ **21. Yesterday and Today • Beatles (Capitol ST-2553)** 1966 **$10,000**

Stereo LP. The words "New Improved Full Dimensional Stereo" appear in a gray banner at the top of the front cover. Cover pictures group wearing butcher smocks and garnished with cuts of meat and pieces of toy dolls. Commonly referred to as the "Butcher Cover." After distributing copies to the media, Capitol sent recipients a recall letter, requesting they return their albums. Aware they had a valuable collectible in their possession, many kept them. Capitol pasted new covers – picturing the Beatles and a trunk – over the Butcher Covers. Original issues, without any modifications, are known as "First State" copies. Cover shows title as *Yesterday And Today*, whereas label reads: *"Yesterday" ... And Today*. Price range of $7,500 to $10,000 is for copies that have been opened.
Variations of this release in the Top 1,000 can be found at Numbers 1; 175; 495; 967.
Members: John Lennon; Paul McCartney, George Harrison; Ringo Starr.
Side 1: *Drive My Car; I'm Only Sleeping; Nowhere Man; Dr. Robert; Yesterday; Act Naturally.*
Side 2: *And Your Bird Can Sing; If I Needed Someone; We Can Work It Out; What Goes On; Day Tripper.*

☐ **22. Do I Love You/Sweeter As the Days Go By • Frank Wilson (Soul 35019)** 1966 **$10,000**

45 rpm. Near-mint price range: $7,500 to $10,000.

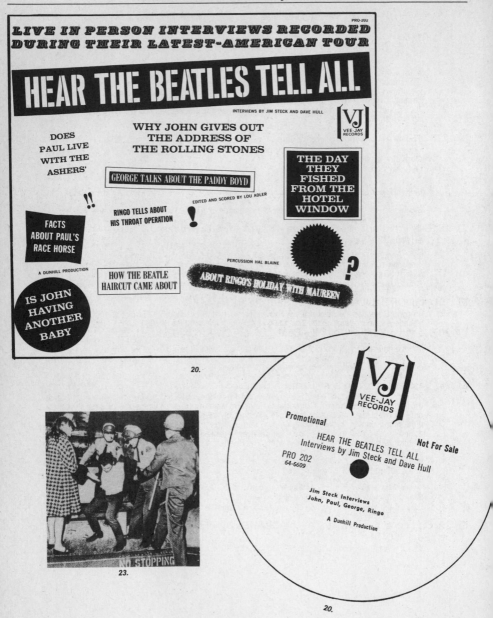

PRO-202

LIVE IN PERSON INTERVIEWS RECORDED
DURING THEIR LATEST-AMERICAN TOUR

HEAR THE BEATLES TELL ALL

INTERVIEWS BY JIM STECK AND DAVE HULL

[VJ] VEE-JAY RECORDS

DOES PAUL LIVE WITH THE ASHERS'

WHY JOHN GIVES OUT THE ADDRESS OF THE ROLLING STONES

THE DAY THEY FISHED FROM THE HOTEL WINDOW

GEORGE TALKS ABOUT THE PADDY BOYD

EDITED AND SCORED BY LOU ADLER

!!

FACTS ABOUT PAUL'S RACE HORSE

RINGO TELLS ABOUT HIS THROAT OPERATION

!

A DUNHILL PRODUCTION

HOW THE BEATLE HAIRCUT CAME ABOUT

PERCUSSION HAL BLAINE

ABOUT RINGO'S HOLIDAY WITH MAUREEN

?

IS JOHN HAVING ANOTHER BABY

20.

NO STOPPING

23.

[VJ] VEE-JAY RECORDS

Promotional   Not For Sale

HEAR THE BEATLES TELL ALL
Interviews by Jim Steck and Dave Hull

PRO 202
64-6609

Jim Steck Interviews
John, Paul, George, Ringo

A Dunhill Production

20.

18

☐ 23. Street Fighting Man/No Expectations • Rolling Stones
  (London 909) 1968 $10,000

📷 Picture sleeve. Approximately a dozen copies are known to exist. Compared to the sleeve, the value of the 45 is negligible. Near-mint price range: $5,000 to $10,000.
Members: Mick Jagger; Keith Richards; Bill Wyman; Charlie Watts.

☐ 24. The Beatles and Frank Ifield on Stage • Beatles & Frank Ifield
  (Vee-Jay LPS-1085) 1964 $9,000

📷 Stereo LP. Front cover has a painted portrait of the Beatles. Issued for a very short time to replace British statesman with Beatles' wig cover. Label variations may affect value. Near-mint price range: $8,000 to $9,000.
A variation of this release in the Top 1,000 can be found at Number 170.
Members: John Lennon; Paul McCartney, George Harrison; Ringo Starr.

Side 1: *Please Please Me* (Beatles)*; Anytime* (Frank Ifield); *Lovesick Blues* (Frank Ifield); *I'm Smiling Now* (Frank Ifield); *Nobody's Darlin' But Mine* (Frank Ifield); *From Me to You* (Beatles).
Side 2: *I Remember You* (Frank Ifield); *Ask Me Why* (Beatles); *Thank You Girl* (Beatles); *The Wayward Wind* (Frank Ifield); *Unchained Melody* (Frank Ifield); *I Listen to My Heart* (Frank Ifield).

☐ 25. Ask Me Why • Beatles (Vee-Jay VJEP 1-903) 1964 $8,500

📷 EP and promotional title sleeve. Same number as Vee-Jay EP *Souvenir of Their Visit to America*. Issued with a limited number of copies of the promotional EP. Came with the large print *Ask Me Why* version of the promotional EP. Used as part of a failed attempt to lower EP prices to that of singles (cover reads: "an EP that is selling like a single ... at single record prices"). Approximately 95% of the value is for the paper sleeve. Near-mint price range: $7,500 to $8,500.
Members: John Lennon; Paul McCartney, George Harrison; Ringo Starr.
Side 1: *Misery; Taste of Honey.*
Side 2: *Ask Me Why; Anna.*

☐ 26. Stormy Weather/Sleepy Cowboy • Five Sharps (Jubilee 5104).......... 1952 $8,000

📷 78 rpm. Since no original 45s have been verified, it is safe to assume none were made. Bootleg 45s are common, but can be identified by their lighter shade of blue paper than was used by Jubilee in the '50s. They also have thicker horizontal lines than originals. Beware of Jubilee 5478, a 1964 issue that, although credited to the Five Sharps, is a completely different recording of *Stormy Weather*. Near-mint price range: $7,000 to $8,000.
Members: Ron Cuffey; Clarence Bassett; Mickey Owens; Robert Ward; Tom Ducket.

☐ 27. Introducing the Beatles • Beatles (Vee-Jay SR-1062)....................... 1963 $8,000

Stereo LP. Black label with circular colorband and oval logo. With *Love Me Do* and *P.S. I Love You* (on later issues these tracks are replaced by *Ask Me Why* and *Please Please Me*). Back cover pictures 25 other Vee-Jay albums (known as "Ad back" cover). Has "Printed In U.S.A." at lower left of front cover (counterfeits lack this print). Front cover also has "Stereophonic" in gray print across a white banner at top. Price range for cover only: $4,000 to $5,000. Cover and disc: $7,000 to $8,000.
Variations of this release in the Top 1,000 can be found at Numbers 7; 65; 93; 169; 202; 218; 543; 559; 760; 789.
Members: John Lennon; Paul McCartney, George Harrison; Ringo Starr.
Side 1: *I Saw Her Standing There; Misery; Anna; Chains; Boys; Love Me Do.*
Side 2: *P.S. I Love You; Baby It's You; Do You Want to Know a Secret; A Taste of Honey; There's a Place; Twist and Shout.*

☐ 28. I'll Be Back/Blank • Elvis Presley (With the Jordanaires)
  (RCA Victor 4-834-115) 1966 $8,000

📷 Single-sided 45 rpm. White label. Reads "For Special Academy Consideration Only." Made specifically for submission to the Academy of Motion Picture Arts and Sciences. Near-mint price range: $6,000 to $8,000.

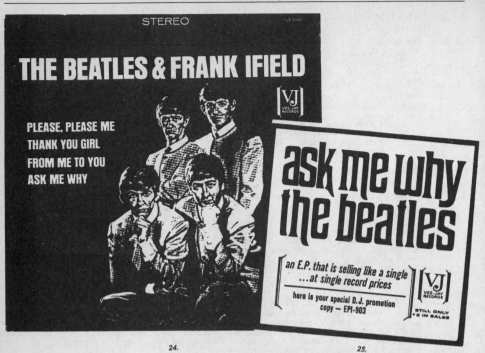

STEREO

THE BEATLES & FRANK IFIELD

PLEASE, PLEASE ME
THANK YOU GIRL
FROM ME TO YOU
ASK ME WHY

VJ VEE-JAY RECORDS

ask me why the beatles

[an E.P. that is selling like a single
...at single record prices]

here is your special D.J. promotion
copy — EPI-903

VJ VEE-JAY RECORDS

STILL ONLY
#2 IN SALES

24.   25.

ASK ME WHY
(McCartney-Lennon)
ANNA
(Alexander)
THE BEATLES

45   45

VJ VEE-JAY RECORDS
PROMOTIONAL COPY

VJ VEE-JAY RECORDS
PROMOTIONAL COPY

45   45

VJEP 1-903

64-3916 — Side 2
Concertone Songs - ASCAP
Hollis Music - BMI

25.

jubilee

5104
(JB-1-116)

Pub: Mills Music
ASCAP

STORMY WEATHER
(Ted Koehler - Harold Arlen)
The Five Sharps

JUBILEE RECORDS CO., NEW YORK, N.Y.

26.

20

☐ 29. Such a Night/Never Ending • Elvis Presley (With Jordanaires)
(RCA Victor 47-8400) 1964   **$7,500**

📷 45 rpm. White label, promotional issue only. Price is based on the one documented sale (1996) of the one known copy. Surprisingly, there are no counterfeits *yet* of this disc. Near-mint price range: $7,000 to $7,500.

☐ 30. Phil Spector Spectacular • Various Artists (Philles 100) 1960s   **$7,500**

LP. Promotional issue only. With letter signed by Phil Spector. Near-mint price range: $5,000 to $7,500.

☐ 31. Bells/You'd Better Run • Bonnie & Little Boys Blue (Nikko 611) 1958   **$7,000**

📷 45 rpm. One known copy. Near-mint price range: $5,000 to $7,000.

☐ 32. Gotta Let You Go/Boogie in the Park • Joe Hill Louis (It's the
Phillips 9001) 1950   **$6,000**

📷 78 rpm. Near-mint price range: $4,000 to $6,000.

☐ 33. I Can't Believe/Lonesome Baby • Hornets & Orchestra (States 127) . 1953   **$6,000**

45 rpm. Black vinyl. Near-mint price range: $4,000 to $6,000.
Members: James "Sonny" Long; Johnny Moore; Ben Iverson; Gus Miller.
Variations of this release in the Top 1,000 can be found at Numbers 13; 252.

☐ 34. Crying in the Chapel/Don't You Think I Ought to Know • Orioles
(Jubilee 5122) 1953   **$6,000**

45 rpm. Red vinyl. Near-mint price range: $4,000 to $6,000.
Members: Sonny Til; Alex Sharp; George Nelson; John Reed; Tom Gaither.

☐ 35. Can't Help Loving That Girl of Mine/I'm Coming Home • Hide-A-Ways
(Ronni 1000) 1954   **$6,000**

📷 45 rpm. Seven known copies. Near-mint price range: $5,000 to $6,000.

☐ 36. Aurelia/White Cliffs of Dover • Pelicans (Parrot 793) 1954   **$6,000**

📷 45 rpm. Red vinyl. (Since 45 was unavailable, the 78 is pictured.) Near-mint price range: $5,000 to $6,000.
A variation of this release in the Top 1,000 can be found at Number 81.

☐ 37. Gatemouth Moore Sings Blues • Gatemouth Moore (King 684) 1960   **$6,000**

LP. Near-mint price range: $4,000 to $6,000.
Side 1: *I'm a Fool to Care; Highway 61 Blues; Gambling Woman; Don't You Know I Love You Baby; Teasin' Brown; Hey Mr. Gatemouth; You're My Specialty Baby; Gotta Walk.*
Side 2: *Something I'm Gonna Be; I Ain't Mad at You Pretty Baby; Did You Ever Try to Cry; Satifsying Papa; Graveyard Disposition; Willa Mae; After Loving a Woman; You're Having Hard Luck.*

☐ 38. Loving You/G.I. Blues • Elvis Presley (RCA Victor LPM-1515) 1960s   **$6,000**

📷 Monaural LP. Picture disc. Photo imbedded in vinyl on both sides is the front cover art of a *G.I. Blues* LP. A one-of-a-kind test pressing discovered by Ed Bonja (Elvis' Tour Manager and photographer in the '70s), while cleaning out Col. Parker's office. When asked about it, Parker described this demo as once being considered for a promotion, but he rejected it because he did not like the way the disc cut off Elvis' name and the movie title. Reportedly from the '60s, though an accurate release date has yet to be confirmed. Since we have yet to confirm its purpose, we cannot categorize this disc as experimental.

Plays five songs from the standard *Loving You* album (*Loving You; Got a Lot o' Livin' to Do; Lonesome Cowboy; Blueberry Hill;* and *True Love*). The remaining five tracks are assorted instrumentals, by as of yet unidentified artists that have nothing whatsoever to do with Elvis. Believed to have been produced in the early to mid-'60s, this is likely the very first RCA Victor picture disc. Near-mint price range: $4,000 to $6,000.

☐ 39. Phil Spector Spectacular • Various Artists (Philles 100) 1960s   **$6,000**

LP. Promotional issue only. Without the letter from Phil Spector. Near-mint price range: $4,000 to $6,000.

RCA VICTOR
ELVIS PRESLEY
with the Jordanaires

4-834-115
(TPKM-5313)
Glady's Music
Inc. - ASCAP
2:02

45
RPM

FOR SPECIAL ACADEMY CONSIDERATION ONLY
I'LL BE BACK
(Sid Wayne-Ben Weisman)
(From the MGM Motion Picture Release "Spinout")
Produced by Joe Pasternak - A Euterpe Production)
(From the RCA Victor Album
LPM-3702 "Spinout")

28.

RCA VICTOR

47-8400
(L2WW-0105)
Raleigh Music
Pub. Co.
BMI
2:57

45
RPM
NOT FOR
SALE

SUCH A NIGHT
(Lincoln Chase)
ELVIS PRESLEY
With The Jordanaires

29.

NIKKO

Suna Music Corp.
Time 2:32

611
45-N-61 A

BELLS
(B. Johnson - Birch)
BONNIE AND
LITTLE BOYS BLUE

31.

IT'S THE
pHILLIps
"HOTTEST THING IN THE COUNTRY"

One Man Band   Vocal—Louis

(Louis - Phillips)
JOE HILL LOUIS
GOTTA LET YOU GO

9001

32.

☐ 40. All Tomorrow's Parties/I'll Be Your Mirror • Velvet Underground & Nico
(Verve 10427).. 1966   **$5,200**
   Picture sleeve and blue label 45 rpm. Produced by Andy Warhol. Sleeve may be a
   promotional issue only. Near-mint price range for sleeve alone: $4,800 to $5,000. Record
   and sleeve: $4,900 to $5,200. For promo label disc, deduct $150 to $250
   Members: Lou Reed; John Cale; Sterling Morrison; Maureen Tucker; Doug Yule; Nico (Christa Paffgen).

☐ 41. Living in the Mountains/I'll Be Thinking of You Little Gal • Gene Autry
(QRS 1044) 1929   **$5,000**

   📷 78 rpm. Near-mint price range: $3,000 to $5,000.

☐ 42. I'll Be Thinking of You Little Gal/Whisper Your Mother's Name • Gene Autry
(Supertone 9705).. 1929   **$5,000**
   78 rpm. Near-mint price range: $3,000 to $5,000.

☐ 43. Hell Hound on My Trail/From Four Until Late • Robert Johnson
(Vocalion 03623) 1937   **$5,000**

   📷 78 rpm. Near-mint price range: $3,000 to $5,000.

☐ 44. My Reverie/Let's Say a Prayer • Larks (Apollo 1184)........................ 1951   **$5,000**

   📷 45 rpm. Orange vinyl. Near-mint price range: $3,000 to $5,000.
   Members: Eugene Mumford; Allen Bunn; Raymond "Pee-Wee" Barnes; Thurmon Ruth; Dave McNeil; Hadie Rowe.

☐ 45. I'll Be Home Again/Amazon Beauty • Hollywood Arist-O-Kats (With Red
Callender Sextette) (Recorded In Hollywood 406) 1953   **$5,000**

   📷 45 rpm. Near-mint price range: $4,000 to $5,000.

☐ 46. Baby It's You/Bounce • Spaniels (Vee-Jay 101)................................. 1953   **$5,000**
   45 rpm. Red vinyl. Near-mint price range: $4,000 to $5,000.
   Members: James "Pookie" Hudson; Jerry Gregory; Ernest Warren; Willie Jackson; Opal Courtney.

☐ 47. About to Lose My Mind/Which One Do I Love • Big Boy Spires & His Trio
(With John Lee Henley) (Chance 1137) 1953   **$5,000**
   45 rpm. Red vinyl. Near-mint price range: $4,000 to $5,000.

☐ 48. Come Back, Come Back/I May Be Wrong • Emperors with Rhythm
(Haven 511).. 1954   **$5,000**

   📷 45 rpm. Red vinyl. Near-mint price range: $4,000 to $5,000.
   A variation of this release in the Top 1,000 can be found at Number 187.

☐ 49. What'll You Do Next/There Is Love in You • Prisonaires ("Confined to
Tennessee State Prison Nashville, Tennessee") (Sun 207)................. 1954   **$5,000**
   45 rpm. Near-mint price range: $4,000 to $5,000.
   Members: Johnny Bragg; John Drew; Marcell Andess; William Stewart.

☐ 50. My Lost Love/Love My Baby • Re-Vels Quartet (Atlas 1035) 1954   **$5,000**
   45 rpm. Near-mint price range: $4,000 to $5,000.

☐ 51. Doll Face/Ooh, I Feel So Good • Vibranaires (Chariot 103) 1954   **$5,000**
   45 rpm. Near-mint price range: $4,000 to $5,000.
   Members: Bobby Thomas; Roosevelt McDuffie; Mike Robinson; Herb Cole; Jimmy Roache.
   A variation of this release in the Top 1,000 can be found at Number 83.

☐ 52. Tell the World/Blues at Three • Dells / Count Morris (Vee-Jay 134)... 1955   **$5,000**
   45 rpm. Red vinyl. Near-mint price range: $4,000 to $5,000.
   Members: Johnny Funches; Mike McGill; Marvin Junior; Vern Allison; Johnny Carter.

☐ 53. It's Almost Christmas/Look What I've Found • Dippers Quintet (With Van
Perry's Combo) (Flayr 500) 1955   **$5,000**

   📷 45 rpm. Two known copies. Near-mint price range: $4,000 to $5,000.

☐ 54. All I Want/Shake-a-Link • Five Chances (Blue Lake 115).................... 1955   **$5,000**

   📷 45 rpm. Red vinyl. Near-mint price range: $4,000 to $5,000.
   Members: Johnny Jones; John Austell; Darnell Austell; Reggie Smith; Howard Pitman; Harold Jones.
   A variation of this release in the Top 1,000 can be found at Number 281.

35.

36.

41.

43.

24

☐ 55. Carolyn/Oh Baby • Five Kids (Maxwell 101) 1955 $5,000

📷 45 rpm. Approximately four known copies. Near-mint price range: $4,000 to $5,000.

☐ 56. I Really Don't Want to Know/Get with It • Flamingos (Parrot 811) 1955 $5,000

45 rpm. Black vinyl. Reads "The Bronzville Record Mfg. Co." at bottom. Counterfeits may show name as "Bronxville." Near-mint price range: $4,000 to $5,000.
Members: Sollie McElroy; John Carter; Zeke Carey; Jake Carey; Paul Wilson; Nate Nelson.

☐ 57. I Had to Let You Go/Rockin' 'n Rollin' with Santa • Hepsters
(Ronel 107) 1955 $5,000

📷 45 rpm. Red vinyl. Two copies known. Near-mint price range: $4,000 to $5,000.

☐ 58. If Only You Were Mine/There Will Come a Time • Five Scalders
(Drummond 3000) 1956 $5,000

45 rpm. Near-mint price range: $4,000 to $5,000.
Members: Mack Rice; Johnny Mayfield; Sol Tilman; Gerald Young; James Bryant.

☐ 59. The Most Talked-About New Personality in the Last Ten Years of Recorded
Music • Elvis Presley (RCA Victor EPB-1254) 1956 $5,000

📷 Two-EPs in a single pocket paper sleeve. White paper sleeve has green print and a green-and-white Elvis photo on the front. Promotional issue only. Contains all 12 tracks from his first LP and EPs: LPM-1254; EPB-1254; EPA-747. Includes a copy of *Dee-Jay Digest*, a newsletter for radio announcers, used within the sleeve to separate the two discs. Counterfeits exist. Two EPs: $1,000 to $2,000. Cover: $2,500 to $3,000. Digest: $25 to $75. Price range for set: $3,500 to $5,000.

Side 1: *Blue Suede Shoes; I'm Counting on You; I Got a Woman.*
Side 2: *One-Sided Love Affair; I Love You Because; Just Because.*
Side 3: *Tutti Frutti; Tryin' to Get to You; I'm Gonna Sit Right Down and Cry (Over You).*
Side 4: *I'll Never Let You Go (Little "Darlin'); Blue Moon; Money Honey.*

☐ 60. Cool Off Baby/Almost • Billy Barrix (Chess 1662) 1957 $5,000

45 rpm. Near-mint price range: $3,000 to $5,000.
Variations of this release in the Top 1,000 can be found at Numbers 19; 636.

☐ 61. I Love You/Trains, Cars, Boats • Climbers (With Orchestra)
(J&S 1658) 1957 $5,000

📷 45 rpm. Near-mint price range: $3,000 to $5,000.
Member: Joe Rivers.

☐ 62. Goodbye Darling/Rock Lilly Rock • Corsairs (Hy-Tone 110) 1958 $5,000

📷 45 rpm. Near-mint price range: $4,000 to $5,000.

☐ 63. That's My Girl/Reality • De Jan & Elgins (Lessie 0099) 1960 $5,000

📷 45 rpm. One copy known. Near-mint price range: $4,000 to $5,000.

☐ 64. I'm Gonna Try to Live My Life All Over/So Long My Darling • Fabulous
Flames (With Original Sunglows) (Harlem 114) 1960 $5,000

📷 45 rpm. Near-mint price range: $4,000 to $5,000.

☐ 65. Introducing the Beatles • Beatles (Vee-Jay SR-1062) 1964 $5,000

📷 Stereo LP. Black label with circular colorband and brackets logo. With *Please Please Me* and *Ask Me Why*. Back cover lists song titles in two large columns. Five cover variations exist of the stereo issue. Near-mint price range: $2,500 to $5,000.
Variations of this release in the Top 1,000 can be found at Numbers 7; 27; 93; 169; 202; 218; 543; 559; 760; 789.
Members: John Lennon; Paul McCartney, George Harrison; Ringo Starr.
Side 1: *I Saw Her Standing There; Misery; Anna; Chains; Boys; Ask Me Why.*
Side 2: *Please Please Me; Baby It's You; Do You Want to Know a Secret; A Taste of Honey; There's a Place; Twist and Shout.*

☐ 66. I Won't Be Coming Back/? • Jay Dee Bryant (Shrine 108) 1966 $5,000

45 rpm. Near-mint price range: $3,000 to $5,000.

44.

45.

48.

53.

☐ 67. Elvis: Aloha from Hawaii Via Satellite • Elvis Presley (RCA
Victor VPSX-6089) 1973 $5,000

📷 Two quadraphonic LPs. Reddish-orange label. Cover: Has a "Chicken of the Sea Sneak
Preview" sticker applied to front, on the shrink wrap. Because these LPs were shrink
wrapped first, the QuadraDisc sticker (on front) and Saturn-shaped contents sticker (on
back) are also on the shrink instead of the actual cover. These copies were distributed within
the Van Camps, or Chicken of the Sea, organization. Promotional issue only. Front has die-
cut (5 ½" diameter) hole which allows inner sleeve to show. Double pocket cover. Includes
an insert card: Pictures Elvis at left, a can of Chicken of the Sea tuna at upper right, and
programming schedule at lower right. Printed on just one side. ($100 to $150) Shrink
stickers: Chicken of the Sea, multi-color (red, yellow, green, black, and white) sticker ($700
to $800); Saturn-shaped contents sticker (black print on gold stock); QuadraDisc sticker
(black, white, and gold). Cover alone: $2,000 to $4,000. Cover with shrink wrap and three
stickers still properly attached: $2,500 to $5,000.

(Disc 1) Side 1: *Introduction: Also Sprach Zarathustra; See See Rider; Burning Love; Something;
    You Gave Me a Mountain; Steamroller Blues.*
(Disc 1) Side 2: *My Way; Love Me; Johnny B. Goode; It's Over; Blue Suede Shoes; I'm So
    Lonesome I Could Cry; I Can't Stop Loving You; Hound Dog.*
(Disc 2) Side 3: *What Now My Love; Fever; Welcome to My World; Suspicious Minds;
    Introductions By Elvis.*
(Disc 2) Side 4: *I'll Remember You; Medley: Long Tall Sally/Whole Lot-ta Shakin' Goin' On; An
    American Trilogy; A Big Hunk O' Love; Can't Help Falling in Love.*
A variation of this release in the Top 1,000 can be found at Number 742.

☐ 68. Elvis Presley • Elvis Presley (RCA Victor SPD-23)............................ 1956 $4,500

📷 Triple-EP set, with cover and insert. Given as a bonus to buyers of a $47.95 Victrola.
Includes six-page brochure titled "How to Use and Enjoy Your RCA Victor Elvis Presley
Autograph, Automatic 45 Victrola Portable Phonograph." Three-EPs: $1,200 to $1,600.
Cover: $2,200 to $2,800. Brochure: $75 to $100. Price range for set: $3,500 to $4,500.
Side 1: *Blue Suede Shoes; I'm Counting on You.*
Side 2: *I Got a Woman; One Sided Love Affair.*
Side 3: *I'm Gonna Sit Right Down and Cry (Over You); I'll Never Let You Go.*
Side 4: *Tutti Frutti; Tryin' to Get to You.*
Side 5: *Don't Be Cruel; I Want You, I Need You, I Love You.*
Side 6: *Hound Dog; My Baby Left Me.*
A variation of this release in the Top 1,000 can be found at Number 191.

☐ 69. Rollin' and Tumblin' (Part 1)/ Rollin' and Tumblin' (Part 2) • Baby Face Leroy
Trio (Parkway 501) 1950 $4,000

📷 78 rpm. Near-mint price range: $2,000 to $4,000.
Session: Muddy Waters; Little Walter.

☐ 70. When I Look at You/Young Girls, Young Girls • Encores
(Checker 760).. 1952 $4,000
45 rpm. Near-mint price range: $3,000 to $4,000.

☐ 71. Red Sails in the Sunset/Be Anything But Be Mine • Five Keys
(Aladdin 3127) 1952 $4,000

📷 45 rpm. Near-mint price range: $3,000 to $4,000.
Members: Rudy West; Ripley Ingram; Maryland Pierce; Dickie Smith; Bernie West.

☐ 72. Stolen Love/In My Lonely Room • Larks (Apollo 1190) 1952 $4,000
45 rpm. Orange vinyl. Near-mint price range: $3,000 to $4,000.
Members: Eugene Mumford; Allen Bunn; Raymond "Pee-Wee" Barnes; Thurmon Ruth; Dave McNeil; Hadie Rowe.
A variation of this release in the Top 1,000 can be found at Number 236.

☐ 73. The Stars Will Remember/Come Back My Love • Buccaneers
(Rama 21)... 1953 $4,000

📷 45 rpm. Near-mint price range: $3,000 to $4,000.
Members: Ernest Smith; Julius Robinson; Richard Gregory; Sam Johnson; Don Marshall.

BLUE LAKE

55-129
B.M.I.

Lake Pub.

ALL I WANT
(Five Chances)
FIVE CHANCES
BL-115
The Bronzville Record Mfg. Co., Chicago

54.

MAXWELL

45 R.P.M.

Jalo Music
Company (BMI)

RECORD NO.
101 A

CAROLYN
(Crowell-Mace-Thomas)
THE FIVE KIDS

55.

Ronel
RECORDS

Adams Vee &
Abbott
BMI
Time 2:42

45-107
(1210

I HAD TO LET YOU GO
(Estelle Young)
THE HEPSTERS
306 S. WABASH AVE. CHICAGO 4. ILL.

57.

the most talked-about new personality
in the last ten years of recorded music

12 great new sides from his new albums!!!
LPM 1254; EPB 1254; EPA 747

ELVIS PRESLEY   RCA VICTOR

59.

28

☐ 74. Good Luck Darling/You Could Be My Love • 5 Crowns (Old
Town 790).. 1953 $4,000

📷 45 rpm. Red vinyl. Near-mint price range: $3,000 to $4,000.
Members: Wilbur Paul; Nicky Clark; John Clark; Jim "Papa" Clark; Dock Green.

☐ 75. Estelle/Promise Love • Belltones (Grand 102) 1954 $4,000

45 rpm. Black vinyl. Blue or yellow label. Near-mint price range: $3,000 to $4,000.
A variation of this release in the Top 1,000 can be found at Number 14.
Members: Fred Walker; Estelle Natson; Irvin Natson; Harry Paschall; Donald Burnett.

☐ 76. Take Everything But You/Cool Whailin Papa • Eddie Carter Quartette
(Grand 107) 1954 $4,000

45 rpm. Reissued crediting the Carter Rays. Near-mint price range: $3,000 to $4,000.

☐ 77. Tony, My Darling/In the Rain • Charmers (With Rhythm Acc.)
(Central 1006)... 1954 $4,000

📷 45 rpm. Near-mint price range: $3,000 to $4,000.
Member: Vicki Burgess; Alfred Todman; George Daniels; James Cook.

☐ 78. Embraceable You/Pa-Pa-Ya Baby • Jumping Jacks (Bruce 115)....... 1954 $4,000

45 rpm. Near-mint price range: $3,000 to $4,000.

☐ 79. 219 Train/My Gal • Moonglows (Chance 1161)................... 1954 $4,000

45 rpm. White and black label. Near-mint price range: $3,000 to $4,000.
Members: Harvey Fuqua; Bobby Lester; Alex Graves; Prentiss Barnes; Buddy Johnson.

☐ 80. Annie Kicked the Bucket/Believe • Nu-Tones (Hollywood Star 798) .. 1954 $4,000

📷 45 rpm. One copy known. Same number used twice and released a year apart. Near-
mint price range: $3,000 to $4,000.

☐ 81. Aurelia/White Cliffs of Dover • Pelicans (Parrot 793)........... 1954 $4,000

45 rpm. Black vinyl. Near-mint price range: $3,000 to $4,000.
A variation of this release in the Top 1,000 can be found at Number 36.

☐ 82. My Baby/Good Time Girls • Swallows (After Hours 104)................... 1954 $4,000

45 rpm. Near-mint price range: $3,000 to $4,000.
Members: Herman "Junior" Denby; Ed Rich; Earl Hurley; Fred Johnson; Norris Mack.

☐ 83. Doll Face/Ooh, I Feel So Good • Vibranaires (After Hours 103)......... 1954 $4,000

📷 45 rpm. Red vinyl. Near-mint price range: $3,000 to $4,000.
Members: Bobby Thomas; Roosevelt McDuffie; Mike Robinson; Herbie Cole; Jimmy Roache.
A variation of this release in the Top 1,000 can be found at Number 51.

☐ 84. Loretta/Please • Coins (Model 2001) 1955 $4,000

📷 45 rpm. Near-mint price range: $3,000 to $4,000.
Members: Don Trotter; Al Perry.

☐ 85. Best of the 5 Keys • Five Keys (Aladdin 806) 1956 $4,000

📷 LP. Maroon label. Bootlegs have the Score reissue cover art, but use the Aladdin name
and number. There is no original Aladdin LP titled *On the Town*. Near-mint price range:
$3,000 to $4,000.
Members: Rudy West; Ripley Ingram; Maryland Pierce; Dickie Smith; Bernie West.
Side 1: *Glory of Love; Oh Baby; My Saddest Hour; Hucklebuck with Jimmy; These Foolish Things;
Christmas Time.*
Side 2: *Red Sails in the Sunset; Too Late, Baby; Teardrops; Be Mine; Love My Loving; Serve
Another Round.*

☐ 86. Delores/Look Out • Four Buddies (Club 51 105) 1956 $4,000

📷 45 rpm. Red vinyl. Reportedly only three copies exist. Near-mint price range: $3,000 to
$4,000.
Members: Leon Harrison; Greg Carroll; Bert Palmer; Tommy Smith.

☐ 87. Heaven Above Me/Millie Brown • Jets (Gee 1020)........... 1956 $4,000

45 rpm. Near-mint price range: $3,000 to $4,000.

☐ 88. Oh Why/? • Sof-Tones (Ceebee 1062)............................ 1957 $4,000

📷 45 rpm. Approximately two copies known. Near-mint price range: $3,000 to $4,000.

J & S
RECORDS
1651 Washington Ave., Bronx 57, N. Y.

UNBREAKABLE
45 R.P.M.

RECORD NO.
J 1658 B

Zells Music (BMI)
2:15

I LOVE YOU
(Sanders)
THE CLIMBERS
WITH ORCHESTRA

61.

HY·TONE
Records

GOODBYE DARLING
(Bernie Valentine-Steve Samuel)
THE CORSAIRS
A-110

62.

LESSIE

W0099A
2:30

FaDuCo B.M.I.
Vocal

THAT'S MY GIRL
(William Davis)
DE JAN
and The Elgins

63.

HARLEM

HM-114-A
Time 2 31
APNO PUB.
B.M.I.

I'M GONNA TRY TO LIVE
MY LIFE ALL OVER
(James Brown)

THE FABULOUS FLAMES
WITH THE ORIGINAL SUNGLOWS

64.

30

☐ 89. For Your Precious Love/Sweet Was the Wine • Jerry Butler & Impressions
(Vee-Jay 280) 1958 $4,000

📷 45 rpm. Near-mint price range: $3,000 to $4,000.
Members: Jerry Butler; Curtis Mayfield; Sam Gooden; Richard Brooks; Arthur Brooks; Fred Cash.

☐ 90. Our Love Is True/One Kiss, One Smile and a Dream • Delrays
(Cord 1001) 1958 $4,000

📷 45 rpm. Near-mint price range: $3,000 to $4,000.

☐ 91. My Gloria/Cool Seabreeze • Lee Scott & Windsors (Back Beat 506). 1958 $4,000

📷 45 rpm. One known copy. Probably on promo only as no commercial copies are yet
known to exist. Near-mint price range: $3,000 to $4,000.

☐ 92. Don't Say Goodbye/On My Happy Way • Trinidads (Formal 1005).... 1959 $4,000
45 rpm. Near-mint price range: $3,000 to $4,000.

☐ 93. Introducing the Beatles • Beatles (Vee-Jay SR-1062) 1963 $4,000
Stereo LP. Black label with circular colorband and oval logo. With *Love Me Do* and *P.S. I
Love You* (on later issues these tracks are replaced by *Ask Me Why* and *Please Please Me*).
Back cover is blank. Front cover has "Stereophonic" in gray print across a white banner at
top. Label has the word "Stereo" on top or on the side. Label has the word "Stereo" on top or
on the side. Near-mint price range: $3,000 to $4,000.
Variations of this release in the Top 1,000 can be found at Numbers 7; 27; 65; 169; 202; 218; 543;
559; 760; 789.
Members: John Lennon; Paul McCartney; George Harrison; Ringo Starr.
Side 1: *I Saw Her Standing There; Misery; Anna; Chains; Boys; Love Me Do.*
Side 2: *P.S. I Love You; Baby It's You; Do You Want to Know a Secret; A Taste of Honey; There's
a Place; Twist and Shout.*

☐ 94. Come on Girl/After Graduation • Four Fifths (Hudson 8101) 1963 $4,000

📷 45 rpm. Blue vinyl. Near-mint price range: $3,000 to $4,000.

☐ 95. Stoned/I Wanna Be Your Man • Rolling Stones (London 9641) 1964 $4,000
45 rpm. Commercial issue. Near-mint price range: $3,000 to $4,000.
Members: Mick Jagger; Keith Richards; Bill Wyman; Brian Jones; Charlie Watts.
A variation of this release in the Top 1,000 can be found at Number 358.

☐ 96. Love in Vain Blues/Preaching Blues • Robert Johnson
(Vocalion 04630) 1938 $3,500
78 rpm. Near-mint price range: $2,500 to $3,500.

☐ 97. Every Beat of My Heart/All Night Long • Royals (Federal 12064) 1952 $3,500
45 rpm. Blue vinyl. *All Night Long* features blues star Wynonie Harris. Near-mint price range:
$2,500 to $3,500.
Members: Henry Booth; Hank Ballard; Charles Sutton; Lawson Smith; Alonzo Tucker; Sonny Woods.
A variation of this release in the Top 1,000 can be found at Number 810.

☐ 98. Dear Ruth/Fine Brown Frame • Buccaneers (With Matthew Child & His
Drifters) (Southern 100/101).. 1953 $3,500

📷 45 rpm. Red vinyl. Near-mint price range: $2,500 to $3,500.
Members: Ernest Smith; Julius Robinson; Richard Gregory; Sam Johnson; Don Marshall.

☐ 99. Just Walkin' in the Rain/Baby Please • Prisonaires ("Confined to Tennessee
State Prison Nashville, Tennessee") (Sun 186) 1953 $3,500
45 rpm. Red vinyl. Near-mint price range: $2,500 to $3,500.
Members: Johnny Bragg; John Drew; Marcell Andess; William Stewart.

☐ 100. Rockin' the Boogie • Amos Milburn (Aladdin 704) 1955 $3,500

📷 10-inch monaural LP. Red vinyl. Near-mint price range: $2,500 to $3,500.
Side 1: *Pot Luck Boogie; Amos' Boogie; Bye-Bye-Boogie; Down the Road Apiece.*
Side 2: *Boogie-Woogie; Chicken-Shack Boogie; Rooming House Boogie; Sax Shack Boogie.*
A variation of this release in the Top 1,000 can be found at Number 618.

65.

67.

68.

68.

69.

☐ 101. Every Night/Come Back Baby • Lyrics (Rhythm 127)....................... 1959   **$3,500**

📷 45 rpm. Same number on both sides. Has an alternative take of *Every Night* compared to track used on 126/127, found elsewhere on this list. Near-mint price range: $2,500 to $3,500.
Member: Carl Henderson.
A variation of this release in the Top 1,000 can be found at Number 326.

☐ 102. I Feel So Bad/Wild in the Country • Elvis Presley (RCA
Victor 37-7880)... 1961   **$3,500**

📷 Compact 33 single with picture sleeve. Second of five mono singles in this somewhat experimental and ultimately failed series. Compact 33s are seven-inch discs with a quarter-inch, LP-size, hole. Picture sleeve alone is $1,500 to $2,000. Price range for both: $2,500 to $3,500.

☐ 103. Star of Love/First Love • Ebbtides (Duane 1022) 1964   **$3,500**

📷 45 rpm. Near-mint price range: $2,500 to $3,500.

☐ 104. Ram • Paul & Linda McCartney (Apple 3375) 1971   **$3,500**

📷 Monaural LP. Promotional issue. Issued in standard stereo cover, but labels indicate "Monaural." Near-mint price range: $3,000 to $3,500.
Side 1: *Too Many People; 3 Legs; Ram On; Dear Boy; Uncle Albert – Admiral Halsey; Smile Away; Heart of the Country.*
Side 2: *Monkberry Moon Delight; Eat at Home; Long Haired Lady; Ram On; The Back Seat of My Car.*

☐ 105. Count Every Star/I'm Gonna Paper My Walls with Your Love • Ravens
(National 9111)... 1950   **$3,000**

📷 45 rpm. Near-mint price range: $2,000 to $3,000.
Members: Ollie Jones; Jimmy Ricks; Leonard Puzey; Warren Suttles; Joe Van Loan; Louis Heyward.

☐ 106. I Don't Believe in Tomorrow/Ooh...It Feels So Good • Larks
(Apollo 430)... 1951   **$3,000**

45 rpm. Near-mint price range: $2,000 to $3,000.
Members: Eugene Mumford; Allen Bunn; Raymond "Pee-Wee" Barnes; Thurmon Ruth; Dave McNeil; Hadie Rowe.

☐ 107. My Lost Love/How Long Must I Wait for You • Larks (Apollo 435) ... 1951   **$3,000**

45 rpm. Near-mint price range: $2,000 to $3,000.
Members: Eugene Mumford; Allen Bunn; Raymond "Pee-Wee" Barnes; Thurmon Ruth; Dave McNeil; Hadie Rowe.

☐ 108. Hopefully Yours/When I Leave These Prison Walls • Larks
(Apollo 1180)... 1951   **$3,000**

📷 45 rpm. Orange vinyl. Near-mint price range: $2,000 to $3,000.
Members: Eugene Mumford; Allen Bunn; Raymond "Pee-Wee" Barnes; Thurmon Ruth; Dave McNeil; Hadie Rowe.
A variation of this release in the Top 1,000 can be found at Number 228.

☐ 109. Where Are You (Now That I Need You)/How Could You • Mello-Moods
(With Schubert Swanston Trio) (Robin 105) 1951   **$3,000**

📷 45 rpm. Near-mint price range: $2,000 to $3,000.
Members: Ray "Buddy" Wooten; Bobby Williams; Monte Owens; Bobby Baylor; Jimmy Bethea.

☐ 110. It's Too Soon to Know/Barbara Lee • Orioles (Jubilee 5000) 1951   **$3,000**

📷 45 rpm. Near-mint price range: $2,000 to $3,000.
Members: Sonny Til; Alex Sharp; George Nelson; John Reed; Tom Gaither.

☐ 111. Eternally/It Ain't the Meat, It's the Motion • Swallows (King 4501).... 1951   **$3,000**

📷 45 rpm. Blue or green vinyl. Near-mint price range: $2,000 to $3,000.
Members: Herman "Junior" Denby; Ed Rich; Earl Hurley; Fred Johnson; Norris Mack.
A variation of this release in the Top 1,000 can be found at Number 765.

☐ 112. Tell Me Why/Roll Roll Pretty Baby • Swallows (King 4515) 1951   **$3,000**

45 rpm. Blue or green vinyl. Near-mint price range: $2,000 to $3,000.
Members: Herman "Junior" Denby; Ed Rich; Earl Hurley; Fred Johnson; Norris Mack.
A variation of this release in the Top 1,000 can be found at Number 497.

☐ 113. Mood Music • Charles Brown (Aladdin 702) 1952   **$3,000**

📷 10-inch LP. Red vinyl. Near-mint price range: $2,000 to $3,000.

71.

73.

74.

77.

Aladdin BEVERLY HILLS, CALIFORNIA
45-3127
(RCA-1882)
Q
Vocal - 3:12
RED SAILS IN THE SUNSET
(H. Williams - J. Kennedy)
THE FIVE KEYS

RAMA
45 RPM   45 RPM
RR-21   Jaga Music
Time. 2:55
COME BACK MY LOVE
(Smith-Halperin)
THE BUCCANEERS
RR-66

Old Town RECORDS, INC.
45 RPM   45 RPM
45-OT 790 B   INST. ACC.
YOU COULD BE MY LOVE
(Patterson)
5 CROWNS
771

Central RECORDS
New York City
Record No.
45-1006
(BMI)
Lynnbrook Music
Time: 2:20
45 R.P.M.
(45-C-108)
Vocal
TONY, MY DARLING
THE CHARMERS
with
Rhythm Acc.

☐ 114. No One to Love Me/Early Sunday Morning • Sha-Weez
(Aladdin 3170) 1952 $3,000

📷 45 rpm. Near-mint price range: $2,000 to $3,000.
Members: Edgar Myles; Warren Myles; James Crawford; Irving Banister.

☐ 115. White Cliffs of Dover/Hey Pappa • Blue Jays (Checker 782) 1953 $3,000

📷 45 rpm. General awareness of this haunting version of *White Cliffs of Dover* increased
substantially after its use in the film, *The Crying Game*. Near-mint price range: $2,500 to
$3,000.

☐ 116. My Girl Awaits Me/Sweetness • Castelles (Grand 101) 1953 $3,000

📷 45 rpm. Glossy blue label. Reportedly 600 made. Near-mint price range: $2,500 to
$3,000.
Members: George Grant; Frank Vance; William Taylor; Ron Everett; Octavius Anthony; Walt Miller.
A variation of this release in the Top 1,000 can be found at Number 245.

☐ 117. It Would Be Heavenly/Baby's Coming Home • Coronets (With Sax Mallard
& Combo) (Chess 1553) 1953 $3,000

📷 45 rpm. Red vinyl. Near-mint price range: $2,500 to $3,000.
Members: Charles Carothers; Lester Russaw; George Lewis; William Griggs; Sam Griggs; Babby Ward.

☐ 118. Keep It a Secret/Why Don't You Believe Me • Five Crowns
(Rainbow 202) 1953 $3,000

45 rpm. Red vinyl. Near-mint price range: $2,000 to $3,000.
Members: Wilbur Paul; Nicky Clark; John Clark; Jim "Papa" Clark; Dock Green.

☐ 119. Golden Teardrops/Carried Away • Flamingos (With Red Holloway's
Orchestra) (Chance 1145) 1953 $3,000

📷 45 rpm. Red vinyl. Near-mint price range: $2,000 to $3,000.
Members: Sollie McElroy; John Carter; Zeke Carey; Jake Carey; Paul Wilson; Nate Nelson.
A variation of this release in the Top 1,000 can be found at Number 585.

☐ 120. Surrender Your Heart/Get on My Train • Love Notes
(Imperial 5254) 1953 $3,000

📷 45 rpm. Near-mint price range: $2,000 to $3,000.

☐ 121. Baby Please/Whistle My Love • Moonglows (Chance 1147) 1953 $3,000

45 rpm. Red vinyl. Near-mint price range: $2,000 to $3,000.
Members: Harvey Fuqua; Bobby Lester; Alex Graves; Prentiss Barnes; Buddy Johnson.

☐ 122. Just a Lonely Christmas/Hey Santa Claus • Moonglows
(Chance 1150) 1953 $3,000

45 rpm. Red vinyl. Near-mint price range: $2,000 to $3,000.
Members: Harvey Fuqua; Bobby Lester; Alex Graves; Prentiss Barnes; Buddy Johnson.

☐ 123. Peddler of Dreams/Dolores • Roscoe Thorne (Atlas 1033) 1953 $3,000

45 rpm. Near-mint price range: $2,000 to $3,000.

☐ 124. Please Tell Me You're Minc/Wondering • Twilighters (With Frank Motley
[Dual Trumpeter] & His Crew) (Marshall 702) 1953 $3,000

📷 45 rpm. Dark red vinyl. (Lighter red vinyl is a $300 to $400 reissue.) Near-mint price
range: $2,500 to $3,000.
Members: Melvin Jennings; Earl Williams; DeRoy Green; Robert Richardson; William Pierce.

☐ 125. Please Tell Me So/Remember When • Cherokees (Grand 110) 1954 $3,000

45 rpm. Yellow label. Rigid disc. Near-mint price range: $2,500 to $3,000.
Member: Russell Carter.

☐ 126. Blue Can't Get No Place with You/Cheatin' Baby • Coins (Gee 10) . 1954 $3,000

45 rpm. Red vinyl. Near-mint price range: $2,000 to $3,000.
Members: Don Trotter; Al Perry.

☐ 127. The Beat of Our Hearts/You Gotta Go Baby • Five Blue Notes
(Sabre 108) 1954 $3,000

📷 45 rpm. White label. Near-mint price range: $2,000 to $3,000.
Members: Fleming Briscoe; Andy Magruder; Jackie Shedrick; Bob Stroud; Moise Vaughan; Louis Smalls.

HOLLYWOOD
STAR
RECORDS

H-798-A   VOCAL

ANNIE KICKED THE BUCKET
(Lucky Hawkins)

NU-TONES

80.

MODEL
RECORDS
Pasadena, Calif.

Model Record
45-2001-B
Berkle Music
BMI 2:16

Vocals
Don Trotter
&
Al Perry

"PLEASE"
(Don Trotter-Al Perry)
Band
"THE COINS"

84.

85.

Ceebee
RECORDS, INC.

45 R.P.M.   NOT FOR SALE

Copyright
Precision Music Co.
B. M. I.

45 - 1062 A
Time: 2:30
written by Sof-Tones

Vocal Group

OH WHY
by
Sof - Tones

88.

CLUB 51
RECORDS CO.

M-5002
L & J Publ.
(B.M.I.)

Vocal
Time 2:50

DELORES
(Buddies)
THE FOUR BUDDIES
Lefty Bates Orchestra
C-105

86.

36

☐ 128. I May Be Small/Nagasaki • Five Chances (Chance 1157)................ 1954 $3,000
  45 rpm. Near-mint price range: $2,500 to $3,000.
  Members: Johnny Jones; John Austell; Darnell Austell; Reggie Smith; Howard Pitman; Harold Jones.

☐ 129. Gloria/Wee Wee Baby • Five Thrills (Parrot 800) 1954 $3,000
  45 rpm. Red vinyl. Near-mint price range: $2,000 to $3,000.
  Members: Levi Jenkins; Gilbert Warren; Oscar Robinson; Fred Washington; Obie Washington; Leon Pace.
  A variation of this release in the Top 1,000 can be found at Number 603.

☐ 130. Dream of a Lifetime/On My Merry Way • Flamingos (Parrot 808)..... 1954 $3,000
  📷 45 rpm. Red vinyl. Reads "The Bronzville Record Mfg. Co." at bottom. Counterfeits may
  show name as "Bronxville." Near-mint price range: $2,000 to $3,000.
  Members: Sollie McElroy; John Carter; Zeke Carey; Jake Carey; Paul Wilson; Nate Nelson.
  A variation of this release in the Top 1,000 can be found at Number 605.

☐ 131. Deed I Do/Talk About the Weather • Gems (Drexel 901) 1954 $3,000
  45 rpm. Red vinyl. Near-mint price range: $2,000 to $3,000.
  Members: Ray Pettis; Bobby Robinson; Wilson James; Dave Taylor; Rip Reed.

☐ 132. Rockin Chair Daddy/Great Medical Menagerist • Harmonica Frank [Frank
  Floyd] (Sun 205) 1954 $3,000
  45 rpm. Near-mint price range: $2,000 to $3,000.

☐ 133. Since I Fell for You/Don't Be No Fool • Love Notes (Riviera 975) 1954 $3,000
  45 rpm. Original label color is a mixture of magenta (red) and cyan (blue) – giving a
  lavender-pink look. Counterfeits are just light pink. Near-mint price range: $2,500 to $3,000.

☐ 134. Please Remember My Heart/South of the Border • Solitaires
  (Old Town 1006/1007)... 1954 $3,000
  45 rpm. Red vinyl. Near-mint price range: $2,000 to $3,000.
  Members: Herman Curtis; Monte Owens; Bobby Williams; Bobby Baylor; Buzzy Willis; Pat Gaston; Milton Love;
  Reggie Barnes; Cecil Holmes; Fred Barksdale; Wally Roker.

☐ 135. Stop Torturing Me/Stop Jibing Baby • Vibes (Formerly the Vibranaires)
  (Chariot 105).. 1954 $3,000
  📷 45 rpm. "Jibing" is a label misprint; "Jiving." Near-mint price range: $2,000 to $3,000.
  Members: Bobby Thomas; Roosevelt McDuffie; Mike Robinson; Herbie Cole; Jimmy Roache; Cleveland Dickerson;
  Dornell Chavous; Matthew McKnight.

☐ 136. Heavenly Father/My Wedding Day • Castelles (Grand 122)............. 1955 $3,000
  45 rpm. Cream color label. Rigid disc. No company address shown. Near-mint price range:
  $2,000 to $3,000.
  Members: George Grant; Frank Vance; William Taylor; Ron Everett; Octavius Anthony; Walt Miller.

☐ 137. Love Will Be Mine/Reward • Incredible Vikings (Winndsock) 1955 $3,000
  45 rpm. No selection number used. One known copy. Near-mint price range: $2,000 to
  $3,000.

☐ 138. Little Senorita/Wedding Bells, Oh Wedding Bells • Paul Lewis "The Mighty
  Swamba" & Swans (Fortune 813) 1955 $3,000
  📷 45 rpm. Purple label. Near-mint price range: $2,500 to $3,000.

☐ 139. Someday/Bow Wow • Pyramids (With Fletcher Smith's Band)
  (C Note 108) 1955 $3,000
  📷 45 rpm. Near-mint price range: $2,000 to $3,000.
  Members: Sidney Correia; Joe Dandy; Melvin White; Kenneth Perdue; Lionel Cobbs; Tom Williams.
  Variations of this release in the Top 1,000 can be found at Numbers 621; 837.

☐ 140. Dear One/Lonesome Tonight • Feathers (Hollywood 1051)............. 1956 $3,000
  45 rpm. Near-mint price range: $2,000 to $3,000.

☐ 141. If Only You Were Mine/There Will Come a Time • Five Scalders
  (Sugar Hill 3000)... 1956 $3,000
  📷 45 rpm. Near-mint price range: $2,000 to $3,000.
  Members: Mack Rice; Johnny Mayfield; Sol Tilman; Gerald Young; James Bryant.

☐ 142. Love Is a Vow/Valerie • Mello-Harps (Do-Re-Mi 203)...................... 1956 $3,000
  📷 45 rpm. Near-mint price range: $2,000 to $3,000.

Vee-Jay RECORDS

FOR YOUR PRECIOUS LOVE
(Brooks & Butler)
JERRY BUTLER
and The Impressions
VJ 280

89.

CORD
RECORD COMPANY
Philadelphia, Pa.

UNBREAKABLE
45 R.P.M.

RECORD NO.
CD-1001 A-45

Published by
SNM Music Corp.
BMI

Directed by
Mickey Johnson

OUR LOVE IS TRUE
(Ben Johnson Jr.)

BY THE
DELRAYS

90.

HUDSON
Division of Fleetwood Records, Inc.
1650 Broadway, New York City

PROMOTIONAL

NOT FOR SALE

RECORD NO.
8101-B
Teedom Music
(BMI) 2:48
(7004-B)

45 RPM
Prod., Arr. &
Cond. by
Four Fifths Pro

AFTER GRADUATION
(J. Kanew-B. Carter)

THE FOUR FIFTHS

94.

Southern

V-101
North. Music Corp.

Vocal with
rhythm
Accomp.

THE BUCCANEERS SING
FINE BROWN FRAME
(Guadalupe Carnero - J. Mayo Williams
with
Matthew Child and his Drifters
101

98.

☐ 143. PRO-12 (RCA Victor Promotion Disc) • Various Artists (RCA
Victor PRO-12) 1956 $3,000

📷 EP. White label, black print. Promotional issue only. Cover: Paper sleeve. Custom made
for WOHO radio, Toledo, Ohio. Front: Reads: "WOHO (1470 KC) Featuring RCA Victor."
RCA Victor logo and number at upper right. Back is blank. We are uncertain as to how and
why this item was offered. EP alone: $750 to $1,000. EP and sleeve: $2,000 to $3,000.
Side 1: *Old Shep* (Elvis Presley); *I'm Moving On* (Hank Snow).
Side 2: *Cattle Call* (Eddy Arnold with Hugo Winterhalter & Chorus); *Four Walls* (Jim Reeves).

☐ 144. Party After Hours • Various Artists (Aladdin 703) 1956 $3,000
10-inch monaural LP. Red vinyl. Near-mint price range: $2,000 to $3,000.
Artists: Amos Milburn, Wynonie Harris, Velma Nelson, Crown Prince Waterford.
A variation of this release in the Top 1,000 can be found at Number 635.

☐ 145. Please Be My Guy/Don't Cry • Crystaliers (Johnson 103) 1957 $3,000
📷 45 rpm. Near-mint price range: $2,000 to $3,000.

☐ 146. Frankie, My Eyes Are on You/Show Me the Way to Your Heart • Little Iris
Culmer (Marlin 803) 1957 $3,000
📷 45 rpm. Three copies known. Near-mint price range: $2,000 to $3,000.

☐ 147. Lamplight/Let Me Share Your Dream • Deltas (Gone 5010) 1957 $3,000
45 rpm. Near-mint price range: $2,000 to $3,000.

☐ 148. Don't Say You're Sorry/Kicking with My Stallion • Kingsmen
(Club 51 108) 1957 $3,000
45 rpm. Near-mint price range: $2,000 to $3,000.

☐ 149. Tears in My Eyes/Spanish Love Song • Magic Tones
(Howfum 3686) 1957 $3,000
45 rpm. Identification number shown since no selection number is used. Near-mint price
range: $2,000 to $3,000.
Members: Gene Hawkins; Arthur Williams; James Williams; Willie Stokes; Joseph Reed.

☐ 150. Blue Christmas/Blue Christmas • Elvis Presley (RCA
Victor H07W-0808) 1957 $3,000
📷 45 rpm. Listed by identification number shown since no selection number is used.
Promotional issue only. Near-mint price range: $2,000 to $3,000.

☐ 151. Jamboree! • Various Artists (Warner Bros) 1957 $3,000
📷 Monaural LP. Soundtrack. No selection number used. Promotional issue only. Front
cover is a slick pasted on generic, unprinted cardboard cover. Notes on back are printed
right on the cardboard (no slick used on back). Original covers have a smooth surface. Front
cover photos have gray-green background hue. Trail-off area on disc has "Jam 1," & "Jam 2"
stamped (not etched) in vinyl. Label is light yellow. Warner "shield" logo has parallel lines as
background, all with sharp, distinct lettering.
Counterfeit identification: Front cover graphics are printed on posterboard. Back cover notes
are pasted on. Cover has textured feel. Front cover photos have pinkish hue background.
Trail-off area has "Jam 1" & "Jam 2" hand-etched. Label is dark yellow. Warner "shield" logo
has black background with broken lettering. Near-mint price range: $2,000 to $3,000.

100.

101.

102.

103.

104.

40

Side 1: *Jamboree* (Count Basie); *Record Hop Tonight* (Andy Martin); *For Children of All Ages* (Connie Francis); *Glad All Over* (Carl Perkins); *Who Are We To Say* (Connie Francie & Paul Carr); *Teachers' Pet* (Frankie Avalon); *Siempre* (Connie Francis); *Cool Baby* (Charlie Gracie); *Sayonara* (Jodie Sands); *Great Balls of Fire* (Jerry Lee Lewis); *Toreador* (Ron Coby).

Side 2: *Your Last Chance* (Lewis Lymon & Teenchords); *If Not for You* (Pau Carr); *Unchain My Heart* (Slim Whitman); *A Broken Promise* (Four Coins); *One O'Clock Jump* (Count Basie); *I Don't Like You No More* (Joe Williams & Count Basie); *Crazy to Care* (Martha Lou); *Cross Over* (Jimmy Bowen); *Hula Love* (Buddy Knox); *Wait and See* (Fats Domino); *Twenty-Four Hours a Day* (Connie Francis & Paul Carr).

☐ 152. Dealers' Prevue • Various Artists (RCA Victor SDS-7-2) 1957 $3,000

📷 EP. White label. Promotional issue only. Paper envelope used to mail SDS-7-2F: Front: Black and white Elvis photo. Reads: "Elvis Presley at His Greatest." The only selection number shown on the mailer is 47/20-7000 (for 45 and 78 rpm singles of *(Let Me Be Your) Teddy Bear / Loving You*. Disc alone: $800 to $1,000. Mailer alone: $1,500 to $2,000. Set: $2,000 to $3,000.

Side 1: *Loving You* (Elvis Presley); *(Let Me Be Your) Teddy Bear* (Elvis Presley); *Now Stop* (Martha Carson); *Just Whistle Or Call* (Martha Carson).

Side 2: *The Wife* (Lou Monte); *Musica Bella* (Lou Monte); *Mailman, Bring Me No More Blues* (Herb Jeffries); *So Shy* (Herb Jeffries).

☐ 153. Dealers' Prevue • Various Artists (RCA Victor SDS-57-39) 1957 $3,000

📷 EP. Includes paper envelope/sleeve. Promotional issue only. Contains edited versions of songs listed. Disc alone: $800 to $1,000. Mailer alone: $1,500 to $2,000. Both: $2,000 to $3,000.

Side 1: *The Old Rugged Cross* (Stuart Hamblen); *Old Time Religion* (Stuart Hamblen); *Jailhouse Rock* (Elvis Presley); *Treat Me Nice* (Elvis Presley); *Till the Last Leaf Shall Fall* (Statesmen Quartet); *Every Hour and Every Day* (Statesmen Quartet).

Side 2: *A Slip of the Lip* (Kathy Barr); *Welcome Mat* (Kathy Barr); *Just Born* (Perry Como); *Ivy Rose* (Perry Como); *Sayonara* (Eddie Fisher); *That's the Way It Goes* (Eddie Fisher).

☐ 154. Boyd Bennett • Boyd Bennett (King 594) 1958 $3,000
LP. Near-mint price range: $2,500 to $3,000.

☐ 155. What Is Your Name Dear/Only Be Mine • Ebbtides (With Butch Ballard Orchestra) (Teen 121) 1958 $3,000

📷 45 rpm. Near-mint price range: $2,000 to $3,000.

☐ 156. My Love Is Real/Believe in Me • Lollypops (Universal International 7420) 1958 $3,000

📷 45 rpm. Near-mint price range: $2,000 to $3,000.
A variation of this release in the Top 1,000 can be found at Number 312.

☐ 157. Just the Way You Are/Only Memories • Marlettes (With Imperial Orchestra) (Howfum) 1958 $3,000

📷 45 rpm. No selection number used. Near-mint price range: $2,000 to $3,000.

☐ 158. Wonderland/Baby • Carribians – Coleman Brooks Anderson (Brooks 2000) 1959 $3,000

📷 45 rpm. At least one source shows the year of release as 1961. We don't know yet which is correct. Near-mint price range: $2,000 to $3,000.

☐ 159. Roses/My Chinese Girl • Five Discs (Dwain 6072) 1959 $3,000

📷 45 rpm. Near-mint price range: $2,000 to $3,000.
Members: Mario deAndrade; Andy Jackson; Paul Albano; Joe Barsalona; Charles DiBella; Frank Arnone; Ed Pardocchi; Tony Basil; Bobby Stewart.

☐ 160. Sorry, Sorry/I Want to Cry • Teenage Moonlighters (Mark 134) 1959 $3,000

📷 45 rpm. Near-mint price range: $2,000 to $3,000.

105.

109.

110.

111.

☐ 161. Tell Me If You Know/That's a Teenage Love • Teen-Kings
(Bee 1115)... 1959 $3,000
45 rpm. Black vinyl. (Red vinyl disc is a 1996 reissue). Near-mint price range: $2,000 to $3,000.

☐ 162. Wedding Bells/Velma • Valiants (Speck 1001).................. 1959 $3,000
📷 45 rpm. Near-mint price range: $2,000 to $3,000.

☐ 163. Why Do I Love You/Please Come Back • Fi-Dels (Bardo 529)........1950s $3,000
45 rpm. Near-mint price range: $2,500 to $3,000.

☐ 164. Don't/Wear My Ring Around Your Neck • Elvis Presley (With Jordanaires)
(RCA Victor SP-45-76) 1960 $3,000
📷 45 rpm single with picture sleeve. Promotional issue only. Picture sleeve alone is $1,000 to $2,000. Price range for both: $2,000 to $3,000.

☐ 165. Darling Angel/Lover's Bells • Royal Boys (Tropelco 1007) 1960 $3,000
📷 45 rpm. Near-mint price range: $2,000 to $3,000.

☐ 166. Can You Remember/Send Me Someone to Love • Celtics
(Al-Jack's 0002) 1962 $3,000
📷 45 rpm. Approximately 200 made. Near-mint price range: $2,000 to $3,000.

☐ 167. When You Walked Out/Sugar Sweet • Arcados (Fam 502).............. 1963 $3,000
📷 45 rpm. One known copy. Near-mint price range: $2,000 to $3,000.

☐ 168. Hello/Burgers, Fries and Shakes • Little June & His Januarys
(Salem 188) 1963 $3,000
📷 45 rpm. Commercial issue. Green-gold label. Near-mint price range: $2,000 to $3,000.
Members: Johnny "June" Coleman; Wilbert Johnson; Lewis Johnson; Claudie Johnson.

☐ 169. Introducing the Beatles • Beatles (Vee-Jay SR-1062)...................... 1964 $3,000
Stereo LP. With *Love Me Do* and *P.S. I Love You* listed on cover and disc, but actually plays *Ask Me Why* and *Please Please Me*. Near-mint price range: $2,500 to $3,000.
Variations of this release in the Top 1,000 can be found at Numbers 7; 27; 65; 93; 202; 218; 543; 559; 760; 789.
Members: John Lennon; Paul McCartney, George Harrison; Ringo Starr.
Side 1: *I Saw Her Standing There; Misery; Anna; Chains; Boys; Ask Me Why.*
Side 2: *Please Please Me; Baby It's You; Do You Want to Know a Secret; A Taste of Honey; There's a Place; Twist and Shout.*

☐ 170. The Beatles and Frank Ifield on Stage • Beatles & Frank Ifield
(Vee-Jay LP-1085) 1964 $3,000
Monaural LP. Front cover has a painted portrait of the Beatles. Issued for a very short time to replace British statesman with Beatles' wig cover. Label variations may affect value. Near-mint price range: $2,500 to $3,000.
A variation of this release in the Top 1,000 can be found at Number 24.
Members: John Lennon; Paul McCartney, George Harrison; Ringo Starr / Frank Ifield.
Side 1: *Please Please Me* (Beatles); *Anytime* (Frank Ifield); *Lovesick Blues* (Frank Ifield); *I'm Smiling Now* (Frank Ifield); *Nobody's Darlin' But Mine* (Frank Ifield); *From Me to You* (Beatles).
Side 2: *I Remember You* (Frank Ifield); *Ask Me Why* (Beatles); *Thank You Girl* (Beatles); *The Wayward Wind* (Frank Ifield); *Unchained Melody* (Frank Ifield); *I Listen to My Heart* (Frank Ifield).

☐ 171. The Beatles Introduce New Songs • Beatles
(Capitol PRO-2720/2721) 1964 $3,000
EP. Promotional issue only. Burgundy label. Has John Lennon and Paul McCartney giving introductory and closing comments for two new Capitol acts – Cilla Black and Peter & Gordon – who perform Lennon-McCartney songs. Known counterfeit does not have machine stamped asterisk in the vinyl trail-off area. Near-mint price range: $2,500 to $3,000.
Members: John Lennon; Paul McCartney, George Harrison; Ringo Starr.

113.

114.

Aladdin
★ BEVERLY HILLS, CALIFORNIA ★

45-3170
(NO-2064)
X

Vocal - 2:54
(BMI)
Aladdin Music Publ

NO ONE TO LOVE ME
(E. Myles - Crawford - W. Myles - Banister)

THE SHA-WEEZ

Checker

U-7547
Shipiro-Bernstein

Vocal
Ascap

WHITE CLIFFS OF DOVER
(Burton-Kent)
THE BLUE JAYS
782

115.

Grand
RECORDS

Record No.
45-101

45 RPM
Pub recorder

MY GIRL AWAITS ME

THE CASTELLES

116.

44

Side 1: *John Lennon Introduces "It's for You" / Cilla Black; John Lennon Sign Off; Paul McCartney Introduces "I Don't Want to See You Again" / Peter & Gordon; Paul McCartney Sign Off.*
Side 2: *It's for You (Cilla Black); I Don't Want to See You Again (Peter & Gordon)*

☐ 172. Boy Crazy/Scuba Duba • Lucy Ann Grassi & Del-Aires
(Volcanic 1002).. 1964 $3,000

📷 45 rpm. One known copy. Near-mint price range: $2,000 to $3,000.

☐ 173. Roustabout Theatre Lobby Spot (Coming Soon)/Roustabout Theatre
Lobby Spot (Now Playing) • Elvis Presley (Paramount
Pictures SP-2413) 1964 $3,000

📷 45 rpm. Promotional issue to theaters for lobby play in advance of and during the run of the *Roustabout* film. This take is different from the one on the *Roustabout* LP and the RCA Victor promo 45. Blue label. Label does not identify Elvis as the singer. Near-mint price range: $2,000 to $3,000.

☐ 174. United Artists Presents *Help!* (Interview) • Beatles (United
Artists UA-Help Show)... 1965 $3,000

📷 LP. Promotional issue only. Single-sided disc. Blue label with black print. Open-end interview (29:50) with the Beatles about the film. Price includes script which represents about $75 to $100 of the value. Near-mint price range: $2,500 to $3,000.
Members: John Lennon; Paul McCartney, George Harrison; Ringo Starr.

☐ 175. Yesterday and Today • Beatles (Capitol T-2553) 1966 $3,000
Monaural LP. Cover pictures group wearing butcher smocks and garnished with cuts of meat and pieces of toy dolls. Commonly referred to as the "Butcher Cover." After distributing copies to the media, Capitol sent recipients a recall letter, requesting they return their albums. Aware they had a valuable collectible in their possession, many kept them. Capitol pasted new covers – picturing the Beatles and a trunk – over the Butcher Covers. Original issues, without any modifications, are known as "First State" copies. Cover shows title as *Yesterday And Today*, whereas label reads: *"Yesterday" ... And Today*. Near-mint price range: $2,000 to $3,000.
Variations of this release in the Top 1,000 can be found at Numbers 1; 21; 495; 967.
Members: John Lennon; Paul McCartney, George Harrison; Ringo Starr.
Side 1: *Drive My Car; I'm Only Sleeping; Nowhere Man; Dr. Robert; Yesterday; Act Naturally.*
Side 2: *And Your Bird Can Sing; If I Needed Someone; We Can Work It Out; What Goes On; Day Tripper.*

☐ 176. The Index • Index (DC) 1968 $3,000
LP. No selection number used. Reportedly 100 made. Identification number in the trail-off is "DC-71." Near-mint price range: $2,500 to $3,000.
Members: Jim Valice; John Ford; Gary Ballew.
A variation of this release in the Top 1,000 can be found at Number 212.

☐ 177. Cowhand's Last Ride/Blue Yodel #12 • Jimmie Rodgers
(Victor 18-6000)... 1933 $2,500

📷 78 rpm picture disc. Near-mint price range: $1,500 to $2,500.

☐ 178. 32-20/Last Fair Deal Gone Down • Robert Johnson
(Oriole 7-04-60) 1937 $2,500

📷 78 rpm. Near-mint price range: $1,500 to $2,500.

☐ 179. Crossroads Blues/Rambling on My Mind • Robert Johnson
(Vocalion 03519) 1937 $2,500
78 rpm. Near-mint price range: $1,500 to $2,500.

☐ 180. Me and the Devil Blues/Little Queen • Robert Johnson
(Vocalion 04108) 1938 $2,500

📷 78 rpm. Near-mint price range: $1,500 to $2,500.

☐ 181. I Guess You're Satisfied/Don't Break My Heart Again • Victorians
(Specialty 411)... 1950 $2,500

📷 45 rpm. Near-mint price range: $1,500 to $2,500.

117.

119.

120.

124.

☐ 182. Angel Baby/Night Has Come • Bill Austin & Hearts (Apollo 444)...... 1952 $2,500
45 rpm. Red vinyl. Near-mint price range: $2,000 to $2,500.

☐ 183. Goodbye My Love/I'll Love You Till My Dying Day • Musketeers
(Roxy 801) 1952 $2,500

📷 78 rpm. Near-mint price range: $2,000 to $2,500.
Members: Norman Thrasher; Noah Howell.

☐ 184. Can't Help Loving You/Pretty Baby • Bachelors (Aladdin 3210)....... 1953 $2,500
45 rpm. Near-mint price range: $2,000 to $2,500.
Members: Walt Taylor; Jim Walton; Herb Fisher; John Bowie; Waverly "Buck" Mason; Charlie Booker.

☐ 185. Over a Cup of Coffee/Baby Can't You See • Castelles (Grand 109) 1954 $2,500
45 rpm. Blue label. Near-mint price range: $2,000 to $2,500.
Members: George Grant; Frank Vance; William Taylor; Ron Everett; Octavius Anthony; Walt Miller.

☐ 186. Marcella/I'm a Fool to Care • Castelles (Grand 114) 1954 $2,500

📷 45 rpm. Cream color label. Rigid disc. No company address shown. Near-mint price
range:
$2,000 to $2,500.
Members: George Grant; Frank Vance; William Taylor; Ron Everett; Octavius Anthony; Walt Miller.

☐ 187. Come Back, Come Back/I May Be Wrong • Emperors with Rhythm
(Haven 511)... 1954 $2,500
45 rpm. Black vinyl. Near-mint price range: $2,000 to $2,500.
A variation of this release in the Top 1,000 can be found at Number 48.

☐ 188. Wolf Call Boogie/Harmonica Jam • Hot Shot Love (Sun 196) 1954 $2,500
45 rpm. Near-mint price range: $2,000 to $2,500.

☐ 189. You Came to Me/Ooh Wee Baby • Five Crowns (With Orchestra)
(Riviera 990) 1955 $2,500

📷 45 rpm. Near-mint price range: $2,000 to $2,500.
Members: Wilbur Paul; Nicky Clark; John Clark; Jim "Papa" Clark; Dock Green.

☐ 190. Johnny Burnette & Rock'n Roll Trio • Johnny Burnette & Rock'n Roll Trio
(Coral 57080)... 1956 $2,500

📷 LP. Counterfeits can be identified by their lack of printing on the spine and hand-etched
identification numbers in the trail-off. Originals have the numbers mechanically stamped.
Canadian issues are worth at least as much as U.S. issues. Near-mint price range: $2,000
to $2,500.
Members (Trio): Johnny Burnette; Dorsey Burnette; Paul Burlison.
Side 1: *Honey Hush; Lonesome Train (On a Lonesome Track); Sweet Love on My Mind; Rock Billy
Boogie; Lonesome Tears in My Eyes; All By Myself.*
Side 2: *The Train Kept A-Rollin'; I Just Found Out; Your Baby Blue Eyes; Chains of Love; I Love
You So; Drinking Wine, Spo-Dee-O-Dee, Drinking Wine.*

☐ 191. Elvis Presley • Elvis Presley (RCA Victor SPD-22)........................... 1956 $2,500

📷 Double-EP set, with cover. Given as a bonus to buyers of a $32.95 Victrola. May have
"Elvis" in either light or dark pink letters on front cover. Counterfeits exist. Two-EPs: $500 to
$750. Cover: $1,500 to $1,750. Price range for set: $2,000 to $2,500.
Side 1: *Blue Suede Shoes; I'm Counting on You.*
Side 2: *I Got a Woman; One Sided Love Affair.*
Side 3: *I'm Gonna Sit Right Down and Cry (Over You); I'll Never Let You Go.*
Side 4: *Tutti Frutti; Tryin' to Get to You.*
A variation of this release in the Top 1,000 can be found at Number 68.

☐ 192. Ooby Dooby/Trying to Get to You • Teen Kings (Je-wel 101) 1956 $2,500

📷 45 rpm. May read "Vocal Roy Oribson," instead of "Orbison," on some labels. Beware
since some counterfeits exist that are difficult to identify. Consult an expert if in doubt. Near-
mint price range: $2,000 to $2,500.
Members: Roy Orbison; Johnny "Peanuts" Wilson; Billy Par Ellis; James Monroe; Jack Kennelly.

Sabre RECORDS, INC.
Joni Music B.M.I.
S-5073
THE BEAT OF OUR HEARTS
(F. Briscoe)
THE FIVE BLUE NOTES
SA-108

127.

DREAM OF A LIFETIME
THE FLAMINGOS

130.

Chariot NEW YORK
45 RPM RECORD
RECORD No. 105 A
TERRIFIC TUNES B.M.I.
Vocal Group
STOP TORTURING ME!
(Bobby Thomas)
THE VIBES
(Formerly The Vibranaires)
Supervision: Joel Turnero
FLAPS RECORDING CO. INC. N.Y.C.

135.

for TRULY GREAT MUSIC
FORTUNE
Reg. U.S. Pat. Off.
FORTUNE RECORDS
DETROIT MICHIGAN
UNBREAKABLE
45 RPM RECORD
RECORD NO. **813** (F-12)
Trianon Publications Time 3:07 (BMI)
Unbreakable Under Normal Use
WEDDING BELLS, OH WEDDING BELLS
(Tommy James)
Paul Lewis (THE MIGHTY SWAMBA)
And
THE SWANS
Music Under Direction Of
GENE NERO

138.

48

☐ 193. Your a Thousand Miles Away/? • Gators (Chuck Lechner "N" His Gators)
(Gator) 1957 $2,500
    45 rpm. No selection number used. Should be "You're," but "Your" is shown on label. Near-mint price range: $2,000 to $2,500.

☐ 194. This Is the End of Love/It's All Over • Klixs (Music City 817) 1957 $2,500
    45 rpm. Red vinyl. Near-mint price range: $1,500 to $2,500.

☐ 195. Jailhouse Rock/Treat Me Nice • Elvis Presley (RCA
Victor 47-7035) 1957 $2,500
    45 rpm. Gold label, dog on top. Gold vinyl. Specific purpose not yet known. May be promotional though not marked as such. Near-mint price range: $1,500 to $2,500.

☐ 196. It Takes Two/I Want • Henry Sawyer & Jupiters (With Music by Mike Tam)
(Planet X 9621) 1957 $2,500
    📷 45 rpm. Three known copies. Near-mint price range: $1,500 to $2,500.

☐ 197. Fountain of Love/Send Me a Picture Baby • Starlarks (Elm 001) 1957 $2,500
    45 rpm. Near-mint price range: $1,500 to $2,500.

☐ 198. Why Did You Leave Me/Why Does It Have to Be • John Shaw & Dell-O's
(With Billy Cooke & Orchestra) (U-C 5002) 1958 $2,500
    📷 45 rpm. Near-mint price range: $1,500 to $2,500.

☐ 199. My Dear/Falling Star • Valquins (Gaity 161/162) 1959 $2,500
    📷 45 rpm. Gold vinyl. Five known copies. Near-mint price range: $1,500 to $2,500.
    Members: John Stafford; Ed Ballard.
    A variation of this release in the Top 1,000 can be found at Number 876.

☐ 200. Hey Boss Man! • Frank Frost (Phillips International 1975) 1961 $2,500
    📷 LP. Near-mint price range: $2,000 to $2,500.
    Side 1: *Everything's Alright; Lucky to Be Living; Jelly Roll King; Baby You're So Kind; Gonna Make You Mine; Now Twist.*
    Side 2: *Big Boss Man; Jack's Jump; So Tired Livin' By Myself; Now What You Gonna Do; Pocket Full of Shells; Just Come on Home.*

☐ 201. My Bonnie/The Saints • Tony Sheridan & Beat Brothers
(Decca 31382) 1962 $2,500
    📷 45 rpm. Promotional issue only. Pink label with black lettering. All Decca pink labels are promotional. Known counterfeits have *My Bonnie* on both sides. This is the first appearance of the Beatles – then billed as the Beat Brothers – on a record in the U.S. Near-mint price range: $2,000 to $2,500.
    A variation of this release in the Top 1,000 can be found at Number 5.
    Members: John Lennon; Paul McCartney, George Harrison; Pete Best.

☐ 202. Introducing the Beatles • Beatles (Vee-Jay LP-1062) 1963 $2,500
    📷 Monaural LP. Black label with circular colorband and oval logo. With *Love Me Do* and *P.S. I Love You* (on later issues these tracks are replaced by *Ask Me Why* and *Please Please Me*). Back cover pictures 25 other Vee-Jay albums (known as "Ad back" cover). Has "Printed In U.S.A." at lower left of front cover (counterfeits lack this). Price range for cover only: $1,400 to $1,600. Cover and disc: $2,000 to $2,500.
    Variations of this release in the Top 1,000 can be found at Numbers 7; 27; 65; 93; 169; 218; 543; 559; 760; 789.
    Members: John Lennon; Paul McCartney, George Harrison; Ringo Starr.
    Side 1: *I Saw Her Standing There; Misery; Anna; Chains; Boys; Love Me Do.*
    Side 2: *P.S. I Love You; Baby It's You; Do You Want to Know a Secret; A Taste of Honey; There's a Place; Twist and Shout.*

☐ 203. Please Please Me/From Me to You • Beatles (Vee-Jay VJ-581) 1964 $2,500
    📷 Picture sleeve. Promotional issue only. Reads "The Record That Started Beatlemania" across top. Does not picture the group. Reads: "(Promotion Copy)." Near-mint price range: $2,000 to $2,500.
    A variation of this release in the Top 1,000 can be found at Number 759.
    Members: John Lennon; Paul McCartney, George Harrison; Ringo Starr.

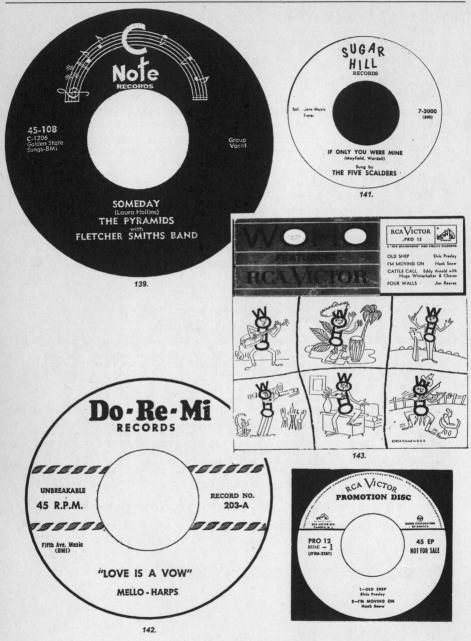

C Note RECORDS

45-108
C-1206
Golden State
Songs-BMI

Group Vocal

SOMEDAY
(Laura Hollins)
THE PYRAMIDS
with
FLETCHER SMITHS BAND

139.

SUGAR HILL RECORDS

Sol. Gore Music Times

7-3000
(300)

IF ONLY YOU WERE MINE
(Mayfield, Wardell)
Sung by
THE FIVE SCALDERS

141.

WOH
FEATURING
RCA VICTOR

RCA VICTOR
PRO 12
A "NEW ORTHOPHONIC" HIGH FIDELITY RECORDING

OLD SHEP   Elvis Presley
I'M MOVING ON   Hank Snow
CATTLE CALL   Eddy Arnold with
                  Hugo Winterhalter & Chorus
FOUR WALLS   Jim Reeves

©RCA Printed in U.S.A.

143.

Do-Re-Mi RECORDS

UNBREAKABLE
45 R.P.M.

RECORD NO.
203-A

Fifth Ave. Music
(BMI)

"LOVE IS A VOW"
MELLO - HARPS

142.

RCA VICTOR
PROMOTION DISC

RCA VICTOR DIV.
CAMDEN, N.J.

RADIO CORPORATION
OF AMERICA

PRO 12
SIDE - 1
(J70H-2287)

45 EP
NOT FOR SALE

1—OLD SHEP
Elvis Presley
2—I'M MOVING ON
Hank Snow

☐ 204. I Want to Hold Your Hand/I Saw Her Standing There • Beatles
(Capitol 5112) 1964 $2,500

📷 Picture sleeve. Promotional issue only distributed in New York by radio station WMCA.
Front side of this sleeve is identical to standard commercial issue. Back pictures six WMCA
dee jays. Contained a commercial copy of the single. Near-mint price range: $2,000 to
$2,500.
Members: John Lennon; Paul McCartney, George Harrison; Ringo Starr.

☐ 205. A Hard Day's Night • Beatles (United Artists UAEP-10029) 1964 $2,500

45 rpm. Promotional issue only. White label. Open-end interview for movie promotion. Made
for radio station use. Record has small play hole. Near-mint price range: $2,000 to $2,500.
Members: John Lennon; Paul McCartney, George Harrison; Ringo Starr.

☐ 206. A Hard Day's Night • Beatles (United Artists UAL-3366) 1964 $2,500

📷 Monaural LP. White label. Promotional issue only. Label reads "Not For Sale." Issued in
either a standard mono cover or one with a black promo stamp. Near-mint price range:
$2,000 to $2,500.
Variations of this release in the Top 1,000 can be found at Numbers 12; 724.
Members: John Lennon; Paul McCartney, George Harrison; Ringo Starr.
Side 1: *A Hard Day's Night; Tell Me Why; I Should Have Known Better; I'm Happy Just to Dance*
with You; And I Love Her.
Side 2: *I Should Have Known Better; And I Love Her; Ringo's Theme; Can't Buy Me Love; A Hard*
Day's Night.

☐ 207. Surprise Gift from the Beatles, Beach Boys and the Kingston Trio
(Eva-Tone 8464) 1964 $2,500

Flexi-disc and mailer/sleeve. Mailer/sleeve is 9½" x 6" with black and red lettering, and black-
and-white photo of each Beatle. Reads: "A Beatles Record Free" on the front and "Free
Beatles Record Inside" on back. Issued with black vinyl, 5" flexi-disc with white print. Disc
price: ?. Price range for mailer/sleeve: $2,000 to $2,500.

☐ 208. Beatles Vs. the Four Seasons • Beatles & 4 Seasons
(Vee-Jay DXS-30) 1964 $2,500

📷 Stereo LP. Double LP with gatefold cover. Cover and disc labels have the print "Stereo."
Repackage set combining two previously released Vee-Jay albums: *Introducing the Beatles*
(Vee-Jay 1062) and *The Golden Hits of the Four Seasons* (Vee-Jay 1065). Many copies
include an 11½ " x 23" color poster, valued separately at $150 to $200. Price range for discs
and cover: $2,000 to $2,500.
Beatles
Side 1: *I Saw Her Standing There; Misery; Anna; Chains; Boys; Ask Me Why.*
Side 2: *Please Please Me; Baby It's You; Do You Want to Know a Secret; A Taste of Honey;*
There's a Place; Twist and Shout.
4 Seasons
Side 1: *Sherry; I've Cried Before; Marlena; Soon (I'll Be Home Again); Ain't That A Shame; Walk*
Like A Man.
Side 2: Connie-O; Big Girls Don't Cry; Starmaker; Candy Girl; Silver
Wings; Peanuts.

☐ 209. Wait for Me/For Your Love • Inconquerables (Flodavieur 803) 1964 $2,500

45 rpm. Near-mint price range: $1,500 to $2,500.

☐ 210. Out of the Bachs • Bachs 1968 $2,500

📷 LP. Neither label name nor selection number used. Reportedly 100 made. Del Val label
reissues exist. Near-mint price range: $1,500 to $2,500.
Members: John Peterman; Black Allison; Ben Harrison.

☐ 211. A Trip Through Hell • C.A. Quintet (Candy Floss 7764) 1968 $2,500

📷 LP. Near-mint price range: $1,500 to $2,500.
Members: Jim Erwin; Ken Erwin; Doug Reynolds; Tom Pohling; Paul Samuels; Rick Johnson; Rick Patron; Donnie
Chapin; Tony Wright.

JOHNSON RECORDS

45 RPM   45 RPM

(BMI) 2:45   103 B

PLEASE BE MY GUY
(Johnson-Santos)
THE CRYSTALIERS

145.

MARLIN RECORDS

UNBREAKABLE
45 R.P.M.

RECORD NO.
803
(C-173)

Sherlyn Pub.
Time 2:40   VOCAL

FRANKIE, MY EYES ARE ON YOU
(Stone-Culmer)
LITTLE IRIS CULMER

146.

RCA VICTOR
FROM THE RCA VICTOR ALBUM
"ELVIS' CHRISTMAS ALBUM"

RCA VICTOR DIV.
CAMDEN, N. J.   RADIO CORPORATION OF AMERICA

Choice Music Inc.
ASCAP

45 R.P.M.
NOT FOR SALE
H07W-0808

BLUE CHRISTMAS
(Billy Hays-Jay Johnson)
ELVIS PRESLEY
2:05

150.

LOVING YOU
(Let Me Be Your) TEDDY BEAR
ELVIS PRESLEY

DEALERS' PREVUE
SDS-7-2
NOT FOR SALE

RCA Victor
RCA VICTOR DIV.
CAMDEN, N. J.

(H2NH-4361)

NOW STOP
JUST WHISTLE OR CALL
MARTHA CARSON

152.

THE OLD RUGGED CROSS - Stuart Hamblen
OLD TIME RELIGION - Stuart Hamblen
JAILHOUSE ROCK - Elvis Presley

DEALERS' PREVUE
SDS-57-39
NOT FOR SALE

RCA Victor
RCA VICTOR DIV.
CAMDEN, N. A.

(H2NH-8568)

TREAT ME NICE - Elvis Presley
TILL THE LAST LEAF SHALL FALL
Statesmen Quartet
EVERY HOUR AND EVERY DAY -
Statesmen Quartet

153.

☐ 212. The Index • Index (DC) 1968 $2,500
  LP. No selection number used. Not issued with cover. Reportedly 100 made. Identification
  number in the trail-off is "DC-4736." Near-mint price range: $1,500 to $2,500.
  Members: Jim Valice; John Ford; Gary Ballew.
  A variation of this release in the Top 1,000 can be found at Number 176.

☐ 213. International Hotel, Las Vegas Nevada, Presents Elvis, August – 1969 –
  August • Elvis Presley (RCA Victor) 1969 $2,500

  📷 Two LPs and numerous inserts in a specially prepared, complimentary gift box given to
  invited guests at the Showroom Internationale on July 31, 1969 (media performance) and
  August 1 (official opening night).

  Box: Oversize, 12¾" x 12¾". Front: Orange RCA Victor logo at lower right. Title is in white,
  6" x 6" box with orange and pink print at upper right. International Hotel logo at upper right.
  Black-and-white Elvis photo, same as first used on *From Memphis to Vegas / From Vegas to
  Memphis*. Back: Black, no printing.

  Box Contents: *Elvis (NBC-TV Special)* RCA Victor LPM-4088 and *From Elvis in Memphis*
  LSP-4155 (both are rigid discs, with orange labels); nine-page press release – a summary of
  Elvis' life and career – page one of which is on RCA Victor Records Public Affairs letterhead;
  RCA Victor 36-page, full-color, 1969 *Elvis' Records & Tapes* catalog (with pink, red and
  white cover); RCA 1969 Elvis pocket calender with a color photo of Elvis in his gold suit on
  one side (calender on reverse); color 8" x 10" Elvis photo, signed "Sincerely, Elvis Presley"
  (back announces Elvis' International Hotel engagement. This photo first appeared as a
  bonus with the *From Elvis in Memphis* LP); and two black-and-white, glossy 8" x 10" Elvis
  photos with blank backs (shots from the NBC-TV Special). Included with box but not actually
  packaged inside it: a single page, reading: "Dear Friend, Enclosed is a special promotion
  package with our compliments. Sincerely, Elvis & the Colonel." Has two black-and-white
  Elvis photos, one at upper left and one at upper right. Box only: $1,500 to $2,000. Complete
  set: $2,000 to $2,500.
  Variations of this release in the Top 1,000 can be found at Numbers 214; 368.

☐ 214. International Hotel, Las Vegas Nevada, Presents Elvis • Elvis Presley
  (RCA Victor) 1969 $2,500
  Known as the "V.I.P. Box," this is the same as the other International Hotel boxes (1969 &
  1970), except does *not* have printed, white 6" x 6" box with International Hotel logo and
  engagement dates. Reportedly made without a date so it could be used for any performance
  or promotion. Box only: $2,000 to $2,500.
  Variations of this release in the Top 1,000 can be found at Numbers 213; 368.

☐ 215. Montgomery's Chapel • Search Party 1969 $2,500
  LP. Approximately a dozen made by this San Francisco band. Neither label name nor
  selection number used. Near-mint price range: $1,500 to $2,500.

☐ 216. Song of a Gypsy • Damon (Ankh) 1970 $2,500
  📷 LP. No selection number used. Reportedly 100 made. Near-mint price range: $2,000 to
  $2,500.

☐ 217. Perpetuum Mobile • Mariani (Sonobeat 1004) 1970s $2,500
  LP. Promotional issue only. Near-mint price range: $2,000 to $2,500.
  Member: Vince Mariani.

☐ 218. Introducing the Beatles • Beatles (Vee-Jay SR-1062) 1964 $2,200
  Stereo LP. With *Ask Me Why* and *Please Please Me*. Includes any of the label or logo
  designs. Price range $2,000 to $2,200.
  Variations of this release in the Top 1,000 can be found at Numbers 7; 27; 65; 93; 169; 202; 543;
  559; 760; 789.
  Members: John Lennon; Paul McCartney; George Harrison; Ringo Starr.
  Side 1: *I Saw Her Standing There; Misery; Anna; Chains; Boys; Ask Me Why.*
  Side 2: *Please Please Me; Baby It's You; Do You Want to Know a Secret; A Taste of Honey;
  There's a Place; Twist and Shout.*

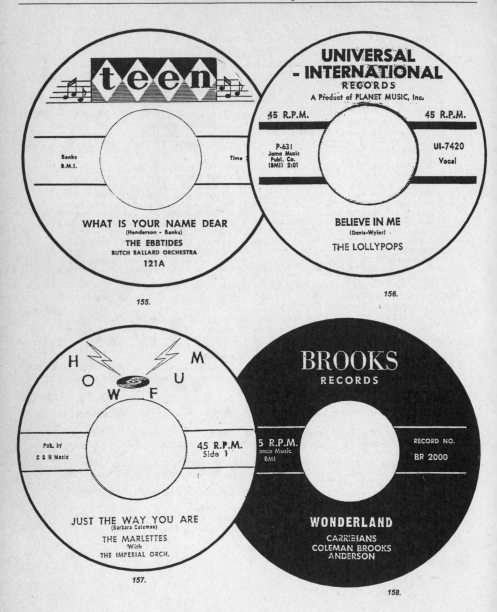

155.

WHAT IS YOUR NAME DEAR
(Henderson - Banks)
THE EBBTIDES
BUTCH BALLARD ORCHESTRA
121A

Banks
B.M.I.

Time

156.

BELIEVE IN ME
(Davis-Wyler)
THE LOLLYPOPS

UNIVERSAL - INTERNATIONAL RECORDS
A Product of PLANET MUSIC, Inc.
45 R.P.M.   45 R.P.M.
P-631
Jomo Music
Publ. Co.
(BMI) 2:01
UI-7420
Vocal

157.

JUST THE WAY YOU ARE
(Barbara Coleman)
THE MARLETTES
With
THE IMPERIAL ORCH.

Pub. by
C & H Music
45 R.P.M.
Side 1

158.

WONDERLAND
CARRIBIANS
COLEMAN BROOKS
ANDERSON

BROOKS RECORDS
5 R.P.M.
anco Music
BMI
RECORD NO.
BR 2000

54

☐ 219. Songs, Pictures and Stories of the Fabulous Beatles • Beatles
(Vee-Jay VJS-1092) 1964 $2,200
Stereo LP. Single disc in gatefold cover of which front is two-third's full width. Disc is actually
Introducing the Beatles (Vee-Jay VJ-1062). Some covers have a sticker/banner from any
one of several of the Beatles U.S. concerts. Add $200 for those. Logo variations may affect
price by as much as $200. Near-mint price range: $2,000 to $2,200.
Members: John Lennon; Paul McCartney, George Harrison; Ringo Starr.
Side 1: *I Saw Her Standing There; Misery; Anna; Chains; Boys; Ask Me Why.*
Side 2: *Please Please Me; Baby It's You; Do You Want to Know a Secret; A Taste of Honey;
There's a Place; Twist and Shout.*

☐ 220. What'cha Gonna Do • Christopher (Chris-Tee 12411) 1970 $2,200
LP. Reportedly 100 made. Near-mint price range: $2,000 to $2,200.
Members: Frank Smoak; Gary Lucas; Steve Nagle; Bill McKee.

☐ 221. Overdrive • Phafner (Dragon) 1971 $2,200
LP. No selection number used. Near-mint price range: $1,800 to $2,200.
Members: Greg Smith; Steve Smith; Dale Shultz; Tom Shultz; Steve Gustafson.

☐ 222. Speedway • Elvis Presley (RCA Victor LPM-3989) 1968 $2,100
Monaural LP. Soundtrack. This is the only standard catalog RCA Victor Presley release
with a solo track by another artist (*Your Groovy Self* by Nancy Sinatra). Cover: Front: Nipper
logo at top center, number at lower left. Seven color Elvis photos. Back: 12 color Elvis
photos. Insert: a color 8" x 10" Elvis (circa 1962) photo, signed "Sincerely, Elvis Presley"
(back lists other RCA Victor Elvis records). Shrink Sticker: red and white, reads: "Special
Bonus, for a limited time only, full color photo of Elvis." Disc alone: $800 to $1,000. Disc,
cover, insert and sticker: $1,700 to $2,100.
Side 1: *Speedway; There Ain't Nothing Like a Song (Duet with Nancy Sinatra); Your Time Hasn't
Come Yet, Baby; Who Are You (Who Am I); He's Your Uncle, Not Your Dad; Let Yourself
Go.*
Side 2: *Your Groovy Self (By Nancy Sinatra); Five Sleepy Heads; Western Union; Mine; Goin'
Home; Suppose.*

☐ 223. I Believe I'll Dust My Broom/Dead Shrimp Blues • Robert Johnson
(Vocalion 03475) 1937 $2,000
78 rpm. Near-mint price range: $1,000 to $2,000.

☐ 224. Come on in My Kitchen/They're Red Hot • Robert Johnson
(Vocalion 03563) 1937 $2,000
78 rpm. Near-mint price range: $1,000 to $2,000.

☐ 225. Milkcow's Calf Blues/Malted Milk • Robert Johnson
(Vocalion 03665) 1937 $2,000
78 rpm. Near-mint price range: $1,000 to $2,000.

☐ 226. Stones in My Passway/I'm a Steady Rolllin' Man • Robert Johnson
(Vocalion 03723) 1937 $2,000
78 rpm. Near-mint price range: $1,000 to $2,000.

☐ 227. Stop Breakin' Down Blues/Honeymoon Blues • Robert Johnson
(Vocalion 04002) 1938 $2,000
78 rpm. Near-mint price range: $1,000 to $2,000.

☐ 228. Hopefully Yours/When I Leave These Prison Walls • Larks
(Apollo 1180) 1951 $2,000
45 rpm. Black vinyl. Near-mint price range: $1,500 to $2,000.
Members: Eugene Mumford; Allen Bunn; Raymond "Pee-Wee" Barnes; Thurmon Ruth; Dave McNeil; Hadie Rowe.
A variation of this release in the Top 1,000 can be found at Number 108.

☐ 229. Tell Me So/Deacon Jones • Orioles (Jubilee 5005) 1951 $2,000
45 rpm. Near-mint price range: $1,500 to $2,000.
Members: Sonny Til; Alex Sharp; George Nelson; John Reed; Tom Gaither.

159.

160.

162.

164.

☐ 230. So Much/Forgive and Forget • Orioles (Jubilee 5016)...................... 1951 $2,000
    45 rpm. Near-mint price range: $1,500 to $2,000.
    Members: Sonny Til; Alex Sharp; George Nelson; John Reed; Tom Gaither.

☐ 231. I Miss You So/You Are My First Love • Orioles (Jubilee 5051)......... 1951 $2,000
    45 rpm. Red vinyl. Near-mint price range: $1,500 to $2,000.
    Members: Sonny Til; Alex Sharp; George Nelson; John Reed; Tom Gaither.
    A variation of this release in the Top 1,000 can be found at Number 396.

☐ 232. You Don't Have to Drop a Heart to Break It/Midnight Blues • Ravens
    (Columbia 39112)... 1951 $2,000
    📷 45 rpm. Near-mint price range: $1,500 to $2,000.
    Members: Ollie Jones; Jimmy Ricks; Leonard Puzey; Warren Suttles; Joe Van Loan; Louis Heyward.

☐ 233. You're Always in My Dreams/Gotta Find My Baby • Ravens
    (Columbia 39194)... 1951 $2,000
    45 rpm. Near-mint price range: $1,500 to $2,000.
    Members: Ollie Jones; Jimmy Ricks; Leonard Puzey; Warren Suttles; Joe Van Loan; Louis Heyward.

☐ 234. You Foolish Thing/Honey, I Don't Want You • Ravens
    (Columbia 39408)... 1951 $2,000
    45 rpm. Near-mint price range: $1,500 to $2,000.
    Members: Ollie Jones; Jimmy Ricks; Leonard Puzey; Warren Suttles; Joe Van Loan; Louis Heyward.

☐ 235. Will You Be Mine/Dearest • Swallows (King 4458).......................... 1951 $2,000
    45 rpm. Near-mint price range: $1,500 to $2,000.
    Members: Herman "Junior" Denby; Ed Rich; Earl Hurley; Fred Johnson; Norris Mack.

☐ 236. Stolen Love/In My Lonely Room • Larks (Apollo 1190) 1952 $2,000
    45 rpm. Black vinyl. Near-mint price range: $1,500 to $2,000.
    Members: Eugene Mumford; Allen Bunn; Raymond "Pee-Wee" Barnes; Thurmon Ruth; Dave McNeil; Hadie Rowe.
    A variation of this release in the Top 1,000 can be found at Number 72.

☐ 237. Hold Me/I Live True to You • Larks (Apollo 1194) 1952 $2,000
    45 rpm. Near-mint price range: $1,500 to $2,000.
    Members: Eugene Mumford; Allen Bunn; Raymond "Pee-Wee" Barnes; Thurmon Ruth; Dave McNeil; Hadie Rowe.

☐ 238. Drivin' Slow/Flat Tire • Johnny London (Sun 175) 1952 $2,000
    📷 78 rpm. First commercial issue on the Sun label. Near-mint price range: $1,000 to
    $2,000.
    Session: Johnny London; Charles Keel; Joe Louis Hall; Julius Drake.

☐ 239. Call on Me/I Tried, Tried and Tried • Mello Moods (With Teacho Wiltshire
    & Band) (Prestige 799) 1952 $2,000
    45 rpm. Near-mint price range: $1,000 to $2,000.
    Members: Ray "Buddy" Wooten; Bobby Williams; Monte Owens; Bobby Baylor; Jimmy Bethea.

☐ 240. I Just Can't Tell No Lie/I've Been Your Dog • Moonglows
    (Champagne 7500)... 1952 $2,000
    📷 45 rpm. Reportedly 1,500 made. Near-mint price range: $1,000 to $2,000.
    Members: Harvey Fuqua; Bobby Lester; Alex Graves; Prentiss Barnes; Buddy Johnson.

☐ 241. Thrill Me, Baby/Hey Fine Mama • Henry Pierce & Five Notes
    (Specialty 461)... 1952 $2,000
    45 rpm. Red vinyl. Near-mint price range: $1,000 to $2,000.

☐ 242. Starting from Tonight/I Know I Love You So • Royals
    (Federal 12077) 1952 $2,000
    45 rpm. Near-mint price range: $1,000 to $2,000.
    Members: Henry Booth; Hank Ballard; Charles Sutton; Lawson Smith; Alonzo Tucker; Sonny Woods.

☐ 243. Moonrise/Fifth Street Blues • Royals (Federal 12088)..................... 1952 $2,000
    45 rpm. Near-mint price range: $1,000 to $2,000.
    Members: Henry Booth; Hank Ballard; Charles Sutton; Lawson Smith; Alonzo Tucker; Sonny Woods.

☐ 244. In the Mission of St. Augustine/You Did Me Wrong • Buccaneers
    (Rama 24)... 1953 $2,000
    45 rpm. Near-mint price range: $1,000 to $2,000.
    Members: Ernest Smith; Julius Robinson; Richard Gregory; Sam Johnson; Don Marshall.

TROPELCO

TK 1007
ZTSP 66479

DARLING ANGEL
(F. Brutton)
THE ROYAL BOYS

165.

AL-Jack's
RECORDS
3615 Woodward Ave., Detroit 2, Mich.

Twilight Pub.
BMI
000.2
Time 2:05

45 R.P.M.
Arr. by
Alonzo Tucker

SEND ME SOMEONE TO LOVE
(W. Pippen-P. Fulton)
THE CELTICS

166.

HOLLYWOOD, CALIF.

WHEN YOU
WALKED OUT
(Dave Johnson) 2:21

FAM-502-A
Vellore Music (BMI)
Produced by
Bob Jones
VOCAL

PROMOTIONAL
COPY
NOT FOR SALE

FAM RECORDS

THE ARCADOS

167.

SALEM
Records

Sebons Publ. Co.
BMI
No. 188

45 RPM
Time 2:30
S-2889

"HELLO"
(J. COLEMAN)
LITTLE JUNE
&
HIS JANUARYS

168.

☐ 245. My Girl Awaits Me/Sweetness • Castelles (Grand 101).................... 1953 $2,000
45 rpm. Flat blue label. Near-mint price range: $1,500 to $2,000.
Members: George Grant; Frank Vance; William Taylor; Ron Everett; Octavius Anthony; Walt Miller.
A variation of this release in the Top 1,000 can be found at Number 116.

☐ 246. No Help Wanted/Seven Lonely Days • Crows (Rama 3).................. 1953 $2,000
45 rpm. Near-mint price range: $1,500 to $2,000.
Members: Viola Watkins; Daniel "Sonny" Norton; Harold Major; Jerry Hamilton; Mark Jackson; Bill Davis.

☐ 247. Call a Doctor/Heartbreaker • Crows (Rama 10)................................ 1953 $2,000
45 rpm. Red vinyl. Some copies may credit the Jewels on one side and the Crows on the other. Near-mint price range: $1,000 to $2,000.
Members: Daniel "Sonny" Norton; Harold Major; Jerry Hamilton; Mark Jackson; Bill Davis.
Variations of this release in the Top 1,000 can be found at Numbers 254; 816.

☐ 248. This Is the Real Thing Now/Crying for My Baby • Billy Dawn Quartet (With Connie Frederick & Orchestra) (Decatur 3001)................................... 1953 $2,000
45 rpm. Near-mint price range: $1,000 to $2,000.
Members: Billy Dawn Smith; Sonny Benton; Donny Sheested; Tommy Smith.

☐ 249. If I Can't Have You/Someday, Someway • Flamingos (Chance 1133)... 1953 $2,000
45 rpm. Red vinyl. Near-mint price range: $1,000 to $2,000.
Members: Sollie McElroy; John Carter; Zeke Carey; Jake Carey; Paul Wilson; Nate Nelson.
A variation of this release in the Top 1,000 can be found at Number 815.

☐ 250. Stormin' and Rainin'/Night and Day • Lowell Fulson (Aladdin 3104) 1953 $2,000
45 rpm. Green vinyl. Near-mint price range: $1,000 to $2,000.

☐ 251. Thrill of Romance/Why-y-y Leave Me This Wa-ay-ay • Gay Tunes (Timely 1002)... 1953 $2,000
45 rpm. Red vinyl. Near-mint price range: $1,000 to $2,000.
Members: Earl Kirton; Wayman Corey; Leroy Williams; Fred Davis; Henry Pinchback.

☐ 252. I Can't Believe/Lonesome Baby • Hornets & Orchestra (States 127)... 1953 $2,000
78 rpm. Near-mint price range: $1,000 to $2,000.
Members: James "Sonny" Long; Johnny Moore; Ben Iverson; Gus Miller.
Variations of this release in the Top 1,000 can be found at Numbers 13; 33.

☐ 253. The Bells/Oh Darling • Jaytones (Timely 1003/1004)....................... 1953 $2,000
📷 45 rpm. Near-mint price range: $1,000 to $2,000.

☐ 254. Heartbreaker/Call a Doctor • Jewels / Crows (Rama 10).................. 1953 $2,000
45 rpm. Red vinyl. Near-mint price range: $1,000 to $2,000.
Variations of this release in the Top 1,000 can be found at Numbers 247; 816.

☐ 255. The Orioles Sing • Orioles (Jubilee 5000) 1953 $2,000
📷 EP. Near-mint price range: $1,000 to $2,000.
Members: Sonny Til; Alex Sharp; George Nelson; John Reed; Tom Gaither.
Side 1: *Too Soon to Know; Forgive and Forget.*
Side 2: *Tell Me So; At Night.*

☐ 256. Silver Bells/Blues Waltz • Ripley Cotton Choppers (Sun 190).......... 1953 $2,000
📷 78 rpm. Near-mint price range: $1,000 to $2,000.

☐ 257. I Can't Forget/Love Nobody • Rockettes (Parrot 789) 1953 $2,000
45 rpm. Near-mint price range: $1,500 to $2,000.

☐ 258. Baby It's You/Bounce • Spaniels (Chance 1141) 1953 $2,000
45 rpm. Red vinyl. Near-mint price range: $1,000 to $2,000.
Members: James "Pookie" Hudson; Jerry Gregory; Ernest Warren; Willie Jackson; Opal Courtney.

☐ 259. My True Love/No More • Swans (Rainbow 233)............................... 1953 $2,000
📷 45 rpm. Red vinyl. Near-mint price range: $1,000 to $2,000.

PARAMOUNT
PICTURES
... Presents ...

45 R.P.M.   Side 2

"ROUSTABOUT"
Theatre Lobby Spot
(NOW PLAYING)
(RECORD PLAYS CONTINUOUSLY
AND AUTOMATICALLY)
SP - 2414

173.

A UNITED ARTISTS'
RELEASE

"HELP!"

33⅓ LP

Special Open-End
Half-Hour Program
with
THE BEATLES
Time: 29:50

UA-Help Show

174.

COWHAND'S LAST RIDE
Sung and Played by JIMMIE RODGERS
A 18-6000

Jimmie Rodgers

RCA

177.

32-20 BLUES
Robert Johnson
ROBERT JOHNSON
7-04-60

178.

☐ 260. Sing a Song of Christmas Cheer/Hanging Up My Christmas Stocking
(Christmas Mambo) • Velvet Sounds & Cosmopolites
(Cosmopolitan 530/531) 1953 $2,000
📷 45 rpm. Near-mint price range: $1,000 to $2,000.
Members: Oliver Johnson; Earl Robbins.

☐ 261. Another Soldier Gone/Joy in the Beulah Land • Violinaires
(Drummond 4000) 1953 $2,000
45 rpm. Group name is misspelled on label as: "Voilinaires." Reportedly the same group as
the Gales, on J-V-B and Mel-O. Near-mint price range: $1,000 to $2,000.

☐ 262. I Want to Be Loved/Get Away Baby • Bees (Imperial 5320) 1954 $2,000
45 rpm. Near-mint price range: $1,000 to $2,000.

☐ 263. This Silver Ring/Wonder Why • Castelles (Grand 103) 1954 $2,000
📷 45 rpm. Glossy yellow label. Rigid disc. No company address shown. Near-mint price
range: $1,000 to $2,000.
Members: George Grant; Frank Vance; William Taylor; Ron Everett; Octavius Anthony; Walt Miller.

☐ 264. Blue Can't Get No Place with You/Cheatin' Baby • Coins (Gee 10) . 1954 $2,000
45 rpm. Black vinyl. Near-mint price range: $1,000 to $2,000.
Members: Don Trotter; Al Perry.

☐ 265. SR Blues/Look at Me Girl • Coins (Gee 11).................................... 1954 $2,000
📷 45 rpm. Near-mint price range: $1,000 to $2,000.
Members: Don Trotter; Al Perry.

☐ 266. The Bells of My Heart/Sweet Baby • Fascinators (Your
Copy 1135)... 1954 $2,000
📷 45 rpm. Red vinyl. Near-mint price range: $1,000 to $2,000.
Members: Jerry Potter; Donald Blackshear; Bob Rivers; Clarence Smith; Earl Richardson.
A variation of this release in the Top 1,000 can be found at Number 769.

☐ 267. Two Loves Have I/Bring My Baby Back • Bill "Bass" Gordon & His
Colonials (Gee 12).. 1954 $2,000
📷 45 rpm. Near-mint price range: $1,000 to $2,000.

☐ 268. Fire in My Heart/You Never Knew • Bobby Hall & Kings
(Harlem 2322).. 1954 $2,000
📷 45 rpm. Red vinyl. Near-mint price range: $1,000 to $2,000.
Members: Robert Hall; Richard Holcomb; Adolphus Holcomb; Gil Wilkes.

☐ 269. I'll Hide My Tears/Got a Little Shadow • Jets (Aladdin 3247) 1954 $2,000
📷 45 rpm. *I'll Hide My Tears* reportedly written by Murray Wilson, father of several of the
Beach Boys. Near-mint price range: $1,000 to $2,000.

☐ 270. Golden Girl/Big Wig Walk • Marbles (Lucky 002) 1954 $2,000
📷 45 rpm. Near-mint price range: $1,000 to $2,000.
Members: Rudy Jackson; Dee Hawkins; Johnny Torrence; James Brown.

☐ 271. Prayer of Love/Father Time • Melotones (Lee Tone 700) 1954 $2,000
45 rpm. Near-mint price range: $1,000 to $2,000.

☐ 272. Tired of Crying Over You/Gonna Buy Me a Telephone • Morris Pejoe
Orchestra (Checker 766) 1954 $2,000
📷 45 rpm. Red vinyl. Near-mint price range: $1,000 to $2,000.

☐ 273. Chimes/Ain't Gonna Do It • Pelicans (Imperial 5307) 1954 $2,000
45 rpm. Near-mint price range: $1,000 to $2,000.

☐ 274. I Wonder Why/Get Lost • Rhythm Aces (Vee-Jay 124) 1954 $2,000
45 rpm. Red vinyl. Near-mint price range: $1,000 to $2,000.

180.

181.

DON'T BREAK MY HEART AGAIN
(J. Kay-L. Simon)

THE VICTORIANS

183.

ROXY

VOCAL

GOODBYE MY LOVE

THE MUSKETEERS

801 B

186.

MARCELLA
THE CASTELLES
114

189.

190.

☐ 275. Blue Valentine/Wonder Why • Solitaires (Old Town 1000) 1954 $2,000

   📷 45 rpm. Red vinyl. Near-mint price range: $1,000 to $2,000.
   Members: Herman Curtis; Monte Owens; Bobby Williams; Bobby Baylor; Buzzy Willis; Pat Gaston; Milton Love;
   Reggie Barnes; Cecil Holmes; Fred Barksdale; Wally Roker.

☐ 276. Faith, Hope and Charity/Lost • Spartans (Banjo Bill and His Rhythm Kings)
   (Capri 7201) 1954 $2,000
   45 rpm. Near-mint price range: $1,000 to $2,000.

☐ 277. (I'm Afraid) The Masquerade Is Over/My Dearest Darling • Clefftones
   (Old Town 1011) 1955 $2,000

   📷 45 rpm. Near-mint price range: $1,000 to $2,000.
   Member: Cas Bridges.

☐ 278. Chop Chop Boom/My Autumn Love • Danderliers (States 147) 1955 $2,000
   45 rpm. Red vinyl. Near-mint price range: $1,500 to $2,000.
   Members: Dallas Taylor; James Campbell; Richard Thomas; Walter Stephenson; Bernard Dixon; Louis Johnson.

☐ 279. No Man Is an Island/Melba • Dreamers (Rollin' 1001) 1955 $2,000

   📷 45 rpm. Outer edge of disc is fairly sharp. Near-mint price range: $1,000 to $2,000.

☐ 280. Can't Stop/Don't Give My Love Away • Fascinators (Blue
   Lake 112) 1955 $2,000
   45 rpm. Near-mint price range: $1,000 to $2,000.
   Members: Jerry Potter; Donald Blackshear; Bob Rivers; Clarence Smith; Earl Richardson.

☐ 281. All I Want/Shake-a-Link • Five Chances (Blue Lake 115) 1955 $2,000
   45 rpm. Black vinyl. Near-mint price range: $1,000 to $2,000.
   Members: Johnny Jones; John Austell; Darnell Austell; Reggie Smith; Howard Pitman; Harold Jones.
   A variation of this release in the Top 1,000 can be found at Number 54.

☐ 282. Let's Fall in Love/We Danced in the Moonlight • Five Stars
   (Treat 505) 1955 $2,000
   45 rpm. Near-mint price range: $1,000 to $2,000.

☐ 283. Milkcow Blues Boogie/You're a Heartbreaker • Elvis Presley (With Scotty
   and Bill) (Sun 215) 1955 $2,000
   78 rpm. Near-mint price range: $1,000 to $2,000.
   A variation of this release in the Top 1,000 can be found at Number 284.
   Members: Elvis Presley; Scotty Moore; Bill Black.

☐ 284. Milkcow Blues Boogie/You're a Heartbreaker • Elvis Presley (With Scotty
   and Bill) (Sun 215) 1955 $2,000

   📷 45 rpm. Near-mint price range: $1,000 to $2,000.
   A variation of this release in the Top 1,000 can be found at Number 283.
   Members: Elvis Presley; Scotty Moore; Bill Black.

☐ 285. Whisper to Me/Olly, Olly, Atsen Free • Rhythm Aces (Vee-Jay 138) 1955 $2,000
   45 rpm. Red vinyl. Near-mint price range: $1,000 to $2,000.

☐ 286. Tell Me Why/Count Every Star • Rockers (With Emmet Carter Combo)
   (Carter 3029) 1955 $2,000

   📷 45 rpm. Black vinyl. Any on red vinyl are bootlegs. Near-mint price range: $1,000 to
   $2,000.
   Member: Art Larson.

☐ 287. My Reckless Heart/They Turned the Party Out Down at Bessie's
   House • Rocketeers (M.J.C. 501) 1955 $2,000

   📷 45 rpm. Near-mint price range: $1,000 to $2,000.

☐ 288. Do-Wah/Don'cha Go • Spaniels (Vee-Jay 131) 1955 $2,000
   45 rpm. Red vinyl. Near-mint price range: $1,000 to $2,000.
   Members: James "Pookie" Hudson; Jerry Gregory; Ernest Warren; Willie Jackson; Opal Courtney.

191.

192.

198.

196.

☐ 289. Giddy-Up and Ding-Dong/You're an Angel • Continentals
(Rama 190).. 1956 $2,000
    45 rpm. Blue label. Near-mint price range: $1,000 to $2,000.
      Members: James Gooden; Sidney Gray; Bill Davis; Demetrius Cleare.

☐ 290. True Love Gone/Wait a Minute Baby • Enchanters (Mercer 1674)... 1956 $2,000
    📷 45 rpm. Near-mint price range: $1,000 to $2,000.

☐ 291. Only the Angels Know/One Word for This • Esquires (Hi-Po 1003) . 1956 $2,000
    📷 45 rpm. Near-mint price range: $1,000 to $2,000.

☐ 292. I'm Traveling Light/My Honey Sweet Pea • Five Lyrics
(Music City 799)... 1956 $2,000
    45 rpm. Near-mint price range: $1,000 to $2,000.
      Members: Robert Rose; Ike Perry.

☐ 293. In the Still of the Nite/Jones Girl • Five Satins (Standord 200) 1956 $2,000
    📷 45 rpm. Red label. Reads "Produced By Martin Kuegull." Three known copies. Near-mint
    price range: $1,000 to $2,000.
      Members: Fred Parris; Louis Peebles; Stan Dortch; Jim Freeman; Ed Martin.
    A variation of this release in the Top 1,000 can be found at Number 628.

☐ 294. Bohemian Daddy/Hope He's True • Marquis (With Sammy Lowe
Orchestra) (Onyx 505).. 1956 $2,000
    📷 45 rpm. Near-mint price range: $1,000 to $2,000.

☐ 295. Ladise/My Doctor of Love • Packards (With Paul Boyers Band)
(Pla-Bac 106)... 1956 $2,000
    📷 45 rpm. Near-mint price range: $1,000 to $2,000.

☐ 296. I Love You the Most/Let's Do the Razzle Dazzle • Rip-Chords
(Abco 105)... 1956 $2,000
    📷 45 rpm. Red vinyl. Near-mint price range: $1,000 to $2,000.
      Members: Leon Arnold; John Gillespie; George Vingard; David Hargrove; Lester Martin.

☐ 297. Come to Me/Little Girl • Shantones (With Orchestra)
(Trilyte 5001) 1956 $2,000
    📷 45 rpm. Approximately three copies known. Near-mint price range: $1,000 to $2,000.

☐ 298. Tell Me You're Mine/Boo Wacka Boo • Velveteers (Spitfire 15) 1956 $2,000
    📷 45 rpm. Near-mint price range: $1,000 to $2,000.

☐ 299. My Darlin' Dear/Angels in Heaven Know I Love You • Climbers
(J&S 1652)... 1957 $2,000
    45 rpm. With straight horizontal lines. Near-mint price range: $1,500 to $2,000.
      Member: Joe Rivers.

☐ 300. Don't Ask Me to Be Lonely/Darling • Dubs (Johnson 102) 1957 $2,000
    45 rpm. Near-mint price range: $1,500 to $2,000.
      Members: Richard Blandon; Billy Carlisle; Cleveland Still; James Miller; Tom Gardner; Tom Grate; Cordell Brown;
      Dave Shelley.

☐ 301. The One I Love/She Must Be from a Different Planet • Fanando's (With
Emmet Carter Combo) (Carter 2050) 1957 $2,000
    45 rpm. Near-mint price range: $1,500 to $2,000.

☐ 302. Dearest Doryce/Rocking Jimmy • Rhythm Cadets (Featuring George
Singleton) (Vesta 501/502)... 1957 $2,000
    45 rpm. Near-mint price range: $1,500 to $2,000.
      Member: George Singleton.

☐ 303. Please Say You'll Be Mine/You've Got to Rock n' Roll • Sunbeams
(Acme 719) 1957 $2,000
    📷 45 rpm. Near-mint price range: $1,500 to $2,000.

▶▶ FRANK FROST ◀◀
WITH THE NIGHT HAWKS

Hey Boss Man!

EVERYTHING'S
LUCKY TO BE LIVING
JELLY ROLL KING
BABY YOU'RE SO KIND
GONNA MAKE YOU MINE
NOW TWIST
BIG BOSS MAN
JACK'S JUMP
SO TIRED LIVING BY MYSELF
NOW WHAT YOU GONNA DO
POCKET FULL OF SHELLS
JUST COME ON HOME

200.

DECCA

MARCA REGISTRADA • MFG'D BY DECCA RECORDS, INC., NEW YORK, U.S.A.

RECORD NO.
31382
(DGG 66 833)A+
(2:58)

Gema (AMRA)

Vocal With
Instrumental
Accompaniment

MY BONNIE
(Arr: Tony Sheridan)

TONY SHERIDAN AND
THE BEAT BROTHERS
RECORDED IN EUROPE BY DEUTSCHE
GRAMMOPHON/POLYDOR · SERIES

201.

RECORDED IN HIGH FIDELITY

Gaity

Pub.
Glen Ray-BMI
Time 2 30

GA 162   199.

Falling Star
by
The Valquins

introducing...
THE BEATLES
ENGLAND'S No.1 VOCAL GROUP

202.

66

☐ 304. Believe in Me/In the Morning • Swans (Steamboat 101) 1957 $2,000
📷 45 rpm. Near-mint price range: $1,500 to $2,000.

☐ 305. You Must Be Born Again/? • Andy Williams & Cavaliers (Our 305).. 1957 $2,000
📷 45 rpm. Near-mint price range: $1,500 to $2,000.

☐ 306. To Look at a Star/Working and Gambling Don't Mix • Arribians
(J.O.B. 1116) 1958 $2,000
45 rpm. Near-mint price range: $1,500 to $2,000.

☐ 307. Would You Do the Same for Me/At the Soda Shop • Candlelighters
(Delta 203)... 1958 $2,000
📷 45 rpm. Near-mint price range: $1,000 to $2,000.

☐ 308. We Are the Chantels • Chantels (End 301) 1958 $2,000
📷 LP. Pictures the quintet on the front cover. Reissues have a reworked cover picturing a
juke box. Near-mint price range: $1,000 to $2,000.
Members: Arlene Smith; Lois Harris; Rene Minus; Sonia Gorring; Jackie Landry.
Side 1: *Maybe; The Plea; Come My Little Baby; Congratulations; Prayee; He's Gone.*
Side 2: *I Love You So; Every Night; Whoever You Are; How Could You Call It Off; Sure of Love; If
You Try.*

☐ 309. Lorraine/The Girl I Walk to School • Joey Dee & Starliters
(Little 813/814).. 1958 $2,000
📷 45 rpm. Near-mint price range: $1,000 to $2,000.

☐ 310. Spellbound By the Moon/Know It All • Enchanters (Stardust 102) ... 1958 $2,000
📷 45 rpm. Near-mint price range: $1,000 to $2,000.

☐ 311. Everyday Holiday/L.A. Lover • Hollywood Saxons (Hareco 102)...... 1958 $2,000
📷 45 rpm. Near-mint price range: $1,000 to $2,000.

☐ 312. My Love Is Real/Believe in Me • Lollypops (Holland 7420) 1958 $2,000
📷 45 rpm. Holland labels may be pasted on top of Universal International ones. Near-mint
price range: $1,500 to $2,000.
A variation of this release in the Top 1,000 can be found at Number 156.

☐ 313. Tender Love/I Want You to Know • Jimmy Moore & Peacocks
(Noble 711).. 1958 $2,000
📷 45 rpm. Near-mint price range: $1,000 to $2,000.

☐ 314. Give Me a Chance/Monkey Business • Pharotones (Timely 1002) .. 1958 $2,000
45 rpm. Near-mint price range: $1,000 to $2,000.

☐ 315. Blue and Lonely/Daddy Needs Baby • Pretenders (Featuring Jimmy Jones
with Rhythm Accompaniment) (Central 2605) 1958 $2,000
📷 45 rpm. Near-mint price range: $1,000 to $2,000.
Members: Jimmy Jones; Bobby Moore; Bill Walker; Mel Walton; Kerry Saxton; Irving Lee Gail.

☐ 316. My Dreams Have Gone/That's What You Mean to Me • Johnny Ross (With
A&R Man Chuck "Tequila" Rio) (Corvette 1006) 1958 $2,000
📷 45 rpm. Near-mint price range: $1,000 to $2,000.

☐ 317. Let There Be Love/Money Talks • Twilighters (Cholly 712).............. 1958 $2,000
📷 45 rpm. Near-mint price range: $1,000 to $2,000.

☐ 318. Broken Heart/Please Say You'll Be True • Vel-Tones (Vel 9178)..... 1958 $2,000
45 rpm. Near-mint price range: $1,000 to $2,000.

☐ 319. Two Loves/Soda Pop • Blenders (Aladdin 3449)............................... 1959 $2,000
📷 45 rpm. Near-mint price range: $1500 to $2,000.

☐ 320. If I Could Hold Your Hand/What Are You Gonna Be • Calendars
(Cyclone 5012) 1959 $2,000
📷 45 rpm. Near-mint price range: $1,000 to $2,000.

203.

204.

206.

208.

☐ 321. Bells Bells/Prayer of Love • Chessmen (Golden Crest 2661) 1959 $2,000
   📷 45 rpm. Near-mint price range: $1,000 to $2,000.
☐ 322. Crying (Over You)/Hold My Hand • Endorsers (Moon 109) 1959 $2,000
   📷 45 rpm. Near-mint price range: $1,000 to $2,000.
☐ 323. The Rockin' 5 Royales • "5" Royales (Apollo 488) 1959 $2,000
   LP. Green label. Near-mint price range: $1,000 to $2,000.
      Members: Lowman Pauling; Johnny Tanner; Jim Moore; Otto Jeffries; Obadiah "Scoop" Carter.
      Side 1: *Baby Don't Do It; Too Much Lovin'; Baby Take All of Me; Courage to Love; You Know I
         Know; Help Me Somebody.*
      Side 2: *What's That; Laundermat* (sic) *Blues; All Righty; I Wanna Thank You; Put Something in It; I
         Like It Like That.*
☐ 324. They Laughed at Me/You Put One Over on Me • Jackie & Starlites
   (Fire & Fury 1000) 1959 $2,000
   📷 45 rpm. Near-mint price range: $1,000 to $2,000.
      Member: Jackie Rue; Alton Jones; George Lassu; John Felix; Billy Montgomery; Charles Hudson.
   A variation of this release in the Top 1,000 can be found at Number 872.
☐ 325. Memory Lane (The Best Songs Little Esther Ever Recorded) • Little Esther
   (King 622) 1959 $2,000
   Monaural LP. This artist is also known as Little Esther Phillips. Near-mint price range: $1,000
   to $2,000.
      Side 1: *Heart to Heart; I Paid My Dues; Tell Him That I Need Him; Ring a Ding Doo; I'll Be There;
         Street Lights; Mainliner.*
      Side 2: *Cherry Wine; Aged and Mellow; The Deacon Moves in; Somebody New; Sweet Lips; The
         Storm; Turn the Lamps Down Low.*
☐ 326. Come Back Baby/Every Night • Lyrics (Rhythm 126/127) 1959 $2,000
   45 rpm. Different selection number on each side of disc. Near-mint price range: $1,000 to
   $2,000.
      Member: Carl Henderson.
   A variation of this release in the Top 1,000 can be found at Number 101.
☐ 327. Never Forget/Rock and Roll Holiday • Marquis (Noble 719) 1959 $2,000
   📷 45 rpm. Repressed crediting the Tabs. Near-mint price range: $1,000 to $2,000.
☐ 328. Just Another Fool/You Crack Me Up • Marvels (Munrab 1008) 1959 $2,000
   📷 45 rpm. Near-mint price range: $1,000 to $2,000.
☐ 329. Love You That's Why/Coming Home • Monarch's (Liban 1002) 1959 $2,000
   📷 45 rpm. Near-mint price range: $1,000 to $2,000.
☐ 330. Whose Love, But Yours/Goin' to the Moon • Quills (Casino 106) 1959 $2,000
   📷 45 rpm. Near-mint price range: $1,000 to $2,000.
☐ 331. Oops/My Girl Is Gone • Tabs (Noble 720) 1959 $2,000
   📷 45 rpm. Near-mint price range: $1,000 to $2,000.
      Members: Bill Gardner; John Johnson; Jim Tanlin; Herb Northern; Ted Forbes.
☐ 332. Guess I'm the Lonely One/Rowdy Mae Is Back in Town • Joe Caldwell
   (M.C. 1) 1950s $2,000
   📷 45 rpm. Near-mint price range: $1,500 to $2,000.
☐ 333. The Vow/? • Capes (Chat 5005) 1950s $2,000
   45 rpm. Near-mint price range: $1,500 to $2,000.
☐ 334. My Confession/After New Years • Del Vues (Featuring W. Voss)
   (U Town 8008) 1950s $2,000
   45 rpm. Near-mint price range: $1,500 to $2,000.
☐ 335. Be My Baby/? • F.D. Johnson (Jan 58) 1950s $2,000
   45 rpm. Near-mint price range: $1,500 to $2,000.

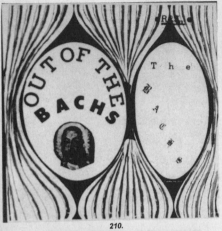

210.

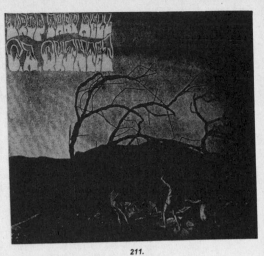

211.

213.

220.

216.

☐ 336. Confusion/She's Just My Size • Clintonian Cubs (My
Brother's 508) 1960 $2,000

  📷 45 rpm. Near-mint price range: $1,000 to $2,000.
  Member: Jimmy Castor.

☐ 337. Bye Bye/Somebody's in Love • Cosmic Rays (With Le Sun Ra & Arkestra)
(Saturn 222) 1960 $2,000

  📷 45 rpm. Near-mint price range: $1,500 to $2,000.

☐ 338. Now I've Confessed/Granny Baby • Deli-Cados (PMP 4979) 1960 $2,000

  📷 45 rpm. Identification number shown since no selection number is used. Near-mint price
  range: $1,500 to $2,000.

☐ 339. Never Let You Go/I'm Falling in Love • Poets (Shade 1001) 1960 $2,000

  📷 45 rpm. Near-mint price range: $1,000 to $2,000.

☐ 340. An Understanding/I'm Trying to Make You Love Me • Rollettes
(Melker 103) 1960 $2,000

  📷 45 rpm. Near-mint price range: $1,000 to $2,000.

☐ 341. I Wish/Blow Winds Blow • Videls (Early 702) 1960 $2,000

  📷 45 rpm. Near-mint price range: $1,000 to $2,000.

☐ 342. Song of a Lover/Compensation Blues • Vals (Unique
Laboratories/Theron) 1961 $2,000

  📷 45 rpm. Near-mint price range: $1,000 to $2,000.
  Members: Bill Gibson; David Wilkerson Jr.; Ernie Morris; Bill Taylor; Clarence Green.

☐ 343. Heavenly Bliss/Please Be Mine • Classic Four [Classic IV]
(Twist 1004) 1962 $2,000
  45 rpm. Near-mint price range: $1,000 to $2,000.

☐ 344. Beneath the Sun/In Between Tears • Equallos (Featuring Willie Logan)
(M&M 30) 1962 $2,000

  📷 45 rpm. Near-mint price range: $1,000 to $2,000.

☐ 345. Wishing Well/Deep Freeze • Ivorys (Darla 1000) 1962 $2,000
  45 rpm. Near-mint price range: $1,000 to $2,000.

☐ 346. How Sweet/No Wonder I Love You • Pacers (Guyden 2064) 1962 $2,000

  📷 45 rpm. Promotional issue. Near-mint price range: $1,000 to $2,000.

☐ 347. Baby/Hold Me Darling • Quarter Notes (Little Star 112) 1962 $2,000
  45 rpm. Near-mint price range: $1,000 to $2,000.

☐ 348. RCA Victor Family Record Center • Various Artists (RCA
Victor PR-121) 1962 $2,000

  📷 EP. Promotional issue only. Not issued with special cover. Near-mint price range: $1,000
  to $2,000.

  Side 1: *Good Luck Charm* (Elvis Presley); *The Way You Look Tonight* (Peter Nero); *Younger Than
    Springtime* (Paul Anka); *Frenesi* (Living Strings).
  Side 2: *Twistin' the Night Away* (Sam Cooke); *Easy Street* (Al Hirt); *Make Someone Happy* (Perry
    Como); *Moon River* (Henry Mancini).

☐ 349. My Heart/I Need Your Love So Bad • Vice-Roys (With Mike Metko Combo)
(Ramco 3715) 1962 $2,000
  45 rpm. Near-mint price range: $1,000 to $2,000.

☐ 350. Please Please Me/Ask Me Why • Beatles (Vee-Jay VJ-498) 1963 $2,000
  45 rpm. Credits "BEATLES." Black label with colorband. Has thick lettering and the VJ in
  brackets logo. Near-mint price range: $1,000 to $2,000.
  Variations of this release in the Top 1,000 can be found at Numbers 378; 379; 388; 488; 541; 542.
  Members: John Lennon; Paul McCartney; George Harrison; Ringo Starr.

222.

223.

232.

238.

☐ 351. Get Married in June/Million and One Dreams • Bel-Larks (With Eternals
Orchestra) (Hammer 6313).. 1963   **$2,000**

> 📷 45 rpm. Near-mint price range: $1,000 to $2,000.

☐ 352. Let's Dance the Screw/Let's Dance the Screw • Crystals
(Philles 111)... 1963   **$2,000**

> 📷 45 rpm. White label. Promotional issue only. Near-mint price range: $1,000 to $2,000.
> Members: Barbara Alston; Lala Brooks; Dee Dee Kennibrew; Patricia Wright; Mary Thomas.

☐ 353. Well, Darling/Over Yonder • Legends (Falco 305)........................... 1963   **$2,000**

> 📷 45 rpm. Near-mint price range: $1,000 to $2,000.

☐ 354. Together/Spooksville • Nu-trends (Lawn 216) 1963   **$2,000**

> 📷 45 rpm. Colored vinyl pressings are bootlegs. Near-mint price range: $1,000 to $2,000.

☐ 355. (Like a) Nightmare/If You Were Mine • Andantes (V.I.P. 25006)...... 1964   **$2,000**
45 rpm. Near-mint price range: $1,000 to $2,000.

☐ 356. The Beatles Talking/You Can't Do That • Beatles (Capitol
Custom 2637) 1964   **$2,000**

> 📷 45 rpm single (red label) and promotional sleeve. Available briefly from radio station
> KFWB and Wallich's Music City stores to celebrate the grand opening of a new location.
> Side 1 has interviews; side 2 is a song. Known counterfeit record does not have the Capitol
> logo. Title sleeve/mailer is a manila 7¼" square envelope with red print. Known counterfeit
> sleeve has a smaller opening flap, about 1½." Original is slightly over 2." Record alone: $800
> to $1,000. Record and sleeve: $1,000 to $2,000.
> Members: John Lennon; Paul McCartney, George Harrison; Ringo Starr.

☐ 357. Open End Interview • Beatles (Capitol Compact 33 PRO-2548/49). 1964   **$2,000**

> 📷 EP and picture insert sheet with script on back. Promotional issue only. Black label with
> colorband. Made to promote the *Meet the Beatles* LP. Has several tracks from LP plus an
> interview. Label reads "Especially prepared for Radio and TV programming Not For Sale."
> Known counterfeit EP does not have colorband. Picture sleeve has the interview script.
> Known counterfeit sleeve lacks the gloss and die cut thumb tab that is on top of one side of
> the original. (Picture sleeve/script alone: $700 to $800.) Near-mint price range: $1,000 to
> $2,000.
> Members: John Lennon; Paul McCartney, George Harrison; Ringo Starr.
> Side 1: *Interview Including "I Want to Hold Your Hand."*
> Side 2: *This Boy; It Won't Be Long.*

☐ 358. Stoned/I Wanna Be Your Man • Rolling Stones (London 9641) 1964   **$2,000**

> 📷 45 rpm. Promotional issue. Near-mint price range: $1,000 to $2,000.
> Members: Mick Jagger; Keith Richards; Bill Wyman; Brian Jones; Charlie Watts.
> A variation of this release in the Top 1,000 can be found at Number 95.

☐ 359. The New Tweedy Brothers • New Tweedy Brothers (Ridon 234)..... 1966   **$2,000**
LP. With hex cover. Near-mint price range: $1,500 to $2,000.

☐ 360. Save for a Rainy Day • Jan & Dean (Columbia 9461) 1967   **$2,000**
LP. At least one sale of this LP has been confirmed. May not be a U.S. issue. Tracks are
remixed from what is heard on the J&D LP of the same title. Does have one track, *Lullaby in
the Rain,* which is not on the J&D LP. Near-mint price range: $1,500 to $2,000.
Members: Jan Berry; Dean Torrence.

☐ 361. Wink • Shaggs (MCM 6311) 1967   **$2,000**
LP. Near-mint price range: $1,500 to $2,000.
Members: Geoff Gillette; Franklin Krakowski; Rick Medich; Ted Poulos; Ray Wheatley.

☐ 362. Smack • Smack (Audio House) 1967   **$2,000**
LP. Reportedly 200 made. No selection number used. Near-mint price range: $1,500 to
$2,000.

240.

255.

256.

253.

74

☐ 363. Elvis' Gold Records, Volume 4 • Elvis Presley (RCA
Victor LPM-3921).. 1968 $2,000

📷 Monaural LP. Black label, "Monaural" at bottom. Cover: Front: RCA Victor logo at upper
right and number at lower left. Has color photo of Elvis in front of a gold record. Back:
Pictures five other Elvis LPs. Disc alone: $750 to $1,000. Disc and cover: $1,500 to $2,000.
Side 1: *Love Letters; Witchcraft; It Hurts Me; What'd I Say; Please Don't Drag That String Around;*
Indescribably Blue.
Side 2: *Devil in Disguise; Lonely Man; A Mess of Blues; Ask Me; Ain't That Loving You Baby; Just*
Tell Her Jim Said Hello.

☐ 364. We Can Work It Out/Day Tripper • Beatles (Capitol/Starline 5555).. 1969 $2,000

45 rpm. Red and white label. "Starline" series. This is the only U.S. Beatles single with this
label style. Discontinued shortly after production when it Capitol learned the label was not
correct for the title. Near-mint price range: $1,500 to $2,000.
Members: John Lennon; Paul McCartney; George Harrison; Ringo Starr.

☐ 365. Don't Leave Me/? • Continentals & Counts of Rhythm (10476).......1960s $2,000

📷 45 rpm. No label name used. Identification number shown since no selection number is
used. Near-mint price range: $1,500 to $2,000.

☐ 366. Lori Anne/The Great Pumpkin • Jack-O-Lanterns
(Goldcrest 163)..1960s $2,000

45 rpm. Near-mint price range: $1,000 to $2,000.

☐ 367. Last Laugh • Brigade (Band 'N' Vocal 1066) 1970 $2,000

LP. Reissues exist on both Del Val and Rockadelic. Near-mint price range: $1,500 to $2,000.
Members: Peter Belknap; Ed Wallo; Mark Hartman; Bob Anderson; Eric Anderson; Tim Vetter; Dennis Steindal.

☐ 368. International Hotel, Las Vegas Nevada, Presents Elvis 1970 • Elvis
Presley (RCA Victor) 1970 $2,000

📷 Specially prepared, complimentary gift box given to invited guests at the Showroom
Internationale on January 26, 1970 (Elvis' opening night).

Box: Oversize, 12¾" x 12¾". Front: Orange RCA Victor logo at lower right. Title is in white,
6" x 6" box with orange and pink print at upper right. International Hotel logo at upper right.
Black-and-white Elvis photo, same as first used on *From Memphis to Vegas / From Vegas to*
Memphis. Back: Black, no printing.

Box Contents: *From Memphis to Vegas/From Vegas to Memphis* LSP-6020 (orange label,
rigid disc LP) and an orange label 45 rpm of *Kentucky Rain/My Little Friend,* with picture
sleeve; nine-page press release – a summary of Elvis' life and career – page one of which is
on RCA Victor Records Public Affairs letterhead; RCA Victor, full-color, spiral-bound 1970
Elvis' Records & Tapes catalog (with red, white and black cover); RCA Victor 1970 Elvis
pocket calender with a black-and-white photo of Elvis in leather suit, from '68 TV Special, on
one side; black-and-white, 8" x 10" Elvis photo, signed "Thanks, Elvis" (back announces
Elvis' International Hotel engagement "January 26th thru February 23rd"); 16-page photo
booklet, color front and back covers, black-and-white photos inside (Elvis photo on front is
identical to the one on the picture sleeve for *Suspicious Minds/You'll Think of Me);* four-page,
complimentary dinner menu, with color front and back covers, black, red and white print
inside (Elvis photo on front is identical to the one on the picture sleeve for *Suspicious*
Minds/You'll Think of Me). Box only: $1,100 to $1,300. Complete set: $1,500 to $2,000.
Variations of this release in the Top 1,000 can be found at Numbers 213; 214.

☐ 369. Robert W. Sarnoff – 25 Years of RCA Leadership • Various Artists (RCA
Victor RWS-0001)... 1973 $2,000

📷 Stereo LP. Orange label. Dynaflex vinyl. In-house promotional issue only. Approximately
50 made as souvenirs for RCA's Robert Sarnoff's retirement party. Includes excerpts of
music released during his years with the company. Near-mint price range: $1,500 to $2,000

rainbow
records
RAINBOW RECORDING CORP.

Record No.
45-233

45 R.P.M.
(45-R-4141)
Kingsbury Music
(BMI)

MY TRUE LOVE

THE SWANS

259.

Cosmopolitan
RECORDS
545 FIFTH AVENUE   N.Y.C., SUITE 812

UNBREAKABLE

45 R.P.M.

RECORD NO.

COS-45-531

Ulysses
Smith Pub. Co.
(ASCAP)

HANGING UP MY CHRISTMAS STOCKING
(Christmas Mambo)
(Joe Grey-U. Smith)
THE VELVET SOUNDS
And THE COSMOPOLITES

260.

Grand
RECORDS

Record No.
45-103

45 R.P.M.
Pub: Slotkin

THIS SILVER RING
(Pagovoy-Epstein)
THE CASTELLES
4103

263.

GEE

Manufactured by
45 RPM

GG 11

Trojan Records, Inc
45 RPM

Blues

Eddie "Tex" Curtis

SR BLUES
(Eddie "Tex" Curtis)
THE COINS
TTR-516

265.

Side 1 - Band 1 (The Post-War Years: Crooners/ Comedy/Mambo) Because (Perry Como); My Two Front Teeth (Spike Jones); Be My Love (Mario Lanza); The Thing (Phil Harris); Anytime (Eddie Fisher); Ghost Riders in the Sky (Vaughn Monroe); Cherry Pink and Apple Blossom White (Perez Prado); Oh My Papa (Eddie Fisher).

Band 2 (From the Golden Classics to the Presley Era) Tchaikovsky Violin Concerto (Jascha Heifetz); Chopin "Polonaise in Ab" (Artur Rubinstein); Puccini "Un-beldi" from Madam Butterfly (Leontyne Price); Liszt "Hungarian Rhapsody No. 2" (Vladmir Horwitz) The Symphony of the Air/Beethoven Symphony No. 9 (Arturo Toscanini); Hound Dog (Elvis Presley); Don't Be Cruel (Elvis Presley); Heartbreak Hotel (Elvis Presley); In the Ghetto (Live) (Elvis Presley).

Band 3 (Broadway's Brightest Lights) Hello Dolly/Fiddler on the Roof; Hair/South Pacific; The Sound of Music.

Band 4 (The Closing Fifties) Day-O (The Banana Boat Song) (Harry Belafonte); Mathilda (Harry Belafonte); Tchaikovsky "Piano Concerto No. 1" (Van Cliburn); The Kennedy Wit (John F. Kennedy).

Side 2 - Band 1 (The Middle Years: Soundtracks/Instrumentals/Country) Victory at Sea (Richard Rodgers-Robert Russell Bennett); Peter Gunn (Henry Mancini); Moon River (Henry Mancini); I Will Follow Him (Little Peggy March); Sugar Lips (Al Hirt); Ballad of the Green Berets (SSgt. Barry Sadler); Bouquet of Roses (shown as "Big Bouquet of Roses") (Eddy Arnold); The Three Bells (Browns); Kiss an Angel Good Morning (Charley Pride); I'm So Afraid of Losing You Again (Charley Pride); He'll Have to Go (Jim Reeves); Tennessee Waltz (Chet Atkins and the Boston Pops).

Band 2 (Rock Begins) Last Train to Clarksville (Monkees); I'm a Believer (Monkees); These Eyes (Guess Who); Light My Fire (Jose, Feliciano); Somebody to Love (Jefferson Airplane).

Band 3 (The New RCA) A Few Words from Neil Armstrong (Neil Armstrong); Grazing in the Grass (Friends of Distinction); Take Me Home Country Roads (John Denver); Everybody Plays the Fool (Main Ingredient); Troglodye (Caveman) (Jimmy Castor Bunch); Space Oddity (David Bowie); It's Impossible (Perry Como); Without You (Harry Nilsson).

Band 4 (Epilog) Keep the Dream Alive/The January 15 Benefit Concert for the Martin Luther King Jr. Center for Social Change/Precious Lord (Linda Hopkins).

☐ 370. Diamond Dogs • David Bowie (RCA Victor 0576)............................. 1974 $2,000
LP. With "Dog Genitals" front cover (picturing, obviously, a dog's genital area). Near-mint price range: $1,500 to $2,000.

☐ 371. We Wrote a Song Together • Neil Diamond (Continuum II 001) 1976 $2,000
12-inch single. Made exclusively for Neil's son Jesse's grade school class. Has Neil and a band composing and recording in a studio – with the children present. Includes an alternative version of *Beautiful Noise*. Neil made and autographed a copy for each child in attendance – estimated to be 30 to 40 copies. Near-mint price range: $1,500 to $2,000.

☐ 372. Beast of Burden/When the Whip Comes Down • Rolling Stones (Rolling Stones 19309) 1978 $2,000
📷 Picture sleeve. Near-mint price range: $1,000 to $2,000.
Members: Mick Jagger; Keith Richards; Bill Wyman; Charlie Watts; Ron Wood.

☐ 373. Too Old to Cry/My Tears Start to Fall • Class-Airs (Honey Bee 81631)..? $2,000
📷 45 rpm. Identification number shown since no selection number is used. Near-mint price range: $1,000 to $2,000.

☐ 374. Job Opening/? • Del-Larks (Queen City 2004) ....? $2,000
45 rpm. Near-mint price range: $1,000 to $2,000.

☐ 375. Burning Sensation/? • Robby Lawson (Kyser 2122)..............................? $2,000
45 rpm. Near-mint price range: $1,000 to $2,000.

☐ 376. Fascinating Girl/? • George Lemons (Gold Soul 102) ....? $2,000
45 rpm. Promotional issue only. Near-mint price range: $1,000 to $2,000.

YOUR COPY INC.
1135 WESTMINSTER, DETROIT, MICH.

YOUR COPY
INCORPORATED PHONO RECORD

UNBREAKABLE
45 R.P.M.

RECORD NO.
45-1135-B

BMI

THE BELLS OF MY HEART
(I. Potter)

THE FASCINATORS
With Musical Accomp.

266.

harlem

45-2322
(45-DA-735-K)
Congress Music
(BMI)

Male Quartet
Vocal Ballad

FIRE IN MY HEART
(Hall - Shod)

BOBBY HALL
And THE KINGS

268.

Aladdin
★ BEVERLY HILLS, CALIFORNIA ★

45-3247
(RR-2088)
Q

Vocal - 3:05

(ASCAP)
Guild Music

I'LL HIDE MY TEARS
(Murry Wilson)

THE JETS

269.

GEE

Manufactured by
45 RPM

Trojan Records, Inc.
45 RPM

GG 12

Jump

TWO LOVES HAVE I
(B. Travers-J. P. Murray)

BILL "BASS" GORDON
and his
COLONIALS

TTR-511

267.

78

☐ 377. Elvis Presley • Elvis Presley (RCA Victor EPA-747) 1956 $1,800

📷 Temporary paper envelope/sleeve. Used until standard EP covers were available. Paper stock is white, with dark blue print. Cover actually reads "Blue Suede Shoes by Elvis Presley" with the other three tracks listed below in smaller type. Counterfeits exist. (Disc value, $20 to $30, is not included.) Price range for sleeve only: $1,000 to $1,800.
Side 1: *Blue Suede Shoes; Tutti Frutti.*
Side 2: *I Got a Woman; Just Because.*

☐ 378. Please Please Me/Ask Me Why • Beatles (Vee-Jay VJ-498) 1963 $1,800
45 rpm. Credits "BEATLES." Black label with colorband. Has thin lettering and oval logo. The number symbol (#) precedes the selection number. Near-mint price range: $1,500 to $1,800.
Variations of this release in the Top 1,000 can be found at Numbers 350; 379; 388; 488; 541; 542.
Members: John Lennon; Paul McCartney, George Harrison; Ringo Starr.

☐ 379. Please Please Me/Ask Me Why • Beatles (Vee-Jay VJ-498) 1963 $1,800

📷 45 rpm. Credits "BEATTLES." Black label with colorband. Has thin lettering and oval logo. The number symbol (#) precedes the selection number on the label. Near-mint price range: $1,500 to $1,800.
Variations of this release in the Top 1,000 can be found at Numbers 350; 378; 388; 488; 541; 542.
Members: John Lennon; Paul McCartney, George Harrison; Ringo Starr.

☐ 380. Second Open End Interview • Beatles (Capitol Compact 33 PRO-2598/99) 1964 $1,800

📷 EP and picture insert sheet with script on back. Promotional issue only. Issued to promote *The Beatles Second Album*. Has three tracks from LP plus an interview. Label reads "Especially prepared for Radio and TV programming Not For Sale." Picture sleeve has the interview script. (Picture sleeve/script alone: $600 to $700.) Near-mint price range: $1,500 to $1,800.
Members: John Lennon; Paul McCartney, George Harrison; Ringo Starr.
Side 1: *Interview Featuring "Roll Over Beethoven."*
Side 2: *Please Mr. Postman; Thank You Girl.*

☐ 381. Yellow Submarine/Eleanor Rigby • Beatles (Apple/Americom) 1969 $1,800
Selection number not known. Round 4" flexi-disc. Light blue vinyl with white print. Available in special vending machines. Near-mint price range: $1,500 to $1,800.
Members: John Lennon; Paul McCartney, George Harrison; Ringo Starr.

☐ 382. Surrender/Lonely Man • Elvis Presley (With Jordanaires) (RCA Victor 37-7850) 1961 $1,700

📷 Compact 33 single with picture sleeve. First of five mono singles in this somewhat experimental and ultimately failed series. Compact 33s are seven-inch discs with a quarter-inch, LP-size, hole. Picture sleeve alone is $800 to $1,000. Price range for both: $1,300 to $1,700.
Variations of this release in the Top 1,000 can be found at Numbers 461; 783.

☐ 383. That's All Right/Blue Moon of Kentucky • Elvis Presley (With Scotty and Bill) (Sun 209) 1954 $1,600

📷 78 rpm. Near-mint price range: $1,400 to $1,600.
A variation of this release in the Top 1,000 can be found at Number 417.
Members: Elvis Presley; Scotty Moore; Bill Black.

Lucky
RECORDS HOLLYWOOD

002-A
Publisher:
Lucky Music-BMI

The Marbles
Sing

GOLDEN GIRL
(Rudy Jackson)

THE MARBLES
45- 002

270.

Old Town
RECORDS
Manufactured by Old Town Record Corp., N. Y. C.

Record No.
O.T. 1000-45
(O.T. 800)

45 R.P.M.
Published by
Robbins Music
ASCAP

WONDER WHY
(Brodsky - Kahn)

THE SOLITAIRES
(O.T. 800)

275.

Old Town
Manufactured by Old Town Record Corp., N.Y.C.

Record No.
O.T. 1011-45
(45-O.T. 900)

45 R.P.M.
Vocal
De Sylva, Brown
& Henderson Inc.

(I'M AFRAID)
THE MASQUERADE IS OVER
(Magidson-Wrubel)

THE CLEFFTONES

277.

Checker

U-7491
Burton Ltd.

Vocal
B.M.I.

GONNA BUY ME A TELEPHONE
(M. Pejoe)
MORRIS PEJOE
and his Band
766

272.

☐ 384. TV Guide Presents Elvis Presley • Elvis Presley (RCA
Victor GB-MW-8705) 1956 $1,600

> 📷 EP with two inserts; no cover. Blue or white label. Single-sided, four-track, open-end interview. Promotional issue only. Inserts: "Suggested continuity," a pink, four-page suggested interview script; and a gray card which provides background on the interview and pictures the September 8-14, 1956 issue of *TV Guide* with Elvis on the cover. Counterfeits exist. Disc: $1,000 to $1,200. Each insert: $150 to $200. Price range for disc and both inserts: $1,400 to $1,600.
>
> Side 1: *"Pelvis" Nickname; Adult's Reaction; First Public Appearance; How "Rockin' Motion" Started.*

☐ 385. (1957) March of Dimes Galaxy of Stars (Discs for Dimes) • Various Artists
(N.F.I.P. GM-8M-0653/0654) 1956 $1,600

> 📷 Monaural LP. White and blue-green label. 16" transcription with 20 entertainers, including Elvis Presley, speaking on behalf of the 1957 March of Dimes campaign. Issued only to radio stations. Promotional issue only. Insert: 16 pages of dee jay announcements. LP alone: $1,350 to $1,500. LP and insert: $1,400 to $1,600.
>
> Artists featured: Howard Miller (Instructions – Not for Broadcast); Eddie Fisher; Julie London; Denise Lor; Jim Lowe; Mills Brothers; Guy Mitchell; Vaughn Monroe; Elvis Presley; Gale Robbins; Pat Boone; Sammy Davis Jr.; Gogi Grant; Bill Hayes; Eartha Kitt; Ray Price; Johnnie Ray; Henri Rene; Dinah Shore; Margaret Whiting; Andy Williams.

☐ 386. (1957) March of Dimes Galaxy of Stars (Disc Jockey Interviews) • Various
Artists (N.F.I.P. GM-8M-0657/0658) 1956 $1,600

> 📷 Monaural LP. White and blue-green label. 16" transcription with six vocal acts, including Elvis Presley, providing an open-end interview on behalf of the 1957 March of Dimes campaign, and introducing one of their songs. Issued only to radio stations. Inserts: Cover letter to Station Managers on National Foundation for Infantile Paralysis (N.F.I.P.) letterhead, listing of National Committee and State Chairmen, five-page script for the open-end interview with Elvis Presley; five, five-page scripts for the open-end interviews with the other stars on this disc. LP alone: $1,350 to $1,500. LP and inserts: $1,400 to $1,600.
>
> Side 1: *I Love My Baby* (Jill Corey); *Love Me Tender* (Elvis Presley); *Baby Doll* (Andy Williams).
> Side 2: *Your Love Is My Love* (Alan Dale); *Paper Doll* (Mills Brothers); *Singing the Blues* (Guy Mitchell).

☐ 387. Jailhouse Rock/Treat Me Nice • Elvis Presley (RCA
Victor 47-7035) 1957 $1,600

> 📷 MGM special press preview theater ticket/sleeve. Sent wrapped around the standard *Jailhouse Rock* picture sleeve ($50 to $75), with a 45 rpm ($30 to $40) inside. Promotional issue only, distributed only to media film reviewers. Counterfeits exist. Price range for package with ticket but without stub attached: $500 to $750. Price range for package with ticket and stub still attached: $1,400 to $1,600.

☐ 388. Please Please Me/Ask Me Why • Beatles (Vee-Jay VJ-498) 1963 $1,600

> 📷 45 rpm. Credits "BEATLES." Black label with colorband. Has thin lettering and oval logo. This is the first Beatles single released in the U.S. Near-mint price range: $1,400 to $1,600.
>
> Variations of this release in the Top 1,000 can be found at Numbers 350; 378; 379; 488; 541; 542.
> Members: John Lennon; Paul McCartney, George Harrison; Ringo Starr.

☐ 389. Help • Azitis (Elco 5555) 1971 $1,600

> LP. Near-mint price range: $1,200 to $1,600.
> Members: Steve Nelson; Michael Welch; Dennis Sullivan; Don Lower.

☐ 390. 32-20/Last Fair Deal Gone Down • Robert Johnson
(Vocalion 03445) 1937 $1,500

> 78 rpm. Near-mint price range: $1,000 to $1,500.

☐ 391. Sweet Home Chicago/Walking Blues • Robert Johnson
(Vocalion 03601) 1937 $1,500

> 78 rpm. Near-mint price range: $1,000 to $1,500.

279.

284.

286.

287.

☐ 392. Stand Up and Be Counted/? • Johnny Clifton & His String Band
   (Center 102) 1950 $1,500
   78 rpm. Near-mint price range: $1,000 to $1,500.
   Member: Bill Haley.

☐ 393. Time Takes Care of Everything/Don't Look Now • Ravens
   (Columbia 1-903).. 1950 $1,500
   Compact 33 single. Near-mint price range: $1,000 to $1,500.
   Members: Ollie Jones; Jimmy Ricks; Leonard Puzey; Warren Suttles; Joe Van Loan; Louis Heyward.

☐ 394. I'm So Crazy for Love/My Baby's Gone • Ravens
   (Columbia 1-925).. 1950 $1,500
   Compact 33 single. Near-mint price range: $1,000 to $1,500.
   Members: Ollie Jones; Jimmy Ricks; Leonard Puzey; Warren Suttles; Joe Van Loan; Louis Heyward.

☐ 395. I Cross My Fingers/Can't Seem to Laugh Anymore • Orioles
   (Jubilee 5040).. 1951 $1,500
   45 rpm. Near-mint price range: $1,000 to $1,500.
   Members: Sonny Til; Alex Sharp; George Nelson; John Reed; Tom Gaither.

☐ 396. I Miss You So/You Are My First Love • Orioles (Jubilee 5051)......... 1951 $1,500
   45 rpm. Black vinyl. Near-mint price range: $1,000 to $1,500.
   Members: Sonny Til; Alex Sharp; George Nelson; John Reed; Tom Gaither.
   A variation of this release can be found in the Top 1,000 at Number 231.

☐ 397. Baby, Please Don't Go/Don't Tell Her • Orioles (Jubilee 5065) 1951 $1,500
   45 rpm. Red vinyl. Near-mint price range: $1,000 to $1,500.
   Members: Sonny Til; Alex Sharp; George Nelson; John Reed; Tom Gaither.

☐ 398. Dorothy Mae/When I Am Gone • Joe Hill Louis (Checker 763) 1952 $1,500
   45 rpm. Near-mint price range: $1,000 to $1,500.

☐ 399. When Boy Meets Girl/Later Baby • Fat Man Matthews & Four Kittens
   (Imperial 5211) 1952 $1,500
   📷 45 rpm. Near-mint price range: $1,000 to $1,500.
   Members: Allen Matthews; Albert Veal; Joseph Gaines; Dudley Royal; John "Buddy" Morris; Frank Rushing.

☐ 400. Don't Cry Baby/See See Rider • Orioles (Jubilee 5092)................... 1952 $1,500
   45 rpm. Red vinyl. Near-mint price range: $1,000 to $1,500.
   Members: Sonny Til; Alex Sharp; George Nelson; John Reed; Tom Gaither.

☐ 401. Blue Serenade/Gonna Let You Go • Baby Face Turner (Vocal Ray Agee)
   (Modern 882) 1952 $1,500
   📷 45 rpm. Near-mint price range: $1,000 to $1,500.
   Session: Sonny Blair (harmonica); Ike Turner (piano).

☐ 402. Heaven Or Fire/Tears and Wine • Dusty Brooks & Four Tones (Featuring
   Juanita Brown) (Sun 182)... 1953 $1,500
   45 rpm. Near-mint price range: $1,000 to $1,500.
   Members: Dusty Brooks (piano); Juanita Brown (vocal); Joe Alexander (vocal); Arathamus Maryland (guitar); Ruby
   Thrasher (bass); Virgil Johnson (drums); Bernard Hunter (vibes). Recorded in Nashville on April 25, 1953.

☐ 403. Baby Come Back to Me/Lonely Mood • Five Echoes (Sabre 102) ... 1953 $1,500
   45 rpm. Red vinyl. Near-mint price range: $1,000 to $1,500.
   Members: Johnny Taylor; Count Sims; Earl Lewis; Herbert Lewis; Jimmy Marshall.

☐ 404. Hurry Home Baby/That's My Desire • Flamingos (Chance 1140)..... 1953 $1,500
   45 rpm. Red vinyl. Near-mint price range: $1,000 to $1,500.
   Members: Sollie McElroy; John Carter; Zeke Carey; Jake Carey; Paul Wilson; Nate Nelson.

☐ 405. The Lovers/Drag It Home, Baby • Jets (Rainbow 201)..................... 1953 $1,500
   78 rpm. Near-mint price range: $1,000 to $1,500.
   Members: Buck Mason; Jim Walton; Walt Taylor; John Bowie; Charlie Booker; Herb Fisher.

☐ 406. Volcano/Gomen Nasai • Jets (7-11 2102) 1953 $1,500
   45 rpm. Near-mint price range: $1,000 to $1,500.

☐ 407. I Miss You So/Till Then • Orioles (Jubilee 5107) 1953 $1,500
   45 rpm. Red vinyl. Near-mint price range: $1,000 to $1,500.

MERCER RECORDS

45 RPM
1674 - EN
FOR DISC JOCKEY
USE ONLY

Tempo Music
ASCAP
(2:50)
fs-992-4

"TRUE LOVE GONE"
(The Enchanters)

THE ENCHANTERS

Musical Direction by:
Maurice King

290.

Hi-Po RECORDS
NASHVILLE, TENNESSEE

UNBREAKABLE

5 R.P.M.

RECORD NO.
1003
SO-78

Time 2:58

ONLY THE ANGELS KNOW
(Esquires)
THE ESQUIRES

291.

ONYX

45 RPM   45 RPM

Walton Music
(Smith)

505

BOHEMIAN DADDY
(Bohemian-Stewart-Mars)
THE MARQUIS
Orch Sammy Lowe
D-1005 A

294.

STANDORD
A Div. of Standard Electronic Mfg. New Haven, Ct.

Side 1
XEP-200

45 RPM
6106 A

IN THE STILL OF THE NITE
F. Parris

The Five Satins

293.

P
B
Pla-Bac
RECORDS

P.B.106B
Pla-bac

45 r.p.m.
Vocal by
The Packards

LADISE
(Scott-Smith)
THE PACKARDS
Paul Boyers Band

295.

MFG. BY PLA-BAC RECORDS, NEW YORK, N.Y.

☐ 408. Crosstown Blues/I Want You for Myself • Snooky Pryor
(Parrot 807) 1953 $1,500
    45 rpm. Red vinyl. Near-mint price range: $1,000 to $1,500.

☐ 409. White Cliffs of Dover/Much Too Much • Lee Andrews & Hearts
(Rainbow 256) 1954 $1,500
    45 rpm. Yellow label. Near-mint price range: $1,000 to $1,500.
    Members: Lee Andrews; Arthur Thompson; Roy Calhoun; Wendell Calhoun; Butch Curry; Ted Weems.

☐ 410. Miss You/I Really Really Love You • Crows (Rama 30) 1954 $1,500
    45 rpm. Red vinyl. Near-mint price range: $1,000 to $1,500.
    Members: Daniel "Sonny" Norton; Harold Major; Jerry Hamilton; Mark Jackson; Bill Davis.

☐ 411. Darling I Know/Christine • El Rays (With Willie Dixon & Orchestra)
(Checker 794) 1954 $1,500
    45 rpm. Near-mint price range: $1,000 to $1,500.
    Members: Marvin Junior; Vern Allison; Mike McGill; Charles Barksdale.

☐ 412. Soft, Sweet and Really Fine/Everybody's Singing the Blues • Five Dukes
of Rhythm (With Gene Moore & His Combo) (Rendezvous 812) 1954 $1,500
    45 rpm. Near-mint price range: $1,000 to $1,500.

☐ 413. So Lonesome/Broke • Five Echoes (Sabre 105) 1954 $1,500
    45 rpm. Red vinyl. Near-mint price range: $1,000 to $1,500.
    Members: Johnny Taylor; Count Sims; Earl Lewis; Herbert Lewis; Jimmy Marshall.

☐ 414. No Other Girl/The World Is Waiting for the Sunrise • Larks
(Lloyds 112) 1954 $1,500
    45 rpm. Near-mint price range: $1,000 to $1,500.
    Members: Eugene Mumford; Allen Bunn; Raymond "Pee-Wee" Barnes; Thurmon Ruth; Dave McNeil; Hadie Rowe.

☐ 415. Big Jay McNeely • Big Jay McNeely (Federal 96) 1954 $1,500
    10-inch LP. Near-mint price range: $1,000 to $1,500.

☐ 416. Good Rockin' Tonight/I Don't Care If the Sun Don't Shine • Elvis Presley
(With Scotty and Bill) (Sun 210) 1954 $1,500
    78 rpm. Near-mint price range: $1,000 to $1,500.
    A variation of this release in the Top 1,000 can be found at Number 487.
    Members: Elvis Presley; Scotty Moore; Bill Black.

☐ 417. That's All Right/Blue Moon of Kentucky • Elvis Presley (With Scotty and
Bill) (Sun 209) 1954 $1,500
    45 rpm. Near-mint price range: $1,000 to $1,500.
    A variation of this release in the Top 1,000 can be found at Number 383.
    Members: Elvis Presley; Scotty Moore; Bill Black.

☐ 418. I'll Be Around/Miss You Tonite • Lynn Roberts & Phantoms
(Oriole 101) 1954 $1,500
    45 rpm. Red vinyl. Near-mint price range: $1,000 to $1,500.
    A variation of this release in the Top 1,000 can be found at Number 828.

☐ 419. Lovely Way to Spend an Evening/You're Still My Baby • Angels
(Grand 121) 1955 $1,500
    45 rpm. Glossy yellow label. Rigid disc. No company address shown. Near-mint price range:
    $1,000 to $1,500.

☐ 420. What Can I Tell Her Now/Let Me Love, Love You • Bells
(Rama 166) 1955 $1,500
    45 rpm. Near-mint price range: $1,000 to $1,500.
    Members: Joe Van Loan; Willie Ray; Willis Sanders; Bob Kornegay.

☐ 421. Darling Patricia/All Is Well, All Is Well • Gales (J-V-B 35) 1955 $1,500
    45 rpm. Reportedly the same group as the Violinaires. Near-mint price range: $1,000 to
    $1,500.

ABCO RECORDS CHICAGO

BMI
2:48

Lawn Music
U3193

I LOVE YOU THE MOST
(Leon Arnold)
THE RIP-CHORDS
G105

296.

TriLyte

5001—AA—45

Time 2:42

COME TO ME
(The Shantones)
THE SHANTONES
WITH ORCH.

297.

SPITFIRE RECORDS
3806 S. San Pedro
Los Angeles, Calif.

45-L-15 A
BMI
Amer. Music

2:50
Vocal

TELL ME YOU'RE MINE
(Hardly-Lyrois-Richards)
THE VELVETEERS

298.

ACME RECORDS

AC-109-A
Beam Pub.
B.M.I

Time: 2:55

"PLEASE SAY YOU'LL BE MINE"
(Edwards-Miller)
SUNBEAMS
45-719

303.

☐ 422. Mystery Train/I Forgot to Remember to Forget • Elvis Presley
(RCA Victor 47-6357) 1955 $1,500

📷 Picture sleeve. The 45 rpm single is on the white "Record Prevue" label. One of a series of promotional "This Is His Life" issues, made for many different RCA Victor artists. Though not numbered, this is the first picture sleeve of any type issued with an Elvis record. Unfortunately, the "life story" is somewhat fabricated. 45 rpm single without picture sleeve is $300 to $400. Price range for both: $1,000 to $1,500.

☐ 423. Yours Alone/Farewell • Bobby Relf & Laurels (Flair 1063) 1955 $1,500

📷 45 rpm. Near-mint price range: $1,000 to $1,500.

☐ 424. Give Me Another Chance/Baby Don't You Cry • Sheiks
(Ef-N-De 1000) 1955 $1,500
45 rpm. Near-mint price range: $1,000 to $1,500.

☐ 425. Keep on Trying/The Switch • Ambassadors (With Johnny L. Chapman
Orchestra) (Air 5065) 1956 $1,500

📷 45 rpm. Approximately 50 made. Near-mint price range: $1,000 to $1,500.

☐ 426. Tongue-Tied Jill/Get with It • Charlie Feathers (Meteor 5032).......... 1956 $1,500

📷 45 rpm. Maroon label. (Since 45 was unavailable, the 78 is pictured.) Near-mint price range: $1,000 to $1,500.
Session: Jody Chastain; Jerry Huffman.

☐ 427. Hello Dear/Bobby Sox Baby • Hi-Liters (Vee-Jay 184) 1956 $1,500
45 rpm. Near-mint price range: $1,000 to $1,500.

☐ 428. Lonesome Road • Lonnie Johnson (King 520) 1956 $1,500

📷 LP. Near-mint price range: $1,000 to $1,500.
Side 1: *Lonesome Road; Backwater Blues; Tomorrow; Call Me Darlin'; So Tired; Careless Love.*
Side 2: *Drunk Again; Working Man's Blues; Jelly Roll Baker; Pleasing You; It's Been So Long; Tomorrow Night.*

☐ 429. Eager Boy/? • Lonesome Drifter (K 5812) 1956 $1,500
45 rpm. Near-mint price range: $1,000 to $1,500.

☐ 430. I Need Someone/Lu La • Ray Dots (Vibro 1651).............................. 1956 $1,500

📷 45 rpm. Near-mint price range: $1,000 to $1,500.

☐ 431. SP-33-4 • Various Artists (RCA Victor SP-33-4).............................. 1956 $1,500

📷 Untitled promotional LP. Not issued with a special cover. Near-mint price range: $1,000 to $1,500.
Side 1: *Magyar Melodies* (Gypsy Sandor); *Pretending* (Andy Russell); *My Bucket's Got a Hole in It* (Bob Scobey); *Dodging a Divorcee* (Skitch Henderson); *Frenesi* (Herb Jeffries); *Usted* (Luis Arcaraz); *Francisco Guayabal* (Deny Mor); *Hot Timbales* (Tito Puente); *El Chicero* (Billo); *Oye Este Ritmo* (M. Lopez); *The Lord's Prayer* (Jerome).
Side 2: *I'm Movin' on to Glory* (Hank Snow); *Babalu* (La Playa); *Twilight in Turkey* (Tommy Dorsey); *Just Say I Love Her* (Lou Monte); *Don't Be Cruel* (Elvis Presley); *I'm Glad I'm Not You* (Grant-Martin); *Holiday for Strings* (Glenn Miller); *Pavan for a Dead Princess* (Fritz Reiner); *Trio in G (Beethoven)* (Heifetz-Primrose); *Marriage of Figaro* (G. Tozzi); *Capriccio* (W. Landowska); *A Mighty Fortress* (Robert Shaw).

☐ 432. Eternally/I Believe • Little Cholly Wright (Cholly 7093) 1956 $1,500
45 rpm. One source indicates *I Believe* as being credited to the Nu-Tones. Near-mint price range: $1,000 to $1,500.

☐ 433. Ring Chimes/Wolf Call • Dots (Rev 3512) 1957 $1,500
45 rpm. Near-mint price range: $1,000 to $1,500.
Member: Jeanette Baker.

☐ 434. A Love Like Yours/Never Look Behind • Lovenotes
(Premium 611)... 1957 $1,500
45 rpm. Reissued almost immediately with artist credit changed to the Trueloves. Near-mint price range: $1,000 to $1,500.
Member: David Haywood.

STEAMBOAT
RECORDS

UNBREAKABLE
45 R.P.M.

RECORD NO.
101 B

Rebecca
Music Publ.

BELIEVE IN ME
(Lucas & Patrick)
THE SWANS

304.

OUR
RECORDS
2667 Long Beach Ave., Los Angeles 53, California

BMI
Elite Pub.

YOU MUST BE BORN AGAIN
(Andy Williams)
ANDY WILLIAMS
AND CAVALIERS

305.

DELTA
RECORDS

UNBREAKABLE
45 R.P.M.

Delta Pub.
BMI

WOULD YOU DO THE SAME FOR ME
(Asberry-Gordon)
THE CANDLELIGHTERS

307.

LITTLE
RECORDS

UNBREAKABLE
45 R.P.M.

RECORD NO.
LIT 813

Emcee Music
BMI

Time 2:35

LORRAINE
(Dee)
JOEY DEE
AND THE STARLITERS

309.

☐ 435. Jerry/Where Are You • Minors (Celeste 3007)................................... 1957 $1,500
    45 rpm. Near-mint price range: $1,000 to $1,500.

☐ 436. SPA 7-61 • Various Artists (RCA Victor SPA 7-61) 1957 $1,500
    📷 Untitled promotional sampler EP. Not issued with special cover. Near-mint price range: $1,000 to $1,500.
    Side 1: Howard University Choir; Versatones; Jeannie Smith; Jim Reeves; Paul Lavalle; Robert Merrill.
    Side 2: Elvis Presley (*Jailhouse Rock*); Billy Mure; Sabres; Gogi Grant; Nick Venet; Lane Brothers.

☐ 437. Billy Ward and His Dominoes • Billy Ward & Dominoes
    (Federal 548).. 1957 $1,500
    LP. Near-mint price range: $1,000 to $1,500.
    Members: Billy Ward; Clyde McPhatter; Charlie White; William Lamont; Bill Brown; Dave McNeil; James Van Loan.
    Side 1: *Tenderly; Over the Rainbow; Learnin' the Blues; When the Swallows Come Back to Capistrano; Harbor Lights; These Foolish Things.*
    Side 2: *Three Coins in the Fountain; Little Things Mean a Lot; Rags to Riches; May I Never Love Again; Lonesome Road; Until the Real Thing Comes Along.*

☐ 438. Clyde McPhatter with Billy Ward & Dominoes • Billy Ward & Dominoes
    with Clyde McPhatter (Federal 559) 1957 $1,500
    LP. Near-mint price range: $1,000 to $1,500.
    Members: Billy Ward; Clyde McPhatter; Charlie White; William Lamont; Bill Brown; Dave McNeil; James Van Loan.
    Side 1: *Sixty Minute Man; That's What You're Doing to Me; Deep Sea Blues; Pedal Pushin' Papa; Don't Leave Me This Way.*
    Side 2: *Have Mercy Baby; I Am with You; Chicken Blues; Weeping Willow Blues; Love, Love, Love; The Bells.*

☐ 439. Baby/I Don't Mind • Flaming Hearts (Inst. Tornadoes) (Vulco 1) 1958 $1,500
    📷 45 rpm. Near-mint price range: $1,000 to $1,500.

☐ 440. Be-Bop Battling Ball/Try This Heart for Size • Eddie Gaines
    (Summit 101).. 1958 $1,500
    45 rpm. Near-mint price range: $1,000 to $1,500.

☐ 441. Confession of Love/Haunting Memories • Halliquins (Juanita 102) .. 1958 $1,500
    📷 45 rpm. Near-mint price range: $1,000 to $1,500.

☐ 442. Twilight/The Wows of Love • Paragons (Winley 227)....................... 1958 $1,500
    📷 45 rpm. Note spelling error: "Wows" should be "Vows." Near-mint price range: $1,000 to $1,500.
    Members: Julius McMichaels; Mack Starr; Al Brown; Don Travis; Ben Frazier; Bill Witt; Rick Jackson. Session: Dave "Baby" Cortez.

☐ 443. Nobody Can Love You/Snap, Crackle and Pop • Supremes
    (Mark 129) 1958 $1,500
    📷 45 rpm. Near-mint price range: $1,000 to $1,500.

☐ 444. Love Is a Vow/Walkie Talkie Baby • Teentones (Featuring Arnold Malone
    with Larry Luple Orchestra) (Rego 1004) 1958 $1,500
    📷 45 rpm. Near-mint price range: $1,000 to $1,500.

☐ 445. A Lonely Boy/Go! Little Susie • Those Four Eldorados
    (Academy 8138) 1958 $1,500
    45 rpm. Near-mint price range: $1,000 to $1,500.

☐ 446. Rock Pretty Mama/? • Billy Adams (Quincy 932)............................. 1959 $1,500
    45 rpm. Near-mint price range: $1,000 to $1,500.

☐ 447. Shake Um Up Rock/? • Benny Cliff (With Benny Cliff Trio)
    (Drift 1441).. 1959 $1,500
    45 rpm. Near-mint price range: $1,000 to $1,500.

☐ 448. Girl of My Dreams/Dolores • Don Juans (Onezy 101) 1959 $1,500
    45 rpm. Near-mint price range: $1,000 to $1,500.

STARDUST RECORDS

UNBREAKABLE
45 R.P.M.

RECORD NO.
102-A

Diana Music
(B.M.I.)

Time: 2:19

THE ENCHANTERS
SING
SPELLBOUND BY THE MOON
(The Enchanters)

310.

HOLLAND RECORDS
507 Fifth Avenue, N. Y. 17, N. Y.

(P-631)
Jame Music
Publ. Co.
(BMI) 2:01

H-7420
Vocal
45 RPM

BELIEVE IN ME
(Davis-Wyler)

THE LOLLYPOPS

312.

NOBLE

Noble Music Co.
NO-601—2:18

Vocal Solo
Jimmy Moore

TENDER LOVE
(Moore)
JIMMY MOORE
and the PEACOCKS
WITH INST. ACCOMP.
- 711—45 -

313.

HARECO

Vendo-Welton
(BMI)
Time 2:36

(1003-A)
Arranged by
JOE LOUIS

EVERYDAY HOLIDAY
(Stan Beverly)
HOLLYWOOD SAXONS
Produced by
G. Olds-L. Johnson-S. Beverly
102

311.

☐ 449. Bells Are Ringing/Pretty Girl • Golden Bells (With Gems of Rhythm Band) (Sure 1002).. 1959   **$1,500**

📷 45 rpm. Near-mint price range: $1,000 to $1,500.

☐ 450. She's My Baby/You're Not Mine At All • Leon Holmes & His Georgia Ramblers (Peach 597)... 1959   **$1,500**

📷 45 rpm. Near-mint price range: $1,000 to $1,500.

☐ 451. *Evelyn/Never Will Part* • Silhouettes (With Dave McRae Orchestra) (Junior 400) 1959   **$1,500**

📷 45 rpm. Near-mint price range: $1,000 to $1,500.

☐ 452. Marlene/? • Sonics (Gaiety 114)... 1959   **$1,500**

45 rpm. Near-mint price range: $1,000 to $1,500.

☐ 453. So Sincere/In My Dreams • Sporttones (With Rhythm Acc.) (Munich 101)... 1959   **$1,500**

45 rpm. Near-mint price range: $1,000 to $1,500.

☐ 454. Just for a Little While/I Love You So • Tender Tones (Ducky 713)... 1959   **$1,500**

📷 45 rpm. Near-mint price range: $1,000 to $1,500.

☐ 455. If She Should Call/Don't Monkey with a Donkey • Voltones (Dynamic 108) 1959   **$1,500**

45 rpm. Near-mint price range: $1,000 to $1,500.

☐ 456. Sweetest Angel/Little Curly Top • Condors (Hunter 2503/2504)....... 1960   **$1,500**

📷 45 rpm. Near-mint price range: $1,000 to $1,500.

☐ 457. It Doesn't Matter/Whisper It • Continentals (Hunter 3503)................ 1960   **$1,500**

📷 45 rpm. Near-mint price range: $1,000 to $1,500.

☐ 458. Mule Skinner Blues • Fendermen (Soma 1240) 1960   **$1,500**

📷 LP. Vinyl appears to be blue when held to a light. Near-mint price range: $1,000 to $1,500.

Members: Phil Humphrey; Jimmy Sundquist; John Hauer; Denny Dale Gudin.
Side 1: *Mule Skinner Blues; Torture; Beach Party; Bertha Lou; Honky Tonk; Lonesome Road.*
Side 2: *Don't You Just Know It; Heartbreakin' Special; Jack of Diamonds; High Noon; Koo-Koo; Caravan.*
A variation of this release in the Top 1,000 can be found at Number 534.

☐ 459. Forever and Ever/Fade-Out • Frankie & C-Notes (Richie 2)............. 1961   **$1,500**

📷 45 rpm. Near-mint price range: $1,000 to $1,500.

☐ 460. Love Walked Out/The Quarrel • Newlyweds (Homogenized Soul 601) 1961   **$1,500**

📷 45 rpm. Near-mint price range: $1,000 to $1,500.

☐ 461. Surrender/Lonely Man • Elvis Presley (With Jordanaires) (RCA Victor 68-7850) 1961   **$1,500**

📷 Stereo compact 33 single. Not issued with a picture sleeve. Near-mint price range: $1,000 to $1,500.
Variations of this release in the Top 1,000 can be found at Numbers 382; 783.

☐ 462. I Love You/Patricia • Supremes (Sara 1032).................................. 1961   **$1,500**

📷 45 rpm. Also released as by the Supremes 4. Near-mint price range: $1,000 to $1,500.
Members: Lovelace Redmond; Homer Walton; Carl Campbell; Phillips Green.

☐ 463. Nay-Oy-Gwor/Mamie Wong • Ben E. Williams (With Steps Four and Del-Reys) (Riff 6102) 1961   **$1,500**

📷 45 rpm. Near-mint price range: $1,000 to $1,500.

☐ 464. Trouble Lover/? • Charters (Mel-O-Dy 104)..................................... 1962   **$1,500**

45 rpm. Near-mint price range: $1,000 to $1,500.

Central RECORDS

UNBREAKABLE
45 R.P.M.

RECORD NO
NA-2605-A

Newkirk Music
(BMI) Time 2:56

BLUE & LONELY
THE PRETENDERS
Featuring JIMMY JONES
WITH RYTHM ACCOMPANIMENT

315.

CHOLLY RECORDS

C-712-AA
Time 2:20

Cholly
BMI

LET THERE BE LOVE
(Baker-Lanier-Blalock)
THE TWILIGHTERS
Vocal Group

317.

Aladdin
★ LOS ANGELES 19, CALIFORNIA ★

45-3449
CMI-3073
X

Vocal - 2:27
Aladdin Mus. Pub.,
Hi-Mi Pub. Co.
BMI

Promotional   Not For Sale

TWO LOVES
(Carl Davis)
THE BLENDERS

319.

CORVETTE RECORDS

45 RPM

Time 2:25
(73758)

MY DREAMS HAVE GONE
(Johnny Ross)
JOHNNY ROSS
A & R MAN CHUCK TEQUILA RIO
C-1006

316.

☐ 465. Breaking Through • Four Tops (Workshop 217) 1962 $1,500

    📷 LP. Near-mint price range: $1,000 to $1,500.
    Members: Levi Stubbs; Lawrence Payton; Abdul "Duke" Fakir; Obie Benson.
    A variation of this release in the Top 1,000 can be found at Number 703.

☐ 466. Lorraine/Come on and Dance • Ambassadors (Playbox 202) 1963 $1,500

    📷 45 rpm. Near-mint price range: $1,000 to $1,500.

☐ 467. Why Don't You Write Me/Sh-Boom • Cardinals (Rose 835) 1963 $1,500

    📷 45 rpm. Near-mint price range: $1,000 to $1,500.

☐ 468. My Love Will Follow You/Everywhere • Continental Gems
    (Guyden 2091)... 1963 $1,500

    📷 45 rpm. Near-mint price range: $1,000 to $1,500.

☐ 469. Tears from My Eyes/This Is the Night • Net Roman (Sahara 102) ... 1963 $1,500

    45 rpm. Less valuable if credited to "Nap" Roman. Near-mint price range: $1,000 to $1,500.
    A variation of this release in the Top 1,000 can be found at Number 717.

☐ 470. Something New • Beatles (Capitol Compact 33 SXA-2180)............. 1964 $1,500

    📷 Compact 33 EP. Black label with colorband. Stereo only. Made for use in jukeboxes. Has
    six tracks from the LP. Issued with hard cover. Front cover has same photo as LP, back is
    blank. Includes juke box inserts. Near-mint price range: $1,000 to $1,500.
    Members: John Lennon; Paul McCartney; George Harrison; Ringo Starr.
    Side 1: *I'll Cry Instead; And I Love Her; Slow Down.*
    Side 2: *If I Fell; Tell Me Why; Matchbox.*

☐ 471. The Savage Young Beatles • Beatles (Savage BM-69) 1964 $1,500

    📷 Monaural LP. Yellow label. Has a glossy orange front cover. Back cover shows address
    of Savage Records. Includes four songs by the Beatles with Tony Sheridan, and four by just
    Tony Sheridan. Near-mint price range: $1,000 to $1,500.
    Members: Tony Sheridan; John Lennon; Paul McCartney; George Harrison; Pete Best.
    Side 1: *Cry for a Shadow; Let's Dance; If You Love Me Baby; What I Say.*
    Side 2: *Why; Sweet Georgia Brown; Ruby Baby; Ya Ya.*

☐ 472. Friday at the Cage A-Go-Go • Fugitives / Oxford Five / Lourds / Individuals
    (Westchester 1005) 1965 $1,500

    LP. Distributed at the Cage A-Go-Go club. Some copies have a sticker on labels showing
    title as *Long Hot Summer*. Not issued with a cover. Near-mint price range: $1,000 to $1,500.

☐ 473. Ebb Tide/For Sentimental Reasons (I Love You) • Righteous Brothers
    (Philles 130)... 1965 $1,500

    45 rpm. Custom label. Has producer Phil Spector's picture on the label. Promotional issue
    only. Near-mint price range: $1,000 to $1,500.
    Members: Bill Medley; Bobby Hatfield.

☐ 474. The Haunted • Haunted (Trans-World 6701) 1966 $1,500

    LP. Canadian release. Near-mint price range: $1,000 to $1,500.
    Members: Dave Wynne; Bob Burgess.

☐ 475. Homemade Apple Pie and Yankee Ingenuity • Grandma's Rockers
    (Fredlo) 1967 $1,500

    📷 LP. Selection number not yet known. Near-mint price range: $1,000 to $1,500.
    Members: Larry ?; Jamie Farnum; Dave Lange; Brian Haas.
    Side I: *Midnight Hour; Louie Louie; Do You Wanna Dance; You Baby; Breakaway; Love; Time
    Won't Let Me.*
    Side II: *Light My Fire; Incense and Peppermint; Talk Talk; Ablue Peppers; So High on Cloud Nine;
    Gimme Some Lovin'; Never Before.*

Cyclone
RECORDS
322 W. 125 St., N. Y. C. - UN 6-1555

45 R.P.M.
Ninny-Ethel Byrd

CYCLONE
5012-B

IF I COULD HOLD YOUR HAND
(Williams)
THE CALENDARS

320.

Golden Crest

aen–Ten
c Pub. Co.
INI

2661-1
1:56

BELLS BELLS
(Steve Mehiel)
THE CHESSMEN

GOLDEN CREST RECORDS, INC. HUNTINGTON STATION, N.Y.

321.

MOON
RECORDS
NEWARK, N. J.

NOT FOR
SALE

DISC JOCKEY
COPY

UNBREAKABLE
45 R.P.M.

RECORD NO.
109 B

C. Shaw Music
& Jaybird Music
B. M. I.

Time
2:18

CRYING
(Over You)
(Endorsers)
ENDORSERS

322.

Fire & Fury

FF 101
45 RPM

THEY LAUGHED AT ME
(Bobby Robinson - Jackie Rue)
Jackie and the Starlites
1000

324.

☐ 476. Special Christmas Programming • Elvis Presley (RCA
Victor 5697) 1967 $1,500

> Monaural LP. Identification number used since no selection number is shown. Promotional issue only for radio stations to air December 3, 1967. Insert: Script sheet with running times and program information ($50 to $100). Near-mint price range: $1,000 to $1,500.
>
> Side 1: *Here Comes Santa Claus; Blue Christmas; O, Little Town of Bethlehem; Silent Night; I'll Be Home for Christmas.*
>
> Side 2: *I Believe; If Everyday Was Like Christmas; How Great Thou Art; His Hand in Mine; Special Elvis Christmas Message/I'll Be Home for Christmas.*

☐ 477. Axis: Bold As Love • Jimi Hendrix (Reprise R-6281) 1968 $1,500

> Monaural LP. Gatefold cover. White label. Promotional issue only. Near-mint price range: $1,000 to $1,500.
>
> Side 1: *Exp; Up from the Skies; Spanish Castle Magic; Wait Until Tomorrow; Ain't No Telling; Little Wing; If 6 Was 9.*
>
> Side 2: *You Got Me Floatin'; Castles Made of Sand; She's So Fine; One Rainy Wish; Little Miss Lover; Bold As Love.*

☐ 478. Music Emporium • Music Emporium (Sentinel 100) 1968 $1,500

> LP. Near-mint price range: $1,000 to $1,500.
> Members: Dave Padwin; Dora Wahl; Carolyn Lee; Casey Cosby.

☐ 479. Calm Before … The Rising Storm • Rising Storm (Remnant 3571).. 1969 $1,500

> LP. Near-mint price range: $1,000 to $1,500.
> Members: Tony Thompson; Todd Cohen; Bob Cohan; Tom Scheft; Charlie Rockwell; Rich Weinberg.

☐ 480. Street Suite • Touch (Mainline 2001) 1969 $1,500

> LP. Reportedly 100 made. Near-mint price range: $1,000 to $1,500.
> Members: Ray Stone; Jerry Schulte.

☐ 481. Live at Papa Joe's • Starliners (Lejac 1001) 1960s $1,500

> LP. Near-mint price range: $1,000 to $1,500.

☐ 482. Maitreya • Apache (Akashic 2777) 1971 $1,500

> LP. Near-mint price range: $1,000 to $1,500.

☐ 483. Moon Blood • Fraction (Angelus 571) 1971 $1,500

> LP. Near-mint price range: $1,000 to $1,500.
> Members: Jim Beach; Don Swanson; Vic Hemme; Curt Swanson.

☐ 484. Kreed • Kreed (Vision of Sound 71-56) 1971 $1,500

> LP. Near-mint price range: $1,000 to $1,500.
> Members: David Cannon; Reed Boyd; Dean Sack; Doug Parent; Nigel Coff.

☐ 485. Philosophy of the World • Shaggs (Third World 3001) 1972 $1,500

> LP. Reportedly 2,000 made. Near-mint price range: $1,000 to $1,500.
> Members: Betty Wiggin; Dorothy Wiggin; Helen Wiggin.

☐ 486. Put It There/Put It There • Paul McCartney (Capitol SPRO 79074) . 1989 $1,500

> 45 rpm. White label, promotional issue only. Planned as the third single from Paul's *Flowers in the Dirt* LP, though cancelled before distribution. At press time, only three copies are known to eixst. Near-mint price range: $1,000 to $1,500.

☐ 487. Good Rockin' Tonight/I Don't Care If the Sun Don't Shine • Elvis Presley
(With Scotty and Bill) (Sun 210) 1954 $1,400

> 45 rpm. Near-mint price range: $1,000 to $1,400.
> A variation of this release in the Top 1,000 can be found at Number 416.
> Members: Elvis Presley; Scotty Moore; Bill Black.

☐ 488. Please Please Me/Ask Me Why • Beatles (Vee-Jay VJ-498) 1963 $1,400

> 45 rpm. Credits "BEATTLES." Black label with colorband. Has thick lettering and oval logo. Near-mint price range: $1,000 to $1,400.
> Variations of this release in the Top 1,000 can be found at Numbers 350; 378; 379; 388; 541; 542.
> Members: John Lennon; Paul McCartney; George Harrison; Ringo Starr.

NOBLE

CASUAL PUB. CO.
BMI
618

VOCAL
THE MARQUIS
TIME: 2:18

NEVER FORGET
(Forbes)

THE MARQUIS

45-719

327.

MUNRAB RECORDS

BD 1008-1

Pioneer : BMI

JUST ANOTHER FOOL
(Leo Deques)

THE MARVELS

328.

LIBAN

Rene Music
B. M. I.
45 RPM
Side 1

VOCAL
Time 2:20
KO8W-2030
LR 1002

LOVE YOU THAT'S WHY
(Thomas)

THE MONARCH'S

LIBAN RECORD CO., CLEVELAND, OHIO

329.

CASINO

45 RPM

Vocal

WHOSE LOVE, BUT YOURS
(The Quills)

THE QUILLS
(G-436)

330.

☐ 489. The Square Root of Two ● Night Shadow (Spectrum
Stereo ST-2001) 1968 **$1,400**

📷 LP. By the Night Shadows, but credited to the "Night Shadow." Price ($1,400) is for LP
with *both* bonuses. 1,000 made for use as follows: a) 294 promotional copies for radio
stations, each one packaged with a bonus, psychedelic poster (Near-mint price range:
$1,200 to $1,400); b) 700 for commercial sale, packaged with a bonus 45 rpm (Near-mint
price range: $775 – $1,050); c) 6 for executive use, packaged with both the poster and the
45. (Near-mint price range: $1,000 to $1,300.) The poster is so scarce that neither the
producer nor any of the band members have been able to locate one.
> Members: Little Phil Ross (vocals); Ronnie Farmer (guitar); Charles Spinks (drums); Bobbie Newell (organ & guitar);
> Aleck Janoulis (bass & vocals); Pat Andrews (drums); Jimi Callaway (guitar); Electric Bob (monologue).
> Side 1: *The Initial Stage: If Not Stoned, Skip the Prologue; Prologue (Acidity-Unity Is Such a Good*
> *Thing); I Can't Believe (Or Why the Hell Did I Ever Get Hung Up on You); Plenty of*
> *Trouble (Thank God We Have Homes for Unwed Mothers); So Much (Self Explanatory);*
> *In the Air (Air Pollution Can Be Great with the Right Kind of Smoke).*
> Side 2: *Final Stage; 60 Second Swinger Song (An Anthology of the Hip Scene); Illusion; (No, This*
> *Isn't a Song About the Great Society); Anything But Lies (All Lovers Are Disguised*
> *Masochists); Turned On (A Psychedelic Charleston for Mom & Dad); The Hot Rod (A*
> *Clean Song for Dirty Minds); The Hot Dog Man (A Party Song Recorded for Speed*
> *Freaks).*

☐ 490. Take a Little Chance/Time Has Made a Change ● Jimmy De Berry
(Sun 185) 1953 **$1,300**
> 45 rpm. Near-mint price range: $1,000 to $1,300.

☐ 491. Call Me Anything, But Call Me/Baby No, No ● Big Memphis Marainey
(Sun 184) 1953 **$1,300**

📷 45 rpm. Near-mint price range: $1,000 to $1,300.

☐ 492. Cotton Crop Blues/Hold Me in Your Arms ● James Cotton
(Sun 206) 1954 **$1,300**
> 45 rpm. Near-mint price range: $1,000 to $1,300.

☐ 493. Rock and Roll Boogie/I Do ● Clouds (Cobra 5001) 1956 **$1,300**
> 45 rpm. Near-mint price range: $1,000 to $1,300.
> Member: Albert Hunter.

☐ 494. High School Dance/These Four Letters ● El Pollos (Studio 999) 1958 **$1,300**

📷 45 rpm. Near-mint price range: $1,000 to $1,300.

☐ 495. Yesterday and Today ● Beatles (Capitol ST-2553) 1966 **$1,300**
> Stereo LP. The words "New Improved Full Dimensional Stereo" are at the top of front cover.
> "Paste-over" or "peeled" covers. The paste-over version has a photo of the Beatles around a
> trunk pasted over an intact "butcher cover." The peeled version shows the "butcher cover"
> after the trunk photo cover has been peeled off. Removing the slick can be a difficult and
> risky process; however, there are professionals who offer this service. Cover shows title as
> *Yesterday And Today,* whereas label reads: *"Yesterday" ... And Today.* Near-mint price
> range: $1,000 to $1,300.
> Variations of this release in the Top 1,000 can be found at Numbers 1; 21; 175; 967.
> Members: John Lennon; Paul McCartney; George Harrison; Ringo Starr.
> Side 1: *Drive My Car; I'm Only Sleeping; Nowhere Man; Dr. Robert; Yesterday; Act Naturally.*
> Side 2: *And Your Bird Can Sing; If I Needed Someone; We Can Work It Out; What Goes On; Day*
> *Tripper.*

☐ 496. It's Chrismas Time/Old MacDonald ● Five Keys (Aladdin 3113) 1951 **$1,200**
> 45 rpm. Near-mint price range: $800 to $1,200.
> Members: Rudy West; Ripley Ingram; Maryland Pierce; Dickie Smith; Bernie West.

☐ 497. Tell Me Why/Roll Roll Pretty Baby ● Swallows (King 4515) 1951 **$1,200**
> 45 rpm. Black vinyl. Near-mint price range: $800 to $1,200.
> Members: Herman "Junior" Denby; Ed Rich; Earl Hurley; Fred Johnson; Norris Mack.
> A variation of this release in the Top 1,000 can be found at Number 112.

N.O.B.L.E
CASUAL PUB. CO.
BMI
621
VOCAL
THE TABS
TIME: 2:12
OOPS
(Johnson)
THE TABS
45-720

331.

My Brother's
513 LENOX AVENUE
NEW YORK CITY
UNBREAKABLE
45 R.P.M.
RECORD NO.
508
(MB-91)
Destry Music
BMI
SHE'S JUST MY SIZE
(J. Pruitt-J. Castor)
CLINTONIAN CUBS

336.

M. C.
973-45-1 A
Time : 2:50
Dan's Music-BMI
Voca
45-1
GUESS I'M THE LONELY ONE
(Joe Caldwell)
JOE CALDWELL

332.

SATURN
RECORDS
Vocal Quartet
Time 2:40
BYE BYE
(Swift)
THE COSMIC RAYS
WITH LE SUN RA
AND ARKESTRA

337.

☐ 498. A Beggar for Your Kisses/Call Baby Call • Diamonds
(Atlantic 981) 1952 $1,200
  📷 45 rpm. Near-mint price range: $800 to $1,200.
  Members: Harold Wright; Ernest Ward; Myles Hardy; Dan Stevens.

☐ 499. Yes Sir, That's My Baby/Old MacDonald • Five Keys
(Aladdin 3118) 1952 $1,200
  45 rpm. Near-mint price range: $800 to $1,200.
  Members: Rudy West; Ripley Ingram; Maryland Pierce; Dickie Smith; Bernie West.

☐ 500. Mistakes/How Long • Five Keys (Aladdin 3131) 1952 $1,200
  45 rpm. Near-mint price range: $800 to $1,200.
  Members: Rudy West; Ripley Ingram; Maryland Pierce; Dickie Smith; Bernie West.

☐ 501. I Hadn't Anyone 'Til You/Hold Me • Five Keys (Aladdin 3136) 1952 $1,200
  45 rpm. Near-mint price range: $800 to $1,200.
  Members: Rudy West; Ripley Ingram; Maryland Pierce; Dickie Smith; Bernie West.

☐ 502. I Cried for You/Serve Another Round • Five Keys (Aladdin 3158).... 1952 $1,200
  45 rpm. Near-mint price range: $800 to $1,200.
  Members: Rudy West; Ripley Ingram; Maryland Pierce; Dickie Smith; Bernie West.

☐ 503. Western Union Man/Jack Pot • Chicago Sunny Boy (Meteor 5004). 1953 $1,200
  45 rpm. Near-mint price range: $800 to $1,200.

☐ 504. I'll Beg/Let Me Take You Out Tonight • 5 Emeralds (S.R.C. 106) 1953 $1,200
  📷 45 rpm. Credits "5 Emeralds." Blue label. Logo has periods between letters. Near-mint
  price range: $800 to $1,200.
  A variation of this release in the Top 1,000 can be found at Number 581.

☐ 505. These Foolish Things/Lonesome Old Story • Five Keys
(Aladdin 3190) 1953 $1,200
  45 rpm. Near-mint price range: $800 to $1,200.
  Members: Rudy West; Ripley Ingram; Maryland Pierce; Dickie Smith; Bernie West.

☐ 506. Easy/Before Long • Jimmy & Walter (Sun 180) 1953 $1,200
  📷 45 rpm. Near-mint price range: $800 to $1,200.
  Members: Jimmy DeBerry; Walter Horton.

☐ 507. I'm Lost/When I Woke Up This Morning • Mello Moods
(Prestige 856) 1953 $1,200
  45 rpm. Near-mint price range: $800 to $1,200.
  Members: Ray "Buddy" Wooten; Bobby Williams; Monte Owens; Bobby Baylor; Jimmy Bethea.

☐ 508. Darling/Pleasure Me • Five Emeralds [5 Emeralds] (S-R-C 107)...... 1954 $1,200
  45 rpm. Near-mint price range: $800 to $1,200.

☐ 509. M-a-y-b-e-l-l/Ain't Goin' to Cry No More • Serenaders (Swing
Time 347) 1954 $1,200
  📷 45 rpm. Near-mint price range: $800 to $1,200.

☐ 510. Chances I've Taken/Lonely • Solitaires (Old Town 1008)................. 1954 $1,200
  45 rpm. Red vinyl. Near-mint price range: $900 to $1,200.
  Members: Herman Curtis; Monte Owens; Bobby Williams; Bobby Baylor; Buzzy Willis; Pat Gaston; Milton Love;
  Reggie Barnes; Cecil Holmes; Fred Barksdale; Wally Roker.

☐ 511. How Could You Hurt Me So/I Was a Fool to Let You Go • Teasers
(Checker 800) 1954 $1,200
  45 rpm. Red Vinyl. Near-mint price range: $800 to $1,200.

☐ 512. Oh Maria/I Hope These Words Will Find You Well • Joe Alexander &
Cubans (Ballad 1008) 1955 $1,200
  📷 45 rpm. Sought-after because this is Chuck Berry's first appearance on record, credited
  on this session as "Charles Berryn." Near-mint price range: $800 to $1,200.
  Members: Joe Alexander; Chuck Berry; Faith Douglas; Freddy Golden.

☐ 513. Candlelight/Monticello • Concords (Harlem 2328) 1955 $1,200
  45 rpm. Near-mint price range: $800 to $1,200.

PMP
RECORDS

(P M P)
B.M.I.
Time: 2:35

NOW I'VE CONFESSED
(H. Perdue)
DELI-CADOS

SHADE
RECORDS

1001X45
2:19

Aries-Tornado
Vocal

NEVER LET YOU GO
(Elmo Jones)
THE POETS

Mfg. 2524 West Pico Blvd.
Los Angeles, Calif.

338.   339.

MELKER

45 RPM

Harris - Manor Music

AN-UNDERSTANDING
(Al Bolin)
ROLLETTES
M-K-103-A

EARLY
Division of Princeton Ent.

45 R.P.M.
Win-Moore Music
BMI
Time 2:25

702
CP-6264
VOCAL &
ORCHESTRA

I WISH
(Early)
THE VIDELS
A Reynolds-Moore
Production

340.   341.

100

☐ 514. Sitting By My Window/Don't Do That! • Five Tinos (Sun 222) 1955 $1,200

     📷 45 rpm. Near-mint price range: $800 to $1,200.
     Members: Melvin Walker; Marvin Walker; Melvin Jones; Haywood Hebron; Luchrie Jordan.

☐ 515. Baby Let's Play House/I'm Left, You're Right, She's Gone • Elvis Presley
     (With Scotty and Bill) (Sun 217) 1955 $1,200

     📷 78 rpm. Near-mint price range: $800 to $1,200.
     A variation of this release in the Top 1,000 can be found at Number 558.
     Members: Elvis Presley; Scotty Moore; Bill Black.

☐ 516. Helen/Lovely Girl • Cardells (Featuring Wm. Gardner)
     (Middle-Tone 011) 1956 $1,200

     📷 45 rpm. Near-mint price range: $800 to $1,200.
     Members: William Gardner; Sonny Mayberry; Robert Carey; Charles Bearden.

☐ 517. Girl Friend/Willow Blues • Five Scalders (With Bill Moore on Tenor Sax)
     (Drummond 3001) 1956 $1,200

     📷 45 rpm. Powder blue label. Near-mint price range: $800 to $1,200.
     Members: Mack Rice; Johnny Mayfield; Sol Tilman; Gerald Young; James Bryant.
     A variation of this release in the Top 1,000 can be found at Number 629.

☐ 518. RCA Radio Victrola Division Spots • Elvis Presley (RCA
     Victor 0401) 1956 $1,200

     📷 Monaural LP. Maroon label, silver print. Single-sided disc with four 50-second radio
     commercials for RCA's Victrolas, as well as for the bonus SPD-22 *Elvis Presley (2 EPs)* and
     SPD-23 *Elvis Presley (3 EPs)*. Elvis is the announcer on all of the spots, which also include
     excerpts of songs from the two SPD extended plays. Issued only to radio stations running
     the spots. Near-mint price range: $800 to $1,200.

☐ 519. Jim Reeves Sings • Jim Reeves (Abbott 5001) 1956 $1,200

     📷 LP. Near-mint price range: $800 to $1,200.

☐ 520. Too Good to Be True/Heavenly Love • Academics (With Kingsmen
     Quintet) (Anchor 101) 1957 $1,200

     📷 45 rpm. Near-mint price range: $800 to $1,200.
     Members: Dave Fisher; Ron Marone; Marty Ganter; Bill Greenberg; Goose Greenberg.

☐ 521. Diddle-Le-Bom/More and More • Love Larks (Mason's 3-070) 1957 $1,200

     📷 45 rpm. Near-mint price range: $800 to $1,200.

☐ 522. Best in Rhythm & Blues • Penguins / Meadowlarks / Medallions / Dootones
     (Dootone 204)... 1957 $1,200

     📷 LP. Red vinyl. Near-mint price range: $800 to $1,200.
     Members: (Penguins) Cleve Duncan; Curtis Williams; Dexter Tisby; Bruce Tate. (Meadowlarks) Don Julian; Ronald
     Barrett; Earl Jones; Glen Reagan.
     Side 1: (Penguins) *Earth Angel; Hey Senorita; Kiss A Fool Goodbye; Ookey Ook; Love Will Make
         Your Mind Go Wild; Baby Let's Make Love.*
     Side 2: (Medallions) *The Letter; Buick 59.* (Meadowlarks) *Heaven And Paradise; I Got Tore Up.*
         (Dootones) *Teller Of Fortune; Ay Si Si Mambo.*

☐ 523. Jeannie/Forever My Love • Thrashers with Joe Ruffin Band
     (Mason's 178-062)... 1957 $1,200

     📷 45 rpm. Black vinyl. Reads: "Mason's Recording Co. 1630 Amsterdam Ave. N.Y.C." Red
     vinyl copies are 1961 reissues. Near-mint price range: $800 to $1,200.

☐ 524. Dreamer from My Heart/All That's Good • Johnny Woodson & Crescendos
     (Spry 108)... 1957 $1,200

     📷 45 rpm. Near-mint price range: $800 to $1,200.

☐ 525. Just Before You Leave/I Love • Dolls (Teenage 1010).................... 1958 $1,200
     45 rpm. Near-mint price range: $800 to $1,200.

☐ 526. Mr. Moonglow/Need Your Love • El Reyes (Jade 501) 1958 $1,200

     📷 45 rpm. Near-mint price range: $800 to $1,200.

UNIQUE
LABORATORIES
Presents

45 RPM

THE SONG OF A LOVER
by
THE VALS
Produced by
THERON RECORD CO.

342.

M AND M

PROMOTIONAL
COPY

NOT FOR SALE

2315-62
Josette Pub. Co.
B.M.I.

N9OW-9668
Side 2
Time: 2:36

BENEATH THE SUN
(W. Logan)
THE EQUALLOS
Featuring WILLIE LOGAN
M-30

344.

Guyden
RECORDS

B. F. Wood Music
ASCAP

SAMPLE COPY

G-TPA 1
Time: 2:30

NOT FOR SALE

HOW SWEET
(Richard Baxter-Thomas Hadden)

THE PACERS
2064

346.

RCA VICTOR
PROMOTIONAL RECORD
NOT FOR SALE

RCA FAMILY RECORD CENTER

PR-121
SIDE 1
N2NQ-1647

33

1—GOOD LUCK CHARM (47-7992)
2—THE WAY YOU LOOK TONIGHT (LPM-2484)
3—YOUNGER THAN SPRINGTIME (LPM-2502)
4—FRENESI (CAL-682)

1. Elvis Presley
2. Peter Nero
3. Paul Anka
4. Living Strings

348.

☐ 527. You Are My Love/Time Out for Love • 5 Fortunes (Ransom 103) 1958 $1,200

  📷 45 rpm. Near-mint price range: $800 to $1,200.

☐ 528. Tell Me Why/Where Are You • Four Bel'Aires (X-Tra 113) 1958 $1,200

  📷 45 rpm. Near-mint price range: $800 to $1,200.

☐ 529. SP-33-10P • Various Artists (RCA Victor SP-33-10P) 1958 $1,200

  📷 Untitled promotional LP. Not issued with special cover. Near-mint price range: $800 to $1,200.

    Side 1: *Under the Bridges of Paris* (Dissell & O'Reilly); *Maria Elena* (Los Indios Tabajaras); *In Spain They Say Si Si* (Tony Martin); *Freilach Merengue* (Johnny Conquet); *The World Is Your Balloon* (Tony Perkins); *Cheerful Little Earfull* (Dave Pell); *Speak Easy* (Clegg).

    Side 2: *Love, Love, Love* (George Feyer); *Oye Negra* (Xavier Cugat); *The Queen's Fancy* (J. Lewis); *Diamonds Are a Girl's Best Friend* (Lena Horne); *Pampa (Adios Pampa Mia)* (Perez Prado); *King Creole* (Elvis Presley); *Medley* (M. Davis).

☐ 530. A Lover's Prayer/Never Gonna Leave Me • Carvettes (Copa 200-1/200-2) 1959 $1,200

  📷 45 rpm. Near-mint price range: $800 to $1,200.

☐ 531. The Rockin' 5 Royales • "5" Royales (Apollo 488)........................... 1959 $1,200

  LP. Yellow label. Near-mint price range: $800 to $1,200.

    Members: Lowman Pauling; Johnny Tanner; Jim Moore; Otto Jeffries; Obadiah "Scoop" Carter.

    Side 1: *Baby Don't Do It; Too Much Lovin'; Baby Take All of Me; Courage to Love; You Know I Know; Help Me Somebody.*

    Side 2: *What's That; Laundermat* (sic) *Blues; All Righty; I Wanna Thank You; Put Something in It; I Like It Like That.*

☐ 532. The Voodoo Man/I Hear the Rain • Kingsfive (With New Redtops) (Trophy 1/2) 1959 $1,200

  45 rpm. Near-mint price range: $800 to $1,200.

☐ 533. Tell Me a Tale/? • Charm Kings (Mark 146).................................... 1960 $1,200

  📷 45 rpm. Near-mint price range: $800 to $1,200.

☐ 534. Mule Skinner Blues • Fendermen (Soma 1240) 1960 $1,200

  LP. Solid black vinyl. The cover stock on at least one known counterfeit is soft and flimsy – not of rigid cardboard like originals. Near-mint price range: $800 to $1,200.

    Members: Phil Humphrey; Jimmy Sundquist; John Hauer; Denny Dale Gudin.

    Side 1: *Mule Skinner Blues; Torture; Beach Party; Bertha Lou; Honky Tonk; Lonesome Road.*

    Side 2: *Don't You Just Know It; Heartbreakin' Special; Jack of Diamonds; High Noon; Koo-Koo; Caravan.*

    A variation of this release in the Top 1,000 can be found at Number 458.

☐ 535. Lest You Forget/Over the Wall • Invictas (Pix 1101) 1960 $1,200

  📷 45 rpm. Near-mint price range: $800 to $1,200.

☐ 536. Let's Rock/? • Barrett Strong (Tamla 54022)................................... 1960 $1,200

  📷 45 rpm. Near-mint price range: $800 to $1,200.

☐ 537. It's You I Love/? • Visions (R&R 3002) 1960 $1,200

  📷 45 rpm. Near-mint price range: $800 to $1,200.

☐ 538. A Little Rock & Roll for Everybody • H-Bomb Ferguson / Escos / Mascots (Audio Lab 1567).. 1961 $1,200

  📷 LP. Near-mint price range: $800 to $1,200.

    Side 1: (H. Bomb Ferguson): *Mary Little Mary; I'm So Lonely; The Mess Around; I'm Crying Boo-Boo Hoo; Lady Queen; Midnight Ramblin' Tonite.*

    Side 2: (The Escos): *Whatcha Bet; Golden Rule of Love; We Dance.* (Mascots): *(Do the) Wiggle; Lonely Rain; That's the Way I Feel.*

☐ 539. Complete Selections from "Surfin' Safari" By the Beach Boys • Beach
Boys / Ray Anthony (Capitol PRO-2185/PRO-2186)............................ 1962 $1,200
     EP. Earliest promotional Beach Boys record. Side 1 has two selections from Ray Anthony's *I
     Almost Lost My Mind* album. Side 2 has *Ten Little Indians* and *Little Miss America*, both from
     the Beach Boys' *Surfin' Safari* LP. Issued with a hard cardboard jacket, which pictures the
     Surfin' Safari LP cover on one side and the Ray Anthony LP on the other. Like most Capitol
     promotional albums, this one is numbered by side rather than by disc. The Ray Anthony side
     is PRO-2185, the Beach Boys side is PRO-2186. Near-mint price range: $800 to $1,200.
       Members: Brian Wilson; Carl Wilson; Dennis Wilson; Mike Love; Al Jardine; David Marks.

☐ 540. The Girl I Left Behind/? • Carlton (Penney 1306) 1962 $1,200
     📷 45 rpm. Reissued crediting "Carlton Beck." Near-mint price range: $800 to $1,200.

☐ 541. Please Please Me/Ask Me Why • Beatles (Vee-Jay VJ-498) 1963 $1,200
     45 rpm. Credits "BEATLES." Black label with colorband. Has thick lettering and oval logo.
     The letters "VJ" precede the selection number. Near-mint price range: $800 to $1,200.
     Variations of this release in the Top 1,000 can be found at Numbers 350; 378; 379; 388; 488; 542.
       Members: John Lennon; Paul McCartney; George Harrison; Ringo Starr.

☐ 542. Please Please Me/Ask Me Why • Beatles (Vee-Jay VJ-498) 1963 $1,200
     📷 45 rpm. Credits "BEATLES." White label with oval logo. Label reads: "Disc Jockey
     Advance Sample – Not For Sale." Near-mint price range: $800 to $1,200.
     Variations of this release in the Top 1,000 can be found at Numbers 350; 378; 379; 388; 488; 541.
       Members: John Lennon; Paul McCartney; George Harrison; Ringo Starr.

☐ 543. Introducing the Beatles • Beatles (Vee-Jay LP-1062) 1964 $1,200
     Monaural LP. Black label, no circular colorband, brackets logo. With *Ask Me Why* and
     Please Please Me. Add $50 to $75 if with a "Featuring Twist and Shout" and "Please Please
     Me" sticker.) Near-mint price range: $800 to $1,200.
     Variations of this release in the Top 1,000 can be found at Numbers 7; 27; 65; 93; 169; 202; 218;
     559; 760; 789.
       Members: John Lennon; Paul McCartney, George Harrison; Ringo Starr.
     Side 1: *I Saw Her Standing There; Misery; Anna; Chains; Boys; Ask Me Why.*
     Side 2: *Please Please Me; Baby It's You; Do You Want to Know a Secret; A Taste of Honey;*
           There's a Place; Twist and Shout.

☐ 544. Meet the Beatles • Beatles (Capitol Compact 33 SXA-2047) 1964 $1,200
     📷 Compact 33 EP. Black label with colorband. Stereo only. Made for use in juke boxes.
     Has six tracks from the LP. Issued with hard cover. Front cover has same photo as LP; back
     is blank. Includes juke box inserts. Near-mint price range: $800 to $1,200.
       Members: John Lennon; Paul McCartney; George Harrison; Ringo Starr.
     Side 1: *It Won't Be Long; This Boy; All My Loving.*
     Side 2: *Don't Bother Me; All I've Got to Do; I Wanna Be Your Man.*

☐ 545. Beatles' Second Album • Beatles (Capitol Compact 33 SXA-2080) . 1964 $1,200
     📷 Compact 33 EP. Black label with colorband. Stereo only. Made for use in jukeboxes. Has
     six tracks from the LP. Issued with hard cover. Front cover has same photo as LP; back is
     blank. Includes juke box inserts. Near-mint price range: $800 to $1,200.
       Members: John Lennon; Paul McCartney, George Harrison; Ringo Starr.
     Side 1: *Thank You Girl; Devil in Her Heart; Money.*
     Side 2: *Long Tall Sally; I Call Your Name; Please Mr. Postman.*

☐ 546. United Artists Presents *A Hard Day's Night* • Beatles (United
Artists 2359/60) 1964 $1,200
     LP. Promotional issue only. Red label. Open-end interview about the film. Issued with a 12-
     page script and programming information, which represents about $75 to $100 of the value.
     Near-mint price range: $800 to $1,200.
       Members: John Lennon; Paul McCartney, George Harrison; Ringo Starr.

☐ 547. Beatlemania Tour Coverage • Beatles (I-N-S Radio News DOC-1) . 1964 $1,200
     LP. Promotional issue only. An open-end interview. Issued in a plain white cover with a one-
     page interview script. Near-mint price range: $800 to $1,200.
       Members: John Lennon; Paul McCartney, George Harrison; Ringo Starr.

STONED
(Jagger; Phelge)

PROMOTIONAL COPY

THE ROLLING STONES
DR 31955
Made in U.S.A.

358.

THE BEATLES TALK AND SING!
WALLICHS MUSIC CITY • KFWB/98

SOUVENIR RECORD

A LIMITED PRESSING CELEBRATING
THE OPENING OF WALLICHS MUSIC CITY
TOPANGA PLAZA • CANOGA PARK
JUNE 9-13, 1964

356.

363.

MUSIC CITY/KFWBEATLES
Limited Pressings - June 8, 1964

SIDE 1
RB-2637
1:40

Promotional
Not For Sale

THE BEATLES
TALKING

356.

CAPITOL COMPACT
33
OPEN-END
INTERVIEW
WITH

Especially prepared for
Radio & TV Programming
Use — Not For Sale
Produced by Jack Wagner

SIDE 1
PRO 2548
Total Time:
6:08

THE BEATLES
Including the Hit Single
"I WANT TO HOLD YOUR HAND" (BMI)
also in the album
"MEET THE BEATLES"

T-2047

357.

ELVIS' GOLD RECORDS

VOLUME 4

RCA VICTOR

Lonely Man
A Mess of Blues
Just Tell Her Joe Said Hello
Please Don't Drag That String Around
Indescribably Blue
Love Letters

Witchcraft
It Hurts Me
Ain't That Loving You Baby
You're the Devil in Disguise
What'd I Say
Ask Me

LPM-3921

106

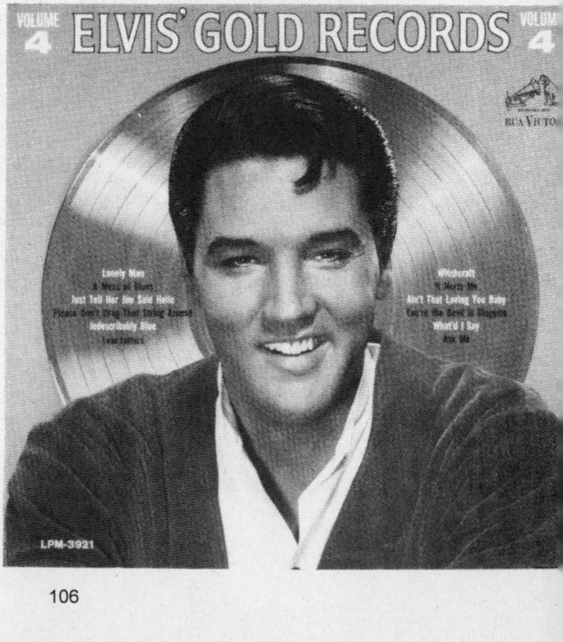

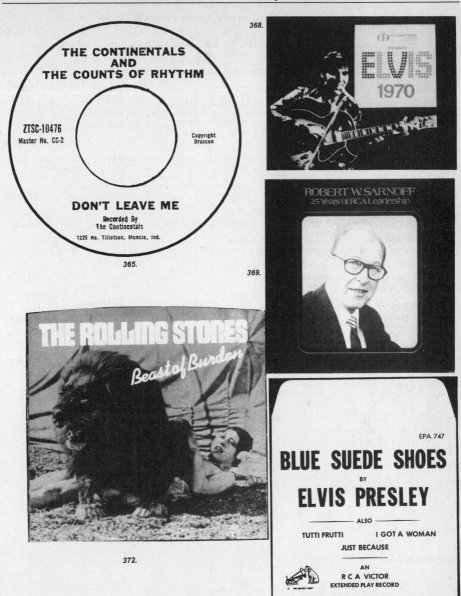

368.

THE CONTINENTALS
AND
THE COUNTS OF RHYTHM

ZTSC-10476
Master No. CC-2

Copyright
Druscon

DON'T LEAVE ME

Recorded By
The Continentals

1225 No. Tillotson, Muncie, Ind.

365.

369.

372.

BLUE SUEDE SHOES
BY
ELVIS PRESLEY

ALSO

TUTTI FRUTTI   I GOT A WOMAN

JUST BECAUSE

AN
R C A VICTOR
EXTENDED PLAY RECORD

EPA 747

377.

☐ 548. A Hard Day's Night/I Should Have Known Better • George Martin
Orchestra (United Artists 750) 1964 $1,200

📷 Picture sleeve. Instrumental versions of two Lennon-McCartney film songs. Sleeve
pictures the Beatles. Near-mint price range: $800 to $1,200.
Members: John Lennon; Paul McCartney, George Harrison; Ringo Starr.

☐ 549. United Artists Presents *Help!* (Interview) • Beatles (United
Artists UA-Help Int).. 1965 $1,200

LP. Promotional issue only. Red label with black print. Open-end interview with the Beatles
and others about the film. Price includes script and programming information, which
represents about $75 to $100 of the value. Near-mint price range: $800 to $1,200.
Members: John Lennon; Paul McCartney, George Harrison; Ringo Starr.

☐ 550. Special Easter Programming Kit • Elvis Presley (RCA
Victor 0651 & 0652)... 1966 $1,200

📷 Gold Standard picture sleeve-mailer and two 45 rpm promo singles, *Joshua Fit the
Battle/Known Only to Him* and *Milky White Way/Swing Down Sweet Chariot* in their sleeves
and an Easter greeting card from Elvis. Has a black-and-white Elvis photo on front. Picture
sleeve-mailer alone is $800 to $1,000. Price range for the complete kit: $800 to $1,200.

☐ 551. Corridor of Faces • Lazy Smoke (Onyx 6903) 1967 $1,200

📷 LP. Near-mint price range: $800 to $1,200.

☐ 552. Marble Phrogg • Marble Phrogg (Derrick 8868)............... 1968 $1,200

📷 LP. Near-mint price range: $800 to $1,200.

☐ 553. Have You Forgotten/Blue Victory • Meridians (Parnaso 107)..........1960s $1,200

📷 45 rpm. Near-mint price range: $800 to $1,200.

☐ 554. Level 6 ½ • Khazad Doom (LPL 892) 1970 $1,200

LP. Near-mint price range: $800 to $1,200.
Members: Jack Eadon; Tom Sievers; Al Yates; Steve Hilkin.

☐ 555. Band on the Run Radio Interview Special with Paul & Linda McCartney •
Paul & Linda McCartney (Capitol/National Features Corp. 2955/2956)1973 $1,200

📷 LP. Promotional only issue. Light Yellow label. Issued in plain white cover with script and
two glossy promo photos. Counterfeits do NOT have "National Features Company" logo on
their label. Near-mint price range: $800 to $1,200.

☐ 556. Beatles Special Limited Edition • Beatles (Apple) 1974 $1,200

Boxed 10-LP set. Includes Apple label copies of the following LPs: ST-2047 *Meet the
Beatles*, ST-2108 *Something New*, ST-2228 *Beatles '65*, ST-2309 *Early Beatles*, ST-2442
Rubber Soul, ST-2576 *Revolver*, SMAS-2653 *Sgt. Pepper's Lonely Hearts Club Band*,
SMAL-2835 *Magical Mystery Tour*, SO-383 *Abbey Road*, SW-385 *Hey Jude*. Box is black
with silver foil title print on one side. Price range for complete set: $800 to $1,200.
Members: John Lennon; Paul McCartney, George Harrison; Ringo Starr.

☐ 557. Dad Is Home/Vilma's Jump-Up • Lynn Tiatt & Comets (Pussy Cat 1) .... ? $1,200

45 rpm. Near-mint price range: $800 to $1,200.

☐ 558. Baby Let's Play House/I'm Left, You're Right, She's Gone • Elvis Presley
(With Scotty and Bill) (Sun 217) 1955 $1,100

📷 45 rpm. Near-mint price range: $800 to $1,100.
A variation of this release in the Top 1,000 can be found at Number 515.
Members: Elvis Presley; Scotty Moore; Bill Black.

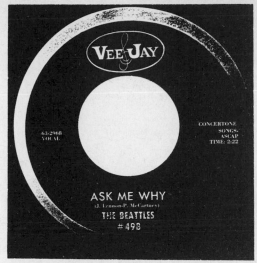

379.

380.

382.

383.

384.

☐ 559. Introducing the Beatles • Beatles (Vee-Jay LP-1062) 1963 $1,100
    Monaural LP. Black label with circular colorband and oval logo. With *Love Me Do* and *P.S. I Love You* (on later issues these tracks are replaced by *Ask Me Why* and *Please Please Me*). Back cover is blank. Has "Printed In U.S.A." at lower left of front cover (counterfeits lack this print). Near-mint price range: $800 to $1,100.
    Variations of this release in the Top 1,000 can be found at Numbers 7; 27; 65; 93; 169; 202; 218; 543; 760; 789.
        Members: John Lennon; Paul McCartney, George Harrison; Ringo Starr.
    Side 1: *I Saw Her Standing There; Misery; Anna; Chains; Boys; Love Me Do.*
    Side 2: *P.S. I Love You; Baby It's You; Do You Want to Know a Secret; A Taste of Honey; There's a Place; Twist and Shout.*

☐ 560. The Sultan/Aurora • Squires (V Records 109)................................... 1963 $1,100
    📷 45 rpm. Instrumental tracks recorded at CKRC (Winnipeg, Manitoba) radio's studio. Features Neil Young on guitar. Near-mint price range: $800 to $1,100.

☐ 561. Beatles Vs. the Four Seasons • Beatles & 4 Seasons
    (Vee-Jay DX-30)... 1964 $1,100
    Monaural LP. Double LP with gatefold cover. Repackage set combining two previously released Vee-Jay albums: *Introducing the Beatles* (Vee-Jay 1062) and *The Golden Hits of the Four Seasons* (Vee-Jay 1065). Many copies include an 11½ " x 23" color poster, valued separately at $150 to $200. Price range for discs and cover: $800 to $1,100.
    Beatles
    Side 1: *I Saw Her Standing There; Misery; Anna; Chains; Boys; Ask Me Why.*
    Side 2: *Please Please Me; Baby It's You; Do You Want to Know a Secret; A Taste of Honey; There's a Place; Twist and Shout.*
    4 Seasons
    Side 1: *Sherry; I've Cried Before; Marlena; Soon (I'll Be Home Again); Ain't That A Shame; Walk Like A Man.*
    Side 2: *Connie-O; Big Girls Don't Cry; Starmaker; Candy Girl; Silver Wings; Peanuts.*

☐ 562. Terraplane Blues/Kind Hearted Woman • Robert Johnson
    (Vocalion 03416) 1937 $1,000
    78 rpm. Near-mint price range: $750 to $1,000.

☐ 563. Pop-Corn Man/Oooo-Oh Boom! • Benny Goodman Orchestra with Martha
    Tilton (Victor 25808) 1939 $1,000
    78 rpm. Near-mint price range: $750 to $1,000.

☐ 564. The Trolley Song/Cocktails for Two • Judy Garland / Tommy Dorsey
    (Vogue).. 1946 $1,000
    78 rpm picture disc. No selection number used. Near-mint price range: $750 to $1,000.

☐ 565. Mean Red Spider/Let Me Be Your Coal Man • James "Sweet Lucy" Carter
    & His Orchestra (20th Century 20-51) 1947 $1,000
    78 rpm. Session includes Muddy Waters. Near-mint price range: $750 to $1,000.

☐ 566. One Foot in Heaven/The Night Is Young and You're So Beautiful • Dean
    Martin (Embassy 124) 1949 $1,000
    📷 78 rpm. One copy known. Near-mint price range: $750 to $1,000.

☐ 567. Chicken Blues/Do Something for Me • Dominoes (Federal 12001).. 1950 $1,000
    45 rpm. Near-mint price range: $750 to $1,000.
        Members: Billy Ward; Clyde McPhatter; Charlie White; William Lamont; Bill Brown; Dave McNeil; James Van Loan.

☐ 568. Deal Me a Hand/Ten Gallon Stetson • Bill Haley (With Saddlemen)
    (Keystone 5101) 1950 $1,000
    📷 78 rpm. Near-mint price range: $750 to $1,000.

☐ 569. Susan Van Dusan/? • Bill Haley (Keystone 5102)............................ 1950 $1,000
    📷 78 rpm. Near-mint price range: $750 to $1,000.

385.

386.

387.

388.

399.

401.

☐ 570. At Night/Every Dog-Gone Time • Orioles (Jubilee 5025)................... 1951 $1,000
     45 rpm. Near-mint price range: $750 to $1,000.
     Members: Sonny Til; Alex Sharp; George Nelson; John Reed; Tom Gaither.

☐ 571. Flame in My Heart/Oh, Oh, Oh Baby • Checkers (King 4558).......... 1952 $1,000
     45 rpm. Near-mint price range: $750 to $1,000.
     Members: Charlie White; Bill Brown.

☐ 572. Night's Curtains/Let Me Come Back • Checkers (King 4581)........... 1952 $1,000
     45 rpm. Near-mint price range: $750 to $1,000.
     Members: Charlie White; Bill Brown.

☐ 573. A Star/You're My Inspiration • Five Crowns (Rainbow 179).............. 1952 $1,000
     45 rpm. Red vinyl. Near-mint price range: $750 to $1,000.
     Members: Wilbur Paul; Nicky Clark; John Clark; Jim "Papa" Clark; Dock Green.

☐ 574. Stop Fooling Around/Troubles of My Own • Shirley Haven & Four Jacks
     (Federal 12092)... 1952 $1,000
     45 rpm. Near-mint price range: $750 to $1,000.

☐ 575. One More Time/Just How Long • Mel-O-Dots (Apollo 1192)............ 1952 $1,000
     45 rpm. Near-mint price range: $750 to $1,000.

☐ 576. Right Back On It/Maggie's Boogie • Peppermint Harris
     (Aladdin 3130) 1952 $1,000
     45 rpm. Real name: Harrison Nelson. Green vinyl. Near-mint price range: $750 to $1,000.

☐ 577. Four Great Voices • Ravens (Rendition 104) 1952 $1,000

     📷 EP. Near-mint price range: $750 to $1,000.
     Members: Ollie Jones; Jimmy Ricks; Leonard Puzey; Warren Suttles.

☐ 578. A Love in My Heart/I'll Never Let Her Go • Royals (Federal 12098). 1952 $1,000
     45 rpm. Near-mint price range: $750 to $1,000.
     Members: Henry Booth; Hank Ballard; Charles Sutton; Lawson Smith; Alonzo Tucker; Sonny Woods.

☐ 579. My Prayer Tonight/Love Wasn't There • Checkers (King 4596) 1953 $1,000
     45 rpm. Near-mint price range: $750 to $1,000.
     Members: Charlie White; Bill Brown.

☐ 580. My Gal Is Gone/Ooh Baby • Five Blue Notes (Sabre 103) 1953 $1,000

     📷 45 rpm. Red vinyl. Near-mint price range: $750 to $1,000.
     Members: Fleming Briscoe; Andy Magruder; Jackie Shedrick; Bob Stroud; Moise Vaughan; Louis Smalls.

☐ 581. I'll Beg/Let Me Take You Out Tonight • Five Emeralds [5 Emeralds]
     (S-R-C 106) 1953 $1,000

     📷 45 rpm. Credits "Five Emeralds." Maroon label. Has hyphens between letters. Near-mint
     price range: $750 to $1,000.
     A variation of this release in the Top 1,000 can be found at Number 504.

☐ 582. Can't Keep from Crying/Come Go My Bail, Louise • Five Keys
     (Aladdin 3167) 1953 $1,000
     45 rpm. Near-mint price range: $750 to $1,000.
     Members: Rudy West; Ripley Ingram; Maryland Pierce; Dickie Smith; Ray Loper; Bernie West; Ulysses Hicks;
     Thomas Threat.

☐ 583. There Ought to Be a Law/Mama • Five Keys (Aladdin 3175) 1953 $1,000
     45 rpm. Near-mint price range: $750 to $1,000.
     Members: Rudy West; Ripley Ingram; Maryland Pierce; Dickie Smith; Bernie West.

☐ 584. Teardrops in Your Eyes/I'm So High • Five Keys (Aladdin 3204) 1953 $1,000
     45 rpm. Near-mint price range: $750 to $1,000.
     Members: Rudy West; Ripley Ingram; Maryland Pierce; Dickie Smith; Bernie West.

☐ 585. Golden Teardrops/Carried Away • Flamingos (With Red Holloway's
     Orchestra) (Chance 1145)... 1953 $1,000
     45 rpm. Black vinyl. Near-mint price range: $750 to $1,000.
     Members: Sollie McElroy; John Carter; Zeke Carey; Jake Carey; Paul Wilson; Nate Nelson.
     A variation of this release in the Top 1,000 can be found at Number 119.

409.

411.

412.

416.

417.

☐ 586. Plan for Love/You Ain't Ready • Flamingos (Chance 1149) 1953 $1,000
     45 rpm. Yellow and black label. Near-mint price range: $750 to $1,000.
     Members: Sollie McElroy; John Carter; Zeke Carey; Jake Carey; Paul Wilson; Nate Nelson.

☐ 587. You Don't Mean Me Right/My Head Goes Acting Up • Four Kings (Music
     By the All Stars) (Fortune 811) 1953 $1,000

     📷 45 rpm. Near-mint price range: $750 to $1,000.

☐ 588. My Inspiration/The Message • Four Plaid Throats
     (Mercury 70143) 1953 $1,000

     📷 45 rpm. Near-mint price range: $750 to $1,000.

☐ 589. Why? Oh, Why/I Love You Baby • Kings (Featuring Bobby Hall)
     (Jax 314).. 1953 $1,000

     📷 45 rpm. Maroon label. Red vinyl. Near-mint price range: $750 to $1,000.
     Members: Robert Hall; Richard Holcomb; Adolphus Holcomb; Gil Wilkes.

☐ 590. Teardrops on My Pillow/Hold Me, Thrill Me, Kiss Me • Orioles
     (Jubilee 5108).. 1953 $1,000
     45 rpm. Red vinyl. Near-mint price range: $750 to $1,000.
     Members: Sonny Til; Alex Sharp; George Nelson; John Reed; Tom Gaither.

☐ 591. I Cover the Waterfront/One More Time • Orioles (Jubilee 5120) 1953 $1,000
     45 rpm. Red vinyl. Near-mint price range: $750 to $1,000.
     Members: Sonny Til; Alex Sharp; George Nelson; John Reed; Tom Gaither.

☐ 592. The Shrine of St. Cecilia/I Feel So Blue • Royals (Federal 12121)... 1953 $1,000
     45 rpm. Near-mint price range: $750 to $1,000.
     Members: Henry Booth; Hank Ballard; Charles Sutton; Lawson Smith; Alonzo Tucker; Sonny Woods.

☐ 593. Baby It's You/Bounce • Spaniels (Vee-Jay 101)............................... 1953 $1,000

     📷 45 rpm. Black vinyl. Maroon label. Near-mint price range: $750 to $1,000.
     Members: James "Pookie" Hudson; Jerry Gregory; Ernest Warren; Willie Jackson; Opal Courtney.

☐ 594. Maybe You'll Be There/Baby Come Back • Lee Andrews & Hearts
     (Rainbow 252) 1954 $1,000
     45 rpm. Red vinyl. Print is small, with the title line being about 1½" long. Near-mint price
     range: $750 to $1,000.
     Members: Lee Andrews; Arthur Thompson; Roy Calhoun; Wendell Calhoun; Butch Curry; Ted Weems.

☐ 595. Biscuit Baking Mama/Superstition • Big Ed & His Combo
     (Checker 790).. 1954 $1,000
     45 rpm. Big Ed is blues singer Eddie Burns. Near-mint price range: $750 to $1,000.

☐ 596. Do You Remember/If You Were the Only Girl • Castelles
     (Grand 105) 1954 $1,000
     45 rpm. Glossy yellow label. Rigid disc. No company address shown. Near-mint price range:
     $750 to $1,000.
     Members: George Grant; Frank Vance; William Taylor; Ron Everett; Octavius Anthony; Walt Miller.

☐ 597. I Was Wrong/The Mambo • Charmers (Timely 1009)....................... 1954 $1,000

     📷 45 rpm. Near-mint price range: $750 to $1,000.
     Member: Vicki Burgess; Alfred Todman; George Daniels; James Cook.

☐ 598. Rainbow of Love/I Had a Thrill • Cherokees (Grand 106)................. 1954 $1,000
     45 rpm. Yellow label. Rigid disc. Near-mint price range: $750 to $1,000.
     Member: Russell Carter.

☐ 599. Why Must I Wonder/Sally Lou • Emeralds (Kicks 3) 1954 $1,000
     45 rpm. Near-mint price range: $750 to $1,000.
     Members: Bobby Parker; Billy Mann.

☐ 600. Someday, Sweetheart/Love My Loving • Five Keys (Aladdin 3228). 1954 $1,000
     45 rpm. Near-mint price range: $750 to $1,000.
     Members: Rudy West; Ripley Ingram; Maryland Pierce; Dickie Smith; Bernie West.

418.

422.

423.

425.

426.

115

☐ 601. Deep in My Heart/How Do You Expect Me to Get It • Five Keys
(Aladdin 3245) 1954 $1,000
    45 rpm. Near-mint price range: $750 to $1,000.
    Members: Rudy West; Ripley Ingram; Maryland Pierce; Dickie Smith; Bernie West.

☐ 602. Feel So Good/My Baby's Gone • Five Thrills (Parrot 796) 1954 $1,000
    45 rpm. Near-mint price range: $750 to $1,000.
    Members: Levi Jenkins; Gilbert Warren; Oscar Robinson; Fred Washington; Obie Washington; Leon Pace.

☐ 603. Gloria/Wee Wee Baby • Five Thrills (Parrot 800) 1954 $1,000
    45 rpm. Black vinyl. Near-mint price range: $750 to $1,000.
    Members: Levi Jenkins; Gilbert Warren; Oscar Robinson; Fred Washington; Obie Washington; Leon Pace.
    A variation of this release in the Top 1,000 can be found at Number 129.

☐ 604. Cross Over the Bridge/Listen to My Plea • Flamingos
(Chance 1154)... 1954 $1,000
    📷 45 rpm. Near-mint price range: $750 to $1,000.
    Members: Sollie McElroy; John Carter; Zeke Carey; Jake Carey; Paul Wilson; Nate Nelson.

☐ 605. Dream of a Lifetime/On My Merry Way • Flamingos (Parrot 808)..... 1954 $1,000
    45 rpm. Black vinyl. Reads "The Bronzville Record Mfg. Co." at bottom. Counterfeits may
    show name as "Bronxville." Near-mint price range: $750 to $1,000.
    Members: Sollie McElroy; John Carter; Zeke Carey; Jake Carey; Paul Wilson; Nate Nelson.
    A variation of this release in the Top 1,000 can be found at Number 130.

☐ 606. Battle of the Saxes • Illinois Jacquet & Lester Young (Aladdin 701) 1954 $1,000
    📷 10–inch LP. Colored vinyl. Near-mint price range: $750 to $1,000.
    Side 1: (Illinois Jacquet): *Flying Home; Blow Illinois Blow; Goofin' Off; Illinois Blows the Blues.*
    Side 2: (Lester Young): *D.B. Blues; Lester Blows Again; Sunny Side of the Street; Jumpin' with*
        Symphony Sid.

☐ 607. When I Grow Too Old to Dream/Crazy Song • Mello Drops
(Imperial 5324) 1954 $1,000
    45 rpm. Near-mint price range: $750 to $1,000.

☐ 608. Secret Love/Real Gone Mama • Moonglows (Chance 1152) 1954 $1,000
    45 rpm. Blue and silver label. Near-mint price range: $750 to $1,000.
    Members: Harvey Fuqua; Bobby Lester; Alex Graves; Prentiss Barnes; Buddy Johnson.
    A variation of this release in the Top 1,000 can be found at Number 753.

☐ 609. The Ravens Featuring Jimmy Ricks • Ravens (Featuring Jimmy Ricks)
(King 310)... 1954 $1,000
    📷 EP. Near-mint price range: $750 to $1,000.
    Members: Ollie Jones; Jimmy Ricks; Leonard Puzey; Warren Suttles; Joe Van Loan; Louis Heyward.
    Side 1: *Honey; Bye Bye Baby Blues.*
    Side 2: *Out of a Dream; My Sugar Is So Refined.*

☐ 610. A Dream Come True/Lucy Lou • Squires (Kicks 1)........................... 1954 $1,000
    📷 45 rpm. Near-mint price range: $750 to $1,000.
    Members: Don Bowman; Dewey Terry; Leon Washington; Chester Pipkin; Bob Armstrong; Lee Goudeau.

☐ 611. Tonight Kathleen/Summer Love • Valentines (Old Town 1009) 1954 $1,000
    📷 45 rpm. Near-mint price range: $750 to $1,000.
    Members: Richard Barrett; Mickey Francis; Ray Briggs; Ron Bright; Don Raysor; Ed Edgehill; Dave "Baby" Cortez;
    Carl Hogan.

☐ 612. Love's Something That's Made for Two/Beggin' for Love • Wrens
(Rama 53).. 1954 $1,000
    45 rpm. Near-mint price range: $750 to $1,000.
    Members: Robert Mansfield; Frenchie Concepcion. George Magnezid; Rocky.

☐ 613. Wine Head Woman/Baby You Just Don't Know • Woodrow Adams
(Meteor 5018) 1955 $1,000
    45 rpm. Near-mint price range: $750 to $1,000.

428.

VIBRO
RECORDS

1651-A
Time: 2:50

Onyx Enterprises,
Asbury Park, N.J.

I NEED SOMEONE
(G. Tillman)

THE RAY DOTS

430.

RCA VICTOR
"HIS MASTER'S VOICE"

SP-33-4
(J2NH-1780)

SIDE 2
NOT FOR SALE

— I'M MOVIN' ON TO GLORY - H. Snow — BABALU - La Playa —
TWILIGHT IN TURKEY - T. Dorsey — JUST SAY I LOVE HER - L. Monte —
DON'T BE CRUEL - E. Presley — I'M GLAD I'M NOT YOU —
Grant Martin — HOLIDAY FOR STRINGS - G. Miller —
PAVAN FOR A DEAD PRINCESS - F. Reiner — TRIO IN C
(BEETHOVEN) - Heifetz Primrose — MARRIAGE OF FIGARO -
G. Tozzi — CAPRICCIO - W. Landowska —
A MIGHTY FORTRESS - R. Shaw

LONG [33⅓] PLAY

431.

RCA VICTOR

SPA 7-61
SIDE 2
(H2NH-7491)

45
EP

NOT FOR
SALE

1—ELVIS PRESLEY (EPA-4114)
2—BILLY MURE (EPA 1-1536)
3—THE SABRES (EPA 4102)
4—GOGI GRANT (EPA 4112)
5—NICK VENET (EPA-4100)
6—LANE BROS. (EPA-4175)

436.

VULCO
RECORDS

Box 122
Ft. Pierce, Fla.

S-1043
45 R.P.M.
Time: 2:33

Lakeland Music Co.
(BMI)

RECORD No
V-1
VOCAL

BABY
(Flaming Hearts)
FLAMING HEARTS
Inst.
TORNADOES

439.

117

☐ 614. Tell Me Baby/Do You Love Me • Lil' Joe Bonner & Idols (With Fabulous
Playboys) (B&S B-Disc-S 1570) 1955 $1,000

📷 45 rpm. Near-mint price range: $750 to $1,000.

☐ 615. My Beauty, My Own/Don't Give It Away • Fascinators
(Your Copy 1136) 1955 $1,000
45 rpm. Near-mint price range: $750 to $1,000.
Members: Jerry Potter; Donald Blackshear; Bob Rivers; Clarence Smith; Earl Richardson.

☐ 616. Ko Ko Mo/I'm Yours • Flamingos (Parrot 812) 1955 $1,000

📷 45 rpm. Red vinyl. Reads "The Bronzville Record Mfg. Co." at bottom. Counterfeits may
show name as "Bronxville." Near-mint price range: $750 to $1,000.
Members: Sollie McElroy; John Carter; Zeke Carey; Jake Carey; Paul Wilson; Nate Nelson.

☐ 617. Cause I Love You So/Is That Exactly What You Wanna Do • Kool Toppers
(Beverly 702) 1955 $1,000

📷 45 rpm. Near-mint price range: $750 to $1,000.

☐ 618. Rockin' the Boogie • Amos Milburn (Aladdin 704) 1955 $1,000
10-inch monaural LP. Black vinyl. Near-mint price range: $750 to $1,000.
Side 1: *Pot Luck Boogie; Amos' Boogie; Bye-Bye-Boogie; Down the Road Apiece.*
Side 2: *Boogie-Woogie; Chicken-Shack Boogie; Rooming House Boogie; Sax Shack Boogie.*
A variation of this release in the Top 1,000 can be found at Number 100.

☐ 619. You're Gone/Here I Am • Roy Perkins (Meladee 112) 1955 $1,000
45 rpm. Near-mint price range: $750 to $1,000.

☐ 620. Mystery Train/I Forgot to Remember to Forget • Elvis Presley (With Scotty
and Bill) (Sun 223) 1955 $1,000

📷 78 rpm. Near-mint price range: $750 to $1,000.
A variation of this release in the Top 1,000 can be found at Number 754.
Members: Elvis Presley; Scotty Moore; Bill Black.

☐ 621. Someday/Bow Wow • Pyramids (With Fletcher Smith's Band)
(Hollywood 1047) 1955 $1,000

📷 45 rpm. Near-mint price range: $750 to $1,000.
Members: Sidney Correia; Joe Dandy; Melvin White; Kenneth Perdue; Lionel Cobbs; Tom Williams.
Variations of this release in the Top 1,000 can be found at Numbers 139; 837.

☐ 622. I'll Forever Love You/Mr. Cool Breeze • Swans (Fortune 822) 1955 $1,000

📷 45 rpm. Near-mint price range: $750 to $1,000.

☐ 623. SPD-15 • Various Artists (RCA Victor SPD-15) 1955 $1,000

📷 Set of 10 black label or gray label (juke box edition) extended plays. Both are dog on top.
Has one Elvis Presley EP, numbered 599-9089, representing sides 7 and 14 of 20. Box and
inserts are yet to be verified. Near-mint price range: $750 to $1,000.
Artists featured: Elvis Presley; others.

☐ 624. Darling Come Back/My Tears • Pat Cordel & Crescents
(Club 1011) 1956 $1,000

📷 45 rpm. Vito Picone and Carman Romano later formed the Elegants. After the break-up
of this group, Pat Cordel joined the June Taylor Dancers. Near-mint price range: $750 to
$1,000.
Members: Pat Croccitto [Cordel]; Vito Picone; Carman Romano; Ronnie Jones.

☐ 625. K.C. Douglas: Dead-Beat Guitar and the Mississippi Blues – Street Corner
Blues 'Bout Women and Automobiles • K.C. Douglas (Cook Road
Recordings 5002) 1956 $1,000

📷 LP. Front cover shows label as only "Road Recordings," whereas label has "Cook Road
Recordings." Near-mint price range: $750 to $1,000.
Side A: *Canned Heat; Catfish; Big Road Blues; Kansas City; I Got the Key; Casey Jones.*
Side B: *Mercury Blues; Blues; I Met the Blues This Morning; I Have My Women; Haid Money.*

Juanita

102
U-22823M
Time: 2:12

HAUNTING MEMORIES
(G. Goldner-J. Wesley)
HALLIQUINS

441.

WINLEY
RECORDS

UNBREAKABLE
45 R.P.M.

RECORD NO.
227 A

Ninny-Ethel Byrd
(BMI) Time 2:37

THE WOWS OF LOVE
(Paragons-Winley)

THE PARAGONS

442.

MARK
MARK RECORDS INC.
UTICA, N.Y.

45 RPM
RN-120-2
Time: 2:30

M
Margi
Publ. Co.

NOBODY CAN LOVE YOU
(Anthony Mitchell)
THE SUPREMES

443.

REGO
RECORDS

UNBREAKABLE
45 RPM

RECORD NO.
1004 B

Douglas (BMI)
2:25

LOVE IS A VOW
(Daniel Elder)
SUNG BY THE
TEENTONES
featuring ARNOLD MALONE

444.

119

Sure
RECORDS

UNBREAKABLE
45 R.P.M.

RECORD NO.
1002-B

Howard Music
BMI (1:31)

PRETTY GIRL
(Robert E. Brown)
THE GOLDEN BELLS
Gems of Rhythm Band
20 East Elizabeth Ave.,
Linden, N. J.

449.

PEACH RECORDS
P. O. Box 111
Jefferson, Georgia

Vocal

SHE'S MY BABY
(Leon Holmes)
LEON HOLMES
and His
Georgia Ramblers

450.

☆ ☆ ☆
Junior
RECORDS

SAMPLE COPY

NOT FOR SALE

UNBREAKABLE
45 R.P.M.

RECORD NO.
400
(610)

Adams Music—
Kae Williams Music
Inc. — BMI

Time 2:27

NEVER WILL PART
(B. Jefferson-D. McRae)
THE SILHOUETTES
Orch. by DAVE McRAE

451.

Ducky
RECORDS
2800 Watson Blvd., Endicott, N. Y.

SAMPLE

NOT FOR SALE

.P.M.
ongkraft
b. (BMI)

RECORD NO.
D-45-713

Produced By
BILL MILLER

JUST FOR A LITTLE WHILE
(Tender Tones & Miller)
TENDER TONES

454.

120

☐ 626. My Girl/China Doll • Downbeats (Gee 1019) 1956 $1,000

  📷 45 rpm. Red and black label. Near-mint price range: $750 to $1,000.

☐ 627. Gloria/Sugar Lips • Five Chances (States 156) 1956 $1,000

  45 rpm. Red vinyl. Near-mint price range: $750 to $1,000.
  Members: Johnny Jones; John Austell; Darnell Austell; Reggie Smith; Howard Pitman; Harold Jones.
  A variation of this release in the Top 1,000 can be found at Number 842.

☐ 628. In the Still of the Nite/Jones Girl • Five Satins (Standord 200) 1956 $1,000

  45 rpm. Red label. Near-mint price range: $750 to $1,000.
  Members: Fred Parris; Louis Peebles; Stan Dortch; Jim Freeman; Ed Martin.
  A variation of this release in the Top 1,000 can be found at Number 293.

☐ 629. Girl Friend/Willow Blues • Five Scalders (With Bill Moore on Tenor Sax)
(Drummond 3001) 1956 $1,000

  45 rpm. Maroon label. Near-mint price range: $750 to $1,000.
  Members: Mack Rice; Johnny Mayfield; Sol Tilman; Gerald Young; James Bryant.
  A variation of this release in the Top 1,000 can be found at Number 517.

☐ 630. I'm So in Love Tonight/Anna Bell • Heptones (Abbco 401) 1956 $1,000

  📷 45 rpm. Serial numbers "105" and "106" are actually more prominent on label than selection no. "401." Near-mint price range: $750 to $1,000.

☐ 631. All I Want Is Love/I've Heard About You • Montclairs (With Douglas
DuBois, Chico Chism & His Jettinaires) (Sonic 104) 1956 $1,000

  📷 45 rpm. Near-mint price range: $750 to $1,000.

☐ 632. What Makes Me Love You Like I Do/Pass It On • Pre-Teens (With Shytan
Five) (J&S 1756)... 1956 $1,000

  📷 45 rpm. Near-mint price range: $750 to $1,000.

☐ 633. Just a Little Loving/The Lonely Telephone • Quintones
(Jordan 1601) 1956 $1,000

  78 rpm. Near-mint price range: $750 to $1,000.

☐ 634. Great Country and Western Hits • Various Artists (RCA
Victor SPD-26).. 1956 $1,000

  📷 10-EP boxed set. Includes insert/separator sheets. Near-mint price range: $750 to $1,000.
  Artists featured: Elvis Presley; Eddy Arnold; Chet Atkins; Johnnie & Jack; Homer & Jethro; Jim, Edward & Maxine Brown; Jim Reeves; Hank Snow; Sons of the Pioneers; Porter Wagoner; Del Wood.

☐ 635. Party After Hours • Various Artists (Aladdin 703) 1956 $1,000

  10-inch maural LP. Black vinyl. Near-mint price range: $750 to $1,000.
  Artists: Amos Milburn, Wynonie Harris, Velma Nelson, Crown Prince Waterford.
  A variation of this release in the Top 1,000 can be found at Number 144.

☐ 636. Cool Off Baby/Almost • Billy Barrix (Chess 1662)........................... 1957 $1,000

  78 rpm. Near-mint price range: $750 to $1,000.
  Variations of this release in the Top 1,000 can be found at Numbers 19; 60.

☐ 637. I'm Long Gone/? • Carl Belew & His Riff Riders (Sowder 248)......... 1957 $1,000

  📷 45 rpm. Near-mint price range: $750 to $1,000.

☐ 638. Whisper/Jungle • Concepts (With Al Browne Orchestra)
(Apache 1515) 1957 $1,000

  📷 45 rpm. Near-mint price range: $750 to $1,000.

☐ 639. Their Greatest Hits • Midnighters (Federal 541) 1957 $1,000

  LP. White cover. Near-mint price range: $750 to $1,000.
  Side 1: *Work with Me Annie; Moonrise; Sexy Ways; Get It; Switchie Witchie Titchie; It's Love Baby (24 Hours a Day)*.
  Side 2: *Annie Had a Baby; She's the One; Annie's Aunt Fannie; Crazy Loving (Stay with Me); Henry's Got Flat Feet; Tore Up over You.*
  Members: Hank Ballard; Henry Booth; Charles Sutton; Sonny Woods; Lawson Smith.
  A variation of this release in the Top 1,000 can be found at Number 16.

HᴜɴTᴇʀ
RECORDS
507 Kennedy Street, N. W.
Atlanta 18, Georgia
Phone 524-5311

Builders Music,
Inc. BMI
Time 2:35

45 2504
Side 2
ZTSC-68310

SWEETEST ANGEL
- T. Brown -
CONDORS

456.

HᴜɴTᴇʀ
RECORDS
507 Kennedy Street, N. W.
Atlanta 18, Georgia
Phone 524-5311

Builders Music,
Inc. - BMI
Time: 3:03
DISC JOCKEY

45-3503
Side 2
ZTSC-68452
NOT FOR SALE

IT DOESN'T MATTER
- Lewis Grant -
THE CONTINENTALS

457.

THE FENDERMEN
MULE SKINNER BLUES

458.

HOMOGENIZED SOUL

Modern Music BMI
Time 2:52
(Q266-102)

A
POLYUNSATURATED
PRODUCTION

LOVE WALKED OUT
(Beazley)
THE NEWLYWEDS
45-601

460.

Richie
RECORDS

45 R.P.M.
Vince Rugo
Music - BMI

R-2-45
Time 2:59
VOCAL

FOREVER AND EVER
(Ciprara-Puce)
FRANKIE
and The C-Notes

459.

☐ 640. Bouquet of Roses/Tweet Tweet • Nunnie Moore & Peacocks
(L&M 1002)... 1957 $1,000

📷 45 rpm. Near-mint price range: $750 to $1,000.

☐ 641. Dance Album • Carl Perkins (Sun 1225) 1957 $1,000

📷 LP. Near-mint price range: $750 to $1,000.
Side 1: *Blue Suede Shoes; Movie Magg; Sure to Fall; Gone, Gone, Gone; Honey Don't; Only You.*
Side 2: *Tennessee; Wrong Yo You; Everybody's Trying to Be My Baby; Matchbox; Your True Love; Boppin' the Blues.*

☐ 642. The Platters • Platters (Federal 549) 1957 $1,000

📷 LP. Near-mint price range: $750 to $1,000.
Members: Tony Williams; David Lynch; Herb Reed; Zola Taylor; Paul Robi.
Side 1: *Only You; Hey Now; I Need You All the Time; Maggie Doesn't Work Here Any More; You Made Me Cry; Tell the World.*
Side 2: *Voo Vee Ah Bee; Give Thanks; Shake It Up Mambo; Love All Night; I'll Cry When You're Gone; Roses of Picardy.*

☐ 643. That Long Black Train/I'm Not Going to Cry • Franklin Stewart
(Lu 501).. 1957 $1,000
45 rpm. Near-mint price range: $750 to $1,000.

☐ 644. How Many Times/Water Water • Twilighters (J-V-B 83) 1957 $1,000

📷 45 rpm. Near-mint price range: $750 to $1,000.

☐ 645. One More Chance/You and Me • Unknowns (X-Tra 102)................. 1957 $1,000

📷 45 rpm. Near-mint price range: $750 to $1,000.

☐ 646. Romeo/What You Do to Me • Velours (With Sammy Lowe Orchestra)
(Onyx 508)... 1957 $1,000

📷 45 rpm. Near-mint price range: $750 to $1,000.
Members: Jerome Ramos; Pete Winston; John Pearson; Don Heywoode; John Cheatdom; Charles Moffett; Keith Williams; Troyce Key.

☐ 647. Mean When I'm Mad/One Kiss • Eddie Cochran (Liberty 55070)..... 1958 $1,000

📷 Picture sleeve. Near-mint price range: $750 to $1,000.

☐ 648. Give Me Your Love/China Girl • Columbus Pharaohs (With Tommy Wills
Orchestra) (Esta 290) 1958 $1,000

📷 45 rpm. Near-mint price range: $750 to $1,000.
Members: Morris Wade; Bobby Taylor; Ron Wilson; Bernard Wilson.

☐ 649. Please Surrender/Rock a Bock • Eldaros (With Ray Parratore & Rhythm
Rockaways) (Vesta 102) 1958 $1,000

📷 45 rpm. Near-mint price range: $750 to $1,000.
Members: Jimmy Singleton; James Crawford; Robert Green; Kenny Tucker; Levy Hall.

☐ 650. Hey Miss Lucy/I'm Batty Over Hatty • Esquerita (Capitol 1075) 1958 $1,000
45 rpm with picture sleeve. Also recorded as Eskew Reeder. Promotional issue only. Near-mint price range: $750 to $1,000.

☐ 651. I Never Told You/Rock with Me Marie • 5 "Gents" (Crest 51657)..... 1958 $1,000

📷 45 rpm. Near-mint price range: $750 to $1,000.

☐ 652. The Five Satins Sing • Five Satins (Ember 100) 1958 $1,000

📷 LP. Multi-color label. Colored vinyl. Near-mint price range: $750 to $1,000.
Members: Fred Parris; Louis Peebles; Stan Dortch; Jim Freeman; Ed Martin.
Side 1: *I'll Remember (In the Still of the Night); Our Anniversary; Wish I Had My Baby; Wonderful Girl; Sugar; I'll Get Along; Again.*
Side 2: *To the Aisle; Pretty Baby; Our Love Is Forever; Oh Happy Day; Jones Girl; Weeping Willow; Moonlight and I.*

461.

462.

463.

465.

466.

☐ 653. Guiding Angel/Baby Come Home • Gales (Mel-O 111) 1958 $1,000

📷 45 rpm. Reportedly the same group as the Violinaires. Near-mint price range: $750 to $1,000.

☐ 654. Suzy-Q • Dale Hawkins (Chess 1429) 1958 $1,000

📷 LP. At least one known counterfeit exists with a black and white cover. Original covers are in full color. Between cover and label, the following spellings of the title track are found: "Suzy-Q," "Susie-Q" and "Suzie Q." Near-mint price range: $750 to $1,000.
Side 1: *Suzie-Q; Don't Treat Me This Way; Juanita; Tornado; Little Pig; Heaven.*
Side II: *Baby Baby; Mrs. Mergritory's Daughter; Take My Heart; Wild, Wild World; See You Soon Baboon; Four Letter Word-Rock.*

☐ 655. Take Me Back/Betty Lou • Bob Jeffries (With Marcels 123)
(Jody 1048)... 1958 $1,000

📷 45 rpm. We're not quite certain if the "123" has to do with the Marcels, or if it means something else. It does appear, however, that 1048 is the selection number. Near-mint price range: $750 to $1,000.

☐ 656. Elaine/This Is the End of Love • Klixs (Music City 823) 1958 $1,000

📷 45 rpm. Near-mint price range: $750 to $1,000.

☐ 657. Walking At Your Will/Tell It to Me Baby • Willie Mitchell & Four Kings
(Stomper Time 1160).. 1958 $1,000

📷 45 rpm. Near-mint price range: $750 to $1,000.

☐ 658. Teenage Sweetheart/Rockin' Yodel • Mystics (Chatam 350/351) 1958 $1,000

📷 45 rpm. Reissued using same label name and number, but credited to the Champs. Near-mint price range: $750 to $1,000.

☐ 659. From Me/My Girl • Plants (With Orchestra) (J&S 1617) 1958 $1,000
45 rpm. Near-mint price range: $750 to $1,000.

☐ 660. Once in a Lifetime/It Ain't True • Sonics (X-Tra 107) 1958 $1,000

📷 45 rpm. Near-mint price range: $750 to $1,000.
Members: Donald Sheffield; Kenny "Butch" Hamilton.

☐ 661. Until You Return/Whomp Whomp • Starlighters (Suncoast 1001).... 1958 $1,000
45 rpm. Near-mint price range: $750 to $1,000.

☐ 662. Promise Me/Never Let Me Go • Tempos (Rhythm 121) 1958 $1,000
45 rpm. Near-mint price range: $750 to $1,000.
Members: Marvin Smith; Jewel Jones; James Maddox; Louis Bradley; Dick Nichens.

☐ 663. Lucky Me/Darling I Fell for You • Castros (Lasso 501) 1959 $1,000

📷 45 rpm. Reportedly 100 made. Near-mint price range: $750 to $1,000.

☐ 664. In My Dreams/Is It Right • Castros (Lasso 502).............................. 1959 $1,000
45 rpm. Reportedly 100 made. Near-mint price range: $750 to $1,000.

☐ 665. Mr. Dee Jay/Yes I Do • Continders (Featuring Clifford Curry)
(Blue Sky 105) 1959 $1,000

📷 45 rpm. Near-mint price range: $750 to $1,000.

☐ 666. Won't You Come In/Pack Your Rags and Go • Cool Breeze & His Band
with Little Cool Breezes (With Jimmy Petty, Rupert Jones & Senders)
(Ebony 1014) 1959 $1,000

📷 45 rpm. Near-mint price range: $750 to $1,000.

☐ 667. I Was a Fool (To Make You Cry)/Teenage Josephine • Golden Nuggets
(With Rocky Rhodes & California Versatones) (Futura 1691) 1959 $1,000

📷 45 rpm. Near-mint price range: $750 to $1,000.

Golden State
EMI
Time: 2:11

R 835

WHY DON'T YOU WRITE ME
(Hollins)
THE CARDINALS

467.

Dandelion -
Crazy Cajun
BMI

G-TCG 1
Time: 2:24

Disk Jockey
Not For Sale

MY LOVE WILL FOLLOW YOU
(L. C. Marshall)
THE CONTINENTAL GEMS
Produced by Huey Meaux
2091

468.

CAPITOL 33 COMPACT
SOMETHING NEW
THE BEATLES
(Recorded in England)
STEREO   SXA-2108
(SXA1-21C2)

1. I'LL CRY INSTEAD
(John Lennon-Paul McCartney)
2. AND I LOVE HER
(John Lennon-Paul McCartney)
3. SLOW DOWN
(Larry Williams)

470.

BEATLES

Recorded by THE BEATLES Hamburg 1961

471.

☐ 668. Look for a Lie/Blue Memories • Jades (With Rocket Flames Band)
   (Christy 114) 1959 $1,000

   📷 45 rpm. Reportedly 100 pressed. Near-mint price range: $750 to $1,000.
   Members: Louis Allen; Art Robinson; Ocie Watkins; Leroy Davis; David McShade.

☐ 669. Bad Girl/I Love You Baby • Miracles (Featuring Bill "Smokey" Robinson)
   (Motown G1) 1959 $1,000

   📷 45 rpm. May or may not have TLX-2207 on label. Near-mint price range: $750 to $1,000.
   Members: William "Smokey" Robinson; Pete Moore; Bobby Rogers; Ron White; Claudette Rogers.

☐ 670. Walkin' Alone/Rag Mop • Willie Mitchell & Four Kings (Stomper
   Time 1163) 1959 $1,000
   45 rpm. Near-mint price range: $750 to $1,000.

☐ 671. Love and Kisses/Casanova • Mixers (Bold 102) 1959 $1,000

   📷 45 rpm. Near-mint price range: $750 to $1,000.

☐ 672. My Valerie/Loved and Lost • Note-Torials (Impala 201) 1959 $1,000
   45 rpm. Near-mint price range: $750 to $1,000.

☐ 673. I Searched the Seven Seas/I Took a Trip Way Over the Sea • Plants
   (J&S 248/249) 1959 $1,000

   📷 45 rpm. Despite having the same name, this is a different group of "Plants" than on J&S
   in 1957 and '58. Near-mint price range: $750 to $1,000.
   Members: James Lawson; Steve McDowell; George Jackson; Thurmon Thrower.

☐ 674. In the Park/In My Heart • Rebels (Kings-X 3362) 1959 $1,000

   📷 45 rpm. Near-mint price range: $750 to $1,000.

☐ 675. Launie, My Love/Which One Will It Be • Valaires (Willett 114) 1959 $1,000

   📷 45 rpm. Near-mint price range: $750 to $1,000.

☐ 676. RCA Victor August 1959 Sampler • Various Artists (RCA
   Victor SP-33-27) 1959 $1,000

   📷 LP. Promotional issue only. Not issued with special cover. All songs except *Blue Moon of
   Kentucky* (Elvis Presley) are true stereo. Near-mint price range: $750 to $1,000.
   Side 1: *Warsaw Concerto* (Hugo Winterhalter's Orchestra); *Volare* (Melachrino Strings and ;
      Orchestra); *Blessed Assurance* (George Beverly Shea); *Wunderbar* (Howard Keel & Anne
      Jeffreys); *Guadalajara* (Xavier Cugat's Orchestra); *Gypsy Lament* (Esquivel's Orchestra);
      The Merry Old Land of Oz (Shorty Rogers' Orchestra).
   Side 2: *Someday* (Jim Reeves); *Blue Moon of Kentucky* (Elvis Presley); *The 3rd Man Theme*
      (Buddy Morrow's Orchestra); *You're Driving Me Crazy* (Perez Prado's Orchestra); *The
      Song Is You* (Pat Suzuki); *Intro; Darling Cora* (Harry Belafonte).

☐ 677. Two Hearts Make One Love/Lost in Dreams • Wisdoms
   (Gaity 169/170) 1959 $1,000

   📷 45 rpm. Near-mint price range: $750 to $1,000.

☐ 678. Let's Rock To-Night/(It's My Fault) You're Gone • Jimmy Grubbs & His
   Music Makers (Mac 468/469) 1950s $1,000

   📷 45 rpm. Near-mint price range: $750 to $1,000.

☐ 679. Hull Records Cordially Invite You to Meet the Avons • Avons
   (Hull 1000) 1960 $1,000

   📷 LP. Near-mint price range: $750 to $1,000.
   Members: Robert Lee; Wendell Lee; William Lee; Irv Watson; Curtis Norris; Franklin Cole; George Coleman.
   Side 1: *What Love Can Do; Baby; What Will I Do; Someone for Everyone; Bonnie; A Girl to Call
      My Own.*
   Side 2: *On the Island; Once Upon a Time; You Are So Close to Me; Our Love Will Never End;
      Fairy Tales; Gonna Catch You Nappin'.*

475.

476.

478.

480.

KREED!

484.

Vee Jay

63-2967
Vocal

Concertone
Songs-ASCAP
Time: 2:00

PLEASE PLEASE ME
(J. Lennon-P. McCartney)
THE BEATLLES
VJ 498

488.

SUN

Famous
ASCAP U-130

Vocal
2:27

I DON'T CARE
IF THE SUN DON'T SnINE
(Mack David)
ELVIS PRESLEY
MEMPHIS, TENNESSEE

487.

SUN

Delta Music
BMI—2:57

Vocal
U-71
Dubrover
Addington

CALL ME ANYTHING, BUT CALL ME
BIG MEMPHIS MARAINEY
ONZIE HORNE COMBO
184
MEMPHIS TENNESSEE

491.

NIGHT SHADDS

ST. GEORGE
AND THE DRAGON
LIGHT SHOW
"SAN FRANCISCO
OF THE SOUTH"

489.

☐ 680. Blue Angel/Shakie Mae • Beatnicks (Key-Lock 913) 1960 $1,000

📷 45 rpm. Near-mint price range: $750 to $1,000.

☐ 681. There's a Moon Out Tonight/Indian Girl • Capris (Planet 1010) 1960 $1,000

📷 45 rpm. Near-mint price range: $750 to $1,000.
Members: Nick "Santos" Santamaria; Mike Mitchell; Vince Narcardo; John Apostol; Frank Reina.

☐ 682. Dreaming/Daddy's Gonna Tell You No Lie • Cosmic Rays (With Sun Ra & Arkestra) (Saturn 401/402) 1960 $1,000

📷 45 rpm. Near-mint price range: $750 to $1,000.

☐ 683. Goodbye Train/? • Jim Foley (Lucky 1001) 1960 $1,000

📷 45 rpm. Lucky also used the selection number 1001 on a release by Ronny & Johnny. Near-mint price range: $750 to $1,000.

☐ 684. Lightnin' and the Blues • Lightnin' Hopkins (Herald 1012)................ 1960 $1,000

LP. Near-mint price range: $750 to $1,000.
Side 1: *Nothin' But the Blues; Don't Think 'Cause You're Pretty; Lightnin's Boogie; Life I Used to Live; Sick Feelin' Blues; Evil Hearted Woman.*
Side 2: *Blues for My Cookie; Sittin' Down Thinkin'; My Baby's Gone; Lonesome in Your Home; Lightnin's Special; My Little Kewpie Doll.*

☐ 685. I Do/Pretty Little Hula Girl • Jokers (With Aztec Combo) (Danco 117)... 1960 $1,000

45 rpm. Near-mint price range: $750 to $1,000.

☐ 686. Rooster Blues • Lightnin' Slim (Excello 8000)................................... 1960 $1000

LP. Real name: Otis Hicks. Near-mint price range: $750 to $1,000.
Side 1: *Rooster Blues; Long Leanie Mama; My Starter Won't Work; G.I. Slim; Lightnin's Troubles; Bed Bug Blues.*
Side 2: *Hoo Doo Blues; It's Might Crazy; Sweet Little Woman; Tom Cat Blues; Feelin' Awful Blues; I'm Leavin' You Baby.*

☐ 687. When I Needed You/? • Little Iva & Her Band (Miracle 2) 1960 $1,000

45 rpm. Near-mint price range: $750 to $1,000.

☐ 688. Each Passing Day/Sally • Jimmy Singleton & Royal Satins (With Hi-Fis) (Devere 006)... 1960 $1,000

📷 45 rpm. Near-mint price range: $750 to $1,000.

☐ 689. Right Now/Night Is So Lonely • Gene Vincent (Capitol 4237) 1960 $1,000

📷 Picture sleeve. Near-mint price range: $750 to $1,000.

☐ 690. Didn't We Have a Nice Time/Open Up Your Heart • Charles Andrea & Hi Tones (Tori Ltd. 2) 1961 $1,000

📷 45 rpm. Near-mint price range: $750 to $1,000.

☐ 691. With All My Heart/Around the World • Billboards (With Red Julian Orchestra) (Vistone 2023) 1961 $1,000

📷 45 rpm. Yellow vinyl. Near-mint price range: $750 to $1,000.

☐ 692. Dry Your Eyes/The Big Sound • Delmiras (Dade 1821) 1961 $1,000

📷 45 rpm. Near-mint price range: $750 to $1,000.
Session: Steve Alaimo.

☐ 693. Don't Call for Me/My Foolish Pride • Implacables (Kain 1004) 1961 $1,000

📷 45 rpm. Reissued as by Johnny Williams. Near-mint price range: $750 to $1,000.

☐ 694. Ring Those Bells/The Cumberland and the Merrimac • Inspirations (Rondack 9787)... 1961 $1,000

📷 45 rpm. Near-mint price range: $750 to $1,000.

☐ 695. Whisper/So Tight • Jokers (Wand 111) 1961 $1,000

📷 45 rpm. Colored vinyl. Near-mint price range: $750 to $1,000.

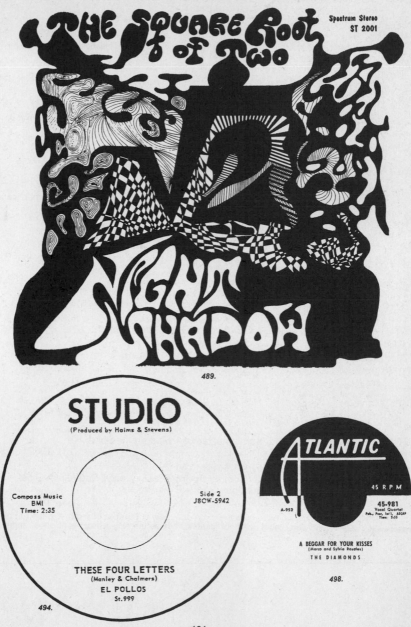

THE SQUARE ROOT of TWO

Spectrum Stereo
ST 2001

NIGHT SHADOW

489.

STUDIO
(Produced by Haims & Stevens)

Compass Music
BMI
Time: 2:35

Side 2
J8OW-5942

THESE FOUR LETTERS
(Manley & Chalmers)
EL POLLOS
St. 999

494.

ATLANTIC

45 R.P.M

45-981
Vocal Quartet
Pab., Peer, Int'l, ASCAP
Time: 3:55

A-952

A BEGGAR FOR YOUR KISSES
(Marco and Sylvia Rosales)
THE DIAMONDS

498.

131

☐ 696. You Told a Lie/Barnyard Dance • Shields (Continental 4072).......... 1961 $1,000
   45 rpm. Near-mint price range: $750 to $1,000.

☐ 697. A Special Message to You from Frank Sinatra • Frank Sinatra
   (Reprise).. 1961 $1,000
   📷 45 rpm. Single-sided disc, made as a Reprise sales and promotional tool. No selection
   number used. Two different pressings exist. Near-mint price range: $750 to $1,000.

☐ 698. Forever and a Day/Please Be My Love • Spirals
   (Admiral 912/913)... 1961 $1,000
   📷 45 rpm. Just two or three known copies. Near-mint price range: $750 to $1,000.

☐ 699. I Want a Guy/Never Again • Supremes (Motown 1008) 1961 $1,000
   📷 45 rpm. Same number is also used on a Contours disc. Near-mint price range: $750 to
   $1,000.
   Members: Diana Ross; Mary Wilson; Florence Ballard.

☐ 700. My Heart Cried/Tina • Tony & Raindrops (Crosley 340)................... 1961 $1,000
   45 rpm. Near-mint price range: $750 to $1,000.

☐ 701. You Can Make It If You Try/? • Clark Vaden & Crescents
   (Dolly 5578) 1961 $1,000
   📷 45 rpm. Identification number shown since no selection number is used. Near-mint price
   range: $750 to $1,000.

☐ 702. The Crystals Twist Uptown • Crystals (Philles 90722)...................... 1962 $1,000
   LP. Capitol Record Club issue. Near-mint price range: $750 to $1,000.
   Side 1: *Uptown; Another Country – Another World; Frankenstein Twist; Oh Yeah, Maybe Baby;*
       Please Hurt Me.
   Side 2: *There's No Other (Like My Baby); On Broadway; What a Nice Way to Turn Seventeen; No*
       One Ever Tells You; Gee Whiz, Look at His Eyes (Twist); I Love You Eddie.
   Members: Barbara Alston; Lala Brooks; Dee Dee Kennibrew; Patricia Wright; Mary Thomas.
   A variation of this release in the Top 1,000 can be found at Number 903.

☐ 703. Jazz Impressions By the Four Tops • Four Tops (Workshop 217) ... 1962 $1,000
   LP. Retitled reissue of *Breaking Through.* Near-mint price range: $750 to $1,000.
   Members: Levi Stubbs; Lawrence Payton; Obie Benson.
   A variation of this release in the Top 1,000 can be found at Number 465.

☐ 704. Late Summer Love/No Good Woman • Grand Prixs (Poncho 10).... 1962 $1,000
   📷 45 rpm. Near-mint price range: $750 to $1,000.

☐ 705. Barbie/What Is a Young Girl Made Of • Kenny & Cadets
   (Randy 422)... 1962 $1,000
   📷 45 rpm. Colored (red and yellow) vinyl. Near-mint price range: $750 to $1,000.
   Members: Brian Wilson; Carl Wilson; Al Jardine; Audree Wilson.

☐ 706. Marvelettes Sing Smash Hits of '62 • Marvelettes (Tamla 229)........ 1962 $1,000
   LP. First issued with this title. Quickly reissued with shortened – not so dated – title: *The*
   Marvelettes Sing. Near-mint price range: $750 to $1,000.
   Members: Gladys Horton; Kathy Anderson; Georgeanna Tillman; Wanda Young; Juanita Cowart; Ann Bogan.

☐ 707. Together (in Your Arms)/Spotlight Dance • Modern Ink Spots
   (Rust 5052)... 1962 $1,000
   📷 45 rpm. Near-mint price range: $750 to $1,000.

☐ 708. Girls! Girls! Girls! Advance (Coming Soon) Theatre Lobby Spot/Girls! Girls!
   Girls! (Now Playing) Theatre Lobby Spot • Elvis Presley
   (Paramount Pictures SP-2017)... 1962 $1,000
   📷 45 rpm. Promotional issue to theaters for lobby play in advance of and during the run of
   Girls! Girls! Girls! film. Label does not identify Elvis as the singer. Near-mint price range:
   $750 to $1,000.

504.

506.

509.

512.

133

☐ 709. Come Back/Got to Get Along • William Wigfall & Lyrics
(Skylight 202)... 1962 $1,000
   📷 45 rpm. Near-mint price range: $750 to $1,000.

☐ 710. From Me to You/Thank You Girl • Beatles (Vee-Jay VJ-522)........... 1963 $1,000
   📷 45 rpm. Black label with colorband and brackets logo. Near-mint price range: $900 to
   $1,000.
   Variations of this release in the Top 1,000 can be found at Numbers 711; 758.
   Members: John Lennon; Paul McCartney, George Harrison; Ringo Starr.

☐ 711. From Me to You/Thank You Girl • Beatles (Vee-Jay VJ-522)........... 1963 $1,000
   📷 45 rpm. Black label with colorband and oval logo. Thin style print. Near-mint price range:
   $900 to $1,000.
   Variations of this release in the Top 1,000 can be found at Numbers 710; 758.
   Members: John Lennon; Paul McCartney, George Harrison; Ringo Starr.

☐ 712. Pardon Me/All At Once • Cezannes (Featuring Cerressa)
(Markay 108) 1963 $1,000
   📷 45 rpm. Near-mint price range: $750 to $1,000.

☐ 713. Dancing with My Lover/There Goes a Young Love • Peter Crawford
(Sandy 1039)... 1963 $1,000
   📷 45 rpm. One known copy. Near-mint price range: $750 to $1,000.

☐ 714. Mixed Up Confusion/Corrina Corrina • Bob Dylan
(Columbia 42656) 1963 $1,000
   45 rpm. Red label. Near-mint price range: $750 to $1,000.
   A variation of this release in the Top 1,000 can be found at Number 919.

☐ 715. Why/Come on Baby • Executives (Revenge 5003) 1963 $1,000
   📷 45 rpm. Near-mint price range: $750 to $1,000.

☐ 716. Summertime Angel/Mr. Misery • Intentions (Jamie 1253)................. 1963 $1,000
   📷 45 rpm. Near-mint price range: $750 to $1,000.

☐ 717. Tears from My Eyes/This Is the Night • Nap [Net] Roman
(Sahara 102)... 1963 $1,000
   📷 45 rpm. More valuable if credited to "Net" Roman. Near-mint price range: $750 to
   $1,000.
   A variation of this release in the Top 1,000 can be found at Number 469.

☐ 718. I'll Cry Tomorrow/If Your Heart Says Yes • Serenaders
(Motown 1046).. 1963 $1,000
   45 rpm. Near-mint price range: $750 to $1,000.
   Members: Sidney Barnes; George Kerr; Timothy Wilson; Luke Gross.

☐ 719. Surfer Joe/Wipe-Out • Surfaris (DFS 11/12)..................................... 1963 $1,000
   📷 45 rpm. Produced by Dale F. Smallin, who made 2,000 copies on his own (DFS) label.
   Near-mint price range: $750 to $1,000.
   Members: Ron Wilson; Jim Fuller; Jim Pash; Pat Connolly; Bob Berryhill; Ken Forssi. Session: Richie Podolor; Chuck
   Girard; Gary Usher.

☐ 720. Your Favorite Singing Groups • Various Artists (Hull 1002) 1963 $1,000
   Monaural LP. Near-mint price range: $750 to $1,000.
   Artists: Avons, Beltones, Carousels, Desires, Elegants, Legends, Miller Sisters, Monotones, Pastels, Sparks,
   Supremes.
   Side 1: *Book of Dance* (Monotones); *Toast to Lovers* (Monotones); *Still Waiting* (Elegants); *Oh Me,
   Oh My* (Pastels); *Drizzle Drizzle* (Supremes); *Baby* (Avons).
   Side 2: *Let It Please Be You* (Desires); *Legend of Love* (Legends); *Roll Back the Rug* (Miller
   Sisters); *Slowly but Surely* (Sparks); *I Talk to My Echo* (Beltones); *Away Over There*
   (Carousels).

☐ 721. Where All Lovers Meet/That's All Right • Vendors (Victorio 128) 1963 $1,000
   45 rpm. Actually a 1962 Invictors' issue [TPE 8221] but with the Victorio/Vendors label on
   top. Near-mint price range: $750 to $1,000.

SITTING BY MY WINDOW
(Tinos)
THE FIVE TINOS
222

514.

HELEN
(W. D. Gardner)
VOCAL BY
THE CARDELLS
Featuring
WM. GARDNER

516.

Baby Let's Play House
(Gunter)
ELVIS PRESLEY
SCOTTY & BILL
217

515.

GIRL FRIEND
McElavine - Waddell
FIVE SCALDERS
BILLi MOORE, Tenor Sax

517.

RCA RADIO VICTROLA DIVISION SPOTS
Form No. 6 P 3565

33⅓ RPM   QM-9E 0401

Band 1   RR-368-B   50 seconds
Band 2   RR-358-B   50 seconds
Band 3   RR-369-B   50 seconds
Band 4   RR-369-B   50 seconds

Produced by
Konyon and Eckhardt, Inc.
November, 1956

518.

135

☐ 722. A Surprise Gift from Your Holiday Innkeeper • Beatles (Capitol/
Holiday Inn) 1964 $1,000

📷 Promotional sleeve/flyer. Yellow paper stock with green print. Pictures the Beatles on front and their first three Capitol LPs on the back. Given gratis to Holiday Inn guests. Flyer either folded around, stapled to, or inserted in commercial copies of early Capitol Beatles singles. Near-mint price range: $750 to $1,000.
Members: John Lennon; Paul McCartney, George Harrison; Ringo Starr.

☐ 723. Ain't She Sweet • Beatles & Swallows (Atco 33-169) 1964 $1,000

📷 Monaural LP. Promotional issue. White label with black print. Label reads "Sample Copy – Not For Sale." Labels and covers on promos do not have "with Tony Sheridan" printed. Has standard commercial cover. Four tracks by the Beatles with Tony Sheridan, and eight tracks by the Swallows. Near-mint price range: $750 to $1,000.
Members: (Beatles) John Lennon; Paul McCartney, George Harrison; Pete Best.
Side 1 (Beatles): *Ain't She Sweet; Sweet Georgia Brown; Take Out Some Insurance on Me Baby; Nobody's Child;* (Swallows): *I Wanna Be Your Man; She Loves You.*
Side 2 (Swallows): *How Do You Do It; Please Please Me; I'll Keep You Satisfied; I'm Telling You Now; I Want to Hold Your Hand; From Me to You.*

☐ 724. A Hard Day's Night • Beatles (United Artists T-90828) 1964 $1,000

Monaural LP. Capitol Record Club issue. Label has "Mfd. By Capitol Records." This is the only verified mono record club issue of a Beatles LP. Near-mint price range: $750 to $1,000. Variations of this release in the Top 1,000 can be found at Numbers 12; 206.
Members: John Lennon; Paul McCartney, George Harrison; Ringo Starr.
Side 1: *A Hard Day's Night; Tell Me Why; I Should Have Known Better (inst.); I'm Happy Just to Dance with You; And I Love Her (inst.).*
Side 2: *I Should Have Known Better; And I Love Her; Ringo's Theme (This Boy) (inst.); Can't Buy Me Love; A Hard Day's Night (inst.).*

☐ 725. Rain/Hey Little Rosie • Demolyrs (With Hash Brown & His Orchestra)
(UWR 900) 1964 $1,000

📷 45 rpm. Near-mint price range: $750 to $1,000.

☐ 726. If I Give My Heart to You/Thunderbird • Freddie & Quantrils
(Karem 1904) 1964 $1,000

45 rpm. Near-mint price range: $750 to $1,000.

☐ 727. Annette & Hayley Mills • Annette Funicello / Hayley Mills (Buena Vista/
Disneyland 3508) 1964 $1,000

📷 Monaural LP. Cover indicates Buena Vista although disc has a (bright yellow) Disneyland label. Issued with paper cover. One side – five tracks – devoted to each artist. Available only by mail order coupon, for $1.98. Its rarity is no doubt helped by poor circulation of magazines with the ad and coupon. Near-mint price range: $750 to $1,000.
Side 1 (Annette): *Pineapple Princess; Tall Paul; Mr. Piano Man; First Name Initial; How Will I Know My Love.*
Side 2 (Hayley Mills): *Flitterin'; Castaway; Let's Get Together; Ding, Ding, Ding; Cobbler, Cobbler.*

☐ 728. I Still Love You/Runaround • Joey & Ovations (Hawk 153) 1964 $1,000

📷 45 rpm. Near-mint price range: $750 to $1,000.

☐ 729. The Rolling Stones • Rolling Stones (London 3375) 1964 $1,000

📷 Monaural LP. White label. Promotional issue only. Near-mint price range: $750 to $1,000.
Members: Mick Jagger; Keith Richards; Bill Wyman; Brian Jones.

☐ 730. This Love Was Real/Anna, My Love • Showcases (Galaxy 732) 1964 $1,000

📷 45 rpm. Near-mint price range: $750 to $1,000.

☐ 731. The Fugitives at Dave's Hideout • Fugitives (Hideout 1001) 1965 $1,000

📷 LP. Near-mint price range: $750 to $1,000.
Members: Gary Quackenbush; Glen Quackenbush; Elmer Clawson.

519.

521.

520.

522.

MASON'S
RECORDING CO.
1630 Amsterdam Ave., N. Y. C.

NO. 0-2
45 RPM

L-178-062

JEANNIE
(Bernard Felton)
THE THRASHERS
with
JOE RUFFIN BAND

523.

Spry

Class Pub.
BMI—Time 2:00

10B-A—45
Vocal

DREAMER FROM MY HEART
(D. Johnson - J. Woodson)
JOHNNY WOODSON
AND THE
CRESCENDOS

524.

JADE
Records
2661 Long Beach Ave., L. A. 58, Calif.

J501-A

MR. MOONGLOW
(H. Wooten)

THE EL REYES

526.

RANSOM
RECORDS

Ransom Publ.
BMI
Time 3:05
CP-3967

VOCAL
45-R103

YOU ARE MY LOVE
(5 Fortunes)

5 FORTUNES

527.

138

X-TRA
RECORDS

45 R.P.M.

RECORD NO.
113-X

Time :45

WHERE ARE YOU
THE FOUR BEL'AIRES

528.

RCA VICTOR
"HIS MASTER'S VOICE"

5P
33-10-P
(12 4P 6274)

SIDE
2
NOT FOR SALE

1—LOVE, LOVE, LOVE — MY HERO - George Feyer
2—OYE NEGRA - X. Cugat
3—THE QUEEN'S FANCY - J. Lewis
4—DIAMONDS ARE A GIRL'S BEST FRIEND - L. Horne
5—PAMPA (ADIOS PAMPA MIA) - P. Prado
6—KING CREOLE - Elvis Presley
7—MEDLEY - M. Davis

LONG 33⅓ PLAY

529.

COPA RECORDS INC

A LOVERS PRAYER
(Harold Atkins)

THE CARVETTES

COPA RECORDS CORP.
1072-5 W. Lynch Street
Jackson, Mississippi

530.

MARK
MARK RECORDS OF NEW YORK

45 R.P.M.

45 R.P.M.

M 146
MA-11-1

Kama Music
Publishing (BMI)
Time 2:26

TELL ME A TALE
(Gary Booker)

THE CHARM KINGS

533.

☐ 732. Why Don't You Love Me/Hitchhike • Spiders (Mascot 112) 1965 $1,000
     45 rpm. Near-mint price range: $750 to $1,000.
     <small>Members: Vince Furnier (a.k.a. Alice Cooper); John Speer; Glen Buxton; Dennis Dunaway; Mike Bruce.</small>

☐ 733. Lay Down and Die, Goodbye/Wonder Who's Loving Her Now • Nazz
     (Very Record 001) 1967 $1,000
     📷 45 rpm. Except for drummer Tom Speer, this band was the same as the Alice Cooper
     Group. *Lay Down and Die, Goodbye* is an earlier version than later released by Alice
     Cooper. There is no connection to Todd Rundgren's Nazz group. Near-mint price range:
     $750 to $1,000.
     <small>Members: Vince "Alice Cooper" Furnier; M. Bruce; G. Buxton; D. Dunaway; T. Speer.</small>

☐ 734. Phases and Faces • Fredric (Forte 80461) 1968 $1,000
     LP. Near-mint price range: $750 to $1,000.
     <small>Members: Joe McCarger; Ron Bera; Steve Thrall.</small>

☐ 735. Magic Lantern • Haymarket Square (Chaparral 201) 1968 $1,000
     LP. Opinions vary as to whether "Magic Lantern" or "Haymarket Square" is the group name.
     Near-mint price range: $750 to $1,000.
     <small>Members: Gloria Lambert; Marc Swenson; Robert Homa; John Kowslowski.</small>

☐ 736. Get Back/Don't Let Me Down • Beatles (Apple/
     Americom 2490/M-335) 1969 $1,000
     Round 4" flexi-disc. Black vinyl with white print. Available in special vending machines. Near-
     mint price range: $750 to $1,000.
     <small>Members: John Lennon; Paul McCartney, George Harrison; Ringo Starr.</small>

☐ 737. In My Diary/At Sundown • Spinners (Motown 1155) 1969 $1,000
     45 rpm. Near-mint price range: $750 to $1,000.
     <small>Members: Bobby Smith; Henry Fambrough; Pervis Jackson; Bill Henderson; G.C. Cameron; Philippe Wynne; Reese
     Palmer; Jim Knowland; Ed Edwards; Chester Simmons.</small>

☐ 738. My Dearest, My Darling (I Miss You)/? • Tim Boyd & Esquires (With Bill
     Gibbs Combo) (Odessa 101) 1960s $1,000
     📷 45 rpm. Near-mint price range: $750 to $1,000.

☐ 739. Bow Street Runners • Bow Street Runners (B.T. Puppy 1026) 1970 $1,000
     LP. Near-mint price range: $750 to $1,000.

☐ 740. Wild Country • Wild Country (LSI 0275) 1970 $1,000
     📷 LP. Near-mint price range: $750 to $1,000.
     <small>Members: Randy Owen; Jeff Cook; Teddy Gentry; John B. Vartanian.</small>
     Side 1: ?
     Side 2: *Tied to the Music; I'll Go on Loving You; I'll Be There, Call on Me; Make It with You in My
     Mind; Music Moves Me; Guess I'm Still in Love with You.*

☐ 741. Mystic Siva • Mystic Siva (VO 19713) 1971 $1,000
     📷 LP. With Gatefold cover. Near-mint price range: $900 to $1,000.
     <small>Members: Dave Mascarin; Al Tozzie; Mark Heckert; Art Trienel;</small>

☐ 742. Elvis: Aloha from Hawaii Via Satellite • Elvis Presley (RCA
     Victor VPSX-6089) 1973 $1,000
     Two quadraphonic LPs. Reddish-orange label. Cover: Front: Has two white stickers, listing
     contents and playing times (contents not printed on covers). There is no Saturn-shaped
     contents sticker, nor is there a QuadraDisc sticker. On this issue, stickers were on shrink
     wrap. Front has die-cut (5 ½" diameter) hole which allows inner sleeve to show. Double
     pocket cover. Promotional issue only. Near-mint price range: $750 to $1,000.
     (Disc 1) Side 1: *Introduction: Also Sprach Zarathustra; See See Rider; Burning Love; Something;
         You Gave Me a Mountain; Steamroller Blues.*
     (Disc 1) Side 2: *My Way; Love Me; Johnny B. Goode; It's Over; Blue Suede Shoes; I'm So
         Lonesome I Could Cry; I Can't Stop Loving You; Hound Dog.*
     (Disc 2) Side 3: *What Now My Love; Fever; Welcome to My World; Suspicious Minds;
         Introductions By Elvis.*
     (Disc 2) Side 4: *I'll Remember You; Medley: Long Tall Sally/Whole Lot-ta Shakin' Goin' On; An
         American Trilogy; A Big Hunk O' Love; Can't Help Falling in Love.*
     A variation of this release in the Top 1,000 can be found at Number 67.

PIX

PIXTON MUSIC
(BMI)

TIME: 2
S—37

LEST YOU FORGET
(Scott, Morris, The Invictas)

THE INVICTAS
PIX—1101

535.

A LITTLE ROCK & ROLL FOR EVERYBODY

H-BOMB FERGUSON
MIDNIGHT RAMBLIN' TONITE
I AM SO LONELY
LADY QUEEN
MARY LITTLE MARY
I'M CRYING BOO-BOO HOO
THE MESS AROUND

THE ESCOS
GOLDEN RULE OF LOVE
WHATCHA BET
WE DANCE

THE MASCOTS
TOO THIS WIGGLE
LONELY RAIN
THAT'S THE WAY I FEEL

538.

TAMLA

MT 54022

Fidelity, Music &
Seagull Music
BMI

LET'S ROCK
(B. Gordy Jr.-R. Davis-G. Gordy)

BARRETT STRONG

536.

R & R

A DIVISION OF
RAINBOW SOUND, INC.

P. O. Box 24500   Dallas, Texas

45 RPM   Side 1
RR-3002   Time 3:45

THE VISIONS
It's You I Love
(LeRoy McCoy)

537.

PENNEY RECORDS

45x1306
BMI
House of Fortun
(PG-2)

Time
2:30

THE GIRL I LEFT BEHIND
(R. Reyen-G. Matola)

CARLTON

540.

141

☐ 743. John Lennon Sings the Great Rock & Roll Hits (Roots) • John Lennon
(Adam VIII Ltd. 8018) 1975 $1,000

📷 LP. Orange label. Available briefly before production and sales were ceased due to legal
action brought against Adam VIII by Apple and John Lennon. Most originals have an
advertisement liner sleeve and a small ad insert. Some originals exist without these two
items. Counterfeits do exist. Copies with discs made of any vinyl other than black are
counterfeits. Colored vinyl originals do not exist. All copies with covers constructed of paper
slicks pasted on cardboard are fakes since originals are made of posterboard. All copies
with unusually large labels are counterfeit. On the back cover of originals, the Adam VIII ads
have photo miniatures that are sharp and clear. On fakes, the print is blurry, particularly on
the "20 Solid Gold Hits" LP ad. The Adam VIII logo on original covers is sharp and clear. It is
blurry and faded on fakes. The number A-8018-A is lightly hand etched on the label of all
originals. Near-mint price range: $750 to $1,000.

Side 1: *Be-Bop-A-Lula; Ain't That a Shame; Stand By M; Sweet Little Sixteen; Rip It Up; Angel
Baby; Do You Want to Dance; You Can't Catch Me.*

Side 2: *Bony Maronie; Peggy Sue; Bring It on Home to Me; Slippin' & Slidin'; Be My Baby;Ya Ya;
Just Because.*

☐ 744. Born to Run • Bruce Springsteen (Columbia 33795) 1975 $1,000

LP. Promotional issue. With script/title cover. Near-mint price range: $750 to $1,000.

☐ 745. Love Comes to Everyone/Soft Touch • George Harrison (Dark
Horse 8844)... 1979 $1,000

📷 Picture sleeve. Near-mint price range: $750 to $1,000.

☐ 746. Xanadu • Various Artists (MCA 10384) 1980 $1,000

📷 LP. Soundtrack. Picture disc. Promotional issue only. Reportedly only 52 made. Near-
mint price range: $750 to $1,000.

Featured artists: Olivia Newton-John, Electric Light Orchestra, Cliff Richard, Gene Kelly, Tubes.

☐ 747. Don't Let Our Love Go Wrong/Stomp, Shake and Twist • Billy Barnette &
Searchers (Mt. Vernon 500) .... ? $1,000

45 rpm. Near-mint price range: $750 to $1,000.

☐ 748. Lady in Green/? • Magnetics (Bonnie 107374)...................................... ? $1,000

45 rpm. We're not sure if "107374" is the selection number. It does seem more like an
identification number. Near-mint price range: $750 to $1,000.

☐ 749. Until/? • Premiers (Echo 6013) .... ? $1,000

📷 45 rpm. Near-mint price range: $750 to $1,000.

☐ 750. The Promotional Album • Rolling Stones (London RSD1)...................... ? $1,000

LP. Near-mint price range: $750 to $1,000.

Members: Mick Jagger; Keith Richards; Bill Wyman; Brian Jones; Charlie Watts.

☐ 751. Wishing/My Money • Walt, Percy & Tracers (Three Rivers) .... ? $1,000

📷 45 rpm. No selection number used. Reissued as by the Roberson Brothers. Near-mint
price range: $750 to $1,000.

Members: Walt Roberson; Percy Roberson.

☐ 752. A Jazz Holiday/Wolverine Blues • Benny Goodman Orchestra
(Vocallon 15656) 1928 $900

78 rpm. First record by Benny Goodman under his own name. Near-mint price range: $700
to $900.

☐ 753. Secret Love/Real Gone Mama • Moonglows (Chance 1152) 1954 $900

📷 45 rpm. Yellow and black label. Near-mint price range: $700 to $900.

Members: Harvey Fuqua; Bobby Lester; Alex Graves; Prentiss Barnes; Buddy Johnson.

A variation of this release in the Top 1,000 can be found at Number 608.

542.

548.

544.

545.

550.

143

☐ 754. Mystery Train/I Forgot to Remember to Forget • Elvis Presley (With Scotty and Bill) (Sun 223).. 1955 $900

📷 45 rpm. Near-mint price range: $700 to $900.
A variation of this release in the Top 1,000 can be found at Number 620.
Members: Elvis Presley; Scotty Moore; Bill Black.

☐ 755. At Home with Screamin' Jay Hawkins • Screamin' Jay Hawkins (Orchestra Under Direction of Leroy Kirkland and O.B. Masingill)
(Epic LN-3448) 1956 $900

📷 LP. Near-mint price range: $700 to $900.
Side 1: *Orange-Colored Sky; Hong Kong; Temptation; I Love Paris; I Put a Spell on You; Swing Low, Sweet Chariot.*
Side 2: *Yellow Coat; Ol' Man River; If You Are But a Dream; Give Me My Boots and Saddle; Deep Purple; You Made Me Love You.*

☐ 756. Koolit/If I Am a Fool • Tommy Blake (Buddy 107) 1958 $900
45 rpm. Near-mint price range: $700 to $900.

☐ 757. The 309/2-3-4 • Rockin' Continentals (Casino 1007)........................ 1962 $900
45 rpm. Near-mint price range: $600 to $900.

☐ 758. From Me to You/Thank You Girl • Beatles (Vee-Jay VJ-522)........... 1963 $900

📷 45 rpm. Black label with brackets logo and thick horizontal silver lines. Near-mint price range: $700 to $900.
Variations of this release in the Top 1,000 can be found at Numbers 710; 711.
Members: John Lennon; Paul McCartney, George Harrison; Ringo Starr.

☐ 759. Please Please Me/From Me to You • Beatles (Vee-Jay VJ-581)...... 1964 $900

📷 45 rpm. Promotional issue. Blue and white label. "Promotional Copy" print is not shown on label. Near-mint price range: $700 to $900.
A variation of this release in the Top 1,000 can be found at Number 203.
Members: John Lennon; Paul McCartney, George Harrison; Ringo Starr.

☐ 760. Introducing the Beatles • Beatles (Vee-Jay LP-1062) 1964 $900
Monaural LP. Black label with circular colorband and brackets logo. With *Love Me Do* and *P.S. I Love You* (on later issues these tracks are replaced by *Ask Me Why* and *Please Please Me*). Back cover lists song titles in two large columns. Near-mint price range: $700 to $900.
Variations of this release in the Top 1,000 can be found at Numbers 7; 27; 65; 93; 169; 202; 218; 543; 559; 789.
Members: John Lennon; Paul McCartney, George Harrison; Ringo Starr.
Side 1: *I Saw Her Standing There; Misery; Anna; Chains; Boys; Love Me Do.*
Side 2: *P.S. I Love You; Baby It's You; Do You Want to Know a Secret; A Taste of Honey; There's a Place; Twist and Shout.*
Members: John Lennon; Paul McCartney, George Harrison; Ringo Starr.

☐ 761. The Other Half • Other Half (7/2 1) 1966 $900
LP. Near-mint price range: $700 to $900.
Members: Andrea Inganni; Bob Collett.

☐ 762. Sometime in New York City • John Lennon & Yoko Ono & Plastic Ono Band (Apple 3392)... 1972 $900

📷 LP. Promotional issue. White labels with black print. Double LP with stock gatefold cover. Near-mint price range: $700 to $900.
Side 1: *Woman Is the Nigger of the World; Sisters O Sisters; Attica State; Born in a Prison; New York City; Sunday, Bloody Sunday; The Luck of the Irish.*
Side 2: *John Sinclair; Angela; We're All Water; Cold Turkey; Don't Worry Kyoko; Well Baby, Please Don't Go; Jamrag; Scum Bag; Au.*

☐ 763. Be-Bop Blues/? • Earl Epps (Minor 103) .... ? $900
45 rpm. Near-mint price range: $700 to $900.

551.

552.

553.

555.

☐ 764. The Glory of Love/Hucklebuck with Jimmy • Five Keys
(Aladdin 3099) 1951 $800
     45 rpm. Near-mint price range: $600 to $800.
     Members: Rudy West; Ripley Ingram; Maryland Pierce; Dickie Smith; Bernie West.

☐ 765. Eternally/It Ain't the Meat, It's the Motion • Swallows (King 4501).... 1951 $800
     45 rpm. Black vinyl. Near-mint price range: $600 to $800.
     Members: Herman "Junior" Denby; Ed Rich; Earl Hurley; Fred Johnson; Norris Mack.
     A variation of this release in the Top 1,000 can be found at Number 111.

☐ 766. You Met a Fool/Goodbye Baby • Four Jacks (Federal 12075) 1952 $800
     45 rpm. Near-mint price range: $600 to $800.

☐ 767. Grandpa Can Boogie Too/Never Again • Four Jacks
(Federal 12093) 1952 $800
     45 rpm. Near-mint price range: $600 to $800.

☐ 768. Sure Cure for the Blues/I Ain't Coming Back Anymore • Shirley Haven &
Four Jacks/Cora Williams & Four Jacks (Federal 12079).................... 1952 $800
     45 rpm. Near-mint price range: $600 to $800.

☐ 769. The Bells of My Heart/Sweet Baby • Fascinators (Your
Copy 1135) 1954 $800
     45 rpm. Black vinyl. Near-mint price range: $600 to $800.
     Members: Jerry Potter; Donald Blackshear; Bob Rivers; Clarence Smith; Earl Richardson.
     A variation of this release in the Top 1,000 can be found at Number 266.

☐ 770. I'm Sorry/Sweet Lulu • Love Notes (With Lucky Warren on Tenor Sax)
(Riviera 970) 1954 $800
     📷 45 rpm. Near-mint price range: $600 to $800.

☐ 771. All Mine/Rose Mary • Five Satins (Standord 100)............................ 1956 $800
     45 rpm. Red label. Any copies on a maroon/brown label are unauthorized reissues. Same
     selection number used for a 1957 Chestnuts issue. Near-mint price range: $600 to $800.
     Members: Fred Parris; Louis Peebles; Stan Dortch; Jim Freeman; Ed Martin.

☐ 772. Gonna Love My Baby/Cause I Love You • Lloyd McCollough
(Republic 7129) 1956 $800
     45 rpm. Near-mint price range: $600 to $800.

☐ 773. Old Shep/Blank • Elvis Presley (RCA Victor CR-15) 1956 $800
     📷 45 rpm single-sided disc. White label, promotional issue only. Near-mint price range:
     $600 to $800.

☐ 774. The Chirping Crickets • Buddy Holly & Crickets (Brunswick 54038). 1957 $800
     📷 LP. Near-mint price range: $600 to $800.
     Side 1: *Oh Boy; Not Fade Away; Maybe Baby; It's Too Late; Tell Me How.*
     Side 2: *That'll Be the Day; I'm Looking for Someone to Love; An Empty Cup (And a Broken Date);*
          Send Me Some Lovin'; Last Night; Rock Me My Baby.

☐ 775. She's the One/Baby • Links (Teenage 1009) 1957 $800
     📷 45 rpm. Near-mint price range: $600 to $800.
     Members: Herb Fisher; James Walton; Wilbert Dobson; Joe Woodley; John Terry.

☐ 776. Their Greatest Jukebox Hits • Hank Ballard & Midnighters
(King 541) 1958 $800
     LP. Repackage of Federal 541. Near-mint price range: $600 to $800.
     Side 1: *Work with Me Annie; Moonrise; Sexy Ways; Get It; Switchie Witchie Titchie; It's Love Baby*
          (24 Hours a Day).
     Side 2: *Annie Had a Baby; She's the One; Annie's Aunt Fannie; Crazy Loving (Stay with Me);*
          Henry's Got Flat Feet; Tore Up over You.

☐ 777. Wedding Bells Gonna Ring/Summer Night Love • Gates featuring Bobby
Ferguson (Peach 716)... 1959 $800
     📷 45 rpm. Near-mint price range: $600 to $800.

SUN

Excellorec BMI

Vocal U-143

Baby Let's Play House
(Gunter)
ELVIS PRESLEY
SCOTTY & BILL
217
MEMPHIS, TENNESSEE

558.

Embassy
RECORD CO.

MANUFACTURED BY EMBASSY RECORD CO · 1607 BROADWAY, NEW YORK

124 B

THE NIGHT IS YOUNG
AND YOU'RE SO BEAUTIFUL
(Rose-Kahal-Suesso)

DEAN MARTIN
with
HAL KANNER ORCHESTRA

LICENSED BY MFGR. FOR NON-COMMERCIAL USE ON PHONOGRAPHS IN HOMES.

566.

Embassy
RECORD CO.

MANUFACTURED BY EMBASSY RECORD CO · 1607 BROADWAY NEW YORK

124 A

ONE FOOT IN HEAVEN
(Roth-Drake-Aycock)

DEAN MARTIN
with
HAL KANNER ORCHESTRA

LICENSED BY MFGR. FOR NON-COMMERCIAL USE ON PHONOGRAPHS IN HOMES.

V *Records*

V-109
Side A

45 RPM

"THE SULTAN"
by "The Squires"
Produced by Bob Bradburn

560.

KEYSTONE
RECORDS

BMI TUNE-SHOP
DEAL ME A HAND
(Artie Clark)
BILL HALEY
and THE SADDLE MEN
with
Billy Williamson
(STEEL GUITAR)
5101-A

568.

147

The Ravens - FOUR GREAT VOICES

For You
Would You Believe Me
Write Me a Letter
Ol' Man River
E.P. 104

on Rendition RECORDS

Sabre RECORDS, INC.
C-5071
Joni Music, B.M.I.
S-103
MY GAL IS GONE
(F. Briscoe)
The Five Blue Notes
580.

577.

KEYSTONE RECORDS
BMI TUNE-SHOP
SUSAN VAN DUSAN
(Irving, Donofrio, Wilson)
BILL HALEY
and THE SADDLE MEN
with
Billy Williamson
(STEEL GUITAR)
5102-A
569.

S-R-C RECORDING
UNBREAKABLE
45 R.P.M.
RECORD NO.
106-A
Time: 2:51
Produced By
State Recording Co.
Ferndale, Mich.
I'LL BEG
(C.C.)
THE FIVE EMERALDS
581.

☐ 778. The Real Elvis • Elvis Presley (RCA Victor EPA-5120) 1959 $800
    EP and cover. Maroon label. Reissue of EPA-940. Disc alone: $625 to $725. Disc and cover: $600 to $800.
    Side 1: *Don't Be Cruel; I Want You, I Need You, I Love You.*
    Side 2: *Hound Dog; My Baby Left Me.*

☐ 779. RCA Victor February Sampler 59-7 • Various Artists (RCA Victor/
    Camden SP-33-59-7) 1959 $800
    📷 Monaural LP. Promotional issue only. Not issued with special cover. Has RCA Victor black label on one side and RCA Victor Camden label on side 2, thus sampling tunes from LPs on both labels. Near-mint price range: $600 to $800.
    Side 1: *Hearts of Paris* (Ray Hartley with Don Walker Orchestra); *The Stranger of Galilee* (Blackwood Brothers); *Countdown* (Buddy Morrow and His Orchestra); *That's All Right* (Elvis Presley).
    Side 2: *Wabash Cannonball* (Eddy Arnold); *The Old Rugged Cross* (Three Suns); *The Sheik of Araby* (Fats Waller); *Colonel Bogey* (Norwegian Military Band).

☐ 780. Lonely Weekends • Charlie Rich (Phillips International 1970).......... 1960 $800
    📷 LP. Near-mint price range: $600 to $800.
    Side 1: *Lonely Weekends; School Days; Whirlwind; Stay; C.C. Rider; Come Back.*
    Side 2: *Gonna Be Waitin'; Apple Blossom Time; Breakup; That's How Much I Love You; Rebound; Juanita.*

☐ 781. Surfer Moon/Humpty Dumpty • Bob & Sheri (Safari 101)................. 1961 $800
    📷 45 rpm. Beach Boy Brian Wilson's first record production. Original commercial copies have a light blue label; promotional copies a white label. Near-perfect counterfeits exist. Near-mint price range: $600 to $800.
    Members: Bob Norberg; Sheri Pomeroy.

☐ 782. Funny/The Stretch • Contours (Motown 1012) 1961 $800
    📷 45 rpm. Near-mint price range: $600 to $800.
    Members: Dennis Edwards; Bill Gordon; Sylvester Potts; Billy Hoggs; Joe Billingslea; Joe Stubbs; Hubert Johnson; Huey Davis.

☐ 783. Surrender/Lonely Man • Elvis Presley (With Jordanaires)
    (RCA Victor 61-7850) 1961 $800
    📷 45 rpm. Living stereo. Near-mint price range: $600 to $800.
    Variations of this release in the Top 1,000 can be found at Numbers 382; 461.

☐ 784. I Love You/Patricia • Supremes 4 (Sara 1032).................................. 1961 $800
    45 rpm. Also released as by the Supremes. Near-mint price range: $600 to $800.
    Members: Lovelace Redmond; Homer Walton; Carl Campbell; Phillips Green.

☐ 785. School Days/Baby Come On • Gliders (Southern Sound 103)......... 1962 $800
    📷 45 rpm. Near-mint price range: $600 to $800.

☐ 786. Where All Lovers Meet/That's All Right • Invictors (TPE 8221) 1962 $800
    45 rpm. Reissued in 1963 with a Victorio label added on top of this one, crediting the Vendors. Near-mint price range: $600 to $800.

☐ 787. Backporch Blues • Smokey Smothers (King 779) 1962 $800
    Monaural LP. Near-mint price range: $600 to $800.
    Side 1: *I Can't Judge Nobody; Come on Rock Little Girl; Honey I Ain't Teasin'; You're Gonna Be Sorry; (What I Done for You) Give It Back; Smokey's Love Sick Blues.*
    Side 2: *I've Been Drinking Muddy Water; Crying Tears; Midnight and Day; Blind and Dumb Man Blues; What Am I Going to Do; I Ain't Gonna Be No Monkey Man No More.*

for TRULY GREAT MUSIC

Fortune
Reg. U.S. Pat. Off.

FORTUNE RECO[RDS]
DETROIT, MICH

UNBREAKABLE
45 RPM
RECORD

RECORD
811

Trianon Publications
(BMI) Time 2:58

Unbreakable Under
Normal Use (F-6)

YOU DON'T MEAN ME RIGHT
(Hartfield-Rawls-Summons-Little)
THE FOUR KINGS
Music by the All Stars

587.

Mercury

70143X45
(YB9648)
Malabar Music Inc.
(BMI) 2:14

Vocal By
The Four
Plaid Throats

MY INSPIRATION
(J. Johnson)
**THE FOUR
PLAID THROATS**

MERCURY RECORD CORPORATION CHICAGO ILLINOIS USA

588.

Chance
RECORDS, INC.
CHICAGO, ILL.

C-5112
1154

Laurel Music
B.M.I.

CROSS OVER THE BRIDGE
(Benjamin - Weiss)
THE FLAMINGOS
with
Red Holloway Orch.

604.

JAX

Record No.
45-314
Blues
Ballad

45 [RPM]
(45-
Andre
B.

"WHY? OH, WHY?"
(Haut - Shad)
The Kings
Featuring
Bobby Hall

589.

Timely

[Division of]
45 RPM

[S]NK Corp. N. Y. C.
45 RPM

5242
Time: 2:08

Simak Music
(BMI)

I WAS WRONG
(Alfred Tadman)
THE CHARMERS
1009-X45

597.

150

☐ 788. The Beatles with Tony Sheridan and Guests • Beatles and Others
(MGM SE-4215) 1964 $800
> Stereo LP. Front cover does *not* have the words "And Others" at the lower left under the
> song title *Why*. Has four tracks by the Beatles with Tony Sheridan, and six tracks by the
> Titans. Near-mint price range: $600 to $800.
>
> Side 1: *My Bonnie; Cry for a Shadow; Johnson Rag; ?*
> Side 2: *The Saints; Rye Beat; You Are My Sunshine; Summertime Beat; Why; Happy New Year
> Beat.*
> Members: Tony Sheridan; John Lennon; Paul McCartney, George Harrison; Pete Best.

☐ 789. Introducing the Beatles • Beatles (Vee-Jay LP-1062) 1964 $800
> Monaural LP. Black label with circular colorband and oval logo. With *Love Me Do* and *P.S. I
> Love You* (on later issues these tracks are replaced by *Ask Me Why* and *Please Please Me*).
> Back cover lists song titles in two large columns. Near-mint price range: $600 to $800.
> Variations of this release in the Top 1,000 can be found at Numbers 7; 27; 65; 93; 169; 202; 218;
> 543; 559; 760.
> Members: John Lennon; Paul McCartney, George Harrison; Ringo Starr.
>
> Side 1: *I Saw Her Standing There; Misery; Anna; Chains; Boys; Love Me Do.*
> Side 2: *P.S. I Love You; Baby It's You; Do You Want to Know a Secret; A Taste of Honey; There's
> a Place; Twist and Shout.*

☐ 790. Hey Joe/51st Anniversary • Jimi Hendrix (Reprise 0572) 1967 $800
> Picture sleeve. Near-mint price range: $400 to $800.

☐ 791. Ballad of John and Yoko/Old Brown Shoe • Beatles (Apple/
Americom 2531/M-382) 1969 $800
> Round 4" flexi-disc. Black vinyl with white print. Available in special vending machines. Near-
> mint price range: $600 to $800.
> Members: John Lennon; Paul McCartney, George Harrison; Ringo Starr.

☐ 792. Give Peace a Chance/Remember Love • John Lennon & Plastic Ono
Band (Americom 435 A/B) 1969 $800
> Flexi-disc. Thin black flexible, "Pocket Disc Series" 4-inch vinyl disc. Has a red cardboard
> cover. Near-mint price range: $600 to $800.

☐ 793. Open Your Box/Greenfield Morning • Yoko Ono (Apple OYB-1) 1970 $800
> 📷 45 rpm. Promotional issue only. White label. Reportedly, Yoko Ono made approximately
> six copies for personal use. Near-mint price range: $600 to $800.

☐ 794. Happy Xmas (War Is Over)/Listen, the Snow Is Falling • John Lennon &
Yoko Ono & Plastic Ono Band (With the Harlem Community Choir) / Yoko
Ono (Apple 47663/4) 1971 $800
> 📷 45 rpm. Promotional issue. White label with large Apple logo. Black vinyl. Known
> counterfeit has photocopy of label on flat paper stock pasted on a black vinyl reissue of the
> single. Print and label quality are noticeably inferior. Originals have semi-gloss label on a
> brittle polystyrene disc. Near-mint price range: $600 to $800.

☐ 795. Principles of the Children • Ya Ho Wa 13 (Higher Key) 1978 $800
> LP. Selection number not known. Near-mint price range: $600 to $800.

☐ 796. You're Wrong/Try Not to Hear • Johnny Garmon (Missile 1) .... ? $800
> 45 rpm. Near-mint price range: $600 to $800.

☐ 797. It's Many a Mile from Me to You/? • Homer Monroe (Silvia 1161) .... ? $800
> 45 rpm. Near-mint price range: $600 to $800.

☐ 798. Campus Boogie/Too Beautiful to Cry • Leonard Sipes & Rhythm Oakies
(Morgan 106) .... ? $800
> 78 rpm. Near-mint price range: $400 to $800.

☐ 799. From the Bottom of My Heart/Melancholy Mood • Frank Sinatra
(Brunswick 8443) 1939 $750
> 78 rpm. Credited to "Harry James & His Orchestra," but is the first recording by Frank
> Sinatra. Near-mint price range: $500 to $750.

KEP-310

THE RAVENS

featuring

Jimmy Ricks

HONEY

BYE BYE BABY BLUES

OUT OF A DREAM

MY SUGAR IS SO REFINED

King 45 EXTENDED PLAY

609.

BATTLE OF THE SAXES

featuring
ILLINOIS JACQUET
and
LESTER YOUNG

long playing 33 1/3 r. p. m.

Aladdin 701

606.

Kicks RECORDS

Colortunes
(BMI)

1-F

A DREAM COME TRUE
(C. Pipkin)
THE SQUIRES
vocal group
with band
Time: 2:39 45 RPM
0

610.

152

☐ 800. Who's Afraid of the Big Bad Wolf • Various Artists (RCA
Victor 224/225/226) 1930s $750
    Soundtrack. Three, six-inch, 78 rpm black and white picture discs. Near-mint price range:
$500 to $750.

☐ 801. Mambo Shevitz/Mambo No. 5 • Crows (With Melino & His Orchestra)
(Tico 1082) 1951 $750
    📷 45 rpm. Red vinyl. Near-mint price range: $500 to $750.
    Members: Daniel "Sonny" Norton; Harold Major; Jerry Hamilton; Mark Jackson; Bill Davis.

☐ 802. Weeping Willow Blues/I Am with You • Dominoes (Federal 12039) . 1951 $750
    45 rpm. Near-mint price range: $500 to $750.
    Members: Billy Ward; Clyde McPhatter; Charlie White; William Lamont; Bill Brown; Dave McNeil; James Van Loan.

☐ 803. Oh Holy Night/The Lord's Prayer • Orioles (Jubilee 5045) 1951 $750
    45 rpm. Near-mint price range: $500 to $750.
    Members: Sonny Til; Alex Sharp; George Nelson; John Reed; Tom Gaither.

☐ 804. Whiffenpoof Song/I Get All My Lovin' on a Saturday Night • Ravens
(Okeh 6825)... 1951 $750
    📷 45 rpm. Near-mint price range: $500 to $750.
    Members: Ollie Jones; Jimmy Ricks; Leonard Puzey; Warren Suttles; Joe Van Loan; Louis Heyward.

☐ 805. Everything But You/That Old Gang of Mine • Ravens (Okeh 6843) . 1951 $750
    📷 45 rpm. Near-mint price range: $500 to $750.
    Members: Ollie Jones; Jimmy Ricks; Leonard Puzey; Warren Suttles; Joe Van Loan; Louis Heyward.

☐ 806. If You Love Me/Dreams of You • Royals (Okeh 6832) 1951 $750
    45 rpm. Near-mint price range: $500 to $750.

☐ 807. That's What You're Doing to Me/When the Swallows Come Back To
Capistrano • Dominoes (Federal 12059).. 1952 $750
    45 rpm. Near-mint price range: $500 to $750.
    Members: Billy Ward; Clyde McPhatter; Charlie White; William Lamont; Bill Brown; Dave McNeil; James Van Loan.

☐ 808. Rock the Joint/Icy Heart • Bill Haley (With Saddlemen)
(Essex 303) 1952 $750
    📷 45 rpm. Colored vinyl. Near-mint price range: $500 to $750.

☐ 809. Lucky/ Don't Trade Your Love for Gold • King Odom Four (With Dick
Jacobs Orchestra) (Abbey 15064)....................................... 1952 $750
    📷 45 rpm. Identification number shown since no selection number is used. Near-mint price
range: $500 to $750.
    Members: Dave Odom; David Bowers; Isaiah Bing; Cleveland Bing.
    Side 1: *For You; Would You Believe Me.*
    Side 2: *Write Me a Letter; Ol' Man River.*

☐ 810. Every Beat of My Heart/All Night Long • Royals (Federal 12064) 1952 $750
    45 rpm. Black vinyl. *All Night Long* features blues star Wynonie Harris. Near-mint price
range: $500 to $750.
    Members: Henry Booth; Hank Ballard; Charles Sutton; Lawson Smith; Alonzo Tucker; Sonny Woods.
    A variation of this release in the Top 1,000 can be found at Number 97.

☐ 811. Don't Be Angry/Blues at Dawn • Sultans (Jubilee 5077) 1952 $750
    45 rpm. Near-mint price range: $500 to $750.

☐ 812. I Was Such a Fool/Midnight • Five Budds (Rama 1)........................... 1953 $750
    45 rpm. Near-mint price range: $500 to $750.

☐ 813. I Want Her Back/I Guess It's All Over Now • Five Budds (Rama 2).. 1953 $750
    45 rpm. Near-mint price range: $500 to $750.

☐ 814. My Saddest Hour/Oh! Babe! • Five Keys (Aladdin 3214) 1953 $750
    📷 45 rpm. Blue label. Near-mint price range: $500 to $750.
    Members: Rudy West; Ripley Ingram; Maryland Pierce; Dickie Smith; Bernie West.

Old Town

Manufactured by Old Town Record Corp., N.Y.C.

Record No.
O.T. 1009-45
(45-OT 813)

45 R.P.M.
BMI

TONIGHT KATHLEEN
(R. Barrett)

THE VALENTINES

611.

CUSTOM-MADE RECORDS
B & S
B-Disc-S

45-R 1570-2

Vocal and Combo

DO YOU LOVE ME
(Lil' Joe Bonner)
LIL' JOE BONNER
and The Idols
Music By
The Fabulous Playboys
B-DISC-S RECORDING CO., DEADWOOD, S. D.

614.

Parrot

P-83231

Vocal

I'M YOURS
(R. Mellin)
THE FLAMINGOS
812
The Bronzeville Record Mfg. Co., Chicago

616.

BEVERLY
KINSTON, NORTH CAROLINA
RECORDS

45 R.P.M.

RECORD NO.
45-702-B
(CP-1536)

Golden State
Songs - BMI

VOCAL

CAUSE I LOVE YOU SO
(Leamon H. Drumgo)
THE KOOL TOPPERS

617.

Good Luck Charm/ Anything That's Part of You, Elvis Presley (1962 compact 33 single and picture sleeve: $24,000)

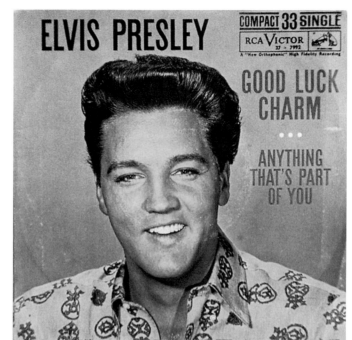

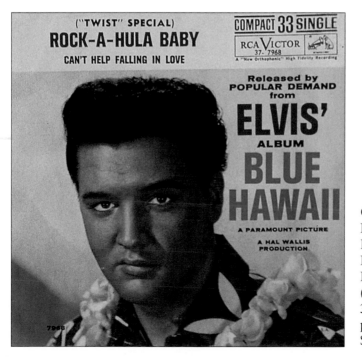

Can't Help Falling in Love/Rock-A-Hula Baby, Elvis Presley (1961 compact 33 single and picture sleeve: $16,000)

Yesterday and Today, Beatles (1966 stereo LP: $25,000)

The Beatles and Frank Ifield on Stage, Beatles and Frank Ifield (1964 stereo LP: $9,000)

Ask Me Why, Beatles (1964 45 rpm EP: $8,500)

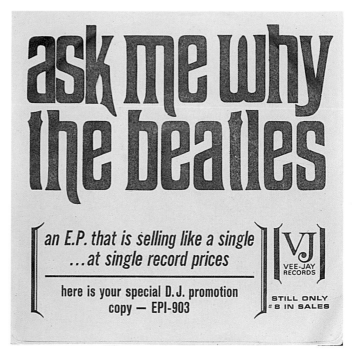

Please Please Me/Ask Me Why, Beattles (1963 45 rpm. Group's name is misspelled: $1,400)

Hopefully Yours/When I Leave
These Prison Walls, Larks (1951
rhythm and blues 45 rpm: $4,000)

Good Luck Darling/You Could
Be My Love, 5 Crowns (1953
rhythm and blues 45 rpm: $4,000)

Doll Face/Ooh, I Feel So Good,
Vibranaires (1954 rhythm and
blues 45 rpm: $5,000)

Billy Ward and His Dominoes, Billy
Ward & Dominoes (1954 10-inch
rhythm and blues LP: $10,000)

We Are the
Chantels,
Chantels
(1958 rhythm
and blues LP:
$2,000)

Axis: Bold As
Love, Jimi
Hendrix
(1968 promo-
tional issue of
popular rock
LP: $1,500)

Jamboree, Various Artists Compilation (1957 film soundtrack LP: $3,000)

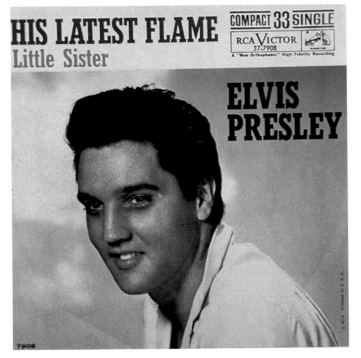

(Marie's the Name) His Latest Flame/Little Sister, Elvis Presley (1962 compact 33 single and picture sleeve: $12,000)

K. C. Douglas:
Dead-Beat
Guitar and the
Mississippi
Blues • Street
Corner Blues
'Bout Women
and Auto-
mobiles, K. C.
Douglas (1956
blues LP:
$1,000)

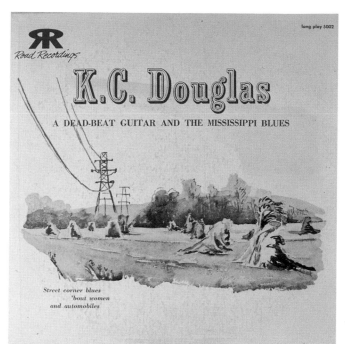

At Home
with
Screamin' Jay
Hawkins,
Screamin' Jay
Hawkins
(1956 blues
LP: $900)

Loving You/G.I. Blues,
Elvis Presley (1960s
picture disc LP: $6,000)

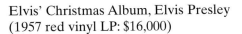

Elvis' Christmas Album, Elvis Presley
(1957 red vinyl LP: $16,000)

☐ 815. If I Can't Have You/Someday, Someway • Flamingos
(Chance 1133)... 1953 $750
    45 rpm. Black vinyl. Near-mint price range: $500 to $750.
    Members: Sollie McElroy; John Carter; Zeke Carey; Jake Carey; Paul Wilson; Nate Nelson; Tommy Hunt; Terry Johnson.
    A variation of this release in the Top 1,000 can be found at Number 249.

☐ 816. Heartbreaker/Call a Doctor • Jewels / Crows (Rama 10)................. 1953 $750
    45 rpm. Black vinyl. May show *Heartbreaker* by the Crows and *Call a Doctor* by the Jewels
    on some labels. Near-mint price range: $500 to $750.
    Variations of this release in the Top 1,000 can be found at Numbers 247; 254.

☐ 817. Foolish One/Gonna Feed My Baby • Rocketeers (Herald 415)........ 1953 $750
    📷 45 rpm. Red vinyl. Near-mint price range: $500 to $750.

☐ 818. Bells Ring Out/House Cleaning • Spaniels (Vee-Jay 103)................ 1953 $750
    📷 45 rpm. Red vinyl. Near-mint price range: $500 to $750.
    Members: James "Pookie" Hudson; Jerry Gregory; Ernest Warren; Willie Jackson; Opal Courtney.

☐ 819. Bells of St. Mary's/Fairest • Lee Andrews & Hearts (Rainbow 259).. 1954 $750
    45 rpm. Yellow label. Near-mint price range: $500 to $750.
    Members: Lee Andrews; Arthur Thompson; Roy Calhoun; Wendell Calhoun; Butch Curry; Ted Weems.

☐ 820. Wedding Bells Are Ringing in My Ears/Times Have Changed • Angels
(Grand 115)... 1954 $750
    45 rpm. Glossy yellow label. No company address shown. Rigid disc. Near-mint price range:
    $500 to $750.

☐ 821. The Beating of My Heart/Why Does It Have to Be Me • Charmers (With
Rhythm Acc.) (Central 1002).. 1954 $750
    📷 45 rpm. Near-mint price range: $500 to $750.
    Member: Vicki Burgess; Alfred Todman; George Daniels; James Cook.

☐ 822. My Heart's Crying for You/Love Me • Chimes (Flair 1051).............. 1954 $750
    📷 45 rpm. Near-mint price range: $500 to $750.
    Members: Cornell Gunter; Young Jessie; Richard Berry; Beverly Thompson; Tom Fox.

☐ 823. One Night with a Fool/Ride Helen Ride • Hollywood Flames (With
Orchestra Acc.) (Lucky 001)... 1954 $750
    45 rpm. Near-mint price range: $500 to $750.
    Members: David Ford; Bobby Byrd; Gaynel Hodge; Clyde Tillis; Earl Nelson; Curtis Williams; Donald Height; Ray Brewster; John Berry; George Home.

☐ 824. Peggy/Oooh-La-La • Hollywood Flames (Lucky 006)....................... 1954 $750
    📷 45 rpm. Near-mint price range: $500 to $750.
    Members: David Ford; Bobby Byrd; Gaynel Hodge; Clyde Tillis; Earl Nelson; Curtis Williams; Donald Height; Ray Brewster; John Berry; George Home.

☐ 825. Goddess of Love/Niki Niki Mambo • Nu-Tones (Hollywood
Star 797)... 1954 $750
    78 rpm. We have yet to learn of any original 45s of this issue. Near-mint price range: $500 to
    $750.

☐ 826. Believe/You're No Barking Dog • Nu-Tones (Hollywood Star 798)... 1954 $750
    78 rpm. Same number used twice. Near-mint price range: $500 to $750.

☐ 827. Can't Get Along/It'll Plumb Get It • Morris Pejoe Orchestra
(Checker 781).. 1954 $750
    45 rpm. Red vinyl. Near-mint price range: $500 to $750.

☐ 828. I'll Be Around/Miss You Tonite • Lynn Roberts & Phantoms
(Oriole 101)... 1954 $750
    45 rpm. Black vinyl. Near-mint price range: $500 to $750.
    A variation of this release in the Top 1,000 can be found at Number 418.

☐ 829. Play It Cool/Let's Make Up • Spaniels (Vee-Jay 116)...................... 1954 $750
    45 rpm. Red vinyl. Near-mint price range: $500 to $750.
    Members: James "Pookie" Hudson; Jerry Gregory; Ernest Warren; Willie Jackson; Opal Courtney.

620.

621.

622.

623.

☐ 830. The Capitol Story • Various Artists (Capitol 197/198) 1954 $750

📷 EP. A Capitol promotional release. Sleeve says "The Capitol Story," but disc reads "The Capitol Record." 100 copies made. Near-mint price range: $500 to $750.
Featured Artists: Frank Sinatra; Dean Martin; Nat King Cole; Peggy Lee; Stan Kenton; Yma Sumac; Jerry Lewis; Johnny Mercer; Jackie Gleason; Billy May; Kay Starr; George Fenneman.

☐ 831. Pleadin' Heart/She Done Me Wrong • Whips (Flair 1025) 1954 $750
45 rpm. Near-mint price range: $500 to $750.

☐ 832. I Cross My Fingers/Wheel Baby Wheel • Bennie Woods & Five Dukes
(Atlas 1040) 1954 $750
45 rpm. Near-mint price range: $500 to $750.

☐ 833. Dearest Darling/A Fool Was I • Chimes (Royal Roost 577) 1955 $750

📷 78 rpm. Near-mint price range: $500 to $750.

☐ 834. Cherie/He Make 'Em Pow Wow • Hide-A-Ways (With Instrumental
Accompaniement) (MGM 55004) 1955 $750

📷 45 rpm. Near-mint price range: $500 to $750.

☐ 835. Floyd's Blues/Any Old Lonesome Day • Floyd Jones
(Vee-Jay 126) 1955 $750
45 rpm. Red vinyl. Near-mint price range: $500 -$750.

☐ 836. Are You Forgetting Me/Drunk • Kidds (Imperial 5335)..................... 1955 $750
45 rpm. Near-mint price range: $500 to $750.

☐ 837. Someday/Bow Wow • Pyramids (With Fletcher Smith's Band)
(C Note 108) 1955 $750
78 rpm. Near-mint price range: $500 to $750.
Members: Sidney Correia; Joe Dandy; Melvin White; Kenneth Perdue; Lionel Cobbs; Tom Williams.
Variations of this release in the Top 1,000 can be found at Numbers 139; 621.

☐ 838. Arline/Sweet Su • Starliters with Jonesy's Combo (Combo 73) 1955 $750

📷 45 rpm. Near-mint price range: $500 to $750.

☐ 839. Are You Sorry/We're Getting Married • Whispers (Gotham 312) 1955 $750

📷 45 rpm. Near-mint price range: $500 to $750.

☐ 840. I Won't Come to Your Wedding/What Makes You Do • Wrens
(Rama 184).. 1955 $750
45 rpm. Near-mint price range: $500 to $750.
Members: Robert Mansfield; Frenchie Concepcion. George Magnezid; Rocky.

☐ 841. Juanita/This Is My Plea • Celebritys (Caroline 2301) 1956 $750

📷 45 rpm. Near-mint price range: $500 to $750.

☐ 842. Gloria/Sugar Lips • Five Chances (States 156) 1956 $750
45 rpm. Black vinyl. Near-mint price range: $500 to $750.
Members: Johnny Jones; John Austell; Darnell Austell; Reggie Smith; Howard Pitman; Harold Jones.
A variation of this release in the Top 1,000 can be found at Number 627.

☐ 843. We Made Romance/Absent Minded • Clay Hammond & Johnnie Young &
Celebritys (Caroline 2302) 1956 $750

📷 45 rpm. Near-mint price range: $500 -$750.

☐ 844. I Love You/Beans • Little Toians (Smalltown).................................... 1956 $750
45 rpm. No selection number used. Near-mint price range: $500 to $750.

☐ 845. I'm Yours/Sweet Lorraine • Mellows (Celeste 3004)....................... 1956 $750
45 rpm. Near-mint price range: $500 to $750.
Members: Lillian Leach; Harry Johnson; John Wilson; Carl Spencer; Arthur Crier.

CLUB RECORDS
Mfg. by Club Records - 1650 Broadway, N.Y.C.
SAMPLE COPY — NOT FOR
UNBREAKABLE
45 R.P.M.
Royal Pub.
Time 2:17 (BMI)
DARLING COME BACK
(Vita Picone)
PAT CORDEL
AND THE CRESCENTS
624.

aBBCo Records
Champ Pub. Co.
BMI
Time: 2:10
Vocal
106
I'M SO IN LOVE TONIGHT
(Smith)
Vocal by
THE HEPTONES
Produced by Paul Skalisky
(Record #401)
630.

GEE
45 RPM   45 RPM
GG-1019
Kahl Music
(BMI)
Jimmy Wright
& his Orch.
MY GIRL
(Phillips-Goldner)
THE DOWNBEATS
(DK-3133)
626.

SONIC RECORDS
ER 104BH
Echo Music
Time: 2:35
Orchestra:
Chico Chism &
His Jettinaires
G8OW-712
ALL I WANT IS LOVE
(Douglas DuBois)
THE MONTCLAIRS
Orchestra Directed by
DOUGLAS DuBois
ECHO PUBLISHING & RECORDING CO. SHREVEPORT, LA.
631.

J & S
1754 ANTHONY AVE., BRONX 57, N. Y.
UNBREAKABLE
45 R.P.M.
RECORD NO.
J 1756
(2:00)
VOCAL
With Orchestra
WHAT MAKES ME LOVE YOU LIKE I DO
(Z. Sanders)
THE PRE-TEENS
WITH
THE SHYTAN FIVE
632.

158

RCA VICTOR

SPD-26
SIDE **6**
599-9141
(H2WH-1996)

45 EP
"NEW Orthophonic"
HIGH FIDELITY

1—BLUE MOON OF KENTUCKY (Bill Monroe)
2—LOVE ME TENDER (from the 20th Century-Fox
CinemaScope production "Love Me Tender")
(Elvis Presley-Vera Matson)

Elvis Presley

634.

SOWDER
RECORDS

OR—248—45
OR-47
Publisher
4 Star Sales—BMI
Time 2.26

Vocal By
Carl Belew

I'M LONG GONE
(C. Belew)
CARL BELEW
& His
Riff Riders

637.

APACHE RECORDS

45 RPM   45 RPM

Thornett
(BMI)

F-1515-A-1
The Concepts

WHISPER
(Johnnie James-S. Browne)
THE CONCEPTS
Music by
AL BROWNE ORCH.

638.

L & M

2819 EIGHTH AVENUE
LOS ANGELES 18, CALIF.

45-1002

Vocal
Naco Pub. Co.
B M I

BOUQUET OF ROSES
(James Moore)
NUNNIE MOORE
and The Peacocks
LM-1006

640.

159

□ 846. Jump Man, Jump • Piano Red [Willie Perryman] (Groove 1001)...... 1956   **$750**
     LP. Near-mint price range: $500 to $750.
       Side 1: *Wrong Yo-Yo; Don't Get Around Much Anymore; Umph-Umph-Umph; Got You on My Mind;*
         Fattenin; Frogs for Snakes; Rockin' with Red.
       Side 2: *Jump Man Jump; Do She Love Me; Real Good Thing; Pay It No Mind; Six O'Clock; Please*
         Tell Me Baby; Jumpin' with Daddy; Goodbye, Goodbye, Goodbye.

□ 847. Elvis • Elvis Presley (RCA Victor LPM-1382)................................... 1956   **$750**
     Monaural LP. Black label, "Long Play" at bottom. Mistakenly pressed with an alternative take
     of *Old Shep*, not available on any other authorized U.S. vinyl release. Any copy with a "15S"
     or "17S" matrix on side 2 (matrix on side 1 is irrelevant) is likely to have the alternative;
     however, playing the track is the way to be certain. May also appear on some "19S"
     pressings; however, price applies to any pressing with the alternative take, regardless of
     identification number. Alternative is different throughout, instrumentally and vocally –
     especially Elvis' phrasing – but here are two lyric variations. Words in all upper case are
     exclusive to the alternative take (which can now be heard on the 1992 CD boxed set *Elvis -*
     The King of Rock 'N' Roll, the Complete '50s Masters): 1) "As the years fast did roll, Old
     Shep he grew old AND his eyes were fast growing dim." 2) "He came to my side and he
     looked up at me, and HE laid his old head on my knee." Price would apply to any other
     pressing with the alternative take, regardless of identification number. LP alone: $500 to
     $600. LP and cover: $500 to $750.
       Side 1: *Rip It Up; Love Me; When My Blue Moon Turns to Gold Again; Long Tall Sally; First in*
         Line; Paralyzed.
       Side 2: *So Glad You're Mine; Old Shep; Reddy Teddy; Anyplace Is Paradise; How's the World*
         Treating You; How Do You Think I Feel.

□ 848. Bop Crazy Baby/It's My Life • Vern Pullens (Spade 1927) 1956   **$750**
     45 rpm. Near-mint price range: $500 to $750.

□ 849. Rock'n Roll'n Robbins • Marty Robbins (Columbia 2601)................. 1956   **$750**
     10-inch LP. Near-mint price range: $500 to $750.
       Side 1: *Long Tall Sally; Tennessee Toddy; Maybelline.*
       Side 2: *Respectfully Miss Brooks; Mean Mama Blues; Long Gone Lonesome Blues.*

□ 850. My Secret Love/Ding Dong Daddy • Carter Rays (Lyric 2001) 1957   **$750**
     45 rpm. Near-mint price range: $500 to $750.

□ 851. Come Go with the Del-Vikings • Del-Vikings (Luniverse 1000) 1957   **$750**
     LP. Near-mint price range: $500 to $750.
       Members: Kripp Johnson; Norman Wright; Clarence Quick; Don Jackson; Gus Backus; Joey Briscoe; David Lerchey;
       Bill Blakely; Ritzi Lee; Billy Woodruff.

□ 852. On the Town • Five Keys (Score 4003) 1957   **$750**
     LP. Repackage of *Best of the 5 Keys,* Aladdin 806. See that listing for bootleg information.
     Near-mint price range: $500 to $750.
       Members: Rudy West; Ripley Ingram; Maryland Pierce; Dickie Smith; Bernie West.
       Side 1: *Glory of Love; Oh Baby; My Saddest Hour; Hucklebuck with Jimmy; These Foolish Things;*
         Christmas Time.
       Side 2: *Red Sails in the Sunset; Too Late, Baby; Teardrops; Be Mine; Love My Loving; Serve*
         Another Round.

□ 853. There's No Return from Love/I Knew It Was You All the Time • Teddy
     Lawson & Lawson Boys (Mansfield 611).. 1957   **$750**
     45 rpm. Near-mint price range: $500 to $750.

□ 854. On the Road with Rock and Roll • Mando & Chili Peppers (Golden
     Crest 3023)... 1957   **$750**
     LP. Near-mint price range: $500 to $750.
       Members: Armando Mandarez; Jesse Perales; Rudy Martinez; Joe Elizando; Jesse Garcia.

641.

642.

644.

645.

☐ 855. Rock 'N Roll Hit Parade, Volume One • Johnny Otis (Dig 104) 1957   **$750**

📷 LP. Mustard color cover, black and white print. Counterfeits exist, some of which have a yellow cover, others have a gold cover. Back photo on originals is clear. Regardless, the discs of originals are rigid – noticeably thicker than the more flexible ones found on fakes. Credits the Jayos, Johnny's group who's other lead vocalists are Mel Williams and Arthur Lee Maye. Session players are: Jackie Kelso (alto sax); Freddie Harmon (tenor and baritone sax); George Washington (trombone); Jimmy Nolan (guitar); Johnny Parker (bass); Don Johnson (trumpet); "Lady Dee" Williams (piano); "Kansas City" Bell (drums). Near-mint price range: $500 to $750.

Side I: *Honey Love; Sh-Boom; Earth Angel; Gee; Sincerely; The Midnight Creeper.*

Side II: *At My Front Door; Long Tall Sally; Only You; One Mint Julep; Hey! Hey! Hey! Hey!; Please Don't Leave Me.*

☐ 856. Would You/Tutti Frutti Man • Jules Savoy (Singing Discovery of Hesperia Inn, Hesperia, Calif.) & Chromatics (Real 1320) 1957   **$750**

📷 45 rpm. Near-mint price range: $500 to $750.

☐ 857. Those Love me Blues/Pretty Pretty Baby • Ruben Siggers & His Fabulous Kool Kats (Vocal by Ephraim Siggers) (Spinks 600) 1957   **$750**

📷 45 rpm. Near-mint price range: $500 to $750.
Members: Ruben Siggers; Ephraim Siggers.

☐ 858. Try the Impossible/Nobody's Home • Lee Andrews & Hearts (Casino 452) 1958   **$750**

📷 45 rpm. Red and white label, with playing cards at top. Near-mint price range: $500 to $750.
Members: Lee Andrews; Arthur Thompson; Roy Calhoun; Wendell Calhoun; Butch Curry; Ted Weems.

☐ 859. Mother Dear/Darling If I Had You • Caliphs (Scatt 111) 1958   **$750**

📷 45 rpm. Near-mint price range: $500 to $750.

☐ 860. Please Don't Crush My Dreams/Soda Pop • Emerals (Triple X 100) 1958   **$750**

📷 45 rpm. Near-mint price range: $500 to $750.
Member: Tony Pabon.

☐ 861. Wish I Was Back in School/Color Cartoon • Goldenrods (Vee-Jay 307) 1958   **$750**

📷 45 rpm. Near-mint price range: $500 to $750.

☐ 862. That'll Be the Day • Buddy Holly (Decca 2575) 1958   **$750**

📷 EP. With liner notes on the back cover. Near-mint price range: $500 to $750.
Side 1: *That'll Be the Day; You Are My One Desire.*
Side 2: *Blue Days, Black Nights; Ting-a-Ling.*

☐ 863. So Long/Baby Don't Go • Pipes (Jacy 001) 1958   **$750**

📷 45 rpm. Near-mint price range: $500 to $750.

☐ 864. Don't Ever Leave Me/How It Feels • Pyramiders (Scott 1205) 1958   **$750**

📷 45 rpm. Near-mint price range: $500 to $750.

☐ 865. Rock 'N' Roll with the Robins • Robins (Whippet 703) 1958   **$750**

LP. Near-mint price range: $500 to $750.
Members: Ty Terrell; Bobby Nunn; Carl Gardner; Bill Richards; Grady Chapman; H.B. Barnum; Roy Richards; Richard Berry.
Side 1: *Cherry Lips; A Fool in Love; Merry-Go-Rock; Since I First Met You; Where's the Fire.*
Side 2: *Out of the Picture; Hurt Me; Every Night; How Long; All of a Sudden My Heart Sings.*

☐ 866. Summer Sunrise/Nature's Beauty • Seaphus Scott & Five Masqueraders (With Billy Gale Orchestra) (Joyce 303) 1958   **$750**

📷 45 rpm. Near-mint price range: $500 to $750.

ONYX

45 RPM   45 R

Disk Jockey Record   NOT FOR
Malone Music   Group V
(BMI)   508

ROMEO
(Cheetdam-Haywoods)
THE VELOURS
Sammy Lowe Orch.
10-5005 A1

646.

MEAN WHEN I'M MAD
. . .
ONE KISS

LIBERTY
5 55070

Eddie Cochran

647.

ESTA
P.O. BOX 233 HAMILTON, OHIO

45—785
2:20
Dodds Music (BMI)
45—290

Vo
o

GIVE ME YOUR LOVE
(The Columbus Pharoahs)
THE COLUMBUS PHARAOHS
with TOMMY WILLS
Orch.

648.

VESTA

45 RPM   45 RPM

EL 102
San-Lyn Music
(BMI) 2:25

Vocal
(RN-14-2)

PLEASE SURRENDER
(R. Green)
THE ELDAROS
Ray Parratoro & the
Rhythm Rockaways

649.

163

☐ 867. Marvella/My Love and Your Love • Spinners (Rhythm 125) 1958 $750
45 rpm. Near-mint price range: $500 to $750.

☐ 868. Rock, Rock, Rock • Various Artists (Roost) 1958 $750

📷 Soundtrack. Monaural LP. No selection number used. 20 tracks credited to seven different lables: Atlantic, Chess, Coral, Gee, MGM, Roost and Vik. Promotional issue only. Near-mint price range: $500 to $750.

Side 1: *Tra L La* (LaVern Baker); *Ever Since I Can Remember* (Bowties); *The Big Beat* (Jimmy Cavallo); *Over and Over Again* (Moonglows); *Right Now, Right Now* (Alan Freed Orch.) *Thanks to You* (3 Chuckles); *Baby Baby* (Frankie Lymon and the Teenagers); *Lonesome Train* (Johnny Burnette) *We're Gonna Rock Tonight* (3 Chuckles); *I Never Had a Sweetheart* (Connie Francis).

Side 2: *You Can't Catch Me* (Chuck Berry); *Little Blue Wren* (Connie Francis); *Rock, Rock, Rock* (Jimmy Cavallo); *The Things Your Heart Needs* (3 Chuckles); *Rock Pretty Baby* (6-Year-Old Ivy Schulman & Bowties); *Would I Be Crying* (Flamingos); *Rock n' Roll Boogie* (Alan Freed Orch.); *Won't You Give Me a Chance* (3 Chuckles); *I Knew from the Start* (Moonglows); *I'm Not a Juvenile Delinquent* (Frankie Lymon & Teenagers).

☐ 869. Be-Boppin' Daddy/? • Mack Banks (Fame 580) 1959 $750
45 rpm. 500 made. Near-mint price range: $500 to $750.

☐ 870. I'm Going to Cry/You're Blue • Corvetts (Moon 100) 1959 $750

📷 45 rpm. Near-mint price range: $500 to $750.
Member: Arthur Conley.

☐ 871. Martini Set • Graham Forbes and Trio (Phillips International 1955) . 1959 $750
LP. Near-mint price range: $500 to $750.

☐ 872. They Laughed at Me/You Put One Over on Me • Jackie & Starlites
(Fire & Fury 1000) 1959 $750
78 rpm. Near-mint price range: $500 to $750.
Member: Jackie Rue; Alton Jones; George Lassu; John Felix; Billy Montgomery; Charles Hudson.
A variation of this release in the Top 1,000 can be found at Number 324.

☐ 873. Blue and Moody • Lula Reed (King 604) 1959 $750
LP. Credits "Lula" Reed; however, some other releases show her as "Lulu" Reed. Near-mint price range: $500 to $750.
Session: Sonny Thompson; Isaac Cole; Bill Johnson.
Side 1: *Watch Dog; I'll Drown in My Tears; Going Back to Mexico; Three Men; Sample Man; Last Night.*
Side 2: *Rock Love; Let's Call It A Day; Bump on a Log; My Poor Heart; Every Second; Jealous Love.*

☐ 874. Hasten Jason/Wouldn't Be Going Steady • The "Singing" Roulettes
(Scepter 1204) 1959 $750

📷 45 rpm. Near-mint price range: $500 to $750.

☐ 875. Lucille/To Be in Love with You • Shantons (With Billy Mure & Orchestra)
(Jay-Mar 241) 1959 $750
45 rpm. Identification number shown since no selection number is used. Near-mint price range: $500 to $750.

☐ 876. My Dear/Falling Star • Valquins (Gaity 161/162) 1959 $750
45 rpm. Black vinyl. Near-mint price range: $500 to $750.
Members: John Stafford; Ed Ballard.
A variation of this release in the Top 1,000 can be found at Number 199.

651.

654.

653.

655.

165

☐ 877. RCA Victor October Christmas Sampler 59-40-41 • Various Artists (RCA
Victor SPS-33-54).. 1959 $750

> 📷 LP. Promotional issue only. Not issued with special cover. All songs except Elvis' *Blue
> Christmas* and *Have Yourself a Merry Little Christmas* (Gisele MacKenzie) are true stereo.
> Near-mint price range: $500 to $750.
>
> Side 1: *Blue Christmas* (Elvis Presley); *Have Yourself a Merry Little Christmas* (Gisele
> MacKenzie); *White Christmas* (John Klein); *Blue Christmas* (Esquivel); *Winter
> Wonderland* (Melachrino Strings); *Santa Claus Is Comin' to Town* (Ralph Hunter).
>
> Side 2 : *O Little Town of Bethlehem* (George Beverly Shea); *Home for the Holidays* (Perry Como);
> *What a Friend We Have in Jesus* (Johnson Family); *A Christmas Festival* (Boston Pops);
> *O Christmas Tree* (Mario Lanza); *Silent Night* (Giorgio Tozzi & Rosalind Elias).

☐ 878. RCA Victor November / December Sampler 59-44 Thru 59-47 • Various
Artists (RCA Victor SPS-33-57) 1959 $750

> 📷 LP. Promotional issue only. Not issued with special cover. Near-mint price range: $500
> to $750.
>
> Side 1: *My Tane* (Jerry Byrd); *It Could Happen to You* (Lena Horne); *Kalamazoo* (New Glenn Miller
> Orchestra); *"Oklahoma" Medley* (Frankie Carle); *San Antonio Rose* (Ames Brothers); *I
> Shall Not Be Moved* (Kay Starr); *Comes Love* (Marty Gold's Orchestra).
>
> Side 2: *I Beg of You* (Elvis Presley); *I'm Sitting on Top of the World* (Dave Gardner); *Camp Meetin'
> Time* (Del Wood); *At the Jazz Band Ball* (Dukes of Dixieland); *I Know That You Know*
> (Chet Atkins); *Cha-Con-Cha* (Tito Puente's Orchestra); *Riff Blues* (Ray Martin and His
> Orchestra).

☐ 879. Bunch of Goodies • Various Artists (Chess 1441) 1959 $750

> 📷 LP. Multi-color vinyl – promotional issue only. Near-mint price range: $500 to $750.
>
> Side 1: *Please Send Me Someone to Love* (Moonglows); *When I'm with You* (Moonglows); *Nadine*
> (Coronets); *Ten Commandments of Love* (Harvey & Moonglows); *Long Lonely Nights*
> (Lee Andrews & Hearts); *You're Everything to Me* (Orchids).
>
> Side 2: *Bad Girl* (Miracles); *In My Diary* (Moonglows); *Teardrops* (Lee Andrews & Hearts);
> *Sincerely* (Moonglows); *Most of All* (Moonglows); *We Go Together* (Moonglows).

☐ 880. Go, Johnny, Go! • Various Artists 1959 $750

> 📷 Soundtrack. Monaural LP. Neither label name nor selection number shown. Promotional
> issue only. Near-mint price range: $500 -$750.
>
> Side 1: *My Love Is Strong* (Jimmy Clanton); *Once Again* (Jimmy Clanton & Sandy Stewart); *Angel
> Face* (Jimmy Clanton); *You'd Better Know It* (Jackie Wilson); *Go, Johnny, Go!* (Chuck
> Berry); *Jay Walker* (Cadillacs); *Jump Children* (Flamingos); *Heavenly Father* (Sandy
> Stewart); *Memphis Tennessee* (Chuck Berry).
>
> Side 2: *Ship on a Stormy Sea* (Jimmy Clanton); *Teenage Heaven* (Eddie Cochran); *Playmates*
> (Sandy Stewart); *Oh! My Head* (Ritchie Valens); *Don't Be Afraid to Love* (Harvey); *Little
> Queenie* (Chuck Berry); *Please Mr. Johnson* (Cadillacs); *Mama, Can I Go Out* (Jo Ann
> Campbell); *It Takes a Long, Long Time* (Jimmy Clanton); *Now the Day Is Over* (Jimmy
> Clanton).

☐ 881. Love Those Goodies • Various Artists (Checker 2973) 1959 $750

> 📷 Monaural LP. Multi-color vinyl – promotional issue only. Cover photo pictures same two
> models as also seen on *Oldies in Hi-Fi*. Near-mint price range: $500 to $750.
>
> Side 1: *Bo Diddley* (Bo Diddley); *I Don't Know What I'll Do* (Sugar Boy [Crawford]); *Country* (Gene
> Barge); *It Ain't No Secret* (Jimmy Witherspoon); *You Better Watch Yourself* (Little Walter);
> *Lima Beans* (Eddie Chamblee).
>
> Side 2: *Reconsider Baby* (Lowell Fulson); *Juke* (Little Walter); *When the Lights Go Out* (Jimmy
> Witherspoon); *That's Why I Love You So* (Al Kent); *Sad Hours* (Little Walter); *Walking the
> Blues* (Willie Dixon).

MUSIC CITY

Gation Pub. Co.
BMI

"ELAINE"
(Bridges)

THE KLIXS

656.

STOMPER TIME
RECORDS
MEMPHIS, TENN.

Jec Pub.
BMI
Time: 2:15

S-102
Vocal
D. Bryant

WALKING AT YOUR WILL
(Donald Bryant)
WILLIE MITCHELL
With The
Four Kings
S-1160

657.

Chatam

45 RPM

CH-350R-45

TEENAGE SWEETHEART
(J. Morris)

THE MYSTICS

CHATAM RECORDS, 164 E. 56th ST., N.Y.C.

658.

X-TRA
RECORDS

ABLE

.M.

RECORD NO.
107-A

(BMI)
2:30

ONCE IN A LIFETIME
(Smith-Gallon)
THE SONICS

660.

167

663.

665.

666.

667.

CHRISTY RECORDS

The Rambolt Music Co.
BMI - 2:01

VOCAL
C-45-114-B

BLUE MEMORIES
(Jaros - McArthur)
THE JADES
with
THE ROCKET FLAMES BAND
Mfg. by CHRISTY RECORDS
Los Gatos. Calif. — U.S.A.

668.

MOTOWN

G 1

Jobete Music
BMI

BAD GIRL
B. Gordy Jr. W. Robinson
THE MIRACLES
Featuring
BILL SMOKEY ROBINSON

669.

J & S
RECORDS
BRONX, N.Y.

45 R.P.M.
Zell's Music
BMI - 2:20

RECORD NO.
248

I Searched The Seven Seas
(THE PLANTS)
THE PLANTS

673.

KINGS-X

Merritt Pub.
Time 2:49

45 RPM
3362-2

IN MY HEART
(Merritt-Sturgell)
THE REBELS

674.

☐ 882. Oldies in Hi Fi • Various Artists (Chess 1439) 1959   **$750**

📷 Monaural LP. Multi-color vinyl – promotional issue only. Cover photo pictures same two models as also seen on *Love Those Goodies*. Near-mint price range: $500 to $750.
Side 1: *I Want to Hug You, Kiss You, Squeeze You* (Buddy & Claudia); *I Don't Know* (Willie Mabon); *Susie-Q* (Dale Hawkins); *Hi Ho Baby* (Jackie Brenston); *Hey Little Girl* (John Godfrey Trio)
Side 2: *Rocket 88* (Jackie Brenston); *Sugaree* (Rusty York); *See You Later, Alligator* (Bobby Charles); *I'm Mad* (Willie Mabon); *Over the Mountain, Across the Sea* (Johnnie & Joe); *All of My Life* (Calvin Bostic).

☐ 883. Down in Mexicali/? • Kappaliers (Shadow 1229) 1950s   **$750**

📷 45 rpm. Near-mint price range: $500 to $750.

☐ 884. Don't Want Your Picture/ ? • Karriann's (Don & Neil with Playboys)
(Pelpal 118) 1950s   **$750**

📷 45 rpm. Near-mint price range: $500 to $750.

☐ 885. The Crests Sing All Biggies • Crests (Coed 901) 1960   **$750**

📷 LP. "Advance Pressing." Promotional issue only. Near-mint price range: $500 to $750
Members: Johnny Maestro; Tom Gough; Harold Torres; Jay Carter; James Ancrum
Side 1: *Earth Angel; Good Golly Miss Molly; My Special Angel; Six Nights a Week; Butterfly; 16 Candles.*
Side 2: *The Angels Listened In; A Rose and a Baby Ruth; I Remember (In the Still of the Night); Party Doll; Silhouettes; Tweedlee Dee.*

☐ 886. Most of All/Come on Baby • Danes (With Marvino Four)
(Le Cam 718) 1960   **$750**

📷 45 rpm. Reissued as by the Team Mates. Near-mint price range: $500 to $750.

☐ 887. It's Now Or Never/A Mess of Blues • Elvis Presley (With Jordanaires)
(RCA Victor 47-7777) 1960   **$750**
45 rpm. Made, mistakenly, with the piano track on *It's Now Or Never* missing. Near-mint price range: $500 to $750.

☐ 888. Look at Me (Vocal)/Look at Me (Instrumental) • Uneeks (Featuring Tiny
Valentine) (Toledo 1501) 1960   **$750**

📷 45 rpm. Group is actually the Uniques (on Gone). Near-mint price range: $500 to $750.

☐ 889. Servant of Love/Sweet Marie • Van Brothers (Poor Boy 111) 1960   **$750**

📷 45 rpm. Near-mint price range: $500 to $750.
Members: Arnold Van Winkel; Lee Van Winkle; Norman Walton.

☐ 890. RCA Victor October 1960 Popular Stereo Sampler • Various Artists (RCA
Victor SPS-33-96) 1960   **$750**

📷 Stereo LP. Promotional issue only. Not issued with special cover. Near-mint price range: $500 to $750.
Side 1: *Flowers for the Cats* (Shorty Rogers); *Am I That Easy to Forget* (Skeeter Davis); *The Battle of San Juan Hill* (Jimmy Driftwood); *Theme: Sunrise Serenade* (No artist credited); *Beg Your Pardon* (Frankie Carle); *Little Drummer Boy* (Hugo & Luigi); *Tonight Is So Right for Love* (Elvis Presley).
Side 2: *One More Dance* (Mariam Makeba); *And the Angels Sing* (Ames Brothers); *Lullaby of Broadway* (Dick Schory's Ensemble); *Zion Stands* (George Beverly Shea); *On That Happy Golden Shore* (Blackwood Brothers); *There's a Promise* (Lyman); *I Need Thee Every Hour* (Laymen Singers); *Wonderful* (Nashville All-Stars).

☐ 891. Walk Don't Run/Home • Ventures (Blue Horizon 101) 1960   **$750**

📷 45 rpm. Reportedly 300 made. Near-mint price range: $500 to $750.

☐ 892. Wonderful Years/? • Barry & Highlights (Planet 1048) 1961   **$750**

📷 45 rpm. Near-mint price range: $500 to $750.

☐ 893. Darling Arlene/? • Frankie Dee (Tee Jay 333) 1961   **$750**

📷 45 rpm. Near-mint price range: $500 to $750.

WILLETT

Vogue Terrace
McKeesport, Pa.

Bourne, Inc.
ASCAP
Time 2:23

Arranged And
Conducted By
TOM EVERETT

114 A

LAUNIE MY LOVE
(Everett-Willett)

THE VALAIRES

675.

RCA Victor

AUGUST 1959 SAMPLER

SPS
33-27
K2NY-4462

SIDE 2

NOT FOR
SALE

1—SOMEDAY (LSP-2001)
2—BLUE MOON OF KENTUCKY (LPM-2011)
3—THE 3RD MAN THEME (LSP-2018)
4—YOU'RE DRIVING ME CRAZY! (LSP-2028)
5—THE SONG IS YOU (LSP-2030)
6—INTRO.; DARLIN' CORA (LSO-6006)
1. Jim Reeves 2. Elvis Presley
3. Buddy Morrow's "Night Train" Orch.
4. Perez Prado's Orch.
5. Pat Suzuki
6. Harry Belafonte

LIVING STEREO

676.

Gaity

RECORDED IN HIGH FIDELITY

Pub:
Glen Ray-BMI
Time: 2:30

GA 169

Two Hearts Make One Love
by
The Wisdoms

MINNEAPOLIS, MINNESOTA

677.

MAC

MACK RECORDS, Norton Bldg., Louisville, Ky.

UNBREAKABLE

45 R.P.M.

RECORD NO.

MR 468

LET'S ROCK TO-NIGHT
(Jimmy Grubbs)

JIMMY GRUBBS
& HIS MUSIC MAKERS

678.

HULL RECORDS Cordially invite you to meet The AVONS

679.

171

☐ 894. This Love of Ours/Over the Rainbow • Delrons (Forum 700) 1961 $750

  📷 45 rpm. Near-mint price range: $500 to $750.

☐ 895. Great Gospel Stars • Gospel Stars (Tamla 222) 1961 $750

  📷 LP. Near-mint price range: $500 to $750.

☐ 896. I'm So in Love/One Chance • Infascinations (Clauwell 004/003)...... 1961 $750

  📷 45 rpm. Polystyrene pressing. Near-mint price range: $500 to $750.

☐ 897. My Lover/Tucson • Neons (Waldon 1001).. 1961 $750

  📷 45 rpm. Near-mint price range: $500 to $750.

☐ 898. Don't Let Love Break Your Heart/Our Love Won't Die • Eldon Rice
    (El Rio 413).. 1961 $750
  45 rpm. Near-mint price range: $500 to $750.

☐ 899. Trembling Hand/Kiss Kiss • Royal Demons (Pek 8101) 1961 $750

  📷 45 rpm. Near-mint price range: $500 to $750.

☐ 900. Long Time Alone/I'm Just a Fool • Danny (Sly) Stewart
    (Luke 1008) 1961 $750

  📷 45 rpm. Reissued on G&S as by Sylvester Stewart. Near-mint price range: $500 to $750.

☐ 901. RCA Victor October '61 Pop Sampler • Various Artists (RCA
    Victor SPS-33-141)... 1961 $750

  📷 Stereo LP. Promotional issue only. Not issued with special cover. Near-mint price range:
  $500 to $750.
  Side 1: *My Blue Heaven* (Henri Rene's Orchestra); *Jerico* (Ray Martin's Orchestra); *I'm Waiting for
     Ships That Never Come In* (Jim Reeves); *Don't Get Around Much Anymore* (Sam Cooke);
     Jingle Bells (Chet Atkins).
  Side 2 : *Blue Hawaii* (Elvis Presley); *You Go to My Head* (New Glenn Miller Orchestra); *Unchained
     Melody* (Floyd Cramer); *Say a Prayer* (Don McNeill); *Rock of Ages* (George Beverly
     Shea); *The Way of the Cross* (Blackwood Brothers).

☐ 902. Some Kinda Wonderful/Is She the One • Cor-Don's [Cor-Dons]
    (Rowe 100) 1962 $750

  📷 45 rpm. Near-mint price range: $500 to $750.

☐ 903. The Crystals Twist Uptown • Crystals (Philles 4000)....................... 1962 $750

  📷 Monaural LP. White label. Promotional issue only. Near-mint price range: $500 to $750.
  Members: Barbara Alston; Lala Brooks; Dee Dee Kennibrew; Patricia Wright; Mary Thomas.
  Side 1: *Uptown; Another Country – Another World; Frankenstein Twist; Oh Yeah, Maybe Baby;
     Please Hurt Me.*
  Side 2: *There's No Other (Like My Baby); On Broadway; What a Nice Way to Turn Seventeen; No
     One Ever Tells You; Gee Whiz, Look at His Eyes (Twist); I Love You Eddie.*
  A variation of this release in the Top 1,000 can be found at Number 702.

☐ 904. Once Upon a Time/The Huddle • Elgins (Joed 716)........................ 1962 $750

  📷 45 rpm. Near-mint price range: $500 to $750.

☐ 905. Aphrodite/I've Gotta Know • Passions (Octavia 8005)..................... 1962 $750

  📷 45 rpm. Near-mint price range: $500 to $750.
  Members: Jim Gallagher; Tony Armato; Al Galione; Vince Acerno; Louis Rotondo.

☐ 906. You've Forgotten Me/Maybe I'm Wrong • Bobby Sanders
    (Kent 382)... 1962 $750
  45 rpm. Near-mint price range: $500 to $750.

☐ 907. Echo in My Heart/Tick Tack Toe • Stereos (Columbia 42626) 1962 $750

  📷 45 rpm. Near-mint price range: $500 to $750.

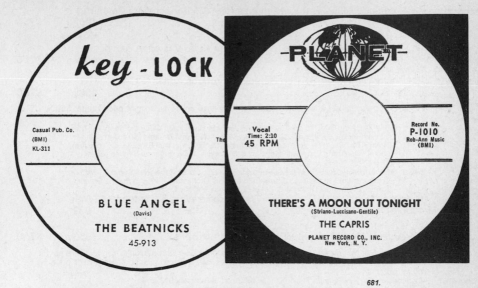

key-LOCK

Casual Pub. Co.
(BMI)
KL-311

The

BLUE ANGEL
(Davis)

THE BEATNICKS
45-913

680.

PLANET

Vocal
Time: 2:10
45 RPM

Record No.
P-1010
Rob-Ann Music
(BMI)

THERE'S A MOON OUT TONIGHT
(Striano-Luccisano-Gentile)

THE CAPRIS

PLANET RECORD CO., INC.
New York, N. Y.

681.

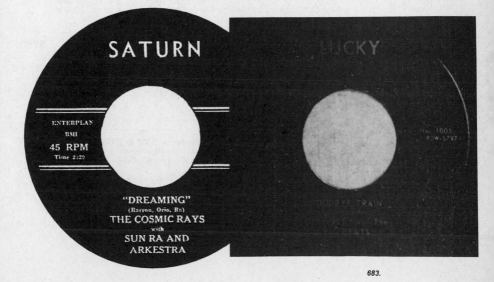

SATURN

ENTERPLAN
BMI
45 RPM
Time 2:29

"DREAMING"
(Barron, Orio, Ra)
THE COSMIC RAYS
with
SUN RA AND
ARKESTRA

682.

LUCKY

No. 1001
ROW-5797

683.

173

☐ 908. The Wedding/Flying Twist • Stick Leg's (sic) (With Butchering Persian's) (Hard-Times 3002) 1962   **$750**

📷 45 rpm. Near-mint price range: $500 to $750.

☐ 909. Baby Doll/Please Don't Leave Me This Way • Leo Valentine & Lyrics (Skylight 201)... 1962   **$750**

45 rpm. Near-mint price range: $500 to $750.

☐ 910. RCA Victor December '62 Pop Sampler • Various Artists (RCA Victor SPS-33-191)... 1962   **$750**

📷 LP. Promotional issue only. Not issued with special cover. Near-mint price range: $500 to $750.

Side 1: *Diane* (Gaylord Carter); *Ivory Tower* (Hank Jones & Dean Kay); *Along the Santa Fe Trail* (Jimmie Haskell Orchestra & Chorus); *Boulevard of Broken Dreams* (Sir Julian at the Organ); *This Could Be the Start of Something* (Sacha Distel with Ray Ellis & Orchestra); *Do It Again* (Sacha Distel with Ray Ellis & Orchestra); *I Don't Wanna Be Tied* (Elvis Presley).

Side 2: *Where Do You Come From* (Elvis Presley); *Next Door to an Angel* (Neil Sedaka); *Joshua* (Tokens); *March of the Toys* (Marty Gold and His Orchestra); *A Kiss to Build a Dream On* (Marty Gold and His Orchestra); *Lover* (Zaccarias and His Orchestra).

☐ 911. Whenever I Get Lonely/That's the Way • Rollie Willis & Contenders (With Matadors) (Saxony 1001) 1962   **$750**

📷 45 rpm. Near-mint price range: $500 to $750.

☐ 912. She Loves You/I'll Get You • Beatles (Swan 4152) 1963   **$750**

📷 45 rpm. Flat (not glossy) white label with red or print. The words "Don't Drop Out" are not on the label. Uses boldface type style. Song titles have quotation marks. Near-mint price range: $650 to $750.
Variations of this release in the Top 1,000 can be found at Numbers 913; 914.
Members: John Lennon; Paul McCartney, George Harrison; Ringo Starr.

☐ 913. She Loves You/I'll Get You • Beatles (Swan 4152) 1963   **$750**

📷 45 rpm. Glossy white label with red print. The words "Don't Drop Out" are on the label. Can be found with or without "Produced by George Martin." Near-mint price range: $500 to $750.
Variations of this release in the Top 1,000 can be found at Numbers 912; 914.
Members: John Lennon; Paul McCartney, George Harrison; Ringo Starr.

☐ 914. She Loves You/I'll Get You • Beatles (Swan 4152) 1963   **$750**

45 rpm. Glossy white label with blue print. The words "Don't Drop Out" are on the label. Near-mint price range: $500 to $750.
Variations of this release in the Top 1,000 can be found at Numbers 912;913.
Members: John Lennon; Paul McCartney, George Harrison; Ringo Starr.

☐ 915. Forever Loving You/Hey Little Girl • Bel-Airs (Sara 6431) 1963   **$750**

📷 45 rpm. Near-mint price range: $500 to $750.
Members: Wayne Demmer; Dennis Gehrke; Bob Wickert; Pete Miller.

☐ 916. He's a Rebel • Crystals (Philles 4001) 1963   **$750**

📷 LP. White label. Promotional issue only. Near-mint price range: $500 to $750.
Members: Barbara Alston; Lala Brooks; Dee Dee Kennibrew; Patricia Wright; Mary Thomas.
Side 1: *He's a Rebel; Uptown; Another Country – Another World; Frankenstein Twist; Oh Yeah, Maybe Baby; He's Sure the Boy I Love.*
Side 2: *There's No Other (Like My Baby); On Broadway; What a Nice Way to Turn Seventeen; No One Ever Tells You; He Hit Me; I Love You Eddie.*

DEVERE RECORDS

UNBREAKABLE
45 R.P.M.

RECORD NO.
HM-006
RN-48-1

Kama Music
Publ. Co. (BMI)

Time 2:34

EACH PASSING DAY
(Wilma R. Lung & Viola Flansburg)
JIMMY SINGLETON
& THE ROYAL SATINS
(ACCOMPANIED BY THE HI-FIS)

688.

GENE VINCENT

Capitol
HIGH FIDELITY
RECORDING

689.

**DIDN'T WE
HAVE A NICE TIME**
(Charles Smith)

TORI
LTD.
Hollywood
Calif.

Contrast
BMI
T - 2X

Produced by
Buddy Harper

CHARLES ANDREA
and
THE HI TONES

690.

VISTONE RECORDS

45 RPM

Da-Tan Music
(BMI)

45 RPM

2023
Time 2:05

WITH ALL MY HEART
(N. German)
THE BILLBOARDS
With The Red Julian Orchestra
Arrangement by J. Hemsley
Dave Polk Production
(205)

691.

☐ 917. Crystals • Crystals (Philles 4003) 1963 $750
   LP. White label. Promotional issue only. Near-mint price range: $500 to $750.
   Members: Barbara Alston; Lala Brooks; Dee Dee Kennibrew; Patricia Wright; Mary Thomas.
   Side 1: *Da Doo Ron Ron; On Broadway; He's a Rebel; Hot Pastrami; There's No Other (Like My Baby); The Wah Watusi.*
   Side 2: *Mashed Potato Time; He's Sure the Boy I Love; Uptown; The Twist; Gee Whiz (Look at His Eyes); Look in My Eyes.*

☐ 918. Does She Love Me/? • D.C. Magnatones (D.C. Magnatones 216)... 1963 $750
   📷 45 rpm. Near-mint price range: $500 to $750.

☐ 919. Mixed Up Confusion/Corrina Corrina • Bob Dylan (Columbia 42656)1963 $750
   📷 45 rpm. White label. Promotional issue only. Near-mint price range: $500 to $750.
   A variation of this release in the Top 1,000 can be found at Number 714.

☐ 920. I Wish.../It's the Last Kiss • Eric (With Plazas & Ralph Casals Trio)
   (Production 612) 1963 $750
   📷 45 rpm. Black vinyl. Purple vinyl copies are 1991 issues. Near-mint price range: $500 to $750.

☐ 921. Blues Boss • Amos Milburn (Motown 608) 1963 $750
   📷 Monaural LP. Near-mint price range: $500 to $750.
   Side 1: *I'll Make It Up to You Somehow; Darling How Long; Baby You Thrill Me; In the Middle of the Night; Don't Be No Fool; My Daily Prayer.*
   Side 2: *Bad, Bad Whiskey; Money; My Baby Gave Me Another Chance; One Scotch, One Bourbon, One Beer; Hold Me Baby; It's a Long, Long Time.*

☐ 922. Meet the Supremes • Supremes (Motown 606)............................... 1963 $750
   📷 LP. Front cover pictures each member sitting on a chair. Near-mint price range: $500 to $750.
   Members: Diana Ross; Mary Wilson; Florence Ballard.

☐ 923. RCA Victor December '63 Pop Sampler • Various Artists (RCA
   Victor SPS-33-247).. 1963 $750
   📷 LP. Promotional issue only. Not issued with special cover. All tracks except *Anytime* (Eddie Fisher) are stereo. Near-mint price range: $500 to $750.
   Side 1: *Main Title from "The Cardinal"* (Jerome Moross); *Dixieland Tango* (Orchestra Conducted by Jerome Moross); *I Can't Stop Loving You* (Hank Locklin); *Oh! Carol* (Neil Sedaka); *Charade* (Main Title) (Henry Mancini and His Orchestra); *Charade* (Vocal) (Henry Mancini and His Orchestra).
   Side 2: *Fun in Acapulco* (Elvis Presley); *One Note* (Joe Daley Trio); *Anytime* (Eddie Fisher); *Womenfolk* (Womenfolk); *Run Molly* (Villagers).

☐ 924. RCA Victor September '63 Pop Sampler • Various Artists (RCA
   Victor SPS-33-219).. 1963 $750
   📷 LP. Promotional issue only. Not issued with special cover. Near-mint price range: $500 to $750.
   Side 1: *900 Miles* (Odetta); *The Midnight Special* (Limeliters); *Guitar Child* (Duane Eddy); *All Keyed Up* (Floyd Cramer); *Don't Tell Me Your Troubles* (Don Gibson); *The Wreck of Number Nine* (Hank Snow); *Nobody Knows the Trouble I've Seen* (Sam Cooke).
   Side 2: *Excerpts* (Three Suns); *Nola* (Sid Ramin and His Orchestra); *Let's Fall in Love* (Voices of Hugo & Luigi Chorus); *Piano Excerpts*: (Frankie Carle/Floyd Cramer/Peter Nero); *Excerpts* (Ann-Margret/Kitty Kallen/Della Reese); *Are You Lonesome Tonight* (Elvis Presley).

☐ 925. Do You Want to Know a Secret/Thank You Girl • Beatles
   (Vee-Jay 587) 1964 $750
   📷 45 rpm. Promotional issue. White and blue label with brackets logo. Label reads: "Promotional copy." A-side title printed on either two or three lines. Near-mint price range: $500 to $750.
   Members: John Lennon; Paul McCartney, George Harrison; Ringo Starr.

DADE
RECORDS

UNBREAKABLE
45 R.P.M.

1007
Vocal

Sherlyn Music
BMI

A Steve Alaimo
Production

DRY YOUR EYES
(Womble and Clarence)
THE DELMIRAS
1821

692.

KAIN

Kain Music Co.
ASCAP 2:30

RECORD NO.
1004
(SO: 1003)

NOT FOR SALE

MY FOOLISH PRIDE
(H. C. Kain)
IMPLACABLES
F.O. Box 955
Mobile, Alabama

693.

RONDACK
RECORDS
Plattsburgh, New York

High Fidelity
45 RPM
Everest Music Co.
(BMI)
PLAT-3567

RO7-9787
(U-27165M)
Prod. by
Ben F. Everest
Vocal

RING THOSE BELLS
(B. Cates)
THE INSPIRATIONS

694.

wand

1650 BROADWAY,
NEW YORK, N.Y.

111 B
Ladex #.5.
Inc. — 2 22

WHISPER
(Cristobel Breeland)
THE JOKERS

695.

177

REPRISE RECORDS · MADE IN U.S.A.

reprise:

*A Special Message
to you from
Frank Sinatra*

697.

★★★★★
ADMIRAL

Fodior Music
(BMI)

(AD-913)
Time 2:20

FOREVER AND A DAY
(Bill Patton)

THE SPIRALS
Produced by SPECOE

AD-913

698.

TAMLA

2648 W. Grand
Boulevard
DISC JOCKEY
ADVANCE SAMPLE
Jobete B.M.I.

Detroit 8. Mich.
TR 1-3340

Time 2:49
H-620

I WANT A GUY
(B. Gordy Jr. - B. Holland - F. Gorman)
THE SUPREMES
Produced By
Berry Gordy, Jr.
T-54038

699.

DOLLY
RECORDS

45 RPM
3:06
M8OW-5578

Bobbs/Conrad
BMI

YOU CAN MAKE IT IF YOU TRY

CLARK VADEN
And The
Crescents

701.

178

☐ 926. This Is Our Wedding Day/Darling Forever • Four Chevelles
(Delft 6408)... 1964   **$750**

📷 45 rpm. Identification number shown since no selection number is used. Near-mint price range: $500 to $750.

☐ 927. Ringo, I Love You/Beatle Blues • Bonnie Jo Mason
(Annette 1000).. 1964   **$750**

📷 45 rpm. Bonnie Jo Mason is a one-time pseudonym for Cher. Near-mint price range: $500 to $750.

☐ 928. RCA Victor April '64 Pop Sampler • Various Artists (RCA
Victor SPS-33-272)... 1964   **$750**

📷 LP. Promotional issue only. Not issued with special cover. All tracks except *Saeta* (Carlos Montoya) are stereo. Near-mint price range: $500 to $750.

Side 1: *The Pink Panther Theme* (Henry Mancini Orchestra); *Prism Song* (Gale Garnett); *It Took a Miracle* (Solomon King); *Give Me This Mountain* (Blackwood Brothers); *I Met God in the Morning* (George Beverly Shea); *What Now My Love* (Frankie Fanelli); *Mayibuye* (Miriam Makeba); *Saeta* (Carlos Montoya).

Side 2: *Exactly Like You* (Ames Brothers); *You Don't Knock* (Don Gibson); *Hobo Flats* (Joe Williams); *Medley: Old Piano Roll Blues* (Frankie Carle); *Jitterbug Waltz* (Chet Atkins); *Kissin' Cousins* (Elvis Presley); *Always in My Heart* (Los Indios Tabajaras).

☐ 929. RCA Victor April '65 Pop Sampler • Various Artists (RCA
Victor SPS-33-331)... 1965   **$750**

📷 LP. Promotional issue only. Not issued with special cover. All tracks except *Chapines* (Juan Serrano) are stereo. Near-mint price range: $500 to $750.

Side 1: *Love Theme from "In Harm's Way"* (Jerry Goldsmith Orchestra); *Oh, What a Beautiful Mornin'* (Ethel Ennis); *Shine on Harvest Moon* (Frankie Carle); *I Could Have Danced All Night* (Peter Nero); *Bossa Antigua* (Paul Desmond Featuring Jim Hall); *Cameroon* (Mariam Makeba); *Hello Dolly* (The Melachrino Stings and Orchestra).

Side 2: *Chapines* (Juan Serrano); *The Meanest Girl in Town* (Elvis Presley); *Never on Sunday* (Mariachi Los Comperos); *The Other Side of You* (Connie Smith); *People* (Joe Williams); *Plastered* (Don Bowman); *I Stepped over the Line* (Don Robertson).

☐ 930. RCA Victor August '65 Pop Sampler • Various Artists (RCA
Victor SPS-33-347)... 1965   **$750**

📷 LP. Promotional issue only. Not issued with special cover. All tracks except *Your Cheatin' Heart* (Elvis Presley) are stereo. Near-mint price range: $500 to $750.

Side 1: *Tatahi Arahoho* (Tahitian Native Group); *In the Middle of a Memory* (Carl Belew); *Get Me to the Church on Time* (Marilyn Maye); *Take a Letter, Miss Gray* (Justin Tubb); *Overture from "My Fair Lady"* (Paul Lavalle); *You've Lost That Lovin' Feelin'* (Floyd Cramer).

Side 2: *Catchin' on Fast* (Peggy March & Bennie Thomas); *The Devil's Grin* (Lorne Greene); *Begin the Beguine* (Los Indios Tabajaras); *Little Ole You* (Jim Reeves); *Twangsville* (Duane Eddy); *Your Cheatin' Heart* (Elvis Presley).

☐ 931. Over the Rainbow/? • Royal-Five (P&L 317) 1966   **$750**

📷 45 rpm. Near-mint price range: $500 to $750.

☐ 932. RCA Victor April '66 Pop Sampler • Various Artists (RCA
Victor SPS-33-403)... 1966   **$750**

📷 Stereo LP. Promotional issue only. Not issued with special cover. Near-mint price range: $500 to $750.

Side 1: *My Fair Sadie* (Various Artists); *It's Just an Old Hawaiian Custom* (Ray Kinney); *Solo and Some Trust in Chariots* (Rod McKuen); *That Old Feeling* (Brook Benton); *Medley: Baia and Solamente Una Vez* (Frankie Carle); *Cheers* (Group 1, Directed By George Wilkins); *Columbus Stockade Blues* (Willie Nelson).

Side 2: *Stand at Your Window* (The Blue Boys with Bud Logan); *Big Boss Man* (Charlie Rich); *Of Thee I Sing* (Tommy Leonetti); *Bill Bailey* (Marilyn Maye); *Frankie and Johnny* (Elvis Presley); *Solo Busanova* (Hugo Montenegro); *Dominique* (The Provocative Strings of Zacharias).

PONCHO
RECORDS

10-A
(10+-A)

Pub:
Lee Andrew

Time 2:15

LATE SUMMER LOVE
(Melvin)

GRAND PRIXS

704.

RANDY
RECORDS

Guild Music Co.
B.M.I.

Time 2:12
(422-B)

BARBIE
-(B. Morgan)
KENNY
and THE CADETS

422

705.

RUST
RECORDS
RUST RECORDS INC
NEW YORK

RECORD NO.
5052
Shelros Music
BMI

PROMOTIONAL
COPY
NOT FOR SALE
Time: 2:35
NO8W 3547
(U-24961M)

TOGETHER
(In Your Arms)
(The Modern Ink Spots)
THE MODERN INK SPOTS

707.

PARAMOUNT
PICTURES

SIDE 1

45 R.P.

"GIRLS! GIRLS! GIRLS"
ADVANCE (COMING SOON)
THEATRE LOBBY SPOT
RECORD PLAYS CONTINUOUSLY AND
AUTOMATICALLY
SP-2017

708.

☐ 933. Action Woman/Pregnant Pig • Electras (Scotty 6720)...................... 1967 $750
     45 rpm. Studio demo. One known copy. Near-mint price range: $500 to $750.
     Members: Earl Bulinski; Bill Bulinski; Jerry Fink; Gary Omerza; Tim Elving.

☐ 934. Special Palm Sunday Programming • Elvis Presley (RCA
     Victor SP-33-461) 1967 $750

     📷 Monaural LP. White label, black print. Reads: "Complete half-hour radio program with spot announcements and selections from the RCA Victor album *How Great Thou Art* (LPM/LSP-3758." Promotional issue only. Insert: Cue sheet with running times and program information. LP alone: $600 to $650. LP and insert: $500 to $750.
     Side 1: *How Great Thou Art; In the Garden; Somebody Bigger Than You and I; Stand by Me.*
     Side 2: *Without Him; Where Could I Go But to the Lord; Where No One Stands Alone; Crying in the Chapel; How Great Thou Art (Excerpt).*

☐ 935. Easter Everywhere • Thirteenth Floor Elevators (International
     Artists 5) 1967 $750
     LP. Monaural. Does NOT have "Masterfonics" stamped in the vinyl trail-off. Near-mint price range: $500 to $750.

☐ 936. Blueprints • American Blues Exchange [A*B*E] (Taylus 1) 1969 $750
     LP. Near-mint price range: $500 to $750.
     Members: Roy Dudley; Roger Briggs; Pete Hartman; Dan Mixer.

☐ 937. Just Like You Did Me/? • Yvonne Vernee (Sonbert 5842)...............1960s $750
     45 rpm. Near-mint price range: $500 to $750.

☐ 938. My Boy/Loving Arms • Elvis Presley (RCA Victor 2458EX) 1974 $750

     📷 45 rpm. Gray label. Includes paper, titles, single-sheet insert. Manufactured in the U.S. for distribution overseas. Couples two songs not issued back-to-back in the U.S. Near-mint price range: $500 to $750.

☐ 939. I'm Gonna Take You Home • Ya Ho Wa 13 (Higher Key 3309) 1975 $750
     LP. Near-mint price range: $500 to $750.

☐ 940. Guitars, Cadillacs, Etc, Etc. • Dwight Yoakam (Oak 2356)............... 1984 $750
     Six-track LP. 1986 Reissue (Reprise 25372) adds four tracks. Near-mint price range: $500 to $750.
     Side 1: *It Won't Hurt; South of Cincinnati; I'll Be Gone.*
     Side 2: *Twenty Years; Ring of Fire; Miner's Prayer.*

☐ 941. Love Forever/? • Barry & Vi-Counts (Fine 102) ....? $750

     📷 45 rpm. Near-mint price range: $500 to $750.

☐ 942. Those Pretty Brown Eyes/Meant to Be • Terry Hull & Starfires
     (Staff 103)..? $750

     📷 45 rpm. Near-mint price range: $500 to $750.

☐ 943. Wailin' Wildcat/? • Little Man Henry (Central 4701) ....? $750
     45 rpm. Near-mint price range: $500 to $750.

☐ 944. Image of Love/? • Publio & Valiants (Menard 6252).............................? $750

     📷 45 rpm. Near-mint price range: $500 to $750.

☐ 945. Believe in Me/Little Baby • Pete Shekeryk & Delua-Tones
     (Ukey 101)...? $750
     45 rpm. Near-mint price range: $500 to $750.

☐ 946. Girl/Nobody Knows • Tejuns (100-Proof 144)....................................? $750

     📷 45 rpm. Near-mint price range: $500 to $750.

☐ 947. When/? • Wee Willie & Mellodiers (Wow 110) ....? $750

     📷 45 rpm. Near-mint price range: $500 to $750.

SKYLIGHT RECORDS.

SL 102 B
ASCAP

San Francisco
45 RPM Time 2:20
PROMOTIONAL
COPY

GOT TO GET ALONG
(Mary E. Johnson)
WILLIAM WIGFALL
AND THE LYRICS

709.

[VJ]

63-321B
Vocal

Gil Music
Corp.-BMI
Time: 1:49

FROM ME TO YOU
(McCartney-Lennon)
THE BEATLES
VJ 522

710.

VEE JAY

63-321
Vocal

Conrad-Pub.
BMI
Time: 2:55

THANK YOU GIRL
(McCartney-Lennon)
THE BEATLES
VJ 522

711.

SANDY
RECORD COMPANY INC.
Box 248   Mobile, Ala.

Dist. Exclusively
by Sandy Record
Co., Inc.

1080-MS
Burnt Oak Pub.
Co., Inc. (BMI)
Time: 2:25
VOCAL

"THERE GOES A YOUNG LOVE"
(P. Crawford)
PETER CRAWFORD
1039-45

713.

MARKAY
RECORDS

45 RPM

House of Fortune
Music Co. (BMI)

45 RPM

(CH-1B)

Time 2:30

PARDON ME
(Kent Harris)
THE CEZANNES
Featuring CERRESSA

108

712.

182

☐ 948. Rum and Coca-Cola/On a Little Street in Singapore • Jackie Heller / Glenn
Miller (Vogue/Philco) 1945 $700

    📷 78 rpm picture disc. Vogue label on one side, Philco on flip. No selection number used.
    Promotional issue. Near-mint price range: $500 to $700.

☐ 949. Happy Bachelor (Blues)/Danger Zone (Crepe on Your Door) • Mercy Dee
(Bayou 013) 1950 $700

    45 rpm. Full name: Mercy Dee Walton. Near-mint price range: $500 to $700.

☐ 950. Heartbreaker/Wanda • Heartbreakers (RCA Victor 4327) 1951 $700

    📷 45 rpm. Near-mint price range: $500 to $700.
    Members: Robert Evans; Lawrence Green; Jim Rose; Junior Davis; Larry Tate.

☐ 951. What Are You Doing New Year's Eve/Lonely Christmas • Orioles
(Jubilee 5017).. 1951 $700

    45 rpm. Near-mint price range: $500 to $700.
    Members: Sonny Til; Alex Sharp; George Nelson; John Reed; Tom Gaither.

☐ 952. Red Cherries/The River • Floyd Dixon (Aladdin 3144) 1952 $700

    45 rpm. Red vinyl. Near-mint price range: $500 to $700.

☐ 953. I Was Wrong/Ooh Rocking Daddy • Moonglows (Chance 1156)...... 1954 $700

    45 rpm. Yellow and black label. Near-mint price range: $500 to $700.
    Members: Harvey Fuqua; Bobby Lester; Alex Graves; Prentiss Barnes; Buddy Johnson.

☐ 954. Split Personality/Lonely Sweetheart • Bill Taylor & Smokey Jo
(Flip 502) 1955 $700

    📷 45 rpm. Near-mint price range: $500 to $700.
    Members: Bill Taylor; Smokey Joe Baugh; Clyde Leoppard; Stan Kesler; Buddy Holobaugh.

☐ 955. Fine Girl/Mambo Fiesta • Calvaes (Cobra 5003)............................. 1956 $700

    📷 45 rpm. Near-mint price range: $500 to $700.

☐ 956. They Were Rockin'/Stop Mambo • Danny Kirkland & His Band
(J-V-B 60) 1957 $700

    📷 45 rpm. Near-mint price range: $500 to $700.

☐ 957. Dear, I Swear/It's You • Plants (With Orchestra) (J&S 1602) 1957 $700

    📷 45 rpm. Label has company address under logo. Near-mint price range: $500 to $700.

☐ 958. My Baby-O/Once Upon a Time • Marv Johnson (Kudo 663)............ 1958 $700

    📷 45 rpm. Near-mint price range: $500 to $700.

☐ 959. You Said You're Leaving Me/Johnny's Got a Girlfriend • Mixers
(Bold 101) 1958 $700

    45 rpm. Near-mint price range: $500 to $700.

☐ 960. Esquerita • Esquerita (Capitol 1186) 1959 $700

    📷 LP. Also recorded as Eskew Reeder. Near-mint price range: $500 to $700.
    Side 1: *Hey, Miss Lucy; Why Did It Take You So Long; She Left Me Crying; Crazy, Crazy Feeling;*
       Get Back Baby; Hole in My Heart.
    Side 2: *I'm Battie over Hattie; Baby, You Can Depend on Me; Believe Me When I Say Rock and*
       Roll Is Here To Stay; I Need You; Maybe Baby; Getting' Plenty Lovin'.

☐ 961. Peace in the Valley • Elvis Presley (RCA Victor EPA-5121)............. 1959 $700

    EP and cover. Maroon label. Reissue of EPA-4054. Disc alone: $575 to $650. Disc and
    cover: $500 to $700.
    Side 1: *(There'll Be) Peace in the Valley (For Me); It Is No Secret (What God Can Do).*
    Side 2: *I Believe; Take My Hand, Precious Lord.*

Revenge
RECORDS

MINK MUSIC
BMI
TIME: 2:20

R-

WHY?
(JEFF ROLLINS)
THE EXECUTIVES
Produced by: SIMKA

715.

Jamie
® 45 RPM

SUMMERTIME ANGEL
(Bob Finiz)

Dandelion Music
BMI
J-TIN 2x
Time: 1:50

THE INTENTIONS
Arranged by Bob Finiz
Produced by Joe Wissert
1253
MFG. BY JAMIE RECORD CO. PHILA., PA.

716.

Sahara

BMI
HOUSE OF SOUND
BILYA BAN MUSIC
TUPPER MUSIC

SH-102-1
TIME: 2:09

TEARS FROM MY EYES
(L. HOGAINS)
NAP ROMAN

717.

DFS

DFS Pub.
DFS-11

Time 3:40

SURFER JOE
(Ron Wilson)
THE SURFARIS

719.

DFS

DFS Pub.
DFS-12

Time 2:12

WIPE-OUT
(The Surfaris)
THE SURFARIS

☐ 962. Date with Elvis • Elvis Presley (RCA Victor LPM-2011)................... 1959　　$700

📷 Monaural LP. Black label, "Long Play" at bottom. Cover: Gatefold, though record pocket is the front instead of back panel and the pocket opening is at top rather than right side (as with most gatefold covers). Front: RCA Victor logo and number at upper right. Contents printed on a red sticker with white lettering, applied to front. No titles are printed on cover itself. Back is an "Elvis 1960" calendar, with March 24 circled in red. Banner: Aluminum foil wraparound banner, proclaiming this LP as one of 24 Alcoa Wrap "New Golden Age of Sound Albums," and announcing a Beautiful Hair Breck New Golden Age of Sound Preview LP. Makes no reference to this specific LP or to Elvis. In fact, a banner from any of the 24 Golden Age of Sound Albums could be used with *A Date with Elvis*. Banner alone: $200 to $300. Cover alone: $250 to $300. Disc, cover and banner: $500 to $700.

Side 1: *Blue Moon of Kentucky; Young and Beautiful; (You're So Square) Baby I Don't Care; Milkcow Blues Boogie; Baby Let's Play House.*

Side 2: *Good Rockin' Tonight; Is It So Strange; We're Gonna Move; I Want to Be Free; I Forgot to Remember to Forget.*

☐ 963. Boogie-Woogie Country Girl/Pins and Needles • N.A. Stephenson
(Westwood 201) .... 1959　　$700
45 rpm. Near-mint price range: $500 to $700.

☐ 964. Baby You Just Wait/? • Spirals (Indigo 500).................................... 1960　　$700
45 rpm. Near-mint price range: $500 to $700.

☐ 965. Over the Rainbow/Loop the Fly • Mustangs (Vest 51)..................... 1963　　$700
📷 45 rpm. Near-mint price range: $500 to $700.

☐ 966. Great American Tour, 1965 Live Beatlemania Concert • Beatles
(Lloyds AG-8146) .... 1965　　$700
LP. Live tracks by the Beatles, with overdubbing by another band – The Liverpool Lads resulting in an overall poor quality product. Near-mint price range: $500 to $700.

☐ 967. Yesterday and Today • Beatles (Capitol ST-2553).......................... 1966　　$700
Monaural LP. "Paste-over" or "peeled" covers. The paste-over version has a photo of the Beatles around a trunk pasted over an intact "butcher cover." The peeled version shows the "butcher cover" after the trunk photo cover has been peeled off. Removing the slick can be a difficult and risky process; however, there are professionals who offer this service. Near-mint price range: $500 to $700.
Variations of this release can be found at Numbers 1; 21; 175; 495.
Members: John Lennon; Paul McCartney, George Harrison; Ringo Starr.
Side 1: *Drive My Car; I'm Only Sleeping; Nowhere Man; Dr. Robert; Yesterday; Act Naturally.*
Side 2: *And Your Bird Can Sing; If I Needed Someone; We Can Work It Out; What Goes On; Day Tripper.*
Members: John Lennon; Paul McCartney, George Harrison; Ringo Starr.

☐ 968. Steve Ellis Songbook • Steve Ellis & Starfires (IGL 105)................. 1967　　$700
📷 LP. Near-mint price range: $500 to $700.
Members: Steve Ellis; Jimmy Groth; Clem Hatting; Dean Sefner; Barry Hanson.
Side 1: *That's How It Feels; Since I Fell for You; Pride of a Man; Her Face.*
Side 2: *Looking Thru Me; On My Face; Walking Around; Baby's Gone.*

☐ 969. Drag Strip Baby/Wasted Past • Johnny Roane (Wagon 1004)............... ?　　$700
📷 45 rpm. Near-mint price range: $500 to $700.

☐ 970. When You Love/People Will Talk • Cliff Butler & Doves
(States 123) .... 1953　　$650
45 rpm. Red vinyl. Near-mint price range: $500 to $650.

☐ 971. Miss Anna B/Something's Wrong with My Lovin Machine • Robert Henry
(King 4624)... 1953　　$650
45 rpm. Near-mint price range: $500 to $650.

☐ 972. Old Battle Ax/Early in the Morning • Robert Henry (King 4646)........ 1953　　$650
45 rpm. Near-mint price range: $500 to $650.

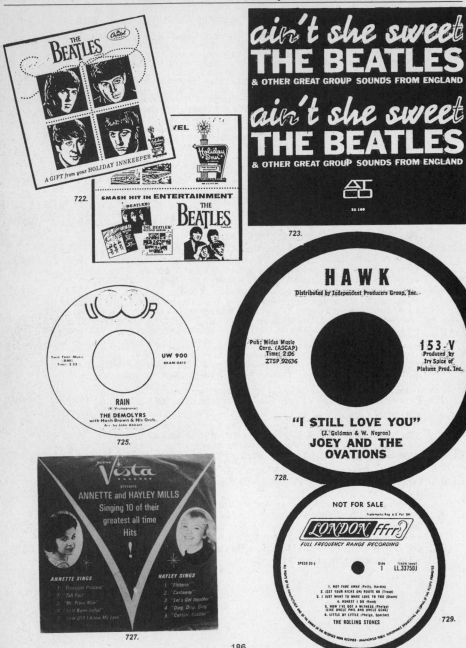

722.

723.

725.

HAWK
Distributed by Independent Producers Group, Inc.

Pub: Midas Music
Corp. (ASCAP)
Time: 2:06
ZTSP 92636

153-V
Produced by
Irv Spice of
Platune Prod. Inc.

"I STILL LOVE YOU"
(J. Goldman & W. Negron)
JOEY AND THE
OVATIONS

728.

727.

NOT FOR SALE

LONDON ffrr
FULL FREQUENCY RANGE RECORDING

SPEED 33⅓

Side
1
LL.33750J

1. NOT FADE AWAY (Petty, Hardin)
2. (GET YOUR KICKS ON) ROUTE 66 (Troup)
3. I JUST WANT TO MAKE LOVE TO YOU (Dixon)
4. HONEST I DO (Reed)
5. NOW I'VE GOT A WITNESS (Phelge)
(LIKE UNCLE PHIL AND UNCLE GENE)
6. LITTLE BY LITTLE (Phelge, Spector)

THE ROLLING STONES

729.

GALAXY®

PROMOTIONAL   NOT FOR SALE

Cireco/Voycon
BMI
TIME: 2:19

732
(F-2406)

THIS LOVE WAS REAL
(Colford-Keyes)
THE SHOWCASES
Produced by Cliff Goldsmith

730.

THE FUGITIVES
at Dave's Hideout

731.

ODESSA

Push Music Co.
BMI (101)

101
Vocal
Time 2:35

MY DEAREST, MY DARLING
(I Miss You)
(T. Boyd)
TIM BOYD &
THE ESQUIRES
Bill Gibbs Combo

738.

VERY
RECORD
1110 E. Turney, Phoenix, Ariz. 85014

S-001
1:58

Produced by
D. Phillips

LAY DOWN AND DIE, GOODBYE
NAZZ
(M. Bruce, G. Buxton, D. Dunaway,
V. Furnier, T. Speer)

733.

WILD COUNTRY

740.

☐ 973. Baby I Need You/My Loving Baby • El Dorados (Vee-Jay 115) 1954 $650
    45 rpm. Red vinyl. Near-mint price range: $500 to $650.
      Members: Pirkle Lee Moses Jr; Arthur Bassett; Louis Bradley; James Maddox; Jewel Jones; Richard Nickens; Johnny Carter; Ted Long; John McCall; Douglas Brown.

☐ 974. America's Favorite Folk Artist • Slim Whitman (Imperial 3004) 1954 $650
    10-inch LP. Colored vinyl. Near-mint price range: $500 to $650.

☐ 975. Gonna Dance All Night/Fallen Angel • Hardrock Gunter (Sun 201).. 1954 $650
    45 rpm. Near-mint price range: $500 to $650.

☐ 976. I Need You All the Time/I'll Cry When You're Gone • Platters
    (Federal 12164) 1954 $650
    45 rpm. Near-mint price range: $500 to $650.
      Members: Tony Williams; David Lynch; Herb Reed; Zola Taylor; Paul Robi.

☐ 977. Memorial Album • Johnny Ace (Duke 70) 1955 $650

    📷 10-inch monaural LP. Near-mint price range: $500 to $650.
    Side 1: *Pledging My Love; Never Let Me Go; Saving My Love for You; Please Forgive Me.*
    Side 2: *The Clock; Cross My Heart; Angel; My Song.*

☐ 978. Tired and Sleepy/Fool's Paradise • Cochran Brothers (Ekko 3001) . 1956 $650

    📷 45 rpm. Near-mint price range: $500 to $650.
      Members: Eddie Cochran; Hank Cochran. (Eddie and Hank are not really brothers.)

☐ 979. Lizzie/Alone on a Rainy Night • Del Rios & Bearcats
    (Meteor 5038) 1956 $650

    📷 45 rpm. Near-mint price range: $500 to $650.

☐ 980. The Way You Look Tonight/Moonlight and You • Jaguars
    (R-Dell 11) 1956 $650

    📷 45 rpm. Red vinyl. Near-mint price range: $500 to $650.

☐ 981. So in Love/It Happened to Me • Re-Vels (With Gene Kutch & Butch
    Ballard Orchestra) (Teen 122) 1956 $650

    📷 45 rpm. Near-mint price range: $500 to $650.

☐ 982. Tears in My Eyes/Magic • Tru-Tones (Chart 634) 1956 $650

    📷 45 rpm. Near-mint price range: $500 to $650.

☐ 983. The Five Keys on Stage! • Five Keys (Capitol 828) 1957 $650

    📷 LP. Black label, reads "Sample Album for Radio-TV Program Use." Cover has white sticker reading "For Promotional Use Only – Not for Sale." In cover photo, group member on left is holding his right hand in what some critics deemed a phallic-like position. Near-mint price range: $500 to $650.
      Members: Rudy West; Ripley Ingram; Maryland Pierce; Dickie Smith; Ray Loper; Bernie West; Ulysses Hicks; Thomas Threat.
    Side 1: *Just for a Thrill; Who Do You Know in Heaven; Maybe You'll Be There; Tiger Lily; C'est la Vie; Dream.*
    Side 2: *Let There Be You; All I Need Is You; The Gypsy; From the Bottom of My Heart; To Each His Own; Boom Boom.*

☐ 984. Little Girl/Two By Two • Johnny Ramistella (Suede 1401) 1958 $650

    📷 45 rpm. Ramistella became popular when he adopted the stage name: Johnny Rivers. Near-mint price range: $500 to $650.

☐ 985. Rattle Shakin' Mama/Cheryl Baby • Mel McGonnigle (Rocket 101) . 1958 $650
    45 rpm. Near-mint price range: $500 to $650.

☐ 986. Ain't That a Dilly/Sugarfoot • Marlon Grisham (Cover 5982) 1959 $650
    45 rpm. Near-mint price range: $500 to $650.

☐ 987. Snaggle Tooth Ann/Night Train • Gene Norman & Rockin' Rockets
    (Snag 101) 1959 $650
    45 rpm. Near-mint price range: $500 to $650.

743.

746.

745.

749.

751.

753.

754.

758.

759.

☐ 988. The Teddy Bears Sing • Teddy Bears (Imperial 12010) 1959   **$650**

📷 Stereo LP. Near-mint price range: $500 to $650.
Members: Phil Spector; Annette Kleinbard; Marshall Leib.

☐ 989. I'm Lonesome for You/Chick-A-Dee • Escos (Background: George Carter, Wilbert Bell & Winfred Gerald. Music by the Swingin' Rocks) (Esta 100) 1959   **$650**

📷 45 rpm. Same selection number also used for a Joe Caldwell release. Near-mint price range: $500 to $650.
Members: Lonnie Carter; Don Peark; Joe Renn; Richard Parker; Roland Bradley.
Session: George Carter; Wilbert Bell; Winfred Gerald; Swingin' Rocks.

☐ 990. First Date with the Ebon-Knights • Ebon-Knights (Stepheny 4001).. 1959   **$650**
LP. Near-mint price range: $500 to $650.

Side 1: *First Date; Stop the World; Only, Only You; Poor Butterfly; I'm Confessin'; Do You Know; Georgia.*

Side 2: *Lonesome Road; Lover Come Back to Me; Why Don't You Happen to Me; Falling in Love; Blues in the Night; That's the Way the Ball Bounces; Numma Numma.*

☐ 991. Wandering/? • Viscounts (Star-Fax 1002) 1950s   **$650**

📷 45 rpm. Near-mint price range: $500 to $650.

☐ 992. For the First Time/Take It from a Fool • Dream Lovers (Len 1006).. 1960   **$650**

📷 45 rpm. Near-mint price range: $500 to $650.
Members: Tommy Ricks; Cleveland Hammock; Cliff Dunn; Morris Gardner; Ray Dunn.

☐ 993. Poor Little Rhode Island/Every Little Girl • Dale Hawkins (Checker 944) 1960   **$650**

📷 45 rpm single with picture sleeve. Sleeve represents about 95% of value. Near-mint price range: $500 to $650.

☐ 994. Are You Lonesome Tonight/I Gotta Know • Elvis Presley (With Jordanaires) (RCA Victor 61-7810) 1960   **$650**

📷 45 rpm. Living stereo. Near-mint price range: $500 to $650.

☐ 995. Runaway • Del Shannon (Big Top 1303)... 1961   **$650**

📷 Stereo LP. Near-mint price range: $500 to $650.

☐ 996. Please Don't Cheat On Me/If You Should Leave Me • Sinceres (Richie 545) 1961   **$650**

📷 45 rpm. No mention of Roulette distribution on label. Near-mint price range: $500 to $650.
Member: Jay Proctor.

☐ 997. Clown Town/At Night • Neil Diamond (Columbia 42809).................. 1963   **$650**
45 rpm. Price is for the commercial release; the promo is valued lower. Near-mint price range: $500 to $650.

☐ 998. Can't Buy Me Love/You Can't Do That • Beatles (Capitol 5150) 1964   **$650**

📷 Picture sleeve. Issued only with a straight cut across the top of the sleeve. Known counterfeit has noticeably inferior quality photos and print. Photo on one known fake is too large to include the top of George's head – same as used on some of the die cut versions of the *I Want to Hold Your Hand* picture sleeve. Another fake includes George's full head, but is of poor quality and uses the wrong paper stock. It is helpful to have an original to determine authenticity. Near-mint price range: $500 to $650.
Members: John Lennon; Paul McCartney, George Harrison; Ringo Starr.

☐ 999. Heart of Stone/What a Shame • Rolling Stones (London 9725) 1965   **$650**

📷 Picture sleeve. Near-mint price range: $500 to $650.
Members: Mick Jagger; Keith Richards; Bill Wyman; Brian Jones; Charlie Watts.

☐ 1000. Special Girl/? • Ernie Simiele & Eratics (Kind A Round 11765)............ ?   **$650**

📷 45 rpm. Also shows "RB 105." It's not clear which is the correct selection number. Near-mint price range: $500 to $650.

762.

770.

773.

TOP 1,000 MOST VALUABLE RECORDS
ALPHABETICALLY BY ARTIST

ACADEMICS
Too Good to Be True/Heavenly Love • Academics (With Kingsmen Quintet)
(Anchor 101) 1957 $1,200
    45 rpm. Near-mint price range: $800 to $1,200.
      Top 1,000 ranking: 520

ACE, Johnny
Memorial Album • Johnny Ace (Duke 70) 1955 $650
    10-inch monaural LP. Near-mint price range: $500 to $650.
      Top 1,000 ranking: 977

ADAMS, Billy
Rock Pretty Mama/? • Billy Adams (Quincy 932)............................. 1959 $1,500
    45 rpm. Near-mint price range: $1,000 to $1,500.
      Top 1,000 ranking: 446

ADAMS, Woodrow
Wine Head Woman/Baby You Just Don't Know • Woodrow Adams
(Meteor 5018)... 1955 $1,000
    45 rpm. Near-mint price range: $750 to $1,000.
      Top 1,000 ranking: 613

ALEXANDER, Joe, & Cubans
Oh Maria/I Hope These Words Will Find You Well • Joe Alexander & Cubans
(Ballad 1008) 1955 $1,200
    45 rpm. Near-mint price range: $800 to $1,200.
      Top 1,000 ranking: 512

AMBASSADORS
Keep on Trying/The Switch • Ambassadors (With Johnny L. Chapman Orchestra)
(Air 5065) 1956 $1,500
    45 rpm. Approximately 50 made. Near-mint price range: $1,000 to $1,500.
      Top 1,000 ranking: 425

AMBASSADORS
Lorraine/Come on and Dance • Ambassadors (Playbox 202) 1963 $1,500
    45 rpm. Near-mint price range: $1,000 to $1,500.
      Top 1,000 ranking: 466

AMERICAN BLUES EXCHANGE
Blueprints • American Blues Exchange [A*B*E] (Taylus 1)............................ 1969 $750
    LP. Near-mint price range: $500 to $750.
      Top 1,000 ranking: 936

ANDANTES
(Like a) Nightmare/If You Were Mine • Andantes (V.I.P. 25006) 1964 $2,000
    45 rpm. Near-mint price range: $1,000 to $2,000.
      Top 1,000 ranking: 355

ANDREA, Charles, & Hi Tones
Didn't We Have a Nice Time/Open Up Your Heart • Charles Andrea & Hi Tones
(Tori Ltd. 2)... 1961 $1,000
    45 rpm. Near-mint price range: $750 to $1,000.
      Top 1,000 ranking: 690

774.

775.

Teenage
RECORD CO.
(PATENT PENDING)
311 WEST 127th ST.,   NEW YORK 26, N.Y.

UNBREAKABLE
45 R.P.M.

RECORD NO.
1009
(121)

Travis Music
(BMI)
2:28

Blues Bailed

SHE'S THE ONE
(D. Bartholomew-P. King)
THE LINKS

PEACH
RECORDS,
INC.
DOUGLASVILLE,
GA. U.S.A.

Lowery Music
Co., Inc. BMI

716
Time: 2:07

WEDDING BELLS GONNA RING
(Bobby Ferguson)
THE GATES
featuring Bobby Ferguson
NR-42

777.

RCA VICTOR

SP
33-59-7
(2708/2520)

SIDE
1
NOT FOR SALE

FEBRUARY SAMPLER 59-7
1—HEARTS OF PARIS (LPRM 1020)
2—THE STRANGER OF GALILEE (LPEM 1039)
3—COUNTDOWN (LPM 1922)
4—THAT'S ALL RIGHT (LPM-1035)
1. Ray Hartley with Dan Walker and Orch.
2. Blackwood Brothers Quartet
3. Buddy Morrow and his Orchestra
4. Elvis Presley

LONG 33⅓ PLAY

779.

ANDREWS, Lee, & Hearts

White Cliffs of Dover/Much Too Much • Lee Andrews & Hearts
(Rainbow 256)... 1954 $1,500
   45 rpm. Yellow label. Near-mint price range: $1,000 to $1,500.
   Top 1,000 ranking: 409
Maybe You'll Be There/Baby Come Back • Lee Andrews & Hearts
(Rainbow 252)... 1954 $1,000
   45 rpm. Red vinyl. Print is small, with the title line being about 1½" long. Near-mint price range:
   $750 to $1,000.
   Top 1,000 ranking: 594
Bells of St. Mary's/Fairest • Lee Andrews & Hearts (Rainbow 259)............... 1954 $750
   45 rpm. Yellow label. Near-mint price range: $500 to $750.
   Top 1,000 ranking: 819
Try the Impossible/Nobody's Home • Lee Andrews & Hearts (Casino 452)... 1958 $750
   45 rpm. Red and white label, with playing cards at top. Near-mint price range: $500 to $750.
   Top 1,000 ranking: 858

ANGELS

Lovely Way to Spend an Evening/You're Still My Baby • Angels
(Grand 121)... 1955 $1,500
   45 rpm. Glossy yellow label. Rigid disc. No company address shown. Near-mint price range:
   $1,000 to $1,500.
   Top 1,000 ranking: 419
Wedding Bells Are Ringing in My Ears/Times Have Changed • Angels
(Grand 115)... 1954 $750
   45 rpm. Glossy yellow label. No company address shown. Rigid disc. Near-mint price range:
   $500 to $750.
   Top 1,000 ranking: 820

ANNETTE / HAYLEY MILLS

Annette & Hayley Mills • Annette Funicello / Hayley Mills (Buena Vista/
Disneyland 3508) 1964 $1,000
   Monaural LP. Cover indicates Buena Vista although disc has a (bright yellow) Disneyland label.
   Issued with paper cover. One side – five tracks – devoted to each artist. Available only by mail
   order coupon, for $1.98. Its rarity is no doubt helped by poor circulation of magazines with the ad
   and coupon. Near-mint price range: $750 to $1,000.
   Top 1,000 ranking: 727

APACHE

Maitreya • Apache (Akashic 2777)... 1971 $1,500
   LP. Near-mint price range: $1,000 to $1,500.
   Top 1,000 ranking: 482

ARCADOS

When You Walked Out/Sugar Sweet • Arcados (Fam 502)........................... 1963 $3,000
   45 rpm. One known copy. Near-mint price range: $2,000 to $3,000.
   Top 1,000 ranking: 167

ARRIBIANS

To Look at a Star/Working and Gambling Don't Mix • Arribians
(J.O.B. 1116)... 1958 $2,000
   45 rpm. Near-mint price range: $1,500 to $2,000.
   Top 1,000 ranking: 306

AUSTIN, Bill, & Hearts

Angel Baby/Night Has Come • Bill Austin & Hearts (Apollo 444)................... 1952 $2,500
   45 rpm. Red vinyl. Near-mint price range: $2,000 to $2,500.
   Top 1,000 ranking: 182

780.

781.

782.

783.

AUTRY, Gene

Living in the Mountains/I'll Be Thinking of You Little Gal • Gene Autry
(QRS 1044) 1929 $5,000
    78 rpm. Near-mint price range: $3,000 to $5,000.
    Top 1,000 ranking: 41
I'll Be Thinking of You Little Gal/Whisper Your Mother's Name • Gene Autry
(Supertone 9705) 1929 $5,000
    78 rpm. Near-mint price range: $3,000 to $5,000.
    Top 1,000 ranking: 42

AVONS

Hull Records Cordially Invite You to Meet the Avons • Avons (Hull 1000) 1960 $1,000
    LP. Near-mint price range: $750 to $1,000.
    Top 1,000 ranking: 679

AZITIS

Help • Azitis (Elco 5555) 1971 $1,600
    LP. Near-mint price range: $1,200 to $1,600.
    Top 1,000 ranking: 389

BABY FACE LEROY TRIO

Rollin' and Tumblin' (Part 1)/ Rollin' and Tumblin' (Part 2) • Baby Face Leroy Trio
(Parkway 501) 1950 $4,000
    78 rpm. Near-mint price range: $2,000 to $4,000.
    Top 1,000 ranking: 69

BACHELORS

Can't Help Loving You/Pretty Baby • Bachelors (Aladdin 3210) 1953 $2,500
    45 rpm. Near-mint price range: $2,000 to $2,500.
    Top 1,000 ranking: 184

BACHS

Out of the Bachs • Bachs.. 1968 $2,500
    LP. Neither label name nor selection number used. Reportedly 100 made. Del Val label reissues
    exist. Near-mint price range: $1,500 to $2,500.
    Top 1,000 ranking: 210

BALLARD, Hank, & Midnighters: see MIDNIGHTERS

BANKS, Mack

Be-Boppin' Daddy/? • Mack Banks (Fame 580)... 1959 $750
    45 rpm. 500 made. Near-mint price range: $500 to $750.
    Top 1,000 ranking: 869

BARNETTE, Billy, & Searchers

Don't Let Our Love Go Wrong/Stomp, Shake and Twist • Billy Barnette &
Searchers (Mt. Vernon 500)... ? $1,000
    45 rpm. Near-mint price range: $750 to $1,000.
    Top 1,000 ranking: 747

BARRIX, Billy

Cool Off Baby/Almost • Billy Barrix (Shreveport)... 1957 $10,000
    45 rpm. Selection number not yet known. Near-mint price range: $7,500 to $10,000.
    Top 1,000 ranking: 19
Cool Off Baby/Almost • Billy Barrix (Chess 1662)... 1957 $5,000
    45 rpm. Near-mint price range: $3,000 to $5,000.
    Top 1,000 ranking: 60
Cool Off Baby/Almost • Billy Barrix (Chess 1662)... 1957 $1,000
    78 rpm. Near-mint price range: $750 to $1,000.
    Top 1,000 ranking: 636

"SCHOOL DAYS"
(Ziennker - Wright - Kessler)

PROMOTION
COPY

Bae Music
Inc., ASCAP
Time: 2:46

SOUTHERN SOUND
MADE IN U.S.A.

THE GLIDERS
SS-103-S

SOUTHERN SOUND - A DIVISION OF SOUTHLAND CORPORATION OF AMERICA - NEW YORK, N.Y.

785.

OPEN YOUR BOX

OYB-1

YOKO ONO/
PLASTIC ONO BAND
MADE SPECIALLY FOR
YOKO ONO

793.

HAPPY XMAS
(War Is Over)

JOHN & YOKO
THE PLASTIC ONO BAND

794.

APPLE

(BMI) 3:30
Produced by
John & Yoko
& Phil Spector

NOT FOR SALE
FOR RADIO STATION
PLAY ONLY
SIDE 1

HAPPY XMAS (WAR IS OVER)
sung by
JOHN & YOKO
& THE PLASTIC ONO BAND
with the HARLEM COMMUNITY CHOIR

TICO
EL REY DEL MAMBO
MADE IN U.S.A. BY TICO RECORDING COMPANY, INC. NEW YORK CITY

45 RPM
RECORD

Vocal

UNBREAKABLE
RECORD NO
45-1082
(45-TR-901)

MAMBO SHEVITZ
(Man O Man)
(Mahler-Melino-Moss)
THE CROWS
With
MELINO
and His Orchestra

801.

198

BARRY & HIGHLIGHTS

Wonderful Years/? • Barry & Highlights (Planet 1048).................................... 1961 $750
   45 rpm. Near-mint price range: $500 to $750.
   Top 1,000 ranking: 892

BARRY & VI-COUNTS

Love Forever/? • Barry & Vi-Counts (Fine 102) .... ? $750
   45 rpm. Near-mint price range: $500 to $750.
   Top 1,000 ranking: 941

BEACH BOYS

Complete Selections from "Surfin' Safari" By the Beach Boys • Beach
   Boys / Ray Anthony (Capitol PRO-2185/PRO-2186) 1962 $1,200
   EP. Earliest promotional Beach Boys record. Side 1 has two selections from Ray Anthony's *I
   Almost Lost My Mind* album. Side 2 has *Ten Little Indians* and *Little Miss America*, both from the
   Beach Boys' *Surfin' Safari* LP. Issued with a hard cardboard jacket, which pictures the *Surfin'
   Safari* LP cover on one side and the Ray Anthony LP on the other. Like most Capitol promotional
   albums, this one is numbered by side rather than by disc. The Ray Anthony side is PRO-2185,
   the Beach Boys side is PRO-2186. Near-mint price range: $800 to $1,200.
   Top 1,000 ranking: 539

BEATLES

Yesterday and Today • Beatles (Capitol ST-2553) 1966 $25,000
   Stereo LP. The words "New Improved Full Dimensional Stereo" appear in a gray banner at the
   top of the front cover. Cover pictures group wearing butcher smocks and garnished with cuts of
   meat and pieces of toy dolls. Commonly referred to as the "Butcher Cover." After distributing
   copies to the media, Capitol sent recipients a recall letter, requesting they return their albums.
   Aware they had a valuable collectible in their possession, many kept them. Capitol pasted new
   covers – picturing the Beatles and a trunk – over the Butcher Covers. Original issues, without
   any modifications, are known as "First State" copies. Cover shows title as *Yesterday And Today,*
   whereas label reads: *"Yesterday" ... And Today.* Price range of $24,000 to $25,000 is for copies
   still in original plastic shrink wrap, primarily copies from the Alan Livingston collection. As of
   press time, three still-sealed "Livingston" copies have each sold for exactly $25,000.
   Top 1,000 ranking: 1
My Bonnie/The Saints • Tony Sheridan & Beat Brothers (Decca 31382) 1962 $15,000
   45 rpm. Price is for commercial issues only. Has Decca's black label with silver print and a multi-
   color stripe across the center of the label. Selection number is printed in the color bar area or
   black area of the label. Black and silver Decca labels without the other colors are counterfeits.
   This is the first appearance of the Beatles – then billed as the Beat Brothers – on a record in the
   U.S. Since Decca quickly lost interest in promoting this release, commercial discs are much
   rarer than promos. Near-mint price range: $12,000 to $15,000.
   Top 1,000 ranking: 5
Introducing the Beatles • Beatles (Vee-Jay SR-1062) 1964 $15,000
   Stereo LP. With *Love Me Do* and *P.S. I Love You.* Back cover lists contents. Oval style label
   logo. Near-mint price range: $10,000 to $15,000.
   Top 1,000 ranking: 7
Anna/Ask Me Why • Beatles (Vee-Jay 8)... 1964 $15,000
   45 rpm. Promotional issue only. White and blue label. Promotes the Vee-Jay EP *Souvenir of
   Their Visit to America.* Used as part of a failed attempt to lower EP prices to that of singles
   (cover reads: "an EP that is selling like a single ... at single record prices"). Near-mint price
   range: $10,000 to $15,000.
   Top 1,000 ranking: 8
A Hard Day's Night • Beatles (United Artists UAS-6366) 1964 $12,000
   Stereo LP. Pink vinyl. Original black label with silver print. Purpose of this disc is not yet known.
   Near-mint price range: $10,000 to $12,000.
   Top 1,000 ranking: 12
Hear the Beatles Tell All • Beatles (Vee-Jay PRO-202)................................. 1964 $10,000
   Monaural LP. Promotional issue. White label with blue print. Label reads "Promotional" on left
   and "Not For Sale" on right. Contains interviews with the group. Only two known copies verified.
   Near-mint price range: $8,000 to $10,000.
   Top 1,000 ranking: 20

804.

808.

805.

809.

Yesterday and Today • Beatles (Capitol ST-2553) 1966 $10,000

     Stereo LP. The words "New Improved Full Dimensional Stereo" appear in a gray banner at the top of the front cover. Cover pictures group wearing butcher smocks and garnished with cuts of meat and pieces of toy dolls. Commonly referred to as the "Butcher Cover." After distributing copies to the media, Capitol sent recipients a recall letter, requesting they return their albums. Aware they had a valuable collectible in their possession, many kept them. Capitol pasted new covers – picturing the Beatles and a trunk – over the Butcher Covers. Original issues, without any modifications, are known as "First State" copies. Cover shows title as *Yesterday And Today*, whereas label reads: *"Yesterday" ... And Today*. Price range of $7,500 to $10,000 is for copies that have been opened.
     Top 1,000 ranking: 21

The Beatles and Frank Ifield on Stage • Beatles & Frank Ifield
(Vee-Jay LPS-1085)... 1964 $9,000

     Stereo LP. Front cover has a painted portrait of the Beatles. Issued for a very short time to replace British statesman with Beatles' wig cover. Label variations may affect value. Near-mint price range: $8,000 to $9,000.
     Top 1,000 ranking: 24

Ask Me Why • Beatles (Vee-Jay VJEP 1-903)... 1964 $8,500

     EP and promotional title sleeve. Same number as Vee-Jay EP *Souvenir of Their Visit to America*. Issued with a limited number of copies of the promotional EP. Came with the large print *Ask Me Why* version of the promotional EP. Used as part of a failed attempt to lower EP prices to that of singles (cover reads: "an EP that is selling like a single ... at single record prices"). Approximately 95% of the value is for the paper sleeve. Near-mint price range: $7,500 to $8,500.
     Top 1,000 ranking: 25

Introducing the Beatles • Beatles (Vee-Jay SR-1062) 1963 $8,000

     Stereo LP. Black label with circular colorband and oval logo. With *Love Me Do* and *P.S. I Love You* (on later issues these tracks are replaced by *Ask Me Why* and *Please Please Me*). Back cover pictures 25 other Vee-Jay albums (known as "Ad back" cover). Has "Printed In U.S.A." at lower left of front cover (counterfeits lack this print). Front cover also has "Stereophonic" in gray print across a white banner at top. Price range for cover only: $4,000 to $5,000. Cover and disc: $7,000 to $8,000.
     Top 1,000 ranking: 27

Introducing the Beatles • Beatles (Vee-Jay SR-1062) 1964 $5,000

     Stereo LP. Black label with circular colorband and brackets logo. With *Please Please Me* and *Ask Me Why*. Back cover lists song titles in two large columns. Five cover variations exist of the stereo issue. Near-mint price range: $2,500 to $5,000.
     Top 1,000 ranking: 65

Introducing the Beatles • Beatles (Vee-Jay SR-1062) 1963 $4,000

     Stereo LP. Black label with circular colorband and oval logo. With *Love Me Do* and *P.S. I Love You* (on later issues these tracks are replaced by *Ask Me Why* and *Please Please Me*). Back cover is blank. Front cover has "Stereophonic" in gray print across a white banner at top. Label has the word "Stereo" on top or on the side. Label has the word "Stereo" on top or on the side. Near-mint price range: $3,000 to $4,000.
     Top 1,000 ranking: 93

Introducing the Beatles • Beatles (Vee-Jay SR-1062) 1964 $3,000

     Stereo LP. With *Love Me Do* and *P.S. I Love You* listed on cover and disc, but actually plays *Ask Me Why* and *Please Please Me*. Near-mint price range: $2,500 to $3,000.
     Top 1,000 ranking: 169

The Beatles and Frank Ifield on Stage • Beatles & Frank Ifield
(Vee-Jay LP-1085).. 1964 $3,000

     Monaural LP. Front cover has a painted portrait of the Beatles. Issued for a very short time to replace British statesman with Beatles' wig cover. Label variations may affect value. Near-mint price range: $2,500 to $3,000.
     Top 1,000 ranking: 170

The Beatles Introduce New Songs • Beatles (Capitol PRO-2720/2721)........ 1964 $3,000

     EP. Promotional issue only. Burgundy label. Has John Lennon and Paul McCartney giving introductory and closing comments for two new Capitol acts – Cilla Black and Peter & Gordon – who perform Lennon-McCartney songs. Known counterfeit does not have machine stamped asterisk in the vinyl trail-off area. Near-mint price range: $2,500 to $3,000.
     Top 1,000 ranking: 171

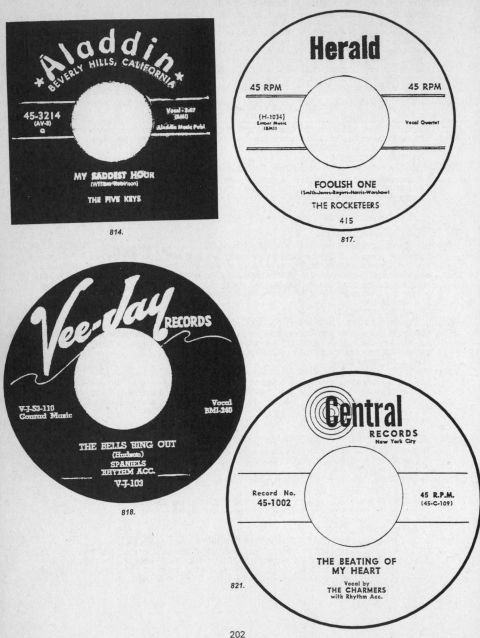

814.

817.

818.

821.

United Artists Presents *Help!* (Interview) • Beatles (United
Artists UA-Help Show) 1965 $3,000
> LP. Promotional issue only. Single-sided disc. Blue label with black print. Open-end interview
> (29:50) with the Beatles about the film. Price includes script which represents about $75 to $100
> of the value. Near-mint price range: $2,500 to $3,000.
> *Top 1,000 ranking: 174*

Yesterday and Today • Beatles (Capitol T-2553)......................... 1966 $3,000
> Monaural LP. Cover pictures group wearing butcher smocks and garnished with cuts of meat
> and pieces of toy dolls. Commonly referred to as the "Butcher Cover." After distributing copies to
> the media, Capitol sent recipients a recall letter, requesting they return their albums. Aware they
> had a valuable collectible in their possession, many kept them. Capitol pasted new covers –
> picturing the Beatles and a trunk – over the Butcher Covers. Original issues, without any
> modifications, are known as "First State" copies. Cover shows title as *Yesterday And Today,*
> whereas label reads: *"Yesterday" ... And Today.* Near-mint price range: $2,000 to $3,000.
> *Top 1,000 ranking: 175*

My Bonnie/The Saints • Tony Sheridan & Beat Brothers (Decca 31382) 1962 $2,500
> 45 rpm. Promotional issue only. Pink label with black lettering. All Decca pink labels are
> promotional. Known counterfeits have *My Bonnie* on both sides. This is the first appearance of
> the Beatles – then billed as the Beat Brothers – on a record in the U.S. Near-mint price range:
> $2,000 to $2,500.
> *Top 1,000 ranking: 201*

Introducing the Beatles • Beatles (Vee-Jay LP-1062).................... 1963 $2,500
> Monaural LP. Black label with circular colorband and oval logo. With *Love Me Do* and *P.S. I
> Love You* (on later issues these tracks are replaced by *Ask Me Why* and *Please Please Me*).
> Back cover pictures 25 other Vee-Jay albums (known as "Ad back" cover). Has "Printed In
> U.S.A." at lower left of front cover (counterfeits lack this). Price range for cover only: $1,400 to
> $1,600. Cover and disc: $2,000 to $2,500.
> *Top 1,000 ranking: 202*

Please Please Me/From Me to You • Beatles (Vee-Jay VJ-581) 1964 $2,500
> Picture sleeve. Promotional issue only. Reads "The Record That Started Beatlemania" across
> top. Does not picture the group. Reads: "(Promotion Copy)." Near-mint price range: $2,000 to
> $2,500.
> *Top 1,000 ranking: 203*

I Want to Hold Your Hand/I Saw Her Standing There • Beatles
(Capitol 5112).. 1964 $2,500
> Picture sleeve. Promotional issue only distributed in New York by radio station WMCA. Front
> side of this sleeve is identical to standard commercial issue. Back pictures six WMCA dee jays.
> Contained a commercial copy of the single. Near-mint price range: $2,000 to $2,500.
> *Top 1,000 ranking: 204*

A Hard Day's Night • Beatles (United Artists UAEP-10029)........................... 1964 $2,500
> 45 rpm. Promotional issue only. White label. Open-end interview for movie promotion. Made for
> radio station use. Record has small play hole. Near-mint price range: $2,000 to $2,500.
> *Top 1,000 ranking: 205*

A Hard Day's Night • Beatles (United Artists UAL-3366) 1964 $2,500
> Monaural LP. White label. Promotional issue only. Label reads "Not For Sale." Issued in either a
> standard mono cover or one with a black promo stamp. Near-mint price range: $2,000 to $2,500.
> *Top 1,000 ranking: 206*

Surprise Gift from the Beatles, Beach Boys and the Kingston Trio
(Eva-Tone 8464) 1964 $2,500
> Flexi-disc and mailer/sleeve. Mailer/sleeve is 9½" x 6" with black and red lettering, and black-
> and-white photo of each Beatle. Reads: "A Beatles Record Free" on the front and "Free Beatles
> Record Inside" on back. Issued with black vinyl, 5" flexi-disc with white print. Disc price: ?. Price
> range for mailer/sleeve: $2,000 to $2,500.
> *Top 1,000 ranking: 207*

Beatles Vs. the Four Seasons • Beatles & 4 Seasons (Vee-Jay DXS-30)..... 1964 $2,500
> Stereo LP. Double LP with gatefold cover. Cover and disc labels have the print "Stereo."
> Repackage set combining two previously released Vee-Jay albums: *Introducing the Beatles*
> (Vee-Jay 1062) and *The Golden Hits of the Four Seasons* (Vee-Jay 1065). Many copies include
> an 11½" x 23" color poster, valued separately at $150 to $200. Price range for discs and cover:
> $2,000 to $2,500.
> *Top 1,000 ranking: 208*

flair
RECORDS

BMI
Flair Pub. Co.
(FL-204)

45x1051
Vocal
Group

MY HEART'S CRYING FOR YOU
(Gunter)

THE CHIMES

822.

THE CAPITOL STORY

THE CAPITOL TOWER
September 27, 1954

Capitol

THE CAPITOL RECORD
Part 1

830.

Lucky
RECORDS HOLLYWOOD

45-006
006-B
Publisher:
Golden State
Songs-BMI
Time: 2:04

Group
Vocal

PEGGY
(Gaynel Hodge)

THE HOLLYWOOD FLAMES

824.

ROYAL ROOST
"Music of the Future"

1164
Rockaway (BMI)

DEAREST DARLING
(T. Woods)

THE CHIMES

833.   577

M-G-M

45 R.P.M.

K55004
54-XY-463

CHERIE
(Atkins-Kirkland)
THE HIDE-A-WAYS
With Instrumental Accompaniment

M.G.M RECORDS—A DIVISION OF LOEW'S INCORPORATED—Made in U.S.A.

834.

204

Introducing the Beatles • Beatles (Vee-Jay SR-1062) 1964 $2,200
Stereo LP. With *Ask Me Why* and *Please Please Me*. Includes any of the label or logo designs.
Price range $2,000 to $2,200.
Top 1,000 ranking: 218

Songs, Pictures and Stories of the Fabulous Beatles • Beatles
(Vee-Jay VJS-1092) 1964 $2,200
Stereo LP. Single disc in gatefold cover of which front is two-third's full width. Disc is actually
Introducing the Beatles (Vee-Jay VJ-1062). Some covers have a sticker/banner from any one of
several of the Beatles U.S. concerts. Add $200 for those. Logo variations may affect price by as
much as $200. Near-mint price range: $2,000 to $2,200.
Top 1,000 ranking: 219

Please Please Me/Ask Me Why • Beatles (Vee-Jay VJ-498) 1963 $2,000
45 rpm. Credits "BEATLES." Black label with colorband. Has thick lettering and the VJ in
brackets logo. Near-mint price range: $1,000 to $2,000.
Top 1,000 ranking: 350

The Beatles Talking/You Can't Do That • Beatles (Capitol Custom 2637) 1964 $2,000
45 rpm single (red label) and promotional sleeve. Available briefly from radio station KFWB and
Wallich's Music City stores to celebrate the grand opening of a new location. Side 1 has
interviews; side 2 is a song. Known counterfeit record does not have the Capitol logo. Title
sleeve/mailer is a manila 7¼" square envelope with red print. Known counterfeit sleeve has a
smaller opening flap, about 1½." Original is slightly over 2." Record alone: $800 to $1,000.
Record and sleeve: $1,000 to $2,000.
Top 1,000 ranking: 356

Open End Interview • Beatles (Capitol Compact 33 PRO-2548/49) 1964 $2,000
EP and picture insert sheet with script on back. Promotional issue only. Black label with
colorband. Made to promote the *Meet the Beatles* LP. Has several tracks from LP plus an
interview. Label reads "Especially prepared for Radio and TV programming Not For Sale."
Known counterfeit sleeve lacks the gloss and die cut thumb tab that is on top of one side of the original.
(Picture sleeve/script alone: $700 to $800.) Near-mint price range: $1,000 to $2,000.
Top 1,000 ranking: 357

We Can Work It Out/Day Tripper • Beatles (Capitol/Starline 5555) 1969 $2,000
45 rpm. Red and white label. "Starline" series. This is the only U.S. Beatles single with this label
style. Discontinued shortly after production when it Capitol learned the label was not correct for
the title. Near-mint price range: $1,500 to $2,000.
Top 1,000 ranking: 364

Please Please Me/Ask Me Why • Beatles (Vee-Jay VJ-498) 1963 $1,800
45 rpm. Credits "BEATTLES." Black label with colorband. Has thin lettering and oval logo. The
number symbol (#) precedes the selection number on the label. Near-mint price range: $1,500 to
$1,800.
Top 1,000 ranking: 378

Please Please Me/Ask Me Why • Beatles (Vee-Jay VJ-498) 1963 $1,800
45 rpm. Credits "BEATLES." Black label with colorband. Has thin lettering and oval logo. The
number symbol (#) precedes the selection number. Near-mint price range: $1,500 to $1,800.
Top 1,000 ranking: 379

Second Open End Interview • Beatles (Capitol Compact 33 PRO-2598/99) . 1964 $1,800
EP and picture insert sheet with script on back. Promotional issue only. Issued to promote *The
Beatles Second Album*. Has three tracks from LP plus an interview. Label reads "Especially
prepared for Radio and TV programming Not For Sale." Picture sleeve has the interview script.
(Picture sleeve/script alone: $600 to $700.) Near-mint price range: $1,500 to $1,800.
Top 1,000 ranking: 380

Yellow Submarine/Eleanor Rigby • Beatles (Apple/Americom) 1969 $1,800
Selection number not known. Round 4" flexi-disc. Light blue vinyl with white print. Available in
special vending machines. Near-mint price range: $1,500 to $1,800.
Top 1,000 ranking: 381

Please Please Me/Ask Me Why • Beatles (Vee-Jay VJ-498) 1963 $1,600
45 rpm. Credits "BEATTLES." Black label with colorband. Has thin lettering and oval logo. This
is the first Beatles single released in the U.S. Near-mint price range: $1,400 to $1,600.
Top 1,000 ranking: 388

Something New • Beatles (Capitol Compact 33 SXA-2180) 1964 $1,500
Compact 33 EP. Black label with colorband. Stereo only. Made for use in jukeboxes. Has six
tracks from the LP. Issued with hard cover. Front cover has same photo as LP, back is blank.
Includes juke box inserts. Near-mint price range: $1,000 to $1,500.
Top 1,000 ranking: 470

45-73-AA
Combo Mus. Pub.
B.M.I.

Time 2:43

ARLINE
STARLITERS
with
Jonesy's Combo

838.

GOTHAM
RECORD CORP., PHILA., PA.

G-7-312

Pub:
Andrea Music
SESAC

ARE YOU SORRY?
(Johnson)
THE WHISPERS

839.

CAROLINE
RECORDS

CR. 2201

Vocal
Time 2:08

THIS IS MY PLEA
(O'Neal)
THE CELEBRITYS
45X2301

841.

CAROLINE
RECORDS

CR. 2203

Vocal
Time 2:30

WE MADE ROMANCE
(Howard)
CLAY HAMMOND & JOHNNIE YOUNG
and
THE CELEBRITYS
45X2302

843.

206

The Savage Young Beatles • Beatles (Savage BM-69)................................. 1964 $1,500
 Monaural LP. Yellow label. Has a glossy orange front cover. Back cover shows address of
 Savage Records. Includes four songs by the Beatles with Tony Sheridan, and four by just Tony
 Sheridan. Near-mint price range: $1,000 to $1,500.
 Top 1,000 ranking: 471

Please Please Me/Ask Me Why • Beatles (Vee-Jay VJ-498)........................ 1963 $1,400
 45 rpm. Credits "BEATTLES." Black label with colorband. Has thick lettering and oval logo.
 Near-mint price range: $1,000 to $1,400.
 Top 1,000 ranking: 488

Yesterday and Today • Beatles (Capitol ST-2553) 1966 $1,300
 Stereo LP. The words "New Improved Full Dimensional Stereo" are at the top of front cover.
 "Paste-over" or "peeled" covers. The paste-over version has a photo of the Beatles around a
 trunk pasted over an intact "butcher cover." The peeled version shows the "butcher cover" after
 the trunk photo cover has been peeled off. Removing the slick can be a difficult and risky
 process; however, there are professionals who offer this service. Cover shows title as *Yesterday
 And Today,* whereas label reads: *"Yesterday" ... And Today.* Near-mint price range: $1,000 to
 $1,300.
 Top 1,000 ranking: 495

Please Please Me/Ask Me Why • Beatles (Vee-Jay VJ-498)........................ 1963 $1,200
 45 rpm. Credits "BEATLES." Black label with colorband. Has thick lettering and oval logo. The
 letters "VJ" precede the selection number. Near-mint price range: $800 to $1,200.
 Top 1,000 ranking: 541

Please Please Me/Ask Me Why • Beatles (Vee-Jay VJ-498)........................ 1963 $1,200
 45 rpm. Credits "BEATTLES." White label with oval logo. Label reads: "Disc Jockey Advance
 Sample Not For Sale." Near-mint price range: $800 to $1,200.
 Top 1,000 ranking: 542

Introducing the Beatles • Beatles (Vee-Jay LP-1062)................................... 1964 $1,200
 Monaural LP. Black label, no circular colorband, brackets logo. With *Ask Me Why* and *Please
 Please Me.* Add $50 to $75 if with a "Featuring Twist and Shout" and "Please Please Me"
 sticker.) Near-mint price range: $800 to $1,200.
 Top 1,000 ranking: 543

Meet the Beatles • Beatles (Capitol Compact 33 SXA-2047) 1964 $1,200
 Compact 33 EP. Black label with colorband. Stereo only. Made for use in juke boxes. Has six
 tracks from the LP. Issued with hard cover. Front cover has same photo as LP; back is blank.
 Includes juke box inserts. Near-mint price range: $800 to $1,200.
 Top 1,000 ranking: 544

Beatles' Second Album • Beatles (Capitol Compact 33 SXA-2080) 1964 $1,200
 Compact 33 EP. Black label with colorband. Stereo only. Made for use in jukeboxes. Has six
 tracks from the LP. Issued with hard cover. Front cover has same photo as LP; back is blank.
 Includes juke box inserts. Near-mint price range: $800 to $1,200.
 Top 1,000 ranking: 545

United Artists Presents *A Hard Day's Night* • Beatles (United
 Artists 2359/60).. 1964 $1,200
 LP. Promotional issue only. Red label. Open-end interview about the film. Issued with a 12-page
 script and programming information, which represents about $75 to $100 of the value. Near-mint
 price range: $800 to $1,200.
 Top 1,000 ranking: 546

Beatlemania Tour Coverage • Beatles (I-N-S Radio News DOC-1)................ 1964 $1,200
 LP. Promotional issue only. An open-end interview. Issued in a plain white cover with a one-
 page interview script. Near-mint price range: $800 to $1,200.
 Top 1,000 ranking: 547

United Artists Presents *Help!* (Interview) • Beatles (United
 Artists UA-Help Int) 1965 $1,200
 LP. Promotional issue only. Red label with black print. Open-end interview with the Beatles and
 others about the film. Price includes script and programming information, which represents
 about $75 to $100 of the value. Near-mint price range: $800 to $1,200.
 Top 1,000 ranking: 549

849.

My Secret Love

(Eddie Carter-Issy Shairerman)

THE CARTER RAYS

850.

There's No Return From Love

(George Weiss-Ray Rivera)

TEDDY LAWSON
AND THE LAWSON BOYS

853.

855.

Beatles Special Limited Edition • Beatles (Apple).. 1974 $1,200
Boxed 10-LP set. Includes Apple label copies of the following LPs: ST-2047 *Meet the Beatles*, ST-2108 *Something New*, ST-2228 *Beatles '65*, ST-2309 *Early Beatles*, ST-2442 *Rubber Soul*, ST-2576 *Revolver*, SMAS-2653 *Sgt. Pepper's Lonely Hearts Club Band*, SMAL-2835 *Magical Mystery Tour*, SO-383 *Abbey Road*, SW-385 *Hey Jude*. Box is black with silver foil title print on one side. Price range for complete set: $800 to $1,200.
Top 1,000 ranking: 556

Introducing the Beatles • Beatles (Vee-Jay LP-1062).................................... 1963 $1,100
Monaural LP. Black label with circular colorband and oval logo. With *Love Me Do* and *P.S. I Love You* (on later issues these tracks are replaced by *Ask Me Why* and *Please Please Me*). Back cover is blank. Has "Printed In U.S.A." at lower left of front cover (counterfeits lack this print). Near-mint price range: $800 to $1,100.
Top 1,000 ranking: 559

Beatles Vs. the Four Seasons • Beatles & 4 Seasons (Vee-Jay DX-30)....... 1964 $1,100
Monaural LP. Double LP with gatefold cover. Repackage set combining two previously released Vee-Jay albums: *Introducing the Beatles* (Vee-Jay 1062) and *The Golden Hits of the Four Seasons* (Vee-Jay 1065). Many copies include an 11½ " x 23" color poster, valued separately at $150 to $200. Price range for discs and cover: $800 to $1,100.
Top 1,000 ranking: 561

From Me to You/Thank You Girl • Beatles (Vee-Jay VJ-522) 1963 $1,000
45 rpm. Black label with colorband and brackets logo. Near-mint price range: $900 to $1,000.
Top 1,000 ranking: 710

From Me to You/Thank You Girl • Beatles (Vee-Jay VJ-522) 1963 $1,000
45 rpm. Black label with colorband and oval logo. Thin style print. Near-mint price range: $900 to $1,000.
Top 1,000 ranking: 711

A Surprise Gift from Your Holiday Innkeeper • Beatles (Capitol/
Holiday Inn)... 1964 $1,000
Promotional sleeve/flyer. Yellow paper stock with green print. Pictures the Beatles on front and their first three Capitol LPs on the back. Given gratis to Holiday Inn guests. Flyer either folded around, stapled to, or inserted in commercial copies of early Capitol Beatles singles. Near-mint price range: $750 to $1,000.
Top 1,000 ranking: 722

Ain't She Sweet • Beatles & Swallows (Atco 33-169) 1964 $1,000
Monaural LP. Promotional issue. White label with black print. Label reads "Sample Copy – Not For Sale." Labels and covers on promos do not have "with Tony Sheridan" printed. Has standard commercial cover. Four tracks by the Beatles with Tony Sheridan, and eight tracks by the Swallows. Near-mint price range: $750 to $1,000.
Top 1,000 ranking: 723

A Hard Day's Night • Beatles (United Artists T-90828) 1964 $1,000
Monaural LP. Capitol Record Club issue. Label has "Mfd. By Capitol Records." This is the only verified mono record club issue of a Beatles LP. Near-mint price range: $750 to $1,000.
Top 1,000 ranking: 724

Get Back/Don't Let Me Down • Beatles (Apple/Americom 2490/M-335)........ 1969 $1,000
Round 4" flexi-disc. Black vinyl with white print. Available in special vending machines. Near-mint price range: $750 to $1,000.
Top 1,000 ranking: 736

From Me to You/Thank You Girl • Beatles (Vee-Jay VJ-522) 1963 $900
45 rpm. Black label with brackets logo and thick horizontal silver lines. Near-mint price range: $700 to $900.
Top 1,000 ranking: 758

Please Please Me/From Me to You • Beatles (Vee-Jay VJ-581) 1964 $900
45 rpm. Promotional issue. Blue and white label. "Promotional Copy" print is not shown on label. Near-mint price range: $700 to $900.
Top 1,000 ranking: 759

Introducing the Beatles • Beatles (Vee-Jay LP-1062).................................... 1964 $900
Monaural LP. Black label with circular colorband and brackets logo. With *Love Me Do* and *P.S. I Love You* (on later issues these tracks are replaced by *Ask Me Why* and *Please Please Me*). Back cover lists song titles in two large columns. Near-mint price range: $700 to $900.
Top 1,000 ranking: 760

REAL
45 R.P.M.
Real-American
'BMI) & CCC Mns.
(BMI) 2:01
1320-x
WOULD YOU
(E. Waller)
JULES SAVOY
Singing Discovery of Hesperia Inn
Hesperia, Calif.
THE CHROMATICS
REAL RECORD CO., PASADENA 3, CALIFORNIA
856.

CASINO
Spinmill Music &
G & H Music
BMI
ML-452
(ML-1003)
Time-2.52
HB-147
TRY THE IMPOSSIBLE
(Curry - Gordon)
LEE ANDREWS AND THE HEARTS
Pancho Villa Orch.
CASINO RECORDS and MANUFACTURING CORP. PHILA., PENNA.
858.

SPINKS
MUSIC COMPANY
SPINKS MUSIC PUB. & RECORDING CO.
AFFILIATED   WITH BMI
45-600-A
(Recorded by Ruben
Siggers and His
Fabulous Kool Kats)
45—600
Vocal By
Ephraim
Siggers
THOSE LOVE ME BLUES
RUBEN SIGGERS
AND HIS FABULOUS KOOL KATS
857.

SCATT
RECORDS
BRONX, N. Y.
UNBREAKABLE
45 R.P.M.
RECORD NO.
SCATT
S-111
Time 2:26
Zell's Music
DARLING IF I HAD YOU
(Zell Sanders)
CALIPHS
859.

The Beatles with Tony Sheridan and Guests • Beatles and Others
(MGM SE-4215) 1964 $800
> Stereo LP. Front cover does *not* have the words "And Others" at the lower left under the song title *Why*. Has four tracks by the Beatles with Tony Sheridan, and six tracks by the Titans. Near-mint price range: $600 to $800.
> *Top 1,000 ranking: 788*

Introducing the Beatles • Beatles (Vee-Jay LP-1062) 1964 $800
> Monaural LP. Black label with circular colorband and oval logo. With *Love Me Do* and *P.S. I Love You* (on later issues these tracks are replaced by *Ask Me Why* and *Please Please Me*). Back cover lists song titles in two large columns. Near-mint price range: $600 to $800.
> *Top 1,000 ranking: 789*

Ballad of John and Yoko/Old Brown Shoe • Beatles (Apple/
Americom 2531/M-382) 1969 $800
> Round 4" flexi-disc. Black vinyl with white print. Available in special vending machines. Near-mint price range: $600 to $800.
> *Top 1,000 ranking: 791*

She Loves You/I'll Get You • Beatles (Swan 4152) 1963 $750
> 45 rpm. Flat (not glossy) white label with red or print. The words "Don't Drop Out" are not on the label. Uses boldface type style. Song titles have quotation marks. Near-mint price range: $650 to $750.
> *Top 1,000 ranking: 912*

She Loves You/I'll Get You • Beatles (Swan 4152) 1963 $750
> 45 rpm. Glossy white label with red print. The words "Don't Drop Out" are on the label. Can be found with or without "Produced by George Martin." Near-mint price range: $500 to $750.
> *Top 1,000 ranking: 913*

She Loves You/I'll Get You • Beatles (Swan 4152) 1963 $750
> 45 rpm. Glossy white label with blue print. The words "Don't Drop Out" are on the label. Near-mint price range: $500 to $750.
> *Top 1,000 ranking: 914*

Do You Want to Know a Secret/Thank You Girl • Beatles (Vee-Jay 587) 1964 $750
> 45 rpm. Promotional issue. White and blue label with brackets logo. Label reads: "Promotional copy." A-side title printed on either two or three lines. Near-mint price range: $500 to $750.
> *Top 1,000 ranking: 925*

Great American Tour, 1965 Live Beatlemania Concert • Beatles
(Lloyds AG-8146) 1965 $700
> LP. Live tracks by the Beatles, with overdubbing by another band – The Liverpool Lads resulting in an overall poor quality product. Near-mint price range: $500 to $700.
> *Top 1,000 ranking: 966*

Yesterday and Today • Beatles (Capitol ST-2553) 1966 $700
> Monaural LP. "Paste-over" or "peeled" covers. The paste-over version has a photo of the Beatles around a trunk pasted over an intact "butcher cover." The peeled version shows the "butcher cover" after the trunk photo cover has been peeled off. Removing the slick can be a difficult and risky process; however, there are professionals who offer this service. Near-mint price range: $500 to $700.
> *Top 1,000 ranking: 967*

Can't Buy Me Love/You Can't Do That • Beatles (Capitol 5150) 1964 $650
> Picture sleeve. Issued only with a straight cut across the top of the sleeve. Known counterfeit has noticeably inferior quality photos and print. Photo on one known fake is too large to include the top of George's head – same as used on some of the die cut versions of the *I Want to Hold Your Hand* picture sleeve. Another fake includes George's full head, but is of poor quality and uses the wrong paper stock. It is helpful to have an original to determine authenticity. Near-mint price range: $500 to $650.
> *Top 1,000 ranking: 998*

BEATNICKS

Blue Angel/Shakie Mae • Beatnicks (Key-Lock 913) 1960 $1,000
> 45 rpm. Near-mint price range: $750 to $1,000.
> *Top 1,000 ranking: 680*

BEES

I Want to Be Loved/Get Away Baby • Bees (Imperial 5320) 1954 $2,000
> 45 rpm. Near-mint price range: $1,000 to $2,000.
> *Top 1,000 ranking: 262*

★ ★ ★
TRIPLE X
RECORDS
271 W. 125th St., N. Y. C.

45 RPM   45 RPM

3X-100A
Triple X Pub.
Co., Inc.
(BMI) 2:40

PLEASE DON'T CRUSH MY DREAMS
(M. Allen-S. Hodge)

THE EMERALS

860.

Vee-Jay RECORDS

SG-1031
Vocal

Time 2:05
Tollie-BMI

WISH I WAS BACK IN SCHOOL
(L. Denham, H. Burnett & C. Carter)

THE GOLDENRODS
VJ 307

861.

THAT'LL BE THE DAY BUDDY HOLLY

862.

JACY
RECORDS

P. O. Box 162   Oakland 3, Calif.

H. Roundtree
Music Publ.
BMI 2:45

45 RPM
J-001-A
VOCAL

SO LONG
(Foreman - Candy's)

THE PIPES

863.

SCOTT
RECORDS

UNBREAKABLE
45 R.P.M.

RECORD NO.
1205
(202)

Sherlyn - Pent
(BMI)

DON'T EVER LEAVE ME
(Freeman)

THE PYRAMIDERS

864.

212

BEL-AIRS
Forever Loving You/Hey Little Girl • Bel-Airs (Sara 6431) 1963 $750
     45 rpm. Near-mint price range: $500 to $750.
     Top 1,000 ranking: 915

BELEW, Carl, & Riff Riders
I'm Long Gone/? • Carl Belew & His Riff Riders (Sowder 248) 1957 $1,000
     45 rpm. Near-mint price range: $750 to $1,000.
     Top 1,000 ranking: 637

BEL-LARKS
Get Married in June/Million and One Dreams • Bel-Larks (With Eternals
     Orchestra) (Hammer 6313) 1963 $2,000
     45 rpm. Near-mint price range: $1,000 to $2,000.
     Top 1,000 ranking: 351

BELLS
What Can I Tell Her Now/Let Me Love, Love You • Bells (Rama 166) 1955 $1,500
     45 rpm. Near-mint price range: $1,000 to $1,500.
     Top 1,000 ranking: 420

BELLTONES
Estelle/Promise Love • Belltones (Grand 102).. 1954 $10,000
     45 rpm. Red vinyl. One known copy. Near-mint price range: $7,500 to $10,000.
     Top 1,000 ranking: 14
Estelle/Promise Love • Belltones (Grand 102).. 1954 $4,000
     45 rpm. Black vinyl. Blue or yellow label. Near-mint price range: $3,000 to $4,000.
     Top 1,000 ranking: 75

BENNETT, Boyd
Boyd Bennett • Boyd Bennett (King 594)... 1958 $3,000
     LP. Counterfeits exist. Near-mint price range: $2,500 to $3,000.
     Top 1,000 ranking: 154

BIG ED & HIS COMBO
Biscuit Baking Mama/Superstition • Big Ed & His Combo (Checker 790)...... 1954 $1,000
     45 rpm. Big Ed is blues singer Eddie Burns. Near-mint price range: $750 to $1,000.
     Top 1,000 ranking: 595

BILLBOARDS
With All My Heart/Around the World • Billboards (With Red Julian Orchestra)
     (Vistone 2023).. 1961 $800
     45 rpm. Yellow vinyl. Near-mint price range: $750 to $1,000.
     Top 1,000 ranking: 691

BLAKE, Tommy
Koolit/If I Am a Fool • Tommy Blake (Buddy 107)... 1958 $900
     45 rpm. Near-mint price range: $700 to $900.
     Top 1,000 ranking: 756

BLENDERS
Two Loves/Soda Pop • Blenders (Aladdin 3449) 1959 $2,000
     45 rpm. Near-mint price range: $1,500 to $2,000.
     Top 1,000 ranking: 319

BLUE JAYS
White Cliffs of Dover/Hey Pappa • Blue Jays (Checker 782) 1953 $3,000
     45 rpm. General awareness of this haunting version of *White Cliffs of Dover* increased
     substantially after its use in the film, *The Crying Game*. Near-mint price range: $2,500 to $3,000.
     Top 1,000 ranking: 115

866.

868.

870.

BOB & SHERI
Surfer Moon/Humpty Dumpty • Bob & Sheri (Safari 101) 1961 $800
  45 rpm. Beach Boy Brian Wilson's first record production. Original commercial copies have a
  light blue label; promotional copies a white label. Near-perfect counterfeits exist. Near-mint price
  range: $600 to $800.
  Top 1,000 ranking: 781

BONNER, Lil' Joe, & Idols
Tell Me Baby/Do You Love Me • Lil' Joe Bonner & Idols (With Fabulous Playboys)
 (B&S B-Disc-S 1570) 1955 $1,000
  45 rpm. Near-mint price range: $750 to $1,000.
  Top 1,000 ranking: 614

BONNIE & LITTLE BOYS BLUE
Bells/You'd Better Run • Bonnie & Little Boys Blue (Nikko 611) 1958 $7,000
  45 rpm. One known copy. Near-mint price range: $5,000 to $7,000.
  Top 1,000 ranking: 31

BOW STREET RUNNERS
Bow Street Runners • Bow Street Runners (B.T. Puppy 1026) 1970 $1,000
  LP. Near-mint price range: $750 to $1,000.
  Top 1,000 ranking: 739

BOWIE, David
Diamond Dogs • David Bowie (RCA Victor 0576) 1974 $2,000
  LP. With "Dog Genitals" front cover (picturing, obviously, a dog's genital area). Near-mint price
  range: $1,500 to $2,000.
  Top 1,000 ranking: 370

BOYD, Tim, & Esquires
My Dearest, My Darling (I Miss You)/? • Tim Boyd & Esquires (With Bill Gibbs
 Combo) (Odessa 101)..1960s $1,000
  45 rpm. Near-mint price range: $750 to $1,000.
  Top 1,000 ranking: 738

BRIGADE
Last Laugh • Brigade (Band 'N' Vocal 1066)... 1970 $2,000
  LP. Reissues exist on both Del Val and Rockadelic. Near-mint price range: $1,500 to $2,000.
  Top 1,000 ranking: 367

BROOKS, Dusty, & Four Tones
Heaven Or Fire/Tears and Wine • Dusty Brooks & Four Tones (Featuring Juanita
 Brown) (Sun 182) 1953 $1,500
  45 rpm. Near-mint price range: $1,000 to $1,500.
  Top 1,000 ranking: 402

BROWN, Charles
Mood Music • Charles Brown (Aladdin 702) 1952 $3,000
  10-inch LP. Red vinyl. Near-mint price range: $2,000 to $3,000.
  Top 1,000 ranking: 113

BRYANT, Jay Dee
I Won't Be Coming Back/? • Jay Dee Bryant (Shrine 108)............................. 1966 $5,000
  45 rpm. Near-mint price range: $3,000 to $5,000.
  Top 1,000 ranking: 66

BUCCANEERS
The Stars Will Remember/Come Back My Love • Buccaneers (Rama 21).... 1953 $4,000
  45 rpm. Near-mint price range: $3,000 to $4,000.
  Top 1,000 ranking: 73

SCEPTER

1674 BROADWAY, N. Y. C.

45 RPM   45 RPM

1204
Scepter Music
(BMI) 2:00   Vocal

HASTEN JASON
(Galante-Galante-Pointe-Acosta)

THE SINGING
ROULETTES

874.

RCA VICTOR

OCTOBER CHRISTMAS SAMPLER 59-40-41

SPS
33-54   SIDE 1
K2NY-548   HOT FOR
SALE

1—BLUE CHRISTMAS (LPM-1951)
2—HAVE YOURSELF A MERRY LITTLE CHRISTMAS
(LPM-2006) 3—WHITE CHRISTMAS (LSP-2023)
4—BLUE CHRISTMAS (LSP-2032)
5—WINTER WONDERLAND (LSP-2044)
6 & 7—SANTA CLAUS IS COMIN' TO TOWN
(LSP-2054) (LSP-2063)
1. Presley 2. MacKenzie 3. Klein
4. Esquivel 5. Melachrino
6. Three Suns
7. R. Hunter Cho.

LIVING STEREO

877.

FROM THE SOUND TRACK
OF THE HAL ROACH PRODUCTION
"GO, JOHNNY, GO!"

1. MY LOVE IS STRONG - Jimmy Clanton
Ace Records (Ace & Figure - BMI)
2. ONCE AGAIN - Jimmy Clanton-Sandy Stewart
(duet not recorded) (Figure - BMI)

SAMPLE COPY   NOT FOR SALE
SIDE 1   LONG PLAYING
33⅓ RPM   MICROGROOVE

3. ANGEL FACE - Jimmy Clanton
Ace Records (Ace & Figure - BMI)
4. YOU'D BETTER KNOW IT - Jackie Wilson
Brunswick Records (Pearl - BMI)
5. GO, JOHNNY GO! - Chuck Berry
Chess Records (ARC - BMI)
6. JAY WALKER - The Cadillacs
Jubilee Records (Figure - BMI)
7. JUMP CHILDREN - The Flamingos
(JONI - BMI)
8. HEAVENLY FATHER - Sandy Stewart
Atco Records (Benell - BMI)
9. MEMPHIS, TENNESSEE
Chuck Berry
Chess Records (ARC - BMI)

880.

RCA VICTOR

NOVEMBER/DECEMBER SAMPLER
59-44 thru 59-47

SPS
33-67   SIDE 2
K2NY-5895   NOT FOR
SALE

1—I BEG OF YOU (LPM-2075) 2—I'M SITTING ON
TOP OF THE WORLD (Except LPM-2083, Side1)
3—CAMP MEETIN' TIME (LSP-2091)
4—AT THE JAZZ BAND BALL (LPM-2007)
5—I KNOW THAT YOU KNOW (LSP-2103)
6—CHA-CON-CHA (LSP-2113)
7—RIFF BLUES (Theme) (LSP-2140)
1. Presley 2. Gardner 3. Wood
4. Dukes of Dixieland
5. Atkins 6. Puento's Orch.
7. Arr and cond by
Martin

LIVING STEREO

878.

From the sound track of the HAL ROACH production

19
NEW
NUMBERS
SUNG
BY A
GALAXY OF
OUTSTANDING
PERFORMERS

"GO, Johnny GO!"

starring ALAN FREED · JIMMY CLANTON · SANDY STEWART · CHUCK BERRY

SPECIAL GUEST ARTISTS
The Late Ritchie VALENS · Jackie WILSON · Eddie COCHRAN · HARVEY of the MOONGLOWS · The CADILLACS · The FLAMINGOS · JoAnn Campbell

NOT FOR SALE

HARVEY AND THE MOONGLOWS
LEE ANDREWS AND THE HEARTS
THE MIRACLES · THE ORCHIDS
CORONETS · THE MOONGLOWS

CHESS LP 1441
High-Fidelity

BUNCH
OF
GOODIES

Ten Commandments Of Love ● When I'm With You ● Long Lonely Nights
Please Send Me Someone To Love ● Teardrops ● In My Diary ● Most Of All
Sincerely ● You're Everything To Me ● We Go Together ● Bad Girl ● Nadine

879.

216

Dear Ruth/Fine Brown Frame • Buccaneers (With Matthew Child & His Drifters) (Southern 100/101) 1953 $3,500
> 45 rpm. Red vinyl. Near-mint price range: $2,500 to $3,500.
> *Top 1,000 ranking: 98*

In the Mission of St. Augustine/You Did Me Wrong • Buccaneers (Rama 24) 1953 $2,000
> 45 rpm. Near-mint price range: $1,000 to $2,000.
> *Top 1,000 ranking: 244*

BURNETTE, Johnny, & Rock'n Roll Trio

Johnny Burnette & Rock'n Roll Trio • Johnny Burnette & Rock'n Roll Trio (Coral 57080) 1956 $2,500
> LP. Counterfeits can be identified by their lack of printing on the spine and hand-etched identification numbers in the trail-off. Originals have the numbers mechanically stamped. Canadian issues are worth at least as much as U.S. issues. Near-mint price range: $2,000 to $2,500.
> *Top 1,000 ranking: 190*

BUTLER, Cliff, & Doves

When You Love/People Will Talk • Cliff Butler & Doves (States 123) 1953 $650
> 45 rpm. Red vinyl. Near-mint price range: $500 to $650.
> *Top 1,000 ranking: 970*

BUTLER, Jerry, & Impressions

For Your Precious Love/Sweet Was the Wine • Jerry Butler & Impressions (Vee-Jay 280) 1958 $4,000
> 45 rpm. Near-mint price range: $3,000 to $4,000.
> *Top 1,000 ranking: 89*

C.A. QUINTET

A Trip Through Hell • C.A. Quintet (Candy Floss 7764) 1968 $2,500
> LP. Near-mint price range: $1,500 to $2,500.
> *Top 1,000 ranking: 211*

CALDWELL, Joe

Guess I'm the Lonely One/Rowdy Mae Is Back in Town • Joe Caldwell (M.C. 1) 1950s $2,000
> 45 rpm. Near-mint price range: $1,500 to $2,000.
> *Top 1,000 ranking: 332*

CALENDARS

If I Could Hold Your Hand/What Are You Gonna Be • Calendars (Cyclone 5012) 1959 $2,000
> 45 rpm. Near-mint price range: $1,000 to $2,000.
> *Top 1,000 ranking: 320*

CALIPHS

Mother Dear/Darling If I Had You • Caliphs (Scatt 111) 1958 $750
> 45 rpm. Near-mint price range: $500 to $750.
> *Top 1,000 ranking: 859*

CALVAES

Fine Girl/Mambo Fiesta • Calvaes (Cobra 5003) 1956 $700
> 45 rpm. Near-mint price range: $500 to $700.
> *Top 1,000 ranking: 955*

CANDLELIGHTERS

Would You Do the Same for Me/At the Soda Shop • Candlelighters (Delta 203) 1958 $2,000
> 45 rpm. Near-mint price range: $1,000 to $2,000.
> *Top 1,000 ranking: 307*

881.

882.

885.

883.

884.

218

CAPES

The Vow/? • Capes (Chat 5005) 1950s $2,000
    45 rpm. Near-mint price range: $1,500 to $2,000.
    Top 1,000 ranking: 333

CAPRIS

There's a Moon Out Tonight/Indian Girl • Capris (Planet 1010) 1960 $1,000
    45 rpm. Near-mint price range: $750 to $1,000.
    Top 1,000 ranking: 681

CARDELLS

Helen/Lovely Girl • Cardells (Featuring Wm. Gardner) (Middle-Tone 011) 1956 $1,200
    45 rpm. Near-mint price range: $800 to $1,200.
    Top 1,000 ranking: 516

CARDINALS

Why Don't You Write Me/Sh-Boom • Cardinals (Rose 835) 1963 $1,500
    45 rpm. Near-mint price range: $1,000 to $1,500.
    Top 1,000 ranking: 467

CARLTON

The Girl I Left Behind/? • Carlton (Penney 1306) 1962 $1,200
    45 rpm. Reissued crediting "Carlton Beck." Near-mint price range: $800 to $1,200.
    Top 1,000 ranking: 540

CARRIBIANS – COLEMAN BROOKS ANDERSON

Wonderland/Baby • Carribians – Coleman Brooks Anderson (Brooks 2000) 1959 $3,000
    45 rpm. At least one source shows the year of release as 1961. We don't know yet which is
    correct. Near-mint price range: $2,000 to $3,000.
    Top 1,000 ranking: 158

CARTER, Eddie, Quartette

Take Everything But You/Cool Whailin Papa • Eddie Carter Quartette
    (Grand 107) 1954 $4,000
    45 rpm. Reissued crediting the Carter Rays. Near-mint price range: $3,000 to $4,000.
    Top 1,000 ranking: 76

CARTER, James

Mean Red Spider/Let Me Be Your Coal Man • James "Sweet Lucy" Carter & His
    Orchestra (20th Century 20-51) 1947 $1,000
    78 rpm. Session includes Muddy Waters. Near-mint price range: $750 to $1,000.
    Top 1,000 ranking: 565

CARTER RAYS

My Secret Love/Ding Dong Daddy • Carter Rays (Lyric 2001) 1957 $750
    45 rpm. Near-mint price range: $500 to $750.
    Top 1,000 ranking: 850

CARVETTES

A Lover's Prayer/Never Gonna Leave Me • Carvettes (Copa 200-1/200-2) .. 1959 $1,200
    45 rpm. Near-mint price range: $800 to $1,200.
    Top 1,000 ranking: 530

CASTELLES

My Girl Awaits Me/Sweetness • Castelles (Grand 101) 1953 $3,000
    45 rpm. Glossy blue label. Reportedly 600 made. Near-mint price range: $2,500 to $3,000.
    Top 1,000 ranking: 116

Heavenly Father/My Wedding Day • Castelles (Grand 122) 1955 $3,000
    45 rpm. Cream color label. Rigid disc. No company address shown. Near-mint price range:
    $2,000 to $3,000.
    Top 1,000 ranking: 136

Le Cam
RECORDS

P. O. Box 11152   Fort Worth, Texas

718
45 RPM   Arc Music
L-128   BMI-2:3

Produced by:
Thomas-Smith

MOST OF ALL
(Fuqua-Freed)
THE DANES
with
MARVINO FOUR

886.

ERMONT
BMI
MO-064001   T1501
Prod. by OZ
Time: 2:30

LOOK AT ME
(J. OSBORNE)
THE UNEEKS
Featuring
TINY VALENTINE

888.

POOR BOY
RECORDS

BOX 1051   MUNCIE, IND.

600-45-

Oleta (BMI)   **45-111**

SERVANT OF LOVE
(Norman Walton)

VAN BROTHERS

889.

RCA VICTOR

OCTOBER 1960 POPULAR STEREO SAMPLER   **1**

SPS
33-96

1—FLOWERS FOR THE CATS (LSP-2110)
2—AM I THAT EASY TO FORGET? (LSP-2197)
3—THE BATTLE OF SAN JUAN HILL (LSP-2228)
4—Theme: SUNRISE SERENADE; BEG YOUR
PARDON (LSP-2233) 5—THE LITTLE DRUMMER
BOY (LSP-2254) 6—TONIGHT IS SO RIGHT
FOR LOVE (LSP-2256)
1. Shorty Rogers 2. Davis 3. Driftwood
4. Carlo 5. Hugo and Luigi with Their
Children's Chorus.
6. Presley

LIVING STEREO

890.

WALK—DON'T RUN
(Johnny Smith)

BLUE HORIZON

101-1
INSTRUMENTAL

45 RPM

Time 2:00

THE VENTURES

891.

BLUE HORIZON RECORDS · SEATTLE, WASHINGTON

Over a Cup of Coffee/Baby Can't You See • Castelles (Grand 109) 1954 $2,500
     45 rpm. Blue label. Near-mint price range: $2,000 to $2,500.
     Top 1,000 ranking: 185

Marcella/I'm a Fool to Care • Castelles (Grand 114) 1954 $2,500
     45 rpm. Cream color label. Rigid disc. No company address shown. Near-mint price range: $2,000 to $2,500.
     Top 1,000 ranking: 186

My Girl Awaits Me/Sweetness • Castelles (Grand 101) 1953 $2,000
     45 rpm. Flat blue label. Near-mint price range: $1,500 to $2,000.
     Top 1,000 ranking: 245

This Silver Ring/Wonder Why • Castelles (Grand 103) 1954 $2,000
     45 rpm. Glossy yellow label. Rigid disc. No company address shown. Near-mint price range: $1,000 to $2,000.
     Top 1,000 ranking: 263

Do You Remember/If You Were the Only Girl • Castelles (Grand 105) 1954 $1,000
     45 rpm. Glossy yellow label. Rigid disc. No company address shown. Near-mint price range: $750 to $1,000.
     Top 1,000 ranking: 596

CASTROS

Lucky Me/Darling I Fell for You • Castros (Lasso 501) 1959 $1,000
     45 rpm. Reportedly 100 made. Near-mint price range: $750 to $1,000.
     Top 1,000 ranking: 663

In My Dreams/Is It Right • Castros (Lasso 502) 1959 $1,000
     45 rpm. Reportedly 100 made. Near-mint price range: $750 to $1,000.
     Top 1,000 ranking: 664

CELEBRITYS

Juanita/This Is My Plea • Celebritys (Caroline 2301) 1956 $750
     45 rpm. Near-mint price range: $500 to $750.
     Top 1,000 ranking: 841

CELTICS

Can You Remember/Send Me Someone to Love • Celtics (Al-Jack's 0002) . 1962 $3,000
     45 rpm. Approximately 200 made. Near-mint price range: $2,000 to $3,000.
     Top 1,000 ranking: 166

CEZANNES

Pardon Me/All At Once • Cezannes (Featuring Cerressa) (Markay 108) 1963 $1,000
     45 rpm. Near-mint price range: $750 to $1,000.
     Top 1,000 ranking: 712

CHANTELS

We Are the Chantels • Chantels (End 301) 1958 $2,000
     LP. Pictures the quintet on the front cover. Reissues have a reworked cover picturing a juke box. Near-mint price range: $1,000 to $2,000.
     Top 1,000 ranking: 308

CHARM KINGS

Tell Me a Tale/? • Charm Kings (Mark 146) 1960 $1,200
     45 rpm. Near-mint price range: $800 to $1,200.
     Top 1,000 ranking: 533

CHARMERS

Tony, My Darling/In the Rain • Charmers (With Rhythm Acc.)
   (Central 1006) 1954 $4,000
     45 rpm. Near-mint price range: $3,000 to $4,000.
     Top 1,000 ranking: 77

I Was Wrong/The Mambo • Charmers (Timely 1009) 1954 $1,000
     45 rpm. Near-mint price range: $750 to $1,000.
     Top 1,000 ranking: 597

PLANET

Vocal
Time: 2:30
45 RPM

Record No.
P-1048
Rob-Ann Music
(BMI)

THE WONDERFUL YEARS
(B. Parker-B. Shore)

BARRY AND THE HIGHLIGHTS

PLANET RECORD CO., INC.
New York, N. Y.

892.

Tee Jay
Baldwin, Long Island, N. Y.

TJ-333
LB-486

DARLING ARLENE
(F. DeTrano)

FRANKIE DEE
Arranged by I. Markoe

893.

FORUM
RECORDS

Selma Music
BMI - 2:30

F700
(61-L-1)

THIS LOVE OF OURS
(A. Shore)

THE DELRONS

894.

TAMLA

THE GREAT GOSPEL STARS

DISC JOCKEY
ADVANCE SAMPLE
Jobete
B.M.I.

SIDE 2
TM-222
#MR-2

1. SWING LOW (1:36)
2. BEHOLD THE SAINTS OF GOD (1:45)
3. LAMB ON THE ALTAR (2:48)
4. HE'S USING ME (2:58)
5. SWEET BYE & BYE (1:48)

Produced By
BERRY GORDY JR.

2648 W. Grand Boulevard
Detroit 8, Michigan
TR. 1-3340

895.

CLAUWELL
42 John Street—S. I. N. Y.

Harris Music Co.
Time: 3:15

Record No.
45-004
Vocal

I'M SO IN LOVE
(David Mapp)

THE INFASCINATIONS

896.

The Beating of My Heart/Why Does It Have to Be Me • Charmers (With Rhythm
Acc.) (Central 1002) 1954 $750
    45 rpm. Near-mint price range: $500 to $750.
    Top 1,000 ranking: 821

CHARTERS
Trouble Lover/? • Charters (Mel-O-Dy 104) 1962 $1,500
    45 rpm. Near-mint price range: $1,000 to $1,500.
    Top 1,000 ranking: 464

CHECKERS
Flame in My Heart/Oh, Oh, Oh Baby • Checkers (King 4558) 1952 $1,000
    45 rpm. Near-mint price range: $750 to $1,000.
    Top 1,000 ranking: 571
Night's Curtains/Let Me Come Back • Checkers (King 4581) 1952 $1,000
    45 rpm. Near-mint price range: $750 to $1,000.
    Top 1,000 ranking: 572
My Prayer Tonight/Love Wasn't There • Checkers (King 4596) 1953 $1,000
    45 rpm. Near-mint price range: $750 to $1,000.
    Top 1,000 ranking: 579

CHEROKEES
Please Tell Me So/Remember When • Cherokees (Grand 110) 1954 $3,000
    45 rpm. Yellow label. Rigid disc. Near-mint price range: $2,500 to $3,000.
    Top 1,000 ranking: 125
Rainbow of Love/I Had a Thrill • Cherokees (Grand 106) 1954 $1,000
    45 rpm. Yellow label. Rigid disc. Near-mint price range: $750 to $1,000.
    Top 1,000 ranking: 598

CHESSMEN
Bells Bells/Prayer of Love • Chessmen (Golden Crest 2661) 1959 $2,000
    45 rpm. Near-mint price range: $1,000 to $2,000.
    Top 1,000 ranking: 321

CHICAGO SUNNY BOY
Western Union Man/Jack Pot • Chicago Sunny Boy (Meteor 5004) 1953 $1,200
    45 rpm. Near-mint price range: $800 to $1,200.
    Top 1,000 ranking: 503

CHIMES
My Heart's Crying for You/Love Me • Chimes (Flair 1051) 1954 $750
    45 rpm. Near-mint price range: $500 to $750.
    Top 1,000 ranking: 822

CHIMES
Dearest Darling/A Fool Was I • Chimes (Royal Roost 577) 1955 $750
    78 rpm. Near-mint price range: $500 to $750.
    Top 1,000 ranking: 833

CHRISTOPHER
What'cha Gonna Do • Christopher (Chris-Tee 12411) 1970 $2,200
    LP. Reportedly 100 made. Near-mint price range: $2,000 to $2,200.
    Top 1,000 ranking: 220

CLASS-AIRS
Too Old to Cry/My Tears Start to Fall • Class-Airs (Honey
Bee 81631) .... ? $2,000
    45 rpm. Identification number shown since no selection number is used. Near-mint price range:
    $1,000 to $2,000.
    Top 1,000 ranking: 373

Waldon Records

45 RPM
WR-1001B

Juanetta Pub. Co.
2:12

MY LOVER
(Demelvin Woodfox-Ricardo King)
THE NEONS

897.

PEK RECORDS
★ ★ ★ ★ ★

CB-2

Pecle Pub.
BMI

Arranged by
D. Howard

TREMBLING HAND
ROYAL DEMONS
8101

899.

LUKE
RECORD CO.
7660 Hollywood Blvd., Hollywood, Calif.

House O' Fortune
(BMI)
(SL-2)
PROMOTIONAL COPY

L & M Producers
Time 2:15
NOT FOR SALE

I'M JUST A FOOL
(Geo. Motola - R. Page)
VOCAL
DANNY (SLY). STEWART
AR-1008-B

900.

901.

RCA VICTOR

OCTOBER '61 POP SAMPLER

1—BLUE HAWAII (LSP-2426)
2—YOU GO TO MY HEAD (LSP-2435)
3—UNCHAINED MELODY (LSP-2444)

SPS
33-141
M2NY-3178

2
STEREO
ORTHOPHONIC
HIGH
FIDELITY

4—SAY A PRAYER (LSP-2325)
5—ROCK OF AGES (LSP-2248)
6—THE WAY OF THE CROSS (LSP-2377)

NOT FOR
SALE

1. Elvis Presley.
2. New Glenn Miller Orchestra, McKinley.
3. Floyd Cramer
4. Don McNeill
5. George Beverly Shea
6. Blackwood Producers
Quartet

LIVING STEREO

224

CLASSIC FOUR
Heavenly Bliss/Please Be Mine • Classic Four [Classic IV] (Twist 1004)....... 1962 $2,000
45 rpm. Near-mint price range: $1,000 to $2,000.
Top 1,000 ranking: 343

CLEFFTONES
(I'm Afraid) The Masquerade Is Over/My Dearest Darling • Clefftones
(Old Town 1011) 1955 $2,000
45 rpm. Near-mint price range: $1,000 to $2,000.
Top 1,000 ranking: 277

CLIFF, Benny
Shake Um Up Rock/? • Benny Cliff (With Benny Cliff Trio) (Drift 1441)......... 1959 $1,500
45 rpm. Near-mint price range: $1,000 to $1,500.
Top 1,000 ranking: 447

CLIFTON, Johnny & His String Band
Stand Up and Be Counted/? • Johnny Clifton & His String Band
(Center 102).. 1950 $1,500
78 rpm. Near-mint price range: $1,000 to $1,500.
Top 1,000 ranking: 392

CLIMBERS
I Love You/Trains, Cars, Boats • Climbers (With Orchestra) (J&S 1658) 1957 $5,000
45 rpm. Near-mint price range: $3,000 to $5,000.
Top 1,000 ranking: 61
My Darlin' Dear/Angels in Heaven Know I Love You • Climbers
(J&S 1652) 1957 $2,000
45 rpm. With straight horizontal lines. Near-mint price range: $1,500 to $2,000.
Top 1,000 ranking: 299

CLINTONIAN CUBS
Confusion/She's Just My Size • Clintonian Cubs (My Brother's 508)............. 1960 $2,000
45 rpm. Near-mint price range: $1,000 to $2,000.
Top 1,000 ranking: 336

CLOUDS
Rock and Roll Boogie/I Do • Clouds (Cobra 5001) 1956 $1,300
45 rpm. Near-mint price range: $1,000 to $1,300.
Top 1,000 ranking: 493

COCHRAN, Eddie
Mean When I'm Mad/One Kiss • Eddie Cochran (Liberty 55070) 1958 $1,000
Picture sleeve. Near-mint price range: $750 to $1,000.
Top 1,000 ranking: 647

COCHRAN BROTHERS
Tired and Sleepy/Fool's Paradise • Cochran Brothers (Ekko 3001) 1956 $650
45 rpm. Near-mint price range: $500 to $650.
Top 1,000 ranking: 978

COINS
Loretta/Please • Coins (Model 2001) 1955 $4,000
45 rpm. Near-mint price range: $3,000 to $4,000.
Top 1,000 ranking: 84
Blue Can't Get No Place with You/Cheatin' Baby • Coins (Gee 10)............... 1954 $3,000
45 rpm. Red vinyl. Near-mint price range: $2,000 to $3,000.
Top 1,000 ranking: 126
Blue Can't Get No Place with You/Cheatin' Baby • Coins (Gee 10).............. 1954 $2,000
45 rpm. Black vinyl. Near-mint price range: $1,000 to $2,000.
Top 1,000 ranking: 264

902.

904.

903.

905.

SR Blues/Look at Me Girl • Coins (Gee 11) 1954 $2,000
    45 rpm. Near-mint price range: $1,000 to $2,000.
    Top 1,000 ranking: 265

COLUMBUS PHARAOHS
Give Me Your Love/China Girl • Columbus Pharaohs (With Tommy Wills
    Orchestra) (Esta 290) 1958 $1,000
    45 rpm. Near-mint price range: $750 to $1,000.
    Top 1,000 ranking: 648

CONCEPTS
Whisper/Jungle • Concepts (With Al Browne Orchestra) (Apache 1515) 1957 $1,000
    45 rpm. Near-mint price range: $750 to $1,000.
    Top 1,000 ranking: 638

CONCORDS
Candlelight/Monticello • Concords (Harlem 2328) 1955 $1,200
    45 rpm. Near-mint price range: $800 to $1,200.
    Top 1,000 ranking: 513

CONDORS
Sweetest Angel/Little Curly Top • Condors (Hunter 2503/2504) 1960 $1,500
    45 rpm. Near-mint price range: $1,000 to $1,500.
    Top 1,000 ranking: 456

CONTINDERS
Mr. Dee Jay/Yes I Do • Continders (Featuring Clifford Curry)
    (Blue Sky 105) 1959 $1,000
    45 rpm. Near-mint price range: $750 to $1,000.
    Top 1,000 ranking: 665

CONTINENTAL GEMS
My Love Will Follow You/Everywhere • Continental Gems (Guyden 2091) ... 1963 $1,500
    45 rpm. Near-mint price range: $1,000 to $1,500.
    Top 1,000 ranking: 468

CONTINENTALS
It Doesn't Matter/Whisper It • Continentals (Hunter 3503) 1960 $1,500
    45 rpm. Near-mint price range: $1,000 to $1,500.
    Top 1,000 ranking: 457

CONTINENTALS
Giddy-Up and Ding-Dong/You're an Angel • Continentals (Rama 190) 1956 $2,000
    45 rpm. Blue label. Near-mint price range: $1,000 to $2,000.
    Top 1,000 ranking: 289

CONTINENTALS & COUNTS OF RHYTHM
Don't Leave Me/? • Continentals & Counts of Rhythm (10476) 1960s $2,000
    45 rpm. No label name used. Identification number shown since no selection number is used.
    Near-mint price range: $1,500 to $2,000.
    Top 1,000 ranking: 365

CONTOURS
Funny/The Stretch • Contours (Motown 1012) 1961 $800
    45 rpm. Near-mint price range: $600 to $800.
    Top 1,000 ranking: 782

COLUMBIA

45 RPM
Publisher:
Deauville Music
Inc. (BMI)
TIME: 2:55

4-42626
ZSP 58444

ECHO IN MY HEART
(D. Jones-L. Dickson)
THE STEREOS
Prod. by Robert Mersy
© "COLUMBIA" MARCAS REG PRINTED IN USA

907.

SAXONY

1001B
N8OW-7012

THAT'S
THE
WAY
(JL TREFZGER)

ROLLIE WILLIS
THE CONTENDERS
THE MATADORS
BEL CANTO PUBLISHING CO. BMI
2:20

911.

HARD-TIMES RECORDS

941-5-3002-A
Time-2:30
Twin-More
Music: All

Vocal
With Orchestra
45-3002

THE WEDDING
(w. Charles F. Sandford)
STICK LEG'S
And The Butchering Persians

908.

RCA VICTOR

DECEMBER '62 POP SAMPLER

1—WHERE DO YOU COME FROM (LSP-2621)
2—NEXT DOOR TO AN ANGEL (LSP-2627)
3—JOSHUA (LSP-2631)
4—MARCH OF THE TOYS (VPS-6012)

SPS
33-191
N2NY-5358

SIDE
2
NOT FOR
SALE

5—A KISS TO BUILD A DREAM ON (VPS-6012)
CAMDEN RELEASE
6—LOVER (CAS-749)

1. Elvis Presley
with The Jordanaires
2. Neil Sedaka; Arr. & cond. by Alan Lorber
3. The Tokens
4, 5. Marty Gold and his Orch.
6. Zaccarias and his
Orch.

LIVING STEREO

910.

228

COOL BREEZE & HIS BAND WITH LITTLE COOL BREEZES

Won't You Come In/Pack Your Rags and Go • Cool Breeze & His Band with Little
Cool Breezes (With Jimmy Petty, Rupert Jones & Senders)
(Ebony 1014) 1959 $1,000
  45 rpm. Near-mint price range: $750 to $1,000.
  Top 1,000 ranking: 666

CORDEL, Pat, & Crescents

Darling Come Back/My Tears • Pat Cordel & Crescents (Club 1011)............ 1956 $1,000
  45 rpm. Vito Picone and Carman Romano later formed the Elegants. After the break-up of this
  group, Pat Cordel joined the June Taylor Dancers. Near-mint price range: $750 to $1,000.
  Top 1,000 ranking: 624

COR-DON'S

Some Kinda Wonderful/Is She the One • Cor-Don's [Cor-Dons]
(Rowe 100)... 1962 $750
  45 rpm. Near-mint price range: $500 to $750.
  Top 1,000 ranking: 902

CORONETS

It Would Be Heavenly/Baby's Coming Home • Coronets (With Sax Mallard &
Combo) (Chess 1553)... 1953 $3,000
  45 rpm. Red vinyl. Near-mint price range: $2,500 to $3,000.
  Top 1,000 ranking: 117

CORONETS & BILL REESE QUINTET: see REESE, Bill, Quintet, & Coronets

CORSAIRS

Goodbye Darling/Rock Lilly Rock • Corsairs (Hy-Tone 110).......................... 1958 $5,000
  45 rpm. Near-mint price range: $4,000 to $5,000.
  Top 1,000 ranking: 62

CORVETTS

I'm Going to Cry/You're Blue • Corvetts (Moon 100)..................................... 1959 $750
  45 rpm. Near-mint price range: $500 to $750.
  Top 1,000 ranking: 870

COSMIC RAYS

Bye Bye/Somebody's in Love • Cosmic Rays (With Le Sun Ra & Arkestra)
(Saturn 222) 1960 $2,000
  45 rpm. Near-mint price range: $1,500 to $2,000.
  Top 1,000 ranking: 337
Dreaming/Daddy's Gonna Tell You No Lie • Cosmic Rays (With Sun Ra &
Arkestra) (Saturn 401/402)... 1960 $1,000
  45 rpm. Near-mint price range: $750 to $1,000.
  Top 1,000 ranking: 682

COTTON, James

Cotton Crop Blues/Hold Me in Your Arms • James Cotton (Sun 206) 1954 $1,300
  45 rpm. Near-mint price range: $1,000 to $1,300.
  Top 1,000 ranking: 492

CRAWFORD, Peter

Dancing with My Lover/There Goes a Young Love • Peter Crawford
(Sandy 1039) 1963 $1,000
  45 rpm. One known copy. Near-mint price range: $750 to $1,000.
  Top 1,000 ranking: 713

Swan

Northern Music Ltd. ASCAP

Time: 2:04

"I'LL GET YOU"
(Lennon - McCartney)
THE BEATLES
S-4152-I

912.

Sara

2:04
BMI

J-6431
Vocal by
Wayne Demmier

(I'LL BE) FOREVER LOVING YOU
the BEL-AIRS
Div. of CUCA RECORD CORP
Sauk City, Wis.

915.

Swan

DON'T
DROP
OUT

Gil Music Corp.
BMI

Time: 2;18
Produced by
George Martin

SHE LOVES YOU
(Lennon-McCartney)
THE BEATLES
S-4152-S

913.

HE*S A REBEL
THE CRYSTALS

INCLUDED IN THIS ALBUM
HE'S SURE THE BOY I LOVE
UPTOWN - THERE'S NO OTHER

916.

D. C. MAGNATONES

45 RPM
Time 2:37

Side 2
MM-216 B

DOES SHE LOVE ME
(Coveli-Saitta-Vabolis)
The D.C. Magnatones

918.

CRESTS

The Crests Sing All Biggies • Crests (Coed 901) 1960 $750
    LP. "Advance Pressing." Promotional issue only. Near-mint price range: $500 to $750.
     Top 1,000 ranking: 885

CROWNS: see MAYE, Arthur Lee, & Crowns

CROWS

No Help Wanted/Seven Lonely Days • Crows (Rama 3) 1953 $2,000
    45 rpm. Near-mint price range: $1,500 to $2,000.
     Top 1,000 ranking: 246
Call a Doctor/Heartbreaker • Crows (Rama 10) 1953 $2,000
    45 rpm. Red vinyl. Some copies may credit the Jewels on one side and the Crows on the other.
    Near-mint price range: $1,000 to $2,000.
     Top 1,000 ranking: 247
Miss You/I Really Really Love You • Crows (Rama 30) 1954 $1,500
    45 rpm. Red vinyl. Near-mint price range: $1,000 to $1,500.
     Top 1,000 ranking: 410
Mambo Shevitz/Mambo No. 5 • Crows (With Melino & His Orchestra)
(Tico 1082) 1951 $750
    45 rpm. Red vinyl. Near-mint price range: $500 to $750.
     Top 1,000 ranking: 801

CRYSTALIERS

Please Be My Guy/Don't Cry • Crystaliers (Johnson 103) 1957 $3,000
    45 rpm. Near-mint price range: $2,000 to $3,000.
     Top 1,000 ranking: 145

CRYSTALS

Let's Dance the Screw/Let's Dance the Screw • Crystals (Philles 111) 1963 $2,000
    45 rpm. White label. Promotional issue only. Near-mint price range: $1,000 to $2,000.
     Top 1,000 ranking: 352
The Crystals Twist Uptown • Crystals (Philles 90722) 1962 $1,000
    LP. Capitol Record Club issue. Near-mint price range: $750 to $1,000.
     Top 1,000 ranking: 702
The Crystals Twist Uptown • Crystals (Philles 4000) 1962 $750
    Monaural LP. White label. Promotional issue only. Near-mint price range: $500 to $750.
     Top 1,000 ranking: 903
He's a Rebel • Crystals (Philles 4001) 1963 $750
    LP. White label. Promotional issue only. Near-mint price range: $500 to $750.
     Top 1,000 ranking: 916
Crystals • Crystals (Philles 4003) 1963 $750
    LP. White label. Promotional issue only. Near-mint price range: $500 to $750.
     Top 1,000 ranking: 917

CULMER, Little Iris

Frankie, My Eyes Are on You/Show Me the Way to Your Heart • Little Iris Culmer
(Marlin 803) 1957 $3,000
    45 rpm. Three copies known. Near-mint price range: $2,000 to $3,000.
     Top 1,000 ranking: 146

D.C. MAGNATONES

Does She Love Me/? • D.C. Magnatones (D.C. Magnatones 216) 1963 $750
    45 rpm. Near-mint price range: $500 to $750.
     Top 1,000 ranking: 918

DAMON

Song of a Gypsy • Damon (Ankh) 1970 $2,500
    LP. No selection number used. Reportedly 100 made. Near-mint price range: $2,000 to $2,500.
     Top 1,000 ranking: 216

COLUMBIA

Produced by
John Hammond

45 RPM

4-42656
2SP 50626

MIXED UP CONFUSION
— B. Dylan
BOB DYLAN
©COLUMBIA/® MARCAS REG. PRINTED IN U.S.A.

919.

MANUFACTURED FOR RALPH SEIJO PRODUCTION CORP. ·· MADE IN U.S.A.

PRODUCTION

RS 63106
InterSound
RSPC
2:33

45 RPM
rsp-612
vocal

PROMOTION COPY

NOT FOR SALE

ERIC
sings
I WISH....
(Mildred Jaeger)
with The Plazas
and Ralph Casals Trio

920.

The return of AMOS MILBURN
"the" blues boss
"I'll make it up to you somehow"

921.

RCA VICTOR

DECEMBER '63 POP SAMPLER

1—FUN IN ACAPULCO (LSP-2756)
2—ONE NOTE (LSP-2763)
3—ANYTIME (LSP-2775 e)
4—WOMENFOLK (LSP-2821)

SPS
33-247
PNRS-3800

SIDE
2

NOT FOR
SALE

5—RUN MOLLY (LSP-2821)

1. Elvis Presley
2. The Joe Daley Trio
3. Eddie Fisher
4. The Womenfolk
5. The Villagers

STEREO

®REGISTERED · MARCA(S) REGISTRADA(S) · RADIO CORPORATION OF AMERICA—MADE IN U.S.A.

923.

MEET THE SUPREMES

MOTOWN RECORD CORP. 606

922.

RCA VICTOR

SEPTEMBER '63 POP
SAMPLER
1—Excerpts: WHEN YOU'RE SMILING
DIGA DIGA DO; MARGIE; THE SHEIK
(LSP-2715)
2—NOLA (LSP-2716)
3—LET'S FALL IN LOVE (LSP-2717)
4—Excerpts: MY IDEAL; SECRETS
THE SWEETEST SOUNDS (LSP-2721)
5—Excerpts: I REALLY DON'T WANT TO KNOW

SPS
33-219
PNRS-4199

BEGIN THE BEGUINE; I HADN'T ANYONE TILL YOU
(LSP-2724)
6—ARE YOU LONESOME TONIGHT? (LSP-2765)
1. The Three Suns 2. Sid Ramin and his Orchestra
3. The Cascading Voices of
The Hugo & Luigi Chorus 4. a. Frankie Carle
b. Floyd Cramer c. Peter Nero
5. a. Ann-Margret b. Kitty Kallan
c. Della Reese 6. Elvis Presley
with The Jordanaires

SIDE
2

NOT FOR
SALE

STEREO

DYNAGROOVE

STEREO

®REGISTERED · MARCA(S) REGISTRADA(S) · RADIO CORPORATION OF AMERICA—MADE IN U.S.A.

924.

232

DANDERLIERS
Chop Chop Boom/My Autumn Love • Danderliers (States 147) 1955 $2,000
    45 rpm. Red vinyl. Near-mint price range: $1,500 to $2,000.
    Top 1,000 ranking: 278

DANES
Most of All/Come on Baby • Danes (With Marvino Four)
(Le Cam 718) 1960 $750
    45 rpm. Reissued as by the Team Mates. Near-mint price range: $500 to $750.
    Top 1,000 ranking: 886

DAWN, Billy, Quartet
This Is the Real Thing Now/Crying for My Baby • Billy Dawn Quartet (With Connie
Frederick & Orchestra) (Decatur 3001) 1953 $2,000
    45 rpm. Near-mint price range: $1,000 to $2,000.
    Top 1,000 ranking: 248

DE BERRY, Jimmy
Take a Little Chance/Time Has Made a Change • Jimmy De Berry
(Sun 185) 1953 $1,300
    45 rpm. Near-mint price range: $1,000 to $1,300.
    Top 1,000 ranking: 490

DEE, Frankie
Darling Arlene/? • Frankie Dee (Tee Jay 333) 1961 $750
    45 rpm. Near-mint price range: $500 to $750.
    Top 1,000 ranking: 893

DEE, Joey & Starliters
Lorraine/The Girl I Walk to School • Joey Dee & Starliters (Little 813/814) ... 1958 $2,000
    45 rpm. Near-mint price range: $1,000 to $2,000.
    Top 1,000 ranking: 309

DEE, Mercy: see MERCY DEE

DE JAN & ELGINS
That's My Girl/Reality • De Jan & Elgins (Lessie 0099) 1960 $5,000
    45 rpm. One copy known. Near-mint price range: $4,000 to $5,000.
    Top 1,000 ranking: 63

DELI-CADOS
Now I've Confessed/Granny Baby • Deli-Cados (PMP 4979) 1960 $2,000
    45 rpm. Identification number shown since no selection number is used. Near-mint price range:
    $1,500 to $12000.
    Top 1,000 ranking: 338

DEL-LARKS
Job Opening/? • Del-Larks (Queen City 2004).. ? $2,000
    45 rpm. Near-mint price range: $1,000 to $2,000.
    Top 1,000 ranking: 374

DELLS / Count Morris
Tell the World/Blues at Three • Dells / Count Morris (Vee-Jay 134) 1955 $5,000
    45 rpm. Red vinyl. Near-mint price range: $4,000 to $5,000.
    Top 1,000 ranking: 52

DELMIRAS
Dry Your Eyes/The Big Sound • Delmiras (Dade 1821)................................. 1961 $1,000
    45 rpm. Near-mint price range: $750 to $1,000.
    Top 1,000 ranking: 692

DO
YOU WANT
TO KNOW A SECRET
(McCartney-Lennon)
THE BEATLES
VJ 587

45   45

VJ   VJ
VEE-JAY   VEE-JAY
RECORDS   RECORDS

PROMOTIONAL   PROMOTIONAL
COPY   COPY

45   45

63-3191 — Vocal
Metric Music - BMI

925.

DELFT RECORDS INC. / DENVER, COLORADO

Side 1   45 rpm
CSS 6408

THIS IS OUR WEDDING DAY
THE FOUR CHEVELLES

926.

927.

RCA VICTOR
APRIL '65 POP
SAMPLER
1—CHAPINES
(LSP-3328) Juan Serrano
2—THE MEANEST GIRL IN TOWN
(LSP-3338) Elvis Presley, with the Jordanaires
3—NEVER ON SUNDAY
(LSP-3340) Mariachi Los Camperos of Natl Cano

SPS   4—THE OTHER SIDE OF YOU   SIDE
33-331   (LSP-3341) Connie Smith   2
SNRS-3311   5—PEOPLE
             (LSP-3343) Joe Williams   NOT FOR
             6—PLASTERED   SALE
             (LSP-3345) Don Bowman
             7—I STEPPED OVER THE LINE
             (LSP-3348) Don Robertson

STEREO   DYNAGROOVE   STEREO

929.

RCA VICTOR
APRIL '64 POP SAMPLER
1—EXACTLY LIKE YOU (LSP-2876 (e)
2—YOU DON'T KNOCK (LSP-2878)
3—HOBO FLATS (LSP-2879)
4—Medley: THE OLD PIANO ROLL BLUES
(LSP-2881)
5—JITTERBUG WALTZ (LSP-2887(e)

SPS   6—KISSIN' COUSINS (LSP-2894)   SIDE
33-272   7—ALWAYS IN MY HEART   2
RNRS-3737   (Siempre en mi Corazon) (LSP-2912)
             1. Ames Brothers   NOT FOR
             2. Don Gibson 3. Joe Williams   SALE
             4. Frankie Carle, His Piano and Orchestra
             5. Chet Atkins 6. Elvis Presley
             7. (The Indians)
             Los Indios Tabajaras

STEREO

928.

RCA VICTOR
AUGUST '65 POP
SAMPLER
1—CATCHIN' ON FAST
(LSP-3408) Peggy March and Bennie Thomas
2—THE DEVIL'S GRIN
(LSP-3409) Lorne Greene

SPS   3—BEGIN THE BEGUINE   SIDE
33-347   (LSP-3413) Los Indios Tabajaras 2
SNRS-5640   4—LITTLE OLE YOU
             (LSP-3427(e) Jim Reeves   NOT FOR
             5—TWANGSVILLE   SALE
             (LSP-3432) Duane Eddy
             6—YOUR CHEATIN' HEART
             (LSP-3450) Elvis Presley
             with The Jordanaires

STEREO DYNAGROOVE

930.

234

DELRAYS
Our Love Is True/One Kiss, One Smile and a Dream • Delrays
(Cord 1001) 1958 $4,000
45 rpm. Near-mint price range: $3,000 to $4,000.
Top 1,000 ranking: 90

DEL RIOS
Lizzie/Alone on a Rainy Night • Del Rios & Bearcats (Meteor 5038) 1956 $650
45 rpm. Near-mint price range: $500 to $650.
Top 1,000 ranking: 979

DELRONS
This Love of Ours/Over the Rainbow • Delrons (Forum 700) 1961 $750
45 rpm. Near-mint price range: $500 to $750.
Top 1,000 ranking: 894

DELTAS
Lamplight/Let Me Share Your Dream • Deltas (Gone 5010) 1957 $3,000
45 rpm. Near-mint price range: $2,000 to $3,000.
Top 1,000 ranking: 147

DEL-VIKINGS
Come Go with the Del-Vikings • Del-Vikings (Luniverse 1000) 1957 $750
LP. Near-mint price range: $500 to $750.
Top 1,000 ranking: 851

DEL VUES
My Confession/After New Years • Del Vues (Featuring W. Voss)
(U Town 8008) 1950s $2,000
45 rpm. Near-mint price range: $1,500 to $2,000.
Top 1,000 ranking: 334

DEMOLYRS
Rain/Hey Little Rosie • Demolyrs (With Hash Brown & His Orchestra)
(UWR 900) 1964 $1,000
45 rpm. Near-mint price range: $750 to $1,000.
Top 1,000 ranking: 725

DIAMOND, Neil
We Wrote a Song Together • Neil Diamond (Continuum II 001) 1976 $2,000
12-inch single. Made exclusively for Neil's son Jesse's grade school class. Has Neil and a band
composing and recording in a studio – with the children present. Includes an alternative version
of *Beautiful Noise*. Neil made and autographed a copy for each child in attendence – estimated
to be 30 to 40 copies. Near-mint price range: $1,500 to $2,000.
Top 1,000 ranking: 371
Clown Town/At Night • Neil Diamond (Columbia 42809) 1963 $650
45 rpm. Price is for the commercial release; the promo is valued lower. Near-mint price range:
$500 to $650.
Top 1,000 ranking: 997

DIAMONDS
A Beggar for Your Kisses/Call Baby Call • Diamonds (Atlantic 981) 1952 $1,200
45 rpm. Near-mint price range: $800 to $1,200.
Top 1,000 ranking: 498

DIPPERS QUINTET
It's Almost Christmas/Look What I've Found • Dippers Quintet (With Van Perry's
Combo) (Flayr 500) 1955 $5,000
45 rpm. Two known copies. Near-mint price range: $4,000 to $5,000.
Top 1,000 ranking: 53

(Somewhere)
OVER THE RAINBOW

P and **L**

A
"Villa-Martin"
Production
Vocal

THE
"ROYAL - FIVE"
317-B

931.

RCA VICTOR

APRIL '66 POP
SAMPLER

1—STAND AT YOUR WINDOW
The Blue Boys with Chorus
featuring Bud Logan (LSP-3529)
2—BIG BOSS MAN
Charlie Rich (LSP-3537)
3—OF THEE I SING
Tommy Leonetti (LSP-3543)

SP
33-403
TNRS-3147

SIDE
2

NOT FOR
SALE

4—BILL BAILEY
Marilyn Maye (LSP-3546)
5—FRANKIE AND JOHNNY
Elvis Presley (LSP-3553)
6—SOLO BUSANOVA
Arr. and cond. by Hugo Montenegro (LSP-3574)
7—DOMINIQUE
The Provocative Strings of
Zacharias (LSP-3597)

STEREO DYNAGROOVE

932.

RCA VICTOR

ELVIS PRESLEY

Special Palm Sunday Programming

SP 33-461
LINHM-1932
TIME: 14:27

SIDE
1

Not For Sale

For DJs only

Complete half-hour program
with spot announcements
and selections from the RCA Victor album
"How Great thou Art" (LPM/LSP-3758)

MONAURAL

934.

**ELVIS
PRESLEY**

MY BOY

938.

STEREO
RCA-2458EX
RCA-2458-II

Rondor Music
(Ldn.) Ltd.
2:53

LOVING ARMS
(Tom Jans)
(from the LP "Good Times")

DIXON, Floyd
Red Cherries/The River • Floyd Dixon (Aladdin 3144)................................... 1952 $700
    45 rpm. Red vinyl. Near-mint price range: $500 to $700.
    Top 1,000 ranking: 952

DOLLS
Just Before You Leave/I Love • Dolls (Teenage 1010).................................. 1958 $1,200
    45 rpm. Near-mint price range: $800 to $1,200.
    Top 1,000 ranking: 525

DOMINOES
Chicken Blues/Do Something for Me • Dominoes (Federal 12001) 1950 $1,000
    45 rpm. Near-mint price range: $750 to $1,000.
    Top 1,000 ranking: 567
Weeping Willow Blues/I Am with You • Dominoes (Federal 12039) 1951 $750
    45 rpm. Near-mint price range: $500 to $750.
    Top 1,000 ranking: 802
That's What You're Doing to Me/When the Swallows Come Back To
    Capistrano • Dominoes (Federal 12059) 1952 $750
    45 rpm. Near-mint price range: $500 to $750.
    Top 1,000 ranking: 807

DON JUANS
Girl of My Dreams/Dolores • Don Juans (Onezy 101)................................... 1959 $1,500
    45 rpm. Near-mint price range: $1,000 to $1,500.
    Top 1,000 ranking: 448

DOTS
Ring Chimes/Wolf Call • Dots (Rev 3512)... 1957 $1,500
    45 rpm. Near-mint price range: $1,000 to $1,500.
    Top 1,000 ranking: 433

DOUGLAS, K.C.
K.C. Douglas: Dead-Beat Guitar and the Mississippi Blues – Street Corner Blues
    'Bout Women and Automobiles • K.C. Douglas (Cook Road
    Recordings 5002)... 1956 $1,000
    LP. Front cover shows label as only "Road Recordings," whereas label has "Cook Road
    Recordings." Near-mint price range: $750 to $1,000.
    Top 1,000 ranking: 625

DOWNBEATS
My Girl/China Doll • Downbeats (Gee 1019).. 1956 $1,000
    45 rpm. Red and black label. Near-mint price range: $750 to $1,000.
    Top 1,000 ranking: 626

DREAM LOVERS
For the First Time/Take It from a Fool • Dream Lovers (Len 1006) 1960 $650
    45 rpm. Near-mint price range: $500 to $650.
    Top 1,000 ranking: 992

DREAMERS
No Man Is an Island/Melba • Dreamers (Rollin' 1001) 1955 $2,000
    45 rpm. Outer edge of disc is fairly sharp. Near-mint price range: $1,000 to $2,000.
    Top 1,000 ranking: 279

DUBS
Don't Ask Me to Be Lonely/Darling • Dubs (Johnson 102)............................. 1957 $2,000
    45 rpm. Near-mint price range: $1,500 to $2,000.
    Top 1,000 ranking: 300

FINE RECORDS

4630 Kosarek

Babe Wes Music, BMI
Time: 2:33
Fine 102

Corpus Christi, Texas

LOVE FOREVER
(Keller, Childers, Mulinix)
BARRY
&
THE VI-COUNTS

941.

STAFF

45 R.P.M.
Florentine Music
BMI
Time 2:05

RECORD NO.
103 B
(2-TH)

THOSE PRETTY BROWN EYES
(Huff-Hawthorne)
TERRY HULL
AND THE STARFIRES

942.

"MENARD
MEANS MUSIC

MENARD

RECORDS

Box 1335
San Antonio 6, Texas

6252 A
Karden Music
BMI

VOCAL
2:18
A&R: Emil Menard Jr.

IMAGE OF LOVE
(Casillas-Menard)
PUBLIO AND
THE VALIANTS

944.

100 - PROOF Records

45 RPM
MM-144 A

Side 1

GIRL
(S. Doucette)
THE TEJUNS

946.

DYLAN, Bob

The Freewheelin' Bob Dylan • Bob Dylan (Columbia CL-1986) 1963 $15,000
> Monaural LP – Commercial or promotional. Has *Let Me Die in My Footsteps, Talkin' John Birch Society Blues, Gamblin' Willie's Dead Man's Hand* and *Rocks and Gravel* (which may also be shown as *Solid Gravel*). We have seen promotional (white label – monaural) copies that do have the correct titles on the labels; however, we know of no copies that have them on the cover. We have yet to see commercial (red label) copies that list the four controversial tracks. Therefore, we suggest verification of the tracks by listening to the LP, rather than accepting the printed information. Some copies of the disc with the rare tracks even have reissue labels. Identification numbers of this press are XLP-58717-1A and XLP-58718-1A.) Near-mint price range: $10,000 to $15,000.
> ***Top 1,000 ranking: 6***

Mixed Up Confusion/Corrina Corrina • Bob Dylan (Columbia 42656) 1963 $1,000
> 45 rpm. Red label. Near-mint price range: $750 to $1,000.
> ***Top 1,000 ranking: 714***

Mixed Up Confusion/Corrina Corrina • Bob Dylan (Columbia 42656) 1963 $750
> 45 rpm. White label. Promotional issue only. Near-mint price range: $500 to $750.
> ***Top 1,000 ranking: 919***

EBBTIDES

Star of Love/First Love • Ebbtides (Duane 1022) 1964 $3,500
> 45 rpm. Near-mint price range: $2,500 to $3,500.
> ***Top 1,000 ranking: 103***

What Is Your Name Dear/Only Be Mine • Ebbtides (With Butch Ballard Orchestra)
(Teen 121) 1958 $3,000
> 45 rpm. Near-mint price range: $2,000 to $3,000.
> ***Top 1,000 ranking: 155***

EBON-KNIGHTS

First Date with the Ebon-Knights • Ebon-Knights (Stepheny 4001) 1959 $650
> LP. Near-mint price range: $500 to $650.
> ***Top 1,000 ranking: 990***

ELDAROS

Please Surrender/Rock a Bock • Eldaros (With Ray Parratore & Rhythm
Rockaways) (Vesta 102) 1958 $1,000
> 45 rpm. Near-mint price range: $750 to $1,000.
> ***Top 1,000 ranking: 649***

EL DORADOS

Baby I Need You/My Loving Baby • El Dorados (Vee-Jay 115) 1954 $650
> 45 rpm. Red vinyl. Near-mint price range: $500 to $650.
> ***Top 1,000 ranking: 973***

ELECTRAS

Action Woman/Pregnant Pig • Electras (Scotty 6720) 1967 $750
> 45 rpm. Studio demo. One known copy. Near-mint price range: $500 to $750.
> ***Top 1,000 ranking: 933***

ELGINS

Once Upon a Time/The Huddle • Elgins (Joed 716) 1962 $750
> 45 rpm. Near-mint price range: $500 to $750.
> ***Top 1,000 ranking: 904***

ELLIS, Steve & Starfires

Steve Ellis Songbook • Steve Ellis & Starfires (IGL 105) 1967 $700
> LP. Near-mint price range: $500 to $700.
> ***Top 1,000 ranking: 968***

WOW

RECORDS

★☆ ☆★

ABILITE
Publishing Co.
BMI

45-110
10-62-A
2:55

WHEN
(Wm. O. White)

WEE WILLIE
and the
MELLODIERS
WOW-1062-A

947.

948.

Flip

RECORDS INC.

Hi-Lo Music
BMI F-17

(Kesler-Taylor)
502

SPLIT PERSONALITY
BILL TAYLOR & SMOKEY JO
Clyde Leappard's
Snearly Ranch Boys

MEMPHIS, TENNESSEE, U.S.A.

954.

RCA VICTOR
RECORD PREVUE
coming attractions

Claiborne-Davis
E1-VW-3672

NOT FOR SALE
47-4327
RELEASE 51-42

HEARTBREAKER
(Robt Trim)

THE HEARTBREAKERS
Time: 2:40

950.

240

EL POLLOS
High School Dance/These Four Letters • El Pollos (Studio 999) ..,................ 1958 $1,300
     45 rpm. Near-mint price range: $1,000 to $1,300.
     Top 1,000 ranking: 494

EL RAYS
Darling I Know/Christine • El Rays (With Willie Dixon & Orchestra)
    (Checker 794) 1954 $1,500
     45 rpm. Near-mint price range: $1,000 to $1,500.
     Top 1,000 ranking: 411

EL REYES
Mr. Moonglow/Need Your Love • El Reyes (Jade 501)................................. 1958 $1,200
     45 rpm. Near-mint price range: $800 to $1,200.
     Top 1,000 ranking: 526

EMERALDS
Why Must I Wonder/Sally Lou • Emeralds (Kicks 3) 1954 $1,000
     45 rpm. Near-mint price range: $750 to $1,000.
     Top 1,000 ranking: 599

EMERALS
Please Don't Crush My Dreams/Soda Pop • Emerals (Triple X 100)............. 1958 $750
     45 rpm. Near-mint price range: $500 to $750.
     Top 1,000 ranking: 860

EMPERORS WITH RHYTHM
Come Back, Come Back/I May Be Wrong • Emperors with Rhythm
    (Haven 511) 1954 $5,000
     45 rpm. Red vinyl. Near-mint price range: $4,000 to $5,000.
     Top 1,000 ranking: 48
Come Back, Come Back/I May Be Wrong • Emperors with Rhythm
    (Haven 511) 1954 $2,500
     45 rpm. Black vinyl. Near-mint price range: $2,000 to $2,500.
     Top 1,000 ranking: 187

ENCHANTERS
True Love Gone/Wait a Minute Baby • Enchanters (Mercer 1674)................ 1956 $2,000
     45 rpm. Near-mint price range: $1,000 to $2,000.
     Top 1,000 ranking: 290
Spellbound By the Moon/Know It All • Enchanters (Stardust 102)................. 1958 $2,000
     45 rpm. Near-mint price range: $1,000 to $2,000.
     Top 1,000 ranking: 310

ENCORES
When I Look at You/Young Girls, Young Girls • Encores (Checker 760)....... 1952 $4,000
     45 rpm. Near-mint price range: $3,000 to $4,000.
     Top 1,000 ranking: 70

ENDORSERS
Crying (Over You)/Hold My Hand • Endorsers (Moon 109) 1959 $2,000
     45 rpm. Near-mint price range: $1,000 to $2,000.
     Top 1,000 ranking: 322

EPPS, Earl
Be-Bop Blues/? • Earl Epps (Minor 103).. ? $900
     45 rpm. Near-mint price range: $700 to $900.
     Top 1,000 ranking: 763

955.

Cobra RECORD CORP.
Armel Music BMI
2:15 U3242
MAMBO FIESTA
(Brown)
CALVAES
5003
MFG. BY COBRA RECORD CO. • CHICAGO

956.

J-V-B Recording Co.
3530 HASTINGS   DETROIT, MICH.
UNBREAKABLE
45 R.P.M.
RECORD NO
60 A X
THEY WERE ROCKIN'
DANNY KIRKLAND
AND HIS BAND

957.

J & S RECORDS
1075 Tiffany St., Bronx 59, N. Y.
UNBREAKABLE
45 R.P.M.
RECORD NO.
J-1602 A
Zell's Music (BMI)
Time 2:27
DEAR I SWEAR
(By "THE PLANTS")
THE PLANTS
WITH ORCHESTRA

958.

A KUDO RECORDING
"Records of Praise"
45 R.P.M.
A-663
Lane-West Higgins
Pub. (BMI) 2:05
Hi-Fidelity
MY BABY-O
(S. Weeds)
MARV JOHNSON
With the Band of
Harold "Beans" Bowles

960.

242

EQUALLOS
Beneath the Sun/In Between Tears • Equallos (Featuring Willie Logan)
(M&M 30) 1962 $2,000
   45 rpm. Near-mint price range: $1,000 to $2,000.
   Top 1,000 ranking: 344

ERIC
I Wish.../It's the Last Kiss • Eric (With Plazas & Ralph Casals Trio)
(Production 612)... 1963 $750
   45 rpm. Black vinyl. Purple vinyl copies are 1991 issues. Near-mint price range: $500 to $750.
   Top 1,000 ranking: 920

ESCOS
I'm Lonesome for You/Chick-A-Dee • Escos (Background: George Carter, Wilbert
Bell & Winfred Gerald. Music by the Swingin' Rocks) (Esta 100)............ 1959 $650
   45 rpm. Same selection number also used for a Joe Caldwell release. Near-mint price range:
   $500 to $650.
   Top 1,000 ranking: 989

ESQUERITA
Hey Miss Lucy/I'm Batty Over Hatty • Esquerita (Capitol 1075)...................... 1958 $1,000
   45 rpm with picture sleeve. Also recorded as Eskew Reeder. Promotional issue only. Near-mint
   price range: $750 to $1,000.
   Top 1,000 ranking: 650
Esquerita • Esquerita (Capitol 1186)... 1959 $700
   LP. Also recorded as Eskew Reeder. Near-mint price range: $500 to $700.
   Top 1,000 ranking: 960

ESQUIRES
Only the Angels Know/One Word for This • Esquires (Hi-Po 1003)............... 1956 $2,000
   45 rpm. Near-mint price range: $1,000 to $2,000.
   Top 1,000 ranking: 291

EXECUTIVES
Why/Come on Baby • Executives (Revenge 5003)....................................... 1963 $1,000
   45 rpm. Near-mint price range: $750 to $1,000.
   Top 1,000 ranking: 715

FABULOUS FLAMES
I'm Gonna Try to Live My Life All Over/So Long My Darling • Fabulous Flames
(With Original Sunglows) (Harlem 114).. 1960 $5,000
   45 rpm. Near-mint price range: $4,000 to $5,000.
   Top 1,000 ranking: 64

FANANDO'S
The One I Love/She Must Be from a Different Planet • Fanando's (With Emmet
Carter Combo) (Carter 2050) 1957 $2,000
   45 rpm. Near-mint price range: $1,500 to $2,000.
   Top 1,000 ranking: 301

FASCINATORS
The Bells of My Heart/Sweet Baby • Fascinators (Your Copy 1135) 1954 $2,000
   45 rpm. Red vinyl. Near-mint price range: $1,000 to $2,000.
   Top 1,000 ranking: 266
Can't Stop/Don't Give My Love Away • Fascinators (Blue Lake 112) 1955 $2,000
   45 rpm. Near-mint price range: $1,000 to $2,000.
   Top 1,000 ranking: 280
My Beauty, My Own/Don't Give It Away • Fascinators (Your Copy 1136) 1955 $1,000
   45 rpm. Near-mint price range: $750 to $1,000.
   Top 1,000 ranking: 615

A DATE WITH ELVIS

RCA VICTOR
LPM-2011

Never Before on L. P.
We're Gonna Move
Blue Moon of Kentucky
I Want to Be Free
Good Rockin' Tonight
Is It So Strange
I Forgot to Remember
to Forget
Young and Beautiful
Baby Let's Play House
Baby I Don't Care
Milkcow Blues Boogie

NEW GOLDEN AGE OF SOUND ALBUM

962.

VEST
VEST RECORD CO., INC.
N.Y.C.

45 RPM
V-51
Nationally Dist. by
R&D Record Sales Inc.

Lee Fost
Time 2:00
Top Artist Production

OVER THE RAINBOW
(H. Arlen - E.Y. Harburg)
THE MUSTANGS
8009

965.

968.

WAGON
RECORDS
Baltimore, Md

45 R.P.M.
Record No
SH 1004
BMI Time 2:30

Vocal with
Instrument
Accompaniment

DRAG STRIP BABY
(Johnny Roane)
JOHNNY ROANE

969.

Memorial Album for
Johnny Ace

Pledging My Love
Never Let Me Go
Saving My Love For You
Please Forgive Me

The Clock
Cross My Heart
Angel
My Song

DUKE

977.

244

The Bells of My Heart/Sweet Baby • Fascinators (Your Copy 1135) 1954 $800
    45 rpm. Black vinyl. Near-mint price range: $600 to $800.
    Top 1,000 ranking: 769

FEATHERS
Dear One/Lonesome Tonight • Feathers (Hollywood 1051) 1956 $3,000
    45 rpm. Near-mint price range: $2,000 to $3,000.
    Top 1,000 ranking: 140

FEATHERS, Charlie
Tongue-Tied Jill/Get with It • Charlie Feathers (Meteor 5032) 1956 $1,500
    45 rpm. Maroon label. Near-mint price range: $1,000 to $1,500.
    Top 1,000 ranking: 426

FENDERMEN
Mule Skinner Blues • Fendermen (Soma 1240).. 1960 $1,500
    LP. Vinyl appears to be blue when held to a light. Near-mint price range: $1,000 to $1,500.
    Top 1,000 ranking: 458
Mule Skinner Blues • Fendermen (Soma 1240).. 1960 $1,200
    LP. Solid black vinyl. The cover stock on at least one known counterfeit is soft and flimsy – not
    of rigid cardboard like originals. Near-mint price range: $800 to $1,200.
    Top 1,000 ranking: 534

FERGUSON, H-Bomb / Escos / Mascots
A Little Rock & Roll for Everybody • H-Bomb Ferguson / Escos / Mascots
    (Audio Lab 1567) 1961 $1,200
    LP. Near-mint price range: $800 to $1,200.
    Top 1,000 ranking: 538

FI-DELS
Why Do I Love You/Please Come Back • Fi-Dels (Bardo 529)......................1950s $3,000
    45 rpm. Near-mint price range: $2,500 to $3,000.
    Top 1,000 ranking: 163

FIVE BLUE NOTES
The Beat of Our Hearts/You Gotta Go Baby • Five Blue Notes (Sabre 108) . 1954 $3,000
    45 rpm. White label. Near-mint price range: $2,000 to $3,000.
    Top 1,000 ranking: 127
My Gal Is Gone/Ooh Baby • Five Blue Notes (Sabre 103) 1953 $1,000
    45 rpm. Red vinyl. Near-mint price range: $750 to $1,000.
    Top 1,000 ranking: 580

FIVE BUDDS
I Was Such a Fool/Midnight • Five Budds (Rama 1)...................................... 1953 $750
    45 rpm. Near-mint price range: $500 to $750.
    Top 1,000 ranking: 812
I Want Her Back/I Guess It's All Over Now • Five Budds (Rama 2)............... 1953 $750
    45 rpm. Near-mint price range: $500 to $750.
    Top 1,000 ranking: 813

FIVE CHANCES
All I Want/Shake-a-Link • Five Chances (Blue Lake 115)............................... 1955 $5,000
    45 rpm. Red vinyl. Near-mint price range: $4,000 to $5,000.
    Top 1,000 ranking: 54
I May Be Small/Nagasaki • Five Chances (Chance 1157)............................. 1954 $3,000
    45 rpm. Near-mint price range: $2,500 to $3,000.
    Top 1,000 ranking: 128
All I Want/Shake-a-Link • Five Chances (Blue Lake 115)............................... 1955 $2,000
    45 rpm. Black vinyl. Near-mint price range: $1,000 to $2,000.
    Top 1,000 ranking: 281

EKKO RECORDS
4949 Hollywood Blvd., Hollywood, California

Old Judge
BMI

3001-B
Time 2:00

Not For Sale

FOOL'S PARADISE
(E. Cochran-J. Capehart-H. Cochran)
COCHRAN BROS.
3001

978.

METEOR

(MR 5063)
Mct. Publ.
BMI 3:00

Vocal
Group

LIZZIE
(W. Dell-Leslo)
THE DEL RIOS
WITH
THE BEARCATS
5038

979.

THE JAGUARS
SING
THE WAY YOU LOOK TONIGHT
(Jerome Kern)

Chappell, Inc.
ASCAP (Time 2:19)
★

R-DELL

RECORD NO.
11

980.

teen

Banks
B.M.I.

Time 2:35

IT HAPPENED TO ME
(Hart - Jackson)
THE RE-VELS
BUTCH BALLARD ORCHESTRA
COND. GENE KUTCH
122B

981.

Gloria/Sugar Lips • Five Chances (States 156) 1956 $1,000
     45 rpm. Red vinyl. Near-mint price range: $750 to $1,000.
     Top 1,000 ranking: 627
Gloria/Sugar Lips • Five Chances (States 156) 1956 $750
     45 rpm. Black vinyl. Near-mint price range: $500 to $750.
     Top 1,000 ranking: 842

5 CROWNS [Five Crowns]

Good Luck Darling/You Could Be My Love • 5 Crowns (Old Town 790) 1953 $4,000
     45 rpm. Red vinyl. Near-mint price range: $3,000 to $4,000.
     Top 1,000 ranking: 74
Keep It a Secret/Why Don't You Believe Me • Five Crowns (Rainbow 202) .. 1953 $3,000
     45 rpm. Red vinyl. Near-mint price range: $2,000 to $3,000.
     Top 1,000 ranking: 118
You Came to Me/Ooh Wee Baby • Five Crowns (With Orchestra)
   (Riviera 990)... 1955 $2,500
     45 rpm. Near-mint price range: $2,000 to $2,500.
     Top 1,000 ranking: 189
A Star/You're My Inspiration • Five Crowns (Rainbow 179)........................... 1952 $1,000
     45 rpm. Red vinyl. Near-mint price range: $750 to $1,000.
     Top 1,000 ranking: 573

FIVE DISCS

Roses/My Chinese Girl • Five Discs (Dwain 6072) 1959 $3,000
     45 rpm. Near-mint price range: $2,000 to $3,000.
     Top 1,000 ranking: 159

FIVE DUKES OF RHYTHM

Soft, Sweet and Really Fine/Everybody's Singing the Blues • Five Dukes of
   Rhythm (With Gene Moore & His Combo) (Rendezvous 812)................ 1954 $1,500
     45 rpm. Near-mint price range: $1,000 to $1,500.
     Top 1,000 ranking: 412

FIVE ECHOES

Baby Come Back to Me/Lonely Mood • Five Echoes (Sabre 102)................. 1953 $1,500
     45 rpm. Red vinyl. Near-mint price range: $1,000 to $1,500.
     Top 1,000 ranking: 403
So Lonesome/Broke • Five Echoes (Sabre 105) 1954 $1,500
     45 rpm. Red vinyl. Near-mint price range: $1,000 to $1,500.
     Top 1,000 ranking: 413

FIVE EMERALDS [5 Emeralds]

I'll Beg/Let Me Take You Out Tonight • 5 Emeralds (S.R.C. 106)................. 1953 $1,200
     45 rpm. Credits "5 Emeralds." Blue label. Logo has periods between letters. Near-mint price
     range: $800 to $1,200.
     Top 1,000 ranking: 504
Darling/Pleasure Me • Five Emeralds [5 Emeralds] (S-R-C 107).................... 1954 $1,200
     45 rpm. Near-mint price range: $800 to $1,200.
     Top 1,000 ranking: 508
I'll Beg/Let Me Take You Out Tonight • Five Emeralds [5 Emeralds]
   (S-R-C 106)... 1953 $1,000
     45 rpm. Credits "Five Emeralds." Maroon label. Has hyphens between letters. Near-mint price
     range: $750 to $1,000.
     Top 1,000 ranking: 581

5 FORTUNES

You Are My Love/Time Out for Love • 5 Fortunes (Ransom 103).................. 1958 $1,200
     45 rpm. Near-mint price range: $800 to $1,200.
     Top 1,000 ranking: 527

984.

982.

983.

5 "GENTS"
I Never Told You/Rock with Me Marie • 5 "Gents" (Crest 51657) 1958 $1,000
  45 rpm. Near-mint price range: $750 to $1,000.
  Top 1,000 ranking: 651

FIVE KEYS
Red Sails in the Sunset/Be Anything But Be Mine • Five Keys
  (Aladdin 3127)... 1952 $4,000
  45 rpm. Near-mint price range: $3,000 to $4,000.
  Top 1,000 ranking: 71
Best of the 5 Keys • Five Keys (Aladdin 806) 1956 $4,000
  LP. Maroon label. Bootlegs have the Score reissue cover art, but use the Aladdin name and
  number. There is no original Aladdin LP titled *On the Town*. Near-mint price range: $3,000 to
  $4,000.
  Top 1,000 ranking: 85
It's Chrismas Time/Old MacDonald • Five Keys (Aladdin 3113) 1951 $1,200
  45 rpm. Near-mint price range: $800 to $1,200.
  Top 1,000 ranking: 496
Yes Sir, That's My Baby/Old MacDonald • Five Keys (Aladdin 3118)............ 1952 $1,200
  45 rpm. Near-mint price range: $800 to $1,200.
  Top 1,000 ranking: 499
Mistakes/How Long • Five Keys (Aladdin 3131) 1952 $1,200
  45 rpm. Near-mint price range: $800 to $1,200.
  Top 1,000 ranking: 500
I Hadn't Anyone 'Til You/Hold Me • Five Keys (Aladdin 3136)...................... 1952 $1,200
  45 rpm. Near-mint price range: $800 to $1,200.
  Top 1,000 ranking: 501
I Cried for You/Serve Another Round • Five Keys (Aladdin 3158).................. 1952 $1,200
  45 rpm. Near-mint price range: $800 to $1,200.
  Top 1,000 ranking: 502
These Foolish Things/Lonesome Old Story • Five Keys (Aladdin 3190)........ 1953 $1,200
  45 rpm. Near-mint price range: $800 to $1,200.
  Top 1,000 ranking: 505
Can't Keep from Crying/Come Go My Bail, Louise • Five Keys
  (Aladdin 3167)... 1953 $1,000
  45 rpm. Near-mint price range: $750 to $1,000.
  Top 1,000 ranking: 582
There Ought to Be a Law/Mama • Five Keys (Aladdin 3175) 1953 $1,000
  45 rpm. Near-mint price range: $750 to $1,000.
  Top 1,000 ranking: 583
Teardrops in Your Eyes/I'm So High • Five Keys (Aladdin 3204) 1953 $1,000
  45 rpm. Near-mint price range: $750 to $1,000.
  Top 1,000 ranking: 584
Someday, Sweetheart/Love My Loving • Five Keys (Aladdin 3228) 1954 $1,000
  45 rpm. Near-mint price range: $750 to $1,000.
  Top 1,000 ranking: 600
Deep in My Heart/How Do You Expect Me to Get It • Five Keys
  (Aladdin 3245)... 1954 $1,000
  45 rpm. Near-mint price range: $750 to $1,000.
  Top 1,000 ranking: 601
The Glory of Love/Hucklebuck with Jimmy • Five Keys (Aladdin 3099)......... 1951 $800
  45 rpm. Near-mint price range: $600 to $800.
  Top 1,000 ranking: 764
My Saddest Hour/Oh! Babe! • Five Keys (Aladdin 3214)............................... 1953 $750
  45 rpm. Blue label. Near-mint price range: $500 to $750.
  Top 1,000 ranking: 814
On the Town • Five Keys (Score 4003).. 1957 $750
  LP. Repackage of *Best of the 5 Keys,* Aladdin 806. See that listing for bootleg information. Near-
  mint price range: $500 to $750.
  Top 1,000 ranking: 852

988.

ESTA
RECORD'S
BOX 233 - HAMILTON, OHIO

UNBREAKABLE
45 R.P.M.

RECORD NO.
100-2
CP-2045

DODDS MUSIC,
BMI
3:27

Vocal By
LONNIE CARTER

I'M LONESOME FOR YOU
(Eva Dodds)
THE ESCOS
Background: George Carter, Wilbert Bell
and Winfred Gerald
MUSIC BY
THE SWINGIN' ROCKS

989.

Star-Fax
Records

Rhinestone
Pub. Co.
BMI
Time 2:08

RECORD NO.
1002
SoN 0063-A

WANDERING
(L. Shelton-R. Sisk)
THE VISCOUNTS

P. O. Box 1368 Huntsville, Alabama

991.

LEN
Records

PHILADELPHIA, PA.

Caldwell Music
BMI

Time 2:14

TAKE IT FROM A FOOL
(D. Hogan)
"THE DREAM LOVERS"
1006B

992.

The Five Keys on Stage! • Five Keys (Capitol 828) 1957 $650
> LP. Black label, reads "Sample Album for Radio-TV Program Use." Cover has white sticker reading "For Promotional Use Only – Not for Sale." In cover photo, group member on left is holding his right hand in what some critics deemed a phallic-like position. Near-mint price range: $500 to $650.
> *Top 1,000 ranking: 983*

FIVE KIDS

Carolyn/Oh Baby • Five Kids (Maxwell 101) 1955 $5,000
> 45 rpm. Approximately four known copies. Near-mint price range: $4,000 to $5,000.
> *Top 1,000 ranking: 55*

FIVE LYRICS

I'm Traveling Light/My Honey Sweet Pea • Five Lyrics (Music City 799) 1956 $2,000
> 45 rpm. Near-mint price range: $1,000 to $2,000.
> *Top 1,000 ranking: 292*

"5" ROYALES

The Rockin' 5 Royales • "5" Royales (Apollo 488) 1959 $2,000
> LP. Green label. Near-mint price range: $1,000 to $2,000.
> *Top 1,000 ranking: 323*

The Rockin' 5 Royales • "5" Royales (Apollo 488) 1959 $1,200
> LP. Yellow label. Near-mint price range: $800 to $1,200.
> *Top 1,000 ranking: 531*

FIVE SATINS

In the Still of the Nite/Jones Girl • Five Satins (Standord 200) 1956 $2,000
> 45 rpm. Red label. Reads "Produced By Martin Kuegull." Three known copies. Near-mint price range: $1,000 to $2,000.
> *Top 1,000 ranking: 293*

In the Still of the Nite/Jones Girl • Five Satins (Standord 200) 1956 $1,000
> 45 rpm. Red label. Near-mint price range: $750 to $1,000.
> *Top 1,000 ranking: 628*

The Five Satins Sing • Five Satins (Ember 100) 1958 $1,000
> LP. Multi-color label. Colored vinyl. Near-mint price range: $750 to $1,000.
> *Top 1,000 ranking: 652*

All Mine/Rose Mary • Five Satins (Standord 100) 1956 $800
> 45 rpm. Red label. Any copies on a maroon/brown label are unauthorized reissues. Same selection number used for a 1957 Chestnuts issue. Near-mint price range: $600 to $800.
> *Top 1,000 ranking: 771*

FIVE SCALDERS

If Only You Were Mine/There Will Come a Time • Five Scalders
(Drummond 3000) 1956 $5,000
> 45 rpm. Near-mint price range: $4,000 to $5,000.
> *Top 1,000 ranking: 58*

If Only You Were Mine/There Will Come a Time • Five Scalders
(Sugar Hill 3000) 1956 $2,000
> 45 rpm. Near-mint price range: $2,000 to $3,000.
> *Top 1,000 ranking: 141*

Girl Friend/Willow Blues • Five Scalders (With Bill Moore on Tenor Sax)
(Drummond 3001) 1956 $1,200
> 45 rpm. Powder blue label. Near-mint price range: $800 to $1,200.
> *Top 1,000 ranking: 517*

Girl Friend/Willow Blues • Five Scalders (With Bill Moore on Tenor Sax)
(Drummond 3001) 1956 $1,000
> 45 rpm. Maroon label. Near-mint price range: $750 to $1,000.
> *Top 1,000 ranking: 629*

993.

994.

995.

996.

FIVE SHARPS

Stormy Weather/Sleepy Cowboy • Five Sharps (Jubilee 5104)..................... 1952 $7,500
    78 rpm. Since no original 45s have been verified, it is safe to assume none were made. Bootleg
    45s are common, but can be identified by their lighter shade of blue paper than was used by
    Jubilee in the '50s. They also have thicker horizontal lines than originals. Beware of Jubilee
    5478, a 1964 issue that, although credited to the Five Sharps, is a completely different recording
    of *Stormy Weather*. Near-mint price range: $7,000 to $8,000.
    Top 1,000 ranking: 26

FIVE STARS

Let's Fall in Love/We Danced in the Moonlight • Five Stars (Treat 505)........ 1955 $2,000
    45 rpm. Near-mint price range: $1,000 to $2,000.
    Top 1,000 ranking: 282

FIVE THRILLS

Gloria/Wee Wee Baby • Five Thrills (Parrot 800)... 1954 $3,000
    45 rpm. Red vinyl. Near-mint price range: $2,000 to $3,000.
    Top 1,000 ranking: 129
Feel So Good/My Baby's Gone • Five Thrills (Parrot 796)............................ 1954 $1,000
    45 rpm. Near-mint price range: $750 to $1,000.
    Top 1,000 ranking: 602
Gloria/Wee Wee Baby • Five Thrills (Parrot 800).. 1954 $1,000
    45 rpm. Black vinyl. Near-mint price range: $750 to $1,000.
    Top 1,000 ranking: 603

FIVE TINOS

Sitting By My Window/Don't Do That! • Five Tinos (Sun 222)........................ 1955 $1,200
    45 rpm. Near-mint price range: $800 to $1,200.
    Top 1,000 ranking: 514

FLAMING HEARTS

Baby/I Don't Mind • Flaming Hearts (Inst. Tornadoes) (Vulco 1) 1958 $1,500
    45 rpm. Near-mint price range: $1,000 to $1,500.
    Top 1,000 ranking: 439

FLAMINGOS

I Really Don't Want to Know/Get with It • Flamingos (Parrot 811) 1955 $5,000
    45 rpm. Black vinyl. Reads "The Bronzville Record Mfg. Co." at bottom. Counterfeits may show
    name as "Bronxville." Near-mint price range: $4,000 to $5,000.
    Top 1,000 ranking: 56
Golden Teardrops/Carried Away • Flamingos (With Red Holloway's Orchestra)
   (Chance 1145) 1953 $3,000
    45 rpm. Red vinyl. Near-mint price range: $2,000 to $3,000.
    Top 1,000 ranking: 119
Dream of a Lifetime/On My Merry Way • Flamingos (Parrot 808).................. 1954 $3,000
    45 rpm. Red vinyl. Reads "The Bronzville Record Mfg. Co." at bottom. Counterfeits may show
    name as "Bronxville." Near-mint price range: $2,000 to $3,000.
    Top 1,000 ranking: 130
If I Can't Have You/Someday, Someway • Flamingos (Chance 1133) 1953 $2,000
    45 rpm. Red vinyl. Near-mint price range: $1,000 to $2,000.
    Top 1,000 ranking: 249
Hurry Home Baby/That's My Desire • Flamingos (Chance 1140) 1953 $1,500
    45 rpm. Red vinyl. Near-mint price range: $1,000 to $1,500.
    Top 1,000 ranking: 404
Golden Teardrops/Carried Away • Flamingos (With Red Holloway's Orchestra)
   (Chance 1145) 1953 $1,000
    45 rpm. Black vinyl. Near-mint price range: $750 to $1,000.
    Top 1,000 ranking: 585
Plan for Love/You Ain't Ready • Flamingos (Chance 1149)........................... 1953 $1,000
    45 rpm. Yellow and black label. Near-mint price range: $750 to $1,000.
    Top 1,000 ranking: 586

999.

1000.

998.

Cross Over the Bridge/Listen to My Plea • Flamingos (Chance 1154) 1954 $1,000
    45 rpm. Near-mint price range: $750 to $1,000.
    Top 1,000 ranking: 604

Dream of a Lifetime/On My Merry Way • Flamingos (Parrot 808).................. 1954 $1,000
    45 rpm. Black vinyl. Reads "The Bronzville Record Mfg. Co." at bottom. Counterfeits may show
    name as "Bronxville." Near-mint price range: $750 to $1,000.
    Top 1,000 ranking: 605

Ko Ko Mo/I'm Yours • Flamingos (Parrot 812) 1955 $1,000
    45 rpm. Red vinyl. Reads "The Bronzville Record Mfg. Co." at bottom. Counterfeits may show
    name as "Bronxville." Near-mint price range: $750 to $1,000.
    Top 1,000 ranking: 616

If I Can't Have You/Someday, Someway • Flamingos (Chance 1133) 1953 $750
    45 rpm. Black vinyl. Near-mint price range: $500 to $750.
    Top 1,000 ranking: 815

FOLEY, Jim

Goodbye Train/? • Jim Foley (Lucky 1001)... 1960 $1,000
    45 rpm. Lucky also used the selection number 1001 on a release by Ronny & Johnny. Near-mint
    price range: $750 to $1,000.
    Top 1,000 ranking: 683

FORBES, Graham and Trio

Martini Set • Graham Forbes and Trio (Phillips International 1955)............... 1959 $750
    LP. Near-mint price range: $500 to $750.
    Top 1,000 ranking: 871

FOUR BEL'AIRES

Tell Me Why/Where Are You • Four Bel'Aires (X-Tra 113)............................. 1958 $1,200
    45 rpm. Near-mint price range: $800 to $1,200.
    Top 1,000 ranking: 528

FOUR BUDDIES

Delores/Look Out • Four Buddies (Club 51 105)... 1956 $4,000
    45 rpm. Red vinyl. Reportedly only three copies exist. Near-mint price range: $3,000 to $4,000.
    Top 1,000 ranking: 86

FOUR CHEVELLES

This Is Our Wedding Day/Darling Forever • Four Chevelles (Delft 6408) 1964 $750
    45 rpm. Identification number shown since no selection number is used. Near-mint price range:
    $500 to $750.
    Top 1,000 ranking: 926

FOUR FIFTHS

Come on Girl/After Graduation • Four Fifths (Hudson 8101) 1963 $4,000
    45 rpm. Blue vinyl. Near-mint price range: $3,000 to $4,000.
    Top 1,000 ranking: 94

FOUR JACKS

You Met a Fool/Goodbye Baby • Four Jacks (Federal 12075) 1952 $800
    45 rpm. Near-mint price range: $600 to $800.
    Top 1,000 ranking: 766

Grandpa Can Boogie Too/Never Again • Four Jacks (Federal 12093).......... 1952 $,800
    45 rpm. Near-mint price range: $600 to $800.
    Top 1,000 ranking: 767

FOUR KINGS

You Don't Mean Me Right/My Head Goes Acting Up • Four Kings (Music By the All
    Stars) (Fortune 811)... 1953 $1,000
    45 rpm. Near-mint price range: $750 to $1,000.
    Top 1,000 ranking: 587

LATE ADDITIONS

The following four label pictures arrived too late to be included in their proper place in the listings:

COOL SEABREEZE
(Al Lewis and The Windsors)
LEE SCOTT and THE WINDSORS

45 R.P.M.
506
MA 5012

PROMOTION RECORD
NOT FOR SALE
ASCAP - 2:39

91.

HOPEFULLY YOURS
THE LARKS
8-1180

108.

Donjo Music
BMI
Vocal
Prod. By
DON PERRY

TOO OLD TO CRY
(A. Gilbert - J. Raymond)
THE CLASS-AIRS

373.

joni Music
Time 2:15

LOVE AND KISSES
(E. Edwards)
THE MIXERS
Bold 102

671.

256

FOUR PLAID THROATS

My Inspiration/The Message • Four Plaid Throats (Mercury 70143).............. 1953 $1,000
45 rpm. Near-mint price range: $750 to $1,000.
Top 1,000 ranking: 588

FOUR TOPS

Breaking Through • Four Tops (Workshop 217) 1962 $1,500
LP. Near-mint price range: $1,000 to $1,500.
Top 1,000 ranking: 465
Jazz Impressions By the Four Tops • Four Tops (Workshop 217)................ 1962 $1,000
LP. Retitled reissue of *Breaking Through*. Near-mint price range: $750 to $1,000.
Top 1,000 ranking: 703

FRACTION

Moon Blood • Fraction (Angelus 571) 1971 $1,500
LP. Near-mint price range: $1,000 to $1,500.
Top 1,000 ranking: 483

FRANKIE & C-NOTES

Forever and Ever/Fade-Out • Frankie & C-Notes (Richie 2)......................... 1961 $1,500
45 rpm. Near-mint price range: $1,000 to $1,500.
Top 1,000 ranking: 459

FREDDIE & QUANTRILS

If I Give My Heart to You/Thunderbird • Freddie & Quantrils (Karem 1904) .. 1964 $1,000
45 rpm. Near-mint price range: $750 to $1,000.
Top 1,000 ranking: 726

FREDRIC

Phases and Faces • Fredric (Forte 80461) 1968 $1,000
LP. Near-mint price range: $750 to $1,000.
Top 1,000 ranking: 734

FROST, Frank

Hey Boss Man! • Frank Frost (Phillips International 1975)........................... 1961 $2,500
LP. Near-mint price range: $2,000 to $2,500.
Top 1,000 ranking: 200

FUGITIVES

The Fugitives at Dave's Hideout • Fugitives (Hideout 1001)........................ 1965 $1,000
LP. Near-mint price range: $750 to $1,000.
Top 1,000 ranking: 731

FUGITIVES / Oxford Five / Lourds / Individuals

Friday at the Cage A-Go-Go • Fugitives / Oxford Five / Lourds / Individuals
(Westchester 1005).. 1965 $1,500
LP. Distributed at the Cage A-Go-Go club. Some copies have a sticker on labels showing title as
Long Hot Summer. Not issued with a cover. Near-mint price range: $1,000 to $1,500.
Top 1,000 ranking: 472

FULSON, Lowell

Stormin' and Rainin'/Night and Day • Lowell Fulson (Aladdin 3104).............. 1953 $2,000
45 rpm. Green vinyl. Near-mint price range: $1,000 to $2,000.
Top 1,000 ranking: 250

GAINES, Eddie

Be-Bop Battling Ball/Try This Heart for Size • Eddie Gaines (Summit 101)... 1958 $1,500
45 rpm. Near-mint price range: $1,000 to $1,500.
Top 1,000 ranking: 440

GALES

Darling Patricia/All Is Well, All Is Well • Gales (J-V-B 35) 1955 $1,500
    45 rpm. Reportedly the same group as the Violinaires. Near-mint price range: $1,000 to $1,500.
    Top 1,000 ranking: 421

Guiding Angel/Baby Come Home • Gales (Mel-O 111) 1958 $1,000
    45 rpm. Reportedly the same group as the Violinaires. Near-mint price range: $750 to $1,000.
    Top 1,000 ranking: 653

GARLAND, Judy, / Tommy Dorsey

The Trolley Song/Cocktails for Two • Judy Garland / Tommy Dorsey
    (Vogue) 1946 $1,000
    78 rpm picture disc. No selection number used. Near-mint price range: $750 to $1,000.
    Top 1,000 ranking: 564

GARMON, Johnny

You're Wrong/Try Not to Hear • Johnny Garmon (Missile 1)............................... ? $800
    45 rpm. Near-mint price range: $600 to $800.
    Top 1,000 ranking: 796

GATES

Wedding Bells Gonna Ring/Summer Night Love • Gates featuring Bobby Ferguson
    (Peach 716) 1959 $800
    45 rpm. Near-mint price range: $600 to $800.
    Top 1,000 ranking: 777

GATORS

Your a Thousand Miles Away/? • Gators (Chuck Lechner "N" His Gators)
    (Gator)... 1957 $2,500
    45 rpm. No selection number used. Should be "You're," but "Your" is shown on label. Near-mint
    price range: $2,000 to $2,500.
    Top 1,000 ranking: 193

GAY TUNES

Thrill of Romance/Why-y-y Leave Me This Wa-ay-ay • Gay Tunes
    (Timely 1002) 1953 $2,000
    45 rpm. Red vinyl. Near-mint price range: $1,000 to $2,000.
    Top 1,000 ranking: 251

GEMS

Deed I Do/Talk About the Weather • Gems (Drexel 901) 1954 $3,000
    45 rpm. Red vinyl. Near-mint price range: $2,000 to $3,000.
    Top 1,000 ranking: 131

GLIDERS

School Days/Baby Come On • Gliders (Southern Sound 103) 1962 $800
    45 rpm. Near-mint price range: $600 to $800.
    Top 1,000 ranking: 785

GOLDEN BELLS

Bells Are Ringing/Pretty Girl • Golden Bells (With Gems of Rhythm Band)
    (Sure 1002) 1959 $1,500
    45 rpm. Near-mint price range: $1,000 to $1,500.
    Top 1,000 ranking: 449

GOLDEN NUGGETS

I Was a Fool (To Make You Cry)/Teenage Josephine • Golden Nuggets (With
    Rocky Rhodes & California Versatones) (Futura 1691) 1959 $1,000
    45 rpm. Near-mint price range: $750 to $1,000.
    Top 1,000 ranking: 667

GOLDENRODS

Wish I Was Back in School/Color Cartoon • Goldenrods (Vee-Jay 307) 1958 $750
45 rpm. Near-mint price range: $500 to $750.
Top 1,000 ranking: 861

GOODMAN, Benny, Orchestra

Pop-Corn Man/Oooo-Oh Boom! • Benny Goodman Orchestra with Martha Tilton
(Victor 25808).. 1939 $1,000
78 rpm. Near-mint price range: $750 to $1,000.
Top 1,000 ranking: 563

A Jazz Holiday/Wolverine Blues • Benny Goodman Orchestra
(Vocallon 15656).. 1928 $900
78 rpm. First record by Benny Goodman under his own name. Near-mint price range: $700 to $900.
Top 1,000 ranking: 752

GORDON, Bill "Bass", & Colonials

Two Loves Have I/Bring My Baby Back • Bill "Bass" Gordon & His Colonials
(Gee 12).. 1954 $2,000
45 rpm. Near-mint price range: $1,000 to $2,000.
Top 1,000 ranking: 267

GOSPEL STARS

Great Gospel Stars • Gospel Stars (Tamla 222).. 1961 $750
LP. Near-mint price range: $500 to $750.
Top 1,000 ranking: 895

GRAND PRIXS

Late Summer Love/No Good Woman • Grand Prixs (Poncho 10) 1962 $1,000
45 rpm. Near-mint price range: $750 to $1,000.
Top 1,000 ranking: 704

GRANDMA'S ROCKERS

Homemade Apple Pie and Yankee Ingenuity • Grandma's Rockers
(Fredlo).. 1967 $1,500
LP. Selection number not yet known. Near-mint price range: $1,000 to $1,500.
Top 1,000 ranking: 475

GRASSI, Lucy Ann, & Del-Aires

Boy Crazy/Scuba Duba • Lucy Ann Grassi & Del-Aires (Volcanic 1002) 1964 $3,000
45 rpm. One known copy. Near-mint price range: $2,000 to $3,000.
Top 1,000 ranking: 172

GRISHAM, Marlon

Ain't That a Dilly/Sugarfoot • Marlon Grisham (Cover 5982)......................... 1959 $650
45 rpm. Near-mint price range: $500 to $650.
Top 1,000 ranking: 986

GRUBBS, Jimmy, & His Music Makers

Let's Rock To-Night/(It's My Fault) You're Gone • Jimmy Grubbs & His Music
Makers (Mac 468/469) 1950s $1,000
45 rpm. Near-mint price range: $750 to $1,000.
Top 1,000 ranking: 678

GUNTER, Hardrock

Gonna Dance All Night/Fallen Angel • Hardrock Gunter (Sun 201)............... 1954 $650
45 rpm. Near-mint price range: $500 to $650.
Top 1,000 ranking: 975

HALEY, Bill
Deal Me a Hand/Ten Gallon Stetson • Bill Haley (With Saddlemen)
(Keystone 5101)... 1950 $1,000
78 rpm. Near-mint price range: $750 to $1,000.
Top 1,000 ranking: 568
Susan Van Dusan/? • Bill Haley (Keystone 5102) 1950 $1,000
78 rpm. Near-mint price range: $750 to $1,000.
Top 1,000 ranking: 569
Rock the Joint/Icy Heart • Bill Haley (With Saddlemen) (Essex 303)............. 1952 $750
45 rpm. Colored vinyl. Near-mint price range: $500 to $750.
Top 1,000 ranking: 808

HALL, Bobby, & Kings
Fire in My Heart/You Never Knew • Bobby Hall & Kings (Harlem 2322)........ 1954 $2,000
45 rpm. Red vinyl. Near-mint price range: $1,000 to $2,000.
Top 1,000 ranking: 268

HALLIQUINS
Confession of Love/Haunting Memories • Halliquins (Juanita 102) 1958 $1,500
45 rpm. Near-mint price range: $1,000 to $1,500.
Top 1,000 ranking: 441

HAMMOND, Clay, & Johnnie Young & Celebritys
We Made Romance/Absent Minded • Clay Hammond & Johnnie Young &
Celebritys (Caroline 2302) 1956 $750
45 rpm. Near-mint price range: $500 -$750.
Top 1,000 ranking: 843

HARMONICA FRANK
Rockin Chair Daddy/Great Medical Menagerist • Harmonica Frank [Frank Floyd]
(Sun 205) 1954 $3,000
45 rpm. Near-mint price range: $2,000 to $3,000.
Top 1,000 ranking: 132

HARPTONES
The Sensational Harptones • Harptones (Bruce 201)................................... 1954 $10,000
EP. Approximately two known. Near-mint price range: $7,500 to $10,000.
Top 1,000 ranking: 15

HARRIS, Peppermint: see PEPPERMINT HARRIS

HARRISON, George
Love Comes to Everyone/Soft Touch • George Harrison (Dark
Horse 8844) 1979 $1,000
Picture sleeve. Near-mint price range: $750 to $1,000.
Top 1,000 ranking: 745

HAUNTED
The Haunted • Haunted (Trans-World 6701) 1966 $1,500
LP. Canadian release. Near-mint price range: $1,000 to $1,500.
Top 1,000 ranking: 474

HAVEN, Shirley, & Four Jacks
Stop Fooling Around/Troubles of My Own • Shirley Haven & Four Jacks
(Federal 12092).. 1952 $1,000
45 rpm. Near-mint price range: $750 to $1,000.
Top 1,000 ranking: 574

HAVEN, Shirley, & Four Jacks / Cora Williams & Four Jacks
Sure Cure for the Blues/I Ain't Coming Back Anymore • Shirley Haven & Four
Jacks/Cora Williams & Four Jacks (Federal 12079) 1952 $800
45 rpm. Near-mint price range: $600 to $800.
Top 1,000 ranking: 768

HAWKINS, Dale
Suzy-Q • Dale Hawkins (Chess 1429) 1958 $1,000
LP. At least one known counterfeit exists with a black and white cover. Original covers are in full
color. Between cover and label, the following spellings of the title track are found: "Suzy-Q,"
"Susie-Q" and "Suzie Q." Near-mint price range: $750 to $1,000.
Top 1,000 ranking: 654
Poor Little Rhode Island/Every Little Girl • Dale Hawkins (Checker 944) 1960 $650
45 rpm single with picture sleeve. Sleeve represents about 95% of value. Near-mint price range:
$500 to $650.
Top 1,000 ranking: 993

HAWKINS, Screamin' Jay
At Home with Screamin' Jay Hawkins • Screamin' Jay Hawkins (Orchestra Under
Direction of Leroy Kirkland and O.B. Masingill) (Epic LN-3448) 1956 $900
LP. Near-mint price range: $700 to $900.
Top 1,000 ranking: 755

HAYMARKET SQUARE
Magic Lantern • Haymarket Square (Chaparral 201) 1968 $1,000
LP. Opinions vary as to whether "Magic Lantern" or "Haymarket Square" is the group name.
Near-mint price range: $750 to $1,000.
Top 1,000 ranking: 735

HEARTBREAKERS
Heartbreaker/Wanda • Heartbreakers (RCA Victor 4327)............................. 1951 $700
45 rpm. Near-mint price range: $500 to $700.
Top 1,000 ranking: 950

HELLER, Jackie / Glenn Miller
Rum and Coca-Cola/On a Little Street in Singapore • Jackie Heller / Glenn Miller
(Vogue/Philco).. 1945 $700
78 rpm picture disc. Vogue label on one side, Philco on flip. No selection number used.
Promotional issue. Near-mint price range: $500 to $700.
Top 1,000 ranking: 948

HENDRIX, Jimi
Axis: Bold As Love • Jimi Hendrix (Reprise R-6281)..................................... 1968 $1,500
Monaural LP. Gatefold cover. White label. Promotional issue only. Near-mint price range: $1,000
to $1,500.
Top 1,000 ranking: 477
Hey Joe/51st Anniversary • Jimi Hendrix (Reprise 0572) 1967 $800
Picture sleeve. Near-mint price range: $400 to $800.
Top 1,000 ranking: 790

HENRY, Robert
Miss Anna B/Something's Wrong with My Lovin Machine • Robert Henry
(King 4624) 1953 $650
45 rpm. Near-mint price range: $500 to $650.
Top 1,000 ranking: 971
Old Battle Ax/Early in the Morning • Robert Henry (King 4646).................... 1953 $650
45 rpm. Near-mint price range: $500 to $650.
Top 1,000 ranking: 972

HEPSTERS
I Had to Let You Go/Rockin' 'n Rollin' with Santa • Hepsters (Ronel 107) 1955 $5,000
45 rpm. Red vinyl. Two copies known. Near-mint price range: $4,000 to $5,000.
Top 1,000 ranking: 57

HEPTONES
I'm So in Love Tonight/Anna Bell • Heptones (Abbco 401)............................ 1956 $1,000
45 rpm. Serial numbers "105" and "106" are actually more prominent on label than selection no.
"401." Near-mint price range: $750 to $1,000.
Top 1,000 ranking: 630

HIDE-A-WAYS
Can't Help Loving That Girl of Mine/I'm Coming Home • Hide-A-Ways
(Ronni 1000) 1954 $6,000
45 rpm. Seven known copies. Near-mint price range: $5,000 to $6,000.
Top 1,000 ranking: 35
Cherie/He Make 'Em Pow Wow • Hide-A-Ways (With Instrumental
Accompaniement) (MGM 55004) 1955 $750
45 rpm. Near-mint price range: $500 to $750.
Top 1,000 ranking: 834

HI-LITERS
Hello Dear/Bobby Sox Baby • Hi-Liters (Vee-Jay 184) 1956 $1,500
45 rpm. Near-mint price range: $1,000 to $1,500.
Top 1,000 ranking: 427

HOLLY, Buddy
The Chirping Crickets • Buddy Holly & Crickets (Brunswick 54038) 1957 $800
LP. Near-mint price range: $600 to $800.
Top 1,000 ranking: 774
That'll Be the Day • Buddy Holly (Decca 2575)... 1958 $750
EP. With liner notes on the back cover. Near-mint price range: $500 to $750.
Top 1,000 ranking: 862

HOLLYWOOD ARIST-O-KATS
I'll Be Home Again/Amazon Beauty • Hollywood Arist-O-Kats (With Red Callender
Sextette) (Recorded In Hollywood 406) 1953 $5,000
45 rpm. Near-mint price range: $4,000 to $5,000.
Top 1,000 ranking: 45

HOLLYWOOD FLAMES
One Night with a Fool/Ride Helen Ride • Hollywood Flames (With Orchestra Acc.)
(Lucky 001) 1954 $750
45 rpm. Near-mint price range: $500 to $750.
Top 1,000 ranking: 823
Peggy/Oooh-La-La • Hollywood Flames (Lucky 006) 1954 $750
45 rpm. Near-mint price range: $500 to $750.
Top 1,000 ranking: 824

HOLLYWOOD SAXONS
Everyday Holiday/L.A. Lover • Hollywood Saxons (Hareco 102).................... 1958 $2,000
45 rpm. Near-mint price range: $1,000 to $2,000.
Top 1,000 ranking: 311

HOLMES, Leon, & His Georgia Ramblers
She's My Baby/You're Not Mine At All • Leon Holmes & His Georgia Ramblers
(Peach 597) 1959 $1,500
45 rpm. Near-mint price range: $1,000 to $1,500.
Top 1,000 ranking: 450

HOPKINS, Lightnin'

Lightnin' and the Blues • Lightnin' Hopkins (Herald 1012) 1960 $1,000
LP. Near-mint price range: $750 to $1,000.
Top 1,000 ranking: 684

HORNETS & ORCHESTRA

I Can't Believe/Lonesome Baby • Hornets & Orchestra (States 127) 1953 $10,000
45 rpm. Red vinyl. The wide price range here reflects both one known sale of, and one offer
which was declined for the red vinyl pressing – though our valuation isn't quite as high as the
1988 sale price. Near-mint price range: $7,500 to $10,000.
Top 1,000 ranking: 13

I Can't Believe/Lonesome Baby • Hornets & Orchestra (States 127) 1953 $6,000
45 rpm. Black vinyl. Near-mint price range: $4,000 to $6,000.
Top 1,000 ranking: 33

I Can't Believe/Lonesome Baby • Hornets & Orchestra (States 127) 1953 $2,000
78 rpm. Near-mint price range: $1,000 to $2,000.
Top 1,000 ranking: 252

HOT SHOT LOVE: see LOVE, Hot Shot

HULL, Terry, & Starfires

Those Pretty Brown Eyes/Meant to Be • Terry Hull & Starfires (Staff 103) .... ? $750
45 rpm. Near-mint price range: $500 to $750.
Top 1,000 ranking: 942

IMPLACABLES

Don't Call for Me/My Foolish Pride • Implacables (Kain 1004) 1961 $1,000
45 rpm. Reissued as by Johnny Williams. Near-mint price range: $750 to $1,000.
Top 1,000 ranking: 693

INCONQUERABLES

Wait for Me/For Your Love • Inconquerables (Flodavieur 803) 1964 $2,500
45 rpm. Near-mint price range: $1,500 to $2,500.
Top 1,000 ranking: 209

INCREDIBLE VIKINGS

Love Will Be Mine/Reward • Incredible Vikings (Winndsock) 1955 $3,000
45 rpm. No selection number used. One known copy. Near-mint price range: $2,000 to $3,000.
Top 1,000 ranking: 137

INDEX

The Index • Index (DC) 1968 $3,000
LP. No selection number used. Reportedly 100 made. Identification number in the trail-off is
"DC-71." Near-mint price range: $2,500 to $3,000.
Top 1,000 ranking: 176

The Index • Index (DC) 1968 $2,500
LP. No selection number used. Not issued with cover. Reportedly 100 made. Identification
number in the trail-off is "DC-4736." Near-mint price range: $1,500 to $2,500.
Top 1,000 ranking: 212

INFASCINATIONS

I'm So in Love/One Chance • Infascinations (Clauwell 004/003) 1961 $750
45 rpm. Polystyrene pressing. Near-mint price range: $500 to $750.
Top 1,000 ranking: 896

INSPIRATIONS

Ring Those Bells/The Cumberland and the Merrimac • Inspirations
(Rondack 9787)... 1961 $1,000
45 rpm. Near-mint price range: $750 to $1,000.
Top 1,000 ranking: 694

INTENTIONS
Summertime Angel/Mr. Misery • Intentions (Jamie 1253) 1963 $1,000
    45 rpm. Near-mint price range: $750 to $1,000.
    Top 1,000 ranking: 716

INVICTAS
Lest You Forget/Over the Wall • Invictas (Pix 1101) 1960 $1,200
    45 rpm. Near-mint price range: $800 to $1,200.
    Top 1,000 ranking: 535

INVICTORS
Where All Lovers Meet/That's All Right • Invictors (TPE 8221) 1962 $800
    45 rpm. Reissued in 1963 with a Victorio label added on top of this one, crediting the Vendors.
    Near-mint price range: $600 to $800.
    Top 1,000 ranking: 786

IVORYS
Wishing Well/Deep Freeze • Ivorys (Darla 1000) 1962 $2,000
    45 rpm. Near-mint price range: $1,000 to $2,000.
    Top 1,000 ranking: 345

JACKIE & STARLITES
They Laughed at Me/You Put One Over on Me • Jackie & Starlites
(Fire & Fury 1000) 1959 $2,000
    45 rpm. Near-mint price range: $1,000 to $2,000.
    Top 1,000 ranking: 324
They Laughed at Me/You Put One Over on Me • Jackie & Starlites
(Fire & Fury 1000) 1959 $750
    78 rpm. Near-mint price range: $500 to $750.
    Top 1,000 ranking: 872

JACK-O-LANTERNS
Lori Anne/The Great Pumpkin • Jack-O-Lanterns (Goldcrest 163) 1960s $2,000
    45 rpm. Near-mint price range: $1,000 to $2,000.
    Top 1,000 ranking: 366

JACQUET, Illinois, & Lester Young
Battle of the Saxes • Illinois Jacquet & Lester Young (Aladdin 701) 1954 $1,000
    10–inch LP. Colored vinyl. Near-mint price range: $750 to $1,000.
    Top 1,000 ranking: 606

JADES
Look for a Lie/Blue Memories • Jades (With Rocket Flames Band)
(Christy 114) 1959 $1,000
    45 rpm. Reportedly 100 pressed. Near-mint price range: $750 to $1,000.
    Top 1,000 ranking: 668

JAGUARS
The Way You Look Tonight/Moonlight and You • Jaguars (R-Dell 11) 1956 $650
    45 rpm. Red vinyl. Near-mint price range: $500 to $650.
    Top 1,000 ranking: 980

JAMES, Harry, & His Orchestra: see SINATRA, Frank

JAN & DEAN
Save for a Rainy Day • Jan & Dean (Columbia 9461) 1967 $2,000
    LP. At least one sale of this LP has been confirmed. May not be a U.S. issue. Tracks are
    remixed from what is heard on the J&D LP of the same title. Does have one track, *Lullaby in the*
    Rain, which is not on the J&D LP. Near-mint price range: $1,500 to $2,000.
    Top 1,000 ranking: 360

JAYTONES
The Bells/Oh Darling • Jaytones (Timely 1003/1004) 1953 $2,000
    45 rpm. Near-mint price range: $1,000 to $2,000.
    Top 1,000 ranking: 253

JEFFRIES, Bob
Take Me Back/Betty Lou • Bob Jeffries (With Marcels 123) (Jody 1048)....... 1958 $1,000
    45 rpm. We're not quite certain if the "123" has to do with the Marcels, or if it means something
    else. It does appear, however, that 1048 is the selection number. Near-mint price range: $750 to
    $1,000.
    Top 1,000 ranking: 655

JETS
The Lovers/Drag It Home, Baby • Jets (Rainbow 201) 1953 $1,500
    78 rpm. Near-mint price range: $1,000 to $1,500.
    Top 1,000 ranking: 405

JETS
Volcano/Gomen Nasai • Jets (7-11 2102)... 1953 $1,500
    45 rpm. Near-mint price range: $1,000 to $1,500.
    Top 1,000 ranking: 406

JETS
I'll Hide My Tears/Got a Little Shadow • Jets (Aladdin 3247)......................... 1954 $2,000
    45 rpm. *I'll Hide My Tears* reportedly written by Murray Wilson, father of several of the Beach
    Boys. Near-mint price range: $1,000 to $2,000.
    Top 1,000 ranking: 269

JETS
Heaven Above Me/Millie Brown • Jets (Gee 1020) 1956 $4,000
    45 rpm. Near-mint price range: $3,000 to $4,000.
    Top 1,000 ranking: 87

JEWELS / CROWS
Heartbreaker/Call a Doctor • Jewels / Crows (Rama 10) 1953 $2,000
    45 rpm. Red vinyl. Near-mint price range: $1,000 to $2,000.
    Top 1,000 ranking: 254
Heartbreaker/Call a Doctor • Jewels / Crows (Rama 10) 1953 $750
    45 rpm. Black vinyl. May show *Heartbreaker* by the Crows and *Call a Doctor* by the Jewels on
    some labels. Near-mint price range: $500 to $750.
    Top 1,000 ranking: 816

JIMMY & WALTER
Easy/Before Long • Jimmy & Walter (Sun 180) 1953 $1,200
    45 rpm. Near-mint price range: $800 to $1,200.
    Top 1,000 ranking: 506

JOEY & OVATIONS
I Still Love You/Runaround • Joey & Ovations (Hawk 153) 1964 $1,000
    45 rpm. Near-mint price range: $750 to $1,000.
    Top 1,000 ranking: 728

JOHNSON, F.D.
Be My Baby/? • F.D. Johnson (Jan 58)..1950s $2,000
    45 rpm. Near-mint price range: $1,500 to $2,000.
    Top 1,000 ranking: 335

JOHNSON, Lonnie
Lonesome Road • Lonnie Johnson (King 520) 1956 $1,500
    LP. Near-mint price range: $1,000 to $1,500.
    Top 1,000 ranking: 428

JOHNSON, Marv
My Baby-O/Once Upon a Time • Marv Johnson (Kudo 663) 1958 $700
  45 rpm. Near-mint price range: $500 to $700.
  Top 1,000 ranking: 958

JOHNSON, Robert
Hell Hound on My Trail/From Four Until Late • Robert Johnson
  (Vocalion 03623).. 1937 $5,000
  78 rpm. Near-mint price range: $3,000 to $5,000.
  Top 1,000 ranking: 43
Love in Vain Blues/Preaching Blues • Robert Johnson (Vocalion 04630) 1938 $3,500
  78 rpm. Near-mint price range: $2,500 to $3,500.
  Top 1,000 ranking: 96
32-20/Last Fair Deal Gone Down • Robert Johnson (Oriole 7-04-60)............ 1937 $2,500
  78 rpm. Near-mint price range: $1,500 to $2,500.
  Top 1,000 ranking: 178
Crossroads Blues/Rambling on My Mind • Robert Johnson
  (Vocalion 03519).. 1937 $2,500
  78 rpm. Near-mint price range: $1,500 to $2,500.
  Top 1,000 ranking: 179
Me and the Devil Blues/Little Queen • Robert Johnson (Vocalion 04108)..... 1938 $2,500
  78 rpm. Near-mint price range: $1,500 to $2,500.
  Top 1,000 ranking: 180
I Believe I'll Dust My Broom/Dead Shrimp Blues • Robert Johnson
  (Vocalion 03475).. 1937 $2,000
  78 rpm. Near-mint price range: $1,000 to $2,000.
  Top 1,000 ranking: 223
Come on in My Kitchen/They're Red Hot • Robert Johnson
  (Vocalion 03563).. 1937 $2,000
  78 rpm. Near-mint price range: $1,000 to $2,000.
  Top 1,000 ranking: 224
Milkcow's Calf Blues/Malted Milk • Robert Johnson (Vocalion 03665)........... 1937 $2,000
  78 rpm. Near-mint price range: $1,000 to $2,000.
  Top 1,000 ranking: 225
Stones in My Passway/I'm a Steady Rolllin' Man • Robert Johnson
  (Vocalion 03723).. 1937 $2,000
  78 rpm. Near-mint price range: $1,000 to $2,000.
  Top 1,000 ranking: 226
Stop Breakin' Down Blues/Honeymoon Blues • Robert Johnson
  (Vocalion 04002).. 1938 $2,000
  78 rpm. Near-mint price range: $1,000 to $2,000.
  Top 1,000 ranking: 227
32-20/Last Fair Deal Gone Down • Robert Johnson (Vocalion 03445).......... 1937 $1,500
  78 rpm. Near-mint price range: $1,000 to $1,500.
  Top 1,000 ranking: 390
Sweet Home Chicago/Walking Blues • Robert Johnson (Vocalion 03601).... 1937 $1,500
  78 rpm. Near-mint price range: $1,000 to $1,500.
  Top 1,000 ranking: 391
Terraplane Blues/Kind Hearted Woman • Robert Johnson
  (Vocalion 03416).. 1937 $1,000
  78 rpm. Near-mint price range: $750 to $1,000.
  Top 1,000 ranking: 562

JOKERS
I Do/Pretty Little Hula Girl • Jokers (With Aztec Combo) (Danco 117)........... 1960 $1,000
  45 rpm. Near-mint price range: $750 to $1,000.
  Top 1,000 ranking: 685
Whisper/So Tight • Jokers (Wand 111)... 1961 $1,000
  45 rpm. Colored vinyl. Near-mint price range: $750 to $1,000.
  Top 1,000 ranking: 695

JONES, Floyd
Floyd's Blues/Any Old Lonesome Day • Floyd Jones (Vee-Jay 126)............. 1955 $750
  45 rpm. Red vinyl. Near-mint price range: $500 -$750.
  Top 1,000 ranking: 835

JUMPING JACKS
Embraceable You/Pa-Pa-Ya Baby • Jumping Jacks (Bruce 115).................. 1954 $4,000
  45 rpm. Near-mint price range: $3,000 to $4,000.
  Top 1,000 ranking: 78

KAPPELIERS
Down in Mexicali/? • Kappaliers (Shadow 1229) 1950s $750
  45 rpm. Near-mint price range: $500 to $750.
  Top 1,000 ranking: 883

KARRIANN'S
Don't Want Your Picture/ ? • Karriann's (Don & Neil with Playboys)
  (Pelpal 118)...1950s $750
  45 rpm. Near-mint price range: $500 to $750.
  Top 1,000 ranking: 884

KENNY & CADETS
Barbie/What Is a Young Girl Made Of • Kenny & Cadets (Randy 422).......... 1962 $1,000
  45 rpm. Colored (red and yellow) vinyl. Near-mint price range: $750 to $1,000.
  Top 1,000 ranking: 705

KHAZAD DOOM
Level 6 ½ • Khazad Doom (LPL 892)... 1970 $1,200
  LP. Near-mint price range: $800 to $1,200.
  Top 1,000 ranking: 554

KIDDS
Are You Forgetting Me/Drunk • Kidds (Imperial 5335)................................... 1955 $750
  45 rpm. Near-mint price range: $500 to $750.
  Top 1,000 ranking: 836

KINGS
Why? Oh, Why/I Love You Baby • Kings (Featuring Bobby Hall) (Jax 314) .. 1953 $1,000
  45 rpm. Maroon label. Red vinyl. Near-mint price range: $750 to $1,000.
  Top 1,000 ranking: 589

KINGSMEN
Don't Say You're Sorry/Kicking with My Stallion • Kingsmen (Club 51 108) .. 1957 $3,000
  45 rpm. Near-mint price range: $2,000 to $3,000.
  Top 1,000 ranking: 148

KINGSFIVE
The Voodoo Man/I Hear the Rain • Kingsfive (With New Redtops)
  (Trophy 1/2)... 1959 $1,200
  45 rpm. Near-mint price range: $800 to $1,200.
  Top 1,000 ranking: 532

KIRKLAND, Danny, & His Band
They Were Rockin'/Stop Mambo • Danny Kirkland & His Band (J-V-B 60).... 1957 $700
  45 rpm. Near-mint price range: $500 to $700.
  Top 1,000 ranking: 956

KLIXS
This Is the End of Love/It's All Over • Klixs (Music City 817) 1957 $2,500
  45 rpm. Red vinyl. Near-mint price range: $1,500 to $2,500.
  Top 1,000 ranking: 194

Elaine/This Is the End of Love • Klixs (Music City 823) 1958 $1,000
45 rpm. Near-mint price range: $750 to $1,000.
Top 1,000 ranking: 656

KOOL TOPPERS
Cause I Love You So/Is That Exactly What You Wanna Do • Kool Toppers
(Beverly 702)... 1955 $1,000
45 rpm. Near-mint price range: $750 to $1,000.
Top 1,000 ranking: 617

KREED
Kreed • Kreed (Vision of Sound 71-56)... 1971 $1,500
LP. Near-mint price range: $1,000 to $1,500.
Top 1,000 ranking: 484

LARKS
My Reverie/Let's Say a Prayer • Larks (Apollo 1184) 1951 $5,000
45 rpm. Orange vinyl. Near-mint price range: $3,000 to $5,000.
Top 1,000 ranking: 44
Stolen Love/In My Lonely Room • Larks (Apollo 1190)................................. 1952 $4,000
45 rpm. Orange vinyl. Near-mint price range: $3,000 to $4,000.
Top 1,000 ranking: 72
I Don't Believe in Tomorrow/Ooh...It Feels So Good • Larks (Apollo 430) 1951 $3,000
45 rpm. Near-mint price range: $2,000 to $3,000.
Top 1,000 ranking: 106
My Lost Love/How Long Must I Wait for You • Larks (Apollo 435)................. 1951 $3,000
45 rpm. Near-mint price range: $2,000 to $3,000.
Top 1,000 ranking: 107
Hopefully Yours/When I Leave These Prison Walls • Larks (Apollo 1180) 1951 $3,000
45 rpm. Orange vinyl. Near-mint price range: $2,000 to $3,000.
Top 1,000 ranking: 108
Hopefully Yours/When I Leave These Prison Walls • Larks (Apollo 1180) 1951 $2,000
45 rpm. Black vinyl. Near-mint price range: $1,500 to $2,000.
Top 1,000 ranking: 228
Stolen Love/In My Lonely Room • Larks (Apollo 1190)................................. 1952 $2,000
45 rpm. Black vinyl. Near-mint price range: $1,500 to $2,000.
Top 1,000 ranking: 236
Hold Me/I Live True to You • Larks (Apollo 1194)... 1952 $2,000
45 rpm. Near-mint price range: $1,500 to $2,000.
Top 1,000 ranking: 237
No Other Girl/The World Is Waiting for the Sunrise • Larks (Lloyds 112) 1954 $1,500
45 rpm. Near-mint price range: $1,000 to $1,500.
Top 1,000 ranking: 414

LAWSON, Robby
Burning Sensation/? • Robby Lawson (Kyser 2122)... ? $2,000
45 rpm. Near-mint price range: $1,000 to $2,000.
Top 1,000 ranking: 375

LAWSON, Teddy, & Lawson Boys
There's No Return from Love/I Knew It Was You All the Time • Teddy Lawson &
Lawson Boys (Mansfield 611) 1957 $750
45 rpm. Near-mint price range: $500 to $750.
Top 1,000 ranking: 853

LAZY SMOKE
Corridor of Faces • Lazy Smoke (Onyx 6903) 1967 $1,200
LP. Near-mint price range: $800 to $1,200.
Top 1,000 ranking: 551

LEGENDS
Well, Darling/Over Yonder • Legends (Falco 305) 1963 $2,000
<small>45 rpm. Near-mint price range: $1,000 to $2,000.
Top 1,000 ranking: 353</small>

LEMONS, George
Fascinating Girl/? • George Lemons (Gold Soul 102) .... ? $2,000
<small>45 rpm. Promotional issue only. Near-mint price range: $1,000 to $2,000.
Top 1,000 ranking: 376</small>

LENNON, John
John Lennon Sings the Great Rock & Roll Hits (Roots) • John Lennon
(Adam VIII Ltd. 8018) 1975 $1,000
<small>LP. Orange label. Available briefly before production and sales were ceased due to legal action brought against Adam VIII by Apple and John Lennon. Most originals have an advertisement liner sleeve and a small ad insert. Some originals exist without these two items. Counterfeits do exist. Copies with discs made of any vinyl other than black are counterfeits. Colored vinyl originals do not exist. All copies with covers constructed of paper slicks pasted on cardboard are fakes since originals are made of posterboard. All copies with unusually large labels are counterfeit. On the back cover of originals, the Adam VIII ads have photo miniatures that are sharp and clear. On fakes, the print is blurry, particularly on the "20 Solid Gold Hits" LP ad. The Adam VIII logo on original covers is sharp and clear. It is blurry and faded on fakes. The number A-8018-A is lightly hand etched on the label of all originals. Near-mint price range: $750 to $1,000.
Top 1,000 ranking: 743</small>

Sometime in New York City • John Lennon & Yoko Ono & Plastic Ono Band (Apple
3392) 1972 $900
<small>LP. Promotional issue. White labels with black print. Double LP with stock gatefold cover. Near-mint price range: $700 to $900.
Top 1,000 ranking: 762</small>

Give Peace a Chance/Remember Love • John Lennon & Plastic Ono Band
(Americom 435 A/B) 1969 $800
<small>Flexi-disc. Thin black flexible, "Pocket Disc Series" 4-inch vinyl disc. Has a red cardboard cover. Near-mint price range: $600 to $800.
Top 1,000 ranking: 792</small>

Happy Xmas (War Is Over)/Listen, the Snow Is Falling • John Lennon & Yoko Ono
& Plastic Ono Band (With the Harlem Community Choir) / Yoko Ono (Apple
47663/4) 1971 $800
<small>45 rpm. Promotional issue. White label with large Apple logo. Black vinyl. Known counterfeit has photocopy of label on flat paper stock pasted on a black vinyl reissue of the single. Print and label quality are noticeably inferior. Originals have semi-gloss label on a brittle polystyrene disc. Near-mint price range: $600 to $800.
Top 1,000 ranking: 794</small>

LEWIS, Paul, & Swans
Little Senorita/Wedding Bells, Oh Wedding Bells • Paul Lewis "The Mighty
Swamba" & Swans (Fortune 813) 1955 $3,000
<small>45 rpm. Purple label. Near-mint price range: $2,500 to $3,000.
Top 1,000 ranking: 138</small>

LIGHTNIN' SLIM
Rooster Blues • Lightnin' Slim (Excello 8000) 1960 $1,000
<small>LP. Real name: Otis Hicks. Near-mint price range: $750 to $1,000.
Top 1,000 ranking: 686</small>

LINKS
She's the One/Baby • Links (Teenage 1009) 1957 $800
<small>45 rpm. Near-mint price range: $600 to $800.
Top 1,000 ranking: 775</small>

LITTLE ESTHER
Memory Lane (The Best Songs Little Esther Ever Recorded) • Little Esther
(King 622) 1959 $2,000
  Monaural LP. This artist is also known as Little Esther Phillips. Near-mint price range: $1,000 to
  $2,000.
  Top 1,000 ranking: 325

LITTLE IVA & HER BAND
When I Needed You/? • Little Iva & Her Band (Miracle 2) 1960 $1,000
  45 rpm. Near-mint price range: $750 to $1,000.
  Top 1,000 ranking: 687

LITTLE JUNE & HIS JANUARYS
Hello/Burgers, Fries and Shakes • Little June & His Januarys (Salem 188) .. 1963 $3,000
  45 rpm. Commercial issue. Green-gold label. Near-mint price range: $2,000 to $3,000.
  Top 1,000 ranking: 168

LITTLE MAN HENRY
Wailin' Wildcat/? • Little Man Henry (Central 4701) .... ? $750
  45 rpm. Near-mint price range: $500 to $750.
  Top 1,000 ranking: 943

LITTLE TOIANS
I Love You/Beans • Little Toians (Smalltown) 1956 $750
  45 rpm. No selection number used. Near-mint price range: $500 to $750.
  Top 1,000 ranking: 844

LOLLYPOPS
My Love Is Real/Believe in Me • Lollypops (Universal
International 7420) 1958 $3,000
  45 rpm. Near-mint price range: $2,000 to $3,000.
  Top 1,000 ranking: 156
My Love Is Real/Believe in Me • Lollypops (Holland 7420) 1958 $2,000
  45 rpm. Holland labels may be pasted on top of Universal International ones. Near-mint price
  range: $1,500 to $2,000.
  Top 1,000 ranking: 312

LONDON, Johnny
Drivin' Slow/Flat Tire • Johnny London (Sun 175) 1952 $2,000
  78 rpm. First commercial issue on the Sun label. Near-mint price range: $1,000 to $2,000.
  Top 1,000 ranking: 238

LONESOME DRIFTER
Eager Boy/? • Lonesome Drifter (K 5812) 1956 $1,500
  45 rpm. Near-mint price range: $1,000 to $1,500.
  Top 1,000 ranking: 429

LOUIS, Joe Hill
Gotta Let You Go/Boogie in the Park • Joe Hill Louis (It's the
Phillips 9001) 1950 $6,000
  78 rpm. Near-mint price range: $4,000 to $6,000.
  Top 1,000 ranking: 32
Dorothy Mae/When I Am Gone • Joe Hill Louis (Checker 763) 1952 $1,500
  45 rpm. Near-mint price range: $1,000 to $1,500.
  Top 1,000 ranking: 398

LOVE, Hot Shot
Wolf Call Boogie/Harmonica Jam • Hot Shot Love (Sun 196) 1954 $2,500
  45 rpm. Near-mint price range: $2,000 to $2,500.
  Top 1,000 ranking: 188

LOVE LARKS
Diddle-Le-Bom/More and More • Love Larks (Mason's 3-070) 1957 $1,200
    45 rpm. Near-mint price range: $800 to $1,200.
    Top 1,000 ranking: 521

LOVE NOTES
Surrender Your Heart/Get on My Train • Love Notes (Imperial 5254) 1953 $3,000
    45 rpm. Near-mint price range: $2,000 to $3,000.
    Top 1,000 ranking: 120
Since I Fell for You/Don't Be No Fool • Love Notes (Riviera 975) 1954 $3,000
    45 rpm. Original label color is a mixture of magenta (red) and cyan (blue) – giving a lavender-
    pink look. Counterfeits are just light pink. Near-mint price range: $2,500 to $3,000.
    Top 1,000 ranking: 133
I'm Sorry/Sweet Lulu • Love Notes (With Lucky Warren on Tenor Sax)
    (Riviera 970).. 1954 $800
    45 rpm. Near-mint price range: $600 to $800.
    Top 1,000 ranking: 770

LOVENOTES
A Love Like Yours/Never Look Behind • Lovenotes (Premium 611).............. 1957 $1,500
    45 rpm. Reissued almost immediately with artist credit changed to the Trueloves. Near-mint
    price range: $1,000 to $1,500.
    Top 1,000 ranking: 434

LYRICS
Every Night/Come Back Baby • Lyrics (Rhythm 127) 1959 $3,500
    45 rpm. Same number on both sides. Has an alternative take of *Every Night* compared to track
    used on 126/127, found elsewhere on this list. Near-mint price range: $2,500 to $3,500.
    Top 1,000 ranking: 101
Come Back Baby/Every Night • Lyrics (Rhythm 126/127) 1959 $2,000
    45 rpm. Different selection number on each side of disc. Near-mint price range: $1,000 to
    $2,000.
    Top 1,000 ranking: 326

MAGIC TONES
Tears in My Eyes/Spanish Love Song • Magic Tones (Howfum 3686).......... 1957 $3,000
    45 rpm. Identification number shown since no selection number is used. Near-mint price range:
    $2,000 to $3,000.
    Top 1,000 ranking: 149

MAGNETICS
Lady in Green/? • Magnetics (Bonnie 107374) .... ? $1,000
    45 rpm. We're not sure if "107374" is the selection number. It does seem more like an
    identification number. Near-mint price range: $750 to $1,000.
    Top 1,000 ranking: 748

MANDO & CHILI PEPPERS
On the Road with Rock and Roll • Mando & Chili Peppers (Golden
    Crest 3023) 1957 $750
    LP. Near-mint price range: $500 to $750.
    Top 1,000 ranking: 854

MARAINEY, Big Memphis
Call Me Anything, But Call Me/Baby No, No • Big Memphis Marainey
    (Sun 184) 1953 $1,300
    45 rpm. Near-mint price range: $1,000 to $1,300.
    Top 1,000 ranking: 491

MARBLE PHROGG
Marble Phrogg • Marble Phrogg (Derrick 8868)... 1968 $1,200
    LP. Near-mint price range: $800 to $1,200.
    Top 1,000 ranking: 552

MARBLES
Golden Girl/Big Wig Walk • Marbles (Lucky 002)... 1954 $2,000
45 rpm. Near-mint price range: $1,000 to $2,000.
Top 1,000 ranking: 270

MARIANI
Perpetuum Mobile • Mariani (Sonobeat 1004)...1970s $2,500
LP. Promotional issue only. Near-mint price range: $2,000 to $2,500.
Top 1,000 ranking: 217

MARLETTES
Just the Way You Are/Only Memories • Marlettes (With Imperial Orchestra)
(Howfum).. 1958 $3,000
45 rpm. No selection number used. Near-mint price range: $2,000 to $3,000.
Top 1,000 ranking: 157

MARQUIS
Bohemian Daddy/Hope He's True • Marquis (With Sammy Lowe Orchestra)
(Onyx 505) 1956 $2,000
45 rpm. Near-mint price range: $1,000 to $2,000.
Top 1,000 ranking: 294
Never Forget/Rock and Roll Holiday • Marquis (Noble 719).......................... 1959 $2,000
45 rpm. Repressed crediting the Tabs. Near-mint price range: $1,000 to $2,000.
Top 1,000 ranking: 327

MARTIN, Dean
One Foot in Heaven/The Night Is Young and You're So Beautiful • Dean Martin
(Embassy 124) 1949 $1,000
78 rpm. One copy known. Near-mint price range: $750 to $1,000.
Top 1,000 ranking: 566

MARTIN, George, Orchestra
A Hard Day's Night/I Should Have Known Better • George Martin Orchestra
(United Artists 750) 1964 $1,200
Picture sleeve. Instrumental versions of two Lennon-McCartney film songs. Sleeve pictures the
Beatles. Near-mint price range: $800 to $1,200.
Top 1,000 ranking: 548

MARVELETTES
Marvelettes Sing Smash Hits of '62 • Marvelettes (Tamla 229)...................... 1962 $1,000
LP. First issued with this title. Quickly reissued with shortened – not so dated – title: *The
Marvelettes Sing.* Near-mint price range: $750 to $1,000.
Top 1,000 ranking: 706

MARVELS
Just Another Fool/You Crack Me Up • Marvels (Munrab 1008)...................... 1959 $2,000
45 rpm. Near-mint price range: $1,000 to $2,000.
Top 1,000 ranking: 328

MASON, Bonnie Jo
Ringo, I Love You/Beatle Blues • Bonnie Jo Mason (Annette 1000)............. 1964 $750
45 rpm. Bonnie Jo Mason is a one-time pseudonym for Cher. Near-mint price range: $500 to
$750.
Top 1,000 ranking: 927

MATTHEWS, Fat Man, & Four Kittens
When Boy Meets Girl/Later Baby • Fat Man Matthews & Four Kittens
(Imperial 5211)... 1952 $1,500
45 rpm. Near-mint price range: $1,000 to $1,500.
Top 1,000 ranking: 399

McCARTNEY, Paul

Ram • Paul & Linda McCartney (Apple 3375).. 1971 $3,500
  Monaural LP. Promotional issue. Issued in standard stereo cover, but labels indicate "Monaural."
  Near-mint price range: $3,000 to $3,500.
  Top 1,000 ranking: 104
Put It There/Put It There • Paul McCartney (Capitol SPRO-79074)............... 1989 $1,500
  45 rpm. White label, promotional issue only. Planned as the third single from Paul's *Flowers in
  the Dirt* LP, though cancelled before distribution. At press time, only three copies are known to
  eixst. Near-mint price range: $1,000 to $1,500.
  Top 1,000 ranking: 486
Band on the Run Radio Interview Special with Paul & Linda McCartney • Paul &
  Linda McCartney (Capitol/National Features Corp. 2955/2956) 1973 $1,200
  LP. Promotional only issue. Light Yellow label. Issued in plain white cover with script and two
  glossy promo photos. Counterfeits do NOT have "National Features Company" logo on their
  label. Near-mint price range: $800 to $1,200.
  Top 1,000 ranking: 555

McCOLLOUGH, Lloyd

Gonna Love My Baby/Cause I Love You • Lloyd McCollough
  (Republic 7129)... 1956 $800
  45 rpm. Near-mint price range: $600 to $800.
  Top 1,000 ranking: 772

McGONNIGLE, Mel

Rattle Shakin' Mama/Cheryl Baby • Mel McGonnigle (Rocket 101)............... 1958 $650
  45 rpm. Near-mint price range: $500 to $650.
  Top 1,000 ranking: 985

McNEELY, Big Jay

Big Jay McNeely • Big Jay McNeely (Federal 96).. 1954 $1,500
  10-inch LP. Near-mint price range: $1,000 to $1,500.
  Top 1,000 ranking: 415

MELLO DROPS

When I Grow Too Old to Dream/Crazy Song • Mello Drops (Imperial 5324) . 1954 $1,000
  45 rpm. Near-mint price range: $750 to $1,000.
  Top 1,000 ranking: 607

MELLO-HARPS

Love Is a Vow/Valerie • Mello-Harps (Do-Re-Mi 203) 1956 $3,000
  45 rpm. Near-mint price range: $2,000 to $3,000.
  Top 1,000 ranking: 142

MELLO MOODS

Where Are You (Now That I Need You)/How Could You • Mello-Moods (With
  Schubert Swanston Trio) (Robin 105)... 1951 $3,000
  45 rpm. Near-mint price range: $2,000 to $3,000.
  Top 1,000 ranking: 109
Call on Me/I Tried, Tried and Tried • Mello Moods (With Teacho Wiltshire & Band)
  (Prestige 799).. 1952 $2,000
  45 rpm. Near-mint price range: $1,000 to $2,000.
  Top 1,000 ranking: 239
I'm Lost/When I Woke Up This Morning • Mello Moods (Prestige 856).......... 1953 $1,200
  45 rpm. Near-mint price range: $800 to $1,200.
  Top 1,000 ranking: 507

MELLOWS

I'm Yours/Sweet Lorraine • Mellows (Celeste 3004)..................................... 1956 $750
  45 rpm. Near-mint price range: $500 to $750.
  Top 1,000 ranking: 845

MEL-O-DOTS
One More Time/Just How Long • Mel-O-Dots (Apollo 1192) 1952 $1,000
    45 rpm. Near-mint price range: $750 to $1,000.
    Top 1,000 ranking: 575

MELOTONES
Prayer of Love/Father Time • Melotones (Lee Tone 700) 1954 $2,000
    45 rpm. Near-mint price range: $1,000 to $2,000.
    Top 1,000 ranking: 271

MERCY DEE
Happy Bachelor (Blues)/Danger Zone (Crepe on Your Door) • Mercy Dee
   (Bayou 013) 1950 $700
    45 rpm. Full name: Mercy Dee Walton. Near-mint price range: $500 to $700.
    Top 1,000 ranking: 949

MERIDIANS
Have You Forgotten/Blue Victory • Meridians (Parnaso 107) 1960s $1,200
    45 rpm. Near-mint price range: $800 to $1,200.
    Top 1,000 ranking: 553

MIDNIGHTERS
Their Greatest Hits • Midnighters (Federal 295-90) 1954 $10,000
    10-inch LP. Near-mint price range: $7,500 to $10,000.
    Top 1,000 ranking: 16
Their Greatest Hits • Midnighters (Federal 541) 1957 $1,000
    LP. White cover. Near-mint price range: $750 to $1,000.
    Top 1,000 ranking: 639
Their Greatest Jukebox Hits • Hank Ballard & Midnighters (King 541) 1958 $800
    LP. Repackage of Federal 541. Near-mint price range: $600 to $800.
    Top 1,000 ranking: 776

MILBURN, Amos
Rockin' the Boogie • Amos Milburn (Aladdin 704) 1955 $3,500
    10-inch monaural LP. Red vinyl. Near-mint price range: $2,500 to $3,500.
    Top 1,000 ranking: 100
Rockin' the Boogie • Amos Milburn (Aladdin 704) 1955 $1,000
    10-inch monaural LP. Black vinyl. Near-mint price range: $750 to $1,000.
    Top 1,000 ranking: 618
Blues Boss • Amos Milburn (Motown 608) 1963 $750
    Monaural LP. Near-mint price range: $500 to $750.
    Top 1,000 ranking: 921

MINORS
Jerry/Where Are You • Minors (Celeste 3007) 1957 $1,500
    45 rpm. Near-mint price range: $1,000 to $1,500.
    Top 1,000 ranking: 435

MIRACLES
Bad Girl/I Love You Baby • Miracles (Featuring Bill "Smokey" Robinson)
   (Motown G1) 1959 $1,000
    45 rpm. May or may not have TLX-2207 on label. Near-mint price range: $750 to $1,000.
    Top 1,000 ranking: 669

MITCHELL, Willie, & Four Kings
Walking At Your Will/Tell It to Me Baby • Willie Mitchell & Four Kings (Stomper
   Time 1160) 1958 $1,000
    45 rpm. Near-mint price range: $750 to $1,000.
    Top 1,000 ranking: 657

Walkin' Alone/Rag Mop • Willie Mitchell & Four Kings (Stomper
Time 1163).. 1959 $1,000
    45 rpm. Near-mint price range: $750 to $1,000.
    Top 1,000 ranking: 670

MIXERS

Love and Kisses/Casanova • Mixers (Bold 102)........................... 1959 $1,000
    45 rpm. Near-mint price range: $750 to $1,000.
    Top 1,000 ranking: 671
You Said You're Leaving Me/Johnny's Got a Girlfriend • Mixers (Bold 101).. 1958 $700
    45 rpm. Near-mint price range: $500 to $700.
    Top 1,000 ranking: 959

MODERN INK SPOTS

Together (in Your Arms)/Spotlight Dance • Modern Ink Spots (Rust 5052)... 1962 $1,000
    45 rpm. Near-mint price range: $750 to $1,000.
    Top 1,000 ranking: 707

MONARCH'S

Love You That's Why/Coming Home • Monarch's (Liban 1002) 1959 $2,000
    45 rpm. Near-mint price range: $1,000 to $2,000.
    Top 1,000 ranking: 329

MONROE, Homer

It's Many a Mile from Me to You/? • Homer Monroe (Silvia 1161)........................ ? $800
    45 rpm. Near-mint price range: $600 to $800.
    Top 1,000 ranking: 797

MONTCLAIRS

All I Want Is Love/I've Heard About You • Montclairs (With Douglas DuBois,
Chico Chism & His Jettinaires) (Sonic 104) 1956 $1,000
    45 rpm. Near-mint price range: $750 to $1,000.
    Top 1,000 ranking: 631

MOONGLOWS

219 Train/My Gal • Moonglows (Chance 1161) 1954 $4,000
    45 rpm. White and black label. Near-mint price range: $3,000 to $4,000.
    Top 1,000 ranking: 79
Baby Please/Whistle My Love • Moonglows (Chance 1147) 1953 $3,000
    45 rpm. Red vinyl. Near-mint price range: $2,000 to $3,000.
    Top 1,000 ranking: 121
Just a Lonely Christmas/Hey Santa Claus • Moonglows (Chance 1150)....... 1953 $3,000
    45 rpm. Red vinyl. Near-mint price range: $2,000 to $3,000.
    Top 1,000 ranking: 122
I Just Can't Tell No Lie/I've Been Your Dog • Moonglows
(Champagne 7500) 1952 $2,000
    45 rpm. Reportedly 1,500 made. Near-mint price range: $1,000 to $2,000.
    Top 1,000 ranking: 240
Secret Love/Real Gone Mama • Moonglows (Chance 1152) 1954 $1,000
    45 rpm. Blue and silver label. Near-mint price range: $750 to $1,000.
    Top 1,000 ranking: 608
Secret Love/Real Gone Mama • Moonglows (Chance 1152) 1954 $900
    45 rpm. Yellow and black label. Near-mint price range: $700 to $900.
    Top 1,000 ranking: 753
I Was Wrong/Ooh Rocking Daddy • Moonglows (Chance 1156).................... 1954 $700
    45 rpm. Yellow and black label. Near-mint price range: $500 to $700.
    Top 1,000 ranking: 953

MOORE, Gatemouth
Gatemouth Moore Sings Blues • Gatemouth Moore (King 684) 1960 $6,000
    LP. Near-mint price range: $4,000 to $6,000.
    Top 1,000 ranking: 37

MOORE, Jimmy, & Peacocks
Tender Love/I Want You to Know • Jimmy Moore & Peacocks (Noble 711).. 1958 $2,000
    45 rpm. Near-mint price range: $1,000 to $2,000.
    Top 1,000 ranking: 313

MOORE, Nunnie, & Peacocks
Bouquet of Roses/Tweet Tweet • Nunnie Moore & Peacocks (L&M 1002) ... 1957 $1,000
    45 rpm. Near-mint price range: $750 to $1,000.
    Top 1,000 ranking: 640

MUSIC EMPORIUM
Music Emporium • Music Emporium (Sentinel 100) 1968 $1,500
    LP. Near-mint price range: $1,000 to $1,500.
    Top 1,000 ranking: 478

MUSKETEERS
Goodbye My Love/I'll Love You Till My Dying Day • Musketeers
  (Roxy 801).. 1952 $2,500
    78 rpm. Near-mint price range: $2,000 to $2,500.
    Top 1,000 ranking: 183

MUSTANGS
Over the Rainbow/Loop the Fly • Mustangs (Vest 51) 1963 $700
    45 rpm. Near-mint price range: $500 to $700.
    Top 1,000 ranking: 965

MYSTIC SIVA
Mystic Siva • Mystic Siva (VO 19713).. 1971 $1,000
    LP. With Gatefold cover. Near-mint price range: $900 to $1,000.
    Top 1,000 ranking: 741

MYSTICS
Teenage Sweetheart/Rockin' Yodel • Mystics (Chatam 350/351)................. 1958 $1,000
    45 rpm. Reissued using same label name and number, but credited to the Champs. Near-mint
    price range: $750 to $1,000.
    Top 1,000 ranking: 658

NAZZ
Lay Down and Die, Goodbye/Wonder Who's Loving Her Now • Nazz
  (Very Record 001).. 1967 $1,000
    45 rpm. Except for drummer Tom Speer, this band was the same as the Alice Cooper Group.
    Lay Down and Die, Goodbye is an earlier version than later released by Alice Cooper. There is
    no connection to Todd Rundgren's Nazz group. Near-mint price range: $750 to $1,000.
    Top 1,000 ranking: 733

NEONS
My Lover/Tucson • Neons (Waldon 1001) 1961 $750
    45 rpm. Near-mint price range: $500 to $750.
    Top 1,000 ranking: 897

NEW TWEEDY BROTHERS
The New Tweedy Brothers • New Tweedy Brothers (Ridon 234) 1966 $2,000
    LP. With hex cover. Near-mint price range: $1,500 to $2,000.
    Top 1,000 ranking: 359

NEWLYWEDS
Love Walked Out/The Quarrel • Newlyweds (Homogenized Soul 601) 1961   **$1,500**
45 rpm. Near-mint price range: $1,000 to $1,500.
Top 1,000 ranking: 460

NIGHT SHADOW
The Square Root of Two • Night Shadow (Spectrum Stereo ST-2001) 1968   **$1,400**
LP. By the Night Shadows, but credited to the "Night Shadow." Price ($1,400) is for LP with *both* bonuses. 1,000 made for use as follows: a) 294 promotional copies for radio stations, each one packaged with a bonus, psychedelic poster (Near-mint price range: $1,200 to $1,400); b) 700 for commectial sale, packaged with a bonus 45 rpm (Near-mint price range: $775 – $1,050); c) 6 for executive use, packaged with both the poster and the 45. (Near-mint price range: $1,000 to $1,300.) The poster is so scarce that neither the producer nor any of the band members have been able to locate one.
Top 1,000 ranking: 489

NORMAN, Gene, & Rockin' Rockets
Snaggle Tooth Ann/Night Train • Gene Norman & Rockin' Rockets
(Snag 101) 1959   **$650**
45 rpm. Near-mint price range: $500 to $650.
Top 1,000 ranking: 987

NOTE-TORIALS
My Valerie/Loved and Lost • Note-Torials (Impala 201) 1959   **$1,000**
45 rpm. Near-mint price range: $750 to $1,000.
Top 1,000 ranking: 672

NU-TONES
Annie Kicked the Bucket/Believe • Nu-Tones (Hollywood Star 798).............. 1954   **$4,000**
45 rpm. One known to exist. Same number used twice and released a year apart. Near-mint price range: $3,000 to $4,000.
Top 1,000 ranking: 80
Goddess of Love/Niki Niki Mambo • Nu-Tones (Hollywood Star 797) 1954   **$750**
78 rpm. We have yet to learn of any original 45s of this issue. Near-mint price range: $500 to $750.
Top 1,000 ranking: 825
Believe/You're No Barking Dog • Nu-Tones (Hollywood Star 798) 1954   **$750**
78 rpm. Same number used twice. Near-mint price range: $500 to $750.
Top 1,000 ranking: 826

NU-TRENDS
Together/Spooksville • Nu-trends (Lawn 216) 1963   **$2,000**
45 rpm. Colored vinyl pressings are bootlegs. Near-mint price range: $1,000 to $2,000.
Top 1,000 ranking: 354

ODOM, King, Four
Lucky/ Don't Trade Your Love for Gold • King Odom Four (With Dick Jacobs
Orchestra) (Abbey 15064).. 1952   **$750**
45 rpm. Identification number shown since no selection number is used. Near-mint price range: $500 to $750.
Top 1,000 ranking: 809

ONO, Yoko
Open Your Box/Greenfield Morning • Yoko Ono (Apple OYB-1) 1970   **$800**
45 rpm. Promotional issue only. White label. Reportedly, Yoko Ono made approximately six copies for personal use. Near-mint price range: $600 to $800.
Top 1,000 ranking: 793

ORIOLES

Crying in the Chapel/Don't You Think I Ought to Know • Orioles
(Jubilee 5122) 1953 $6,000
    45 rpm. Red vinyl. Near-mint price range: $4,000 to $6,000.
    Top 1,000 ranking: 34

It's Too Soon to Know/Barbara Lee • Orioles (Jubilee 5000)......................... 1951 $3,000
    45 rpm. Near-mint price range: $2,000 to $3,000.
    Top 1,000 ranking: 110

Tell Me So/Deacon Jones • Orioles (Jubilee 5005) 1951 $2,000
    45 rpm. Near-mint price range: $1,500 to $2,000.
    Top 1,000 ranking: 229

So Much/Forgive and Forget • Orioles (Jubilee 5016) 1951 $2,000
    45 rpm. Near-mint price range: $1,500 to $2,000.
    Top 1,000 ranking: 230

I Miss You So/You Are My First Love • Orioles (Jubilee 5051)...................... 1951 $2,000
    45 rpm. Red vinyl. Near-mint price range: $1,500 to $2,000.
    Top 1,000 ranking: 231

The Orioles Sing • Orioles (Jubilee 5000).. 1953 $2,000
    EP. Near-mint price range: $1,000 to $2,000.
    Top 1,000 ranking: 255

I Cross My Fingers/Can't Seem to Laugh Anymore • Orioles
(Jubilee 5040) 1951 $1,500
    45 rpm. Near-mint price range: $1,000 to $1,500.
    Top 1,000 ranking: 395

I Miss You So/You Are My First Love • Orioles (Jubilee 5051)...................... 1951 $1,500
    45 rpm. Black vinyl. Near-mint price range: $1,000 to $1,500.
    Top 1,000 ranking: 396

Baby, Please Don't Go/Don't Tell Her • Orioles (Jubilee 5065)...................... 1951 $1,500
    45 rpm. Red vinyl. Near-mint price range: $1,000 to $1,500.
    Top 1,000 ranking: 397

Don't Cry Baby/See See Rider • Orioles (Jubilee 5092) 1952 $1,500
    45 rpm. Red vinyl. Near-mint price range: $1,000 to $1,500.
    Top 1,000 ranking: 400

I Miss You So/Till Then • Orioles (Jubilee 5107).. 1953 $1,500
    45 rpm. Red vinyl. Near-mint price range: $1,000 to $1,500.
    Top 1,000 ranking: 407

At Night/Every Dog-Gone Time • Orioles (Jubilee 5025) 1951 $1,000
    45 rpm. Near-mint price range: $750 to $1,000.
    Top 1,000 ranking: 570

Teardrops on My Pillow/Hold Me, Thrill Me, Kiss Me • Orioles
(Jubilee 5108) 1953 $1,000
    45 rpm. Red vinyl. Near-mint price range: $750 to $1,000.
    Top 1,000 ranking: 590

I Cover the Waterfront/One More Time • Orioles (Jubilee 5120) 1953 $1,000
    45 rpm. Red vinyl. Near-mint price range: $750 to $1,000.
    Top 1,000 ranking: 591

Oh Holy Night/The Lord's Prayer • Orioles (Jubilee 5045)............................ 1951 $750
    45 rpm. Near-mint price range: $500 to $750.
    Top 1,000 ranking: 803

What Are You Doing New Year's Eve/Lonely Christmas • Orioles
(Jubilee 5017) 1951 $700
    45 rpm. Near-mint price range: $500 to $700.
    Top 1,000 ranking: 951

OTHER HALF

The Other Half • Other Half (7/2 1) 1966 $900
    LP. Near-mint price range: $700 to $900.
    Top 1,000 ranking: 761

OTIS, Johnny
Rock 'N Roll Hit Parade, Volume One • Johnny Otis (Dig 104) 1957 $750
> LP. Mustard color cover, black and white print. Counterfeits exist, some of which have a yellow cover, others have a gold cover. Back photo on originals is clear. Regardless, the discs of originals are rigid – noticeably thicker than the more flexible ones found on fakes. Credits the Jayos, Johnny's group who's other lead vocalists are Mel Williams and Arthur Lee Maye. Session players are: Jackie Kelso (alto sax); Freddie Harmon (tenor and baritone sax); George Washington (trombone); Jimmy Nolan (guitar); Johnny Parker (bass); Don Johnson (trumpet); "Lady Dee" Williams (piano); "Kansas City" Bell (drums). Near-mint price range: $500 to $750.
> *Top 1,000 ranking: 855*

PACERS
How Sweet/No Wonder I Love You • Pacers (Guyden 2064) 1962 $2,000
> 45 rpm. Promotional issue. Near-mint price range: $1,000 to $2,000.
> *Top 1,000 ranking: 346*

PACKARDS
Ladise/My Doctor of Love • Packards (With Paul Boyers Band)
(Pla-Bac 106) 1956 $2,000
> 45 rpm. Near-mint price range: $1,000 to $2,000.
> *Top 1,000 ranking: 295*

PARAGONS
Twilight/The Wows of Love • Paragons (Winley 227) 1958 $1,500
> 45 rpm. Note spelling error: "Wows" should be "Vows." Near-mint price range: $1,000 to $1,500.
> *Top 1,000 ranking: 442*

PASSIONS
Aphrodite/I've Gotta Know • Passions (Octavia 8005) 1962 $750
> 45 rpm. Near-mint price range: $500 to $750.
> *Top 1,000 ranking: 905*

PEJOE, Morris, Orchestra
Tired of Crying Over You/Gonna Buy Me a Telephone • Morris Pejoe Orchestra
(Checker 766) 1954 $2,000
> 45 rpm. Red vinyl. Near-mint price range: $1,000 to $2,000.
> *Top 1,000 ranking: 272*

Can't Get Along/It'll Plumb Get It • Morris Pejoe Orchestra (Checker 781).... 1954 $750
> 45 rpm. Red vinyl. Near-mint price range: $500 to $750.
> *Top 1,000 ranking: 827*

PELICANS
Aurelia/White Cliffs of Dover • Pelicans (Parrot 793) 1954 $6,000
> 45 rpm. Red vinyl. Near-mint price range: $5,000 to $6,000.
> *Top 1,000 ranking: 36*

Aurelia/White Cliffs of Dover • Pelicans (Parrot 793) 1954 $4,000
> 45 rpm. Black vinyl. Near-mint price range: $3,000 to $4,000.
> *Top 1,000 ranking: 81*

Chimes/Ain't Gonna Do It • Pelicans (Imperial 5307).................................. 1954 $2,000
> 45 rpm. Near-mint price range: $1,000 to $2,000.
> *Top 1,000 ranking: 273*

PENGUINS / MEADOWLARKS / MEDALLIONS / DOOTONES
Best in Rhythm & Blues • Penguins / Meadowlarks / Medallions / Dootones
(Dootone 204) 1957 $1,200
> LP. Red vinyl. Near-mint price range: $800 to $1,200.
> *Top 1,000 ranking: 522*

PEPPERMINT HARRIS
Right Back On It/Maggie's Boogie • Peppermint Harris (Aladdin 3130) .... 1952　　$1,000
　　45 rpm. Real name: Harrison Nelson. Green vinyl. Near-mint price range: $750 to $1,000.
　　Top 1,000 ranking: 576

PERKINS, Carl
Dance Album • Carl Perkins (Sun 1225) .... 1957　　$1,000
　　LP. Near-mint price range: $750 to $1,000.
　　Top 1,000 ranking: 641

PERKINS, Roy
You're Gone/Here I Am • Roy Perkins (Meladee 112) .... 1955　　$1,000
　　45 rpm. Near-mint price range: $750 to $1,000.
　　Top 1,000 ranking: 619

PHAFNER
Overdrive • Phafner (Dragon) .... 1971　　$2,200
　　LP. No selection number used. Near-mint price range: $1,800 to $2,200.
　　Top 1,000 ranking: 221

PHAROTONES
Give Me a Chance/Monkey Business • Pharotones (Timely 1002) .... 1958　　$2,000
　　45 rpm. Near-mint price range: $1,000 to $2,000.
　　Top 1,000 ranking: 314

PIANO RED [Willie Perryman]
Jump Man, Jump • Piano Red [Willie Perryman] (Groove 1001) .... 1956　　$750
　　LP. Near-mint price range: $500 to $750.
　　Top 1,000 ranking: 846

PIERCE, Henry, & Five Notes
Thrill Me, Baby/Hey Fine Mama • Henry Pierce & Five Notes
　　(Specialty 461) .... 1952　　$2,000
　　45 rpm. Red vinyl. Near-mint price range: $1,000 to $2,000.
　　Top 1,000 ranking: 241

PIPES
So Long/Baby Don't Go • Pipes (Jacy 001) .... 1958　　$750
　　45 rpm. Near-mint price range: $500 to $750.
　　Top 1,000 ranking: 863

PLANTS
From Me/My Girl • Plants (With Orchestra) (J&S 1617) .... 1958　　$1,000
　　45 rpm. Near-mint price range: $750 to $1,000.
　　Top 1,000 ranking: 659
Dear, I Swear/It's You • Plants (With Orchestra) (J&S 1602) .... 1957　　$700
　　45 rpm. Label has company address under logo. Near-mint price range: $500 to $700.
　　Top 1,000 ranking: 957

PLANTS
I Searched the Seven Seas/I Took a Trip Way Over the Sea • Plants
　　(J&S 248/249) .... 1959　　$1,000
　　45 rpm. Despite having the same name, this is a different group of "Plants" than on J&S in 1957
　　and '58. Near-mint price range: $750 to $1,000.
　　Top 1,000 ranking: 673

PLATTERS
The Platters • Platters (Federal 549) .... 1957　　$1,000
　　LP. Near-mint price range: $750 to $1,000.
　　Top 1,000 ranking: 642

I Need You All the Time/I'll Cry When You're Gone • Platters
    (Federal 12164).. 1954 $650
      45 rpm. Near-mint price range: $500 to $650.
      Top 1,000 ranking: 976

POETS

Never Let You Go/I'm Falling in Love • Poets (Shade 1001)......................... 1960 $2,000
      45 rpm. Near-mint price range: $1,000 to $2,000.
      Top 1,000 ranking: 339

PREMIERS

Until/? • Premiers (Echo 6013)... ? $1,000
      45 rpm. Near-mint price range: $750 to $1,000.
      Top 1,000 ranking: 749

PRESLEY, Elvis

Good Luck Charm/Anything That's Part of You • Elvis Presley
    (RCA Victor 37-7992)... 1962 $24,000
      Compact 33 Single with picture sleeve. Fifth of five mono singles in this somewhat experimental
      and ultimately failed series. Compact 33s are seven-inch discs with a quarter-inch, LP-size,
      hole. Price reflects an actual sale and subsequent offers of what is thus far the only known copy.
      Picture sleeve alone is $8,000 to $12,000. Price range for both: $16,000 to $24,000.
      Top 1,000 ranking: 2

Elvis' Christmas Album • Elvis Presley (RCA Victor LOC-1035).................... 1957 $18,000
      Monaural LP. Red vinyl. Black label, "Long Play" at bottom. Value is based on the one known
      sale (Nov. 1997). Stories have circulated of a second copy but we have yet to conrfim its
      existence. Near-mint price range: $15,000 to $18,000.
      Top 1,000 ranking: 3

Can't Help Falling in Love/Rock-A-Hula Baby • Elvis Presley (With Jordanaires)
    (RCA Victor 37-7968)... 1961 $16,000
      Compact 33 single with picture sleeve. Fourth of five mono singles in this somewhat
      experimental and ultimately failed series. Compact 33s are seven-inch discs with a quarter-inch,
      LP-size, hole. Picture sleeve alone is $5,000 to $8,000. Price range for both: $10,000 to
      $16,000.
      Top 1,000 ranking: 4

Elvis/Jaye P. Morgan • Elvis Presley / Jaye P. Morgan (RCA Victor EPA-992 and
    EPA-689) 1956 $12,000
      Two-EP, promotional sampler, though the discs were standard commercial pressings. This
      package was made to encourage retail stores to establish themselves in the music/record
      business. The idea of the Elvis/Jaye P. Morgan coupling was both to emphasize that the Elvis
      EP (EPA-992) sold 1,000 times better than the Jaye P. Morgan EP (EPA-689) and that record
      and phonograph sales were on the rise. Cover: Double pocket jacket. Front: Titles are not
      printed anywhere. RCA Victor logo at upper right, numbers (for both EPs) at lower right. Color
      Elvis photo. Back: Color slick from Jaye P. Morgan EP. Both inside panels have the promotional
      pitch; however, at least two variations exist. One is imprinted for "Mr. L.F. Koranda, Associated
      Merchandising Corp, 1440 Broadway, New York, New York." and another for "Mr. Walter H.
      Awe, Mutual Buying Syndicate, 11 West 42st Street, New York 36, New York." Other than the
      representative's imprint, all text is identical. Since the discs were standard pressings, at least
      95% of the value here is represented by the custom EP cover. Near-mint price range: $8,000 to
      $12,000.
      Top 1,000 ranking: 10

(Marie's the Name) His Latest Flame/Little Sister • Elvis Presley
    (RCA Victor 37-7908)... 1961 $12,000
      Compact 33 single with picture sleeve. Third of five mono singles in this somewhat experimental
      and ultimately failed series. Compact 33s are seven-inch discs with a quarter-inch, LP-size,
      hole. Picture sleeve alone is $4,000 to $6,000. Price range for both: $8,000 to $12,000.
      Top 1,000 ranking: 11

I'll Be Back/Blank • Elvis Presley (With the Jordanaires)
    (RCA Victor 4-834-115)... 1966 $8,000
      45 rpm single-sided disc. White label. Reads "For Special Academy Consideration Only." Made
      for submission to the Academy of Motion Picture Arts and Sciences. Near-mint price range:
      $6,000 to $8,000.
      Top 1,000 ranking: 28

Such a Night/Never Ending • Elvis Presley (With Jordanaires)
(RCA Victor 47-8400).. 1964 $7,500
    45 rpm. White label, promotional issue only. Price is based on the one documented sale (1996)
    of the one known copy. Near-mint price range: $7,000 to $7,500.
    Top 1,000 ranking: 29

Loving You/G.I. Blues • Elvis Presley (RCA Victor LPM-1515).....................1960s $6,000
    Monaural LP. Picture disc. Photo imbedded in vinyl on both sides is the front cover art of a *G.I.*
    Blues LP. A one-of-a-kind test pressing discovered by Ed Bonja (Elvis' Tour Manager and
    photographer in the '70s), while cleaning out Col. Parker's office. When asked about it, Parker
    described this demo as once being considered for a promotion, but he rejected it because he did
    not like the way the disc cut off Elvis' name and the movie title. Reportedly from the '60s, though
    an accurate release date has yet to be confirmed. Since we have yet to confirm its purpose, we
    cannot categorize this disc as experimental.

    Plays five songs from the standard *Loving You* album (*Loving You; Got a Lot o' Livin' to Do;*
    Lonesome Cowboy; Blueberry Hill; and *True Love*). The remaining five tracks are assorted
    instrumentals, by as of yet unidentified artists that have nothing whatsoever to do with Elvis.
    Believed to have been produced in the early to mid-'60s, this is likely the very first RCA Victor
    picture disc. Near-mint price range: $4,000 to $6,000.
    Top 1,000 ranking: 38

The Most Talked-About New Personality in the Last Ten Years of Recorded
Music • Elvis Presley (RCA Victor EPB-1254) 1956 $5,000
    Two-EPs in a single pocket paper sleeve. White paper sleeve has green print and a green-and-
    white Elvis photo on the front. Promotional issue only. Contains all 12 tracks from his first LP
    and EPs: LPM-1254; EPB-1254; EPA-747. Includes a copy of *Dee-Jay Digest*, a newsletter for
    radio announcers, used within the sleeve to separate the two discs. Counterfeits exist. Two EPs:
    $1,000 to $2,000. Cover: $2,500 to $3,000. Digest: $25 to $75. Price range for set: $3,500 to
    $5,000.
    Top 1,000 ranking: 59

Elvis: Aloha from Hawaii Via Satellite • Elvis Presley (RCA
Victor VPSX-6089).. 1973 $5,000
    Two quadraphonic LPs. Reddish-orange label. Cover: Has a "Chicken of the Sea Sneak
    Preview" sticker applied to front, on the shrink wrap. Because these LPs were shrink wrapped
    first, the QuadraDisc sticker (on front) and Saturn-shaped contents sticker (on back) are also on
    the shrink instead of the actual cover. These copies were distributed within the Van Camps, or
    Chicken of the Sea, organization. Promotional issue only. Front has die-cut (5 ½" diameter) hole
    which allows inner sleeve to show. Double pocket cover. Includes an insert card: Pictures Elvis
    at left, a can of Chicken of the Sea tuna at upper right, and programming schedule at lower right.
    Printed on just one side. ($100 to $150) Shrink stickers: Chicken of the Sea, multi-color (red,
    yellow, green, black, and white) sticker ($700 to $800); Saturn-shaped contents sticker (black
    print on gold stock); QuadraDisc sticker (black, white, and gold). Cover alone: $2,000 to $4,000.
    Cover with shrink wrap and three stickers still properly attached: $2,500 to $5,000.
    Top 1,000 ranking: 67

Elvis Presley • Elvis Presley (RCA Victor SPD-23) 1956 $4,500
    Triple-EP set, with cover and insert. Given as a bonus to buyers of a $47.95 Victrola. Includes
    six-page brochure titled "How to Use and Enjoy Your RCA Victor Elvis Presley Autograph,
    Automatic 45 Victrola Portable Phonograph." Three-EPs: $1,200 to $1,600. Cover: $2,200 to
    $2,800. Brochure: $75 to $100. Price range for set: $3,500 to $4,500.
    Top 1,000 ranking: 68

I Feel So Bad/Wild in the Country • Elvis Presley (RCA Victor 37-7880)....... 1961 $3,500
    Compact 33 single with picture sleeve. Second of five mono singles in this somewhat
    experimental and ultimately failed series. Compact 33s are seven-inch discs with a quarter-inch,
    LP-size, hole. Picture sleeve alone is $1,500 to $2,000. Price range for both: $2,500 to $3,500.
    Top 1,000 ranking: 102

Blue Christmas/Blue Christmas • Elvis Presley (RCA Victor H07W-0808) 1957 $3,000
    45 rpm. Listed by identification number shown since no selection number is used.
    Promotional issue only. Near-mint price range: $2,000 to $3,000.
    Top 1,000 ranking: 150

Don't/Wear My Ring Around Your Neck • Elvis Presley (With Jordanaires)
(RCA Victor SP-45-76)... 1960 $3,000
    45 rpm single with picture sleeve. Promotional issue only. Picture sleeve alone is $1,000 to
    $2,000. Price range for both: $2,000 to $3,000.
    Top 1,000 ranking: 164

Roustabout Theatre Lobby Spot (Coming Soon)/Roustabout Theatre Lobby Spot
(Now Playing) • Elvis Presley (Paramount Pictures SP-2413)................ 1964   **$3,000**
    45 rpm. Promotional issue to theaters for lobby play in advance of and during the run of the
Roustabout film. This take is different from the one on the *Roustabout* LP and the RCA Victor
promo 45. Blue label. Label does not identify Elvis as the singer. Near-mint price range: $2,000
to $3,000.
    Top 1,000 ranking: 173

Elvis Presley • Elvis Presley (RCA Victor SPD-22) 1956   **$2,500**
    Double-EP set, with cover. Given as a bonus to buyers of a $32.95 Victrola. May have "Elvis" in
either light or dark pink letters on front cover. Counterfeits exist. Two-EPs: $500 to $750. Cover:
$1,500 to $1,750. Price range for set: $2,000 to $2,500.
    Top 1,000 ranking: 191

Jailhouse Rock/Treat Me Nice • Elvis Presley (RCA Victor 47-7035) 1957   **$2,500**
    45 rpm. Gold label, dog on top. Gold vinyl. Specific purpose not yet known. May be promotional
though not marked as such. Near-mint price range: $1,500 to $2,500.
    Top 1,000 ranking: 195

International Hotel, Las Vegas Nevada, Presents Elvis, August – 1969 – August •
Elvis Presley (RCA Victor).. 1969   **$2,500**
    Two LPs and numerous inserts in a specially prepared, complimentary gift box given to invited
guests at the Showroom Internationale on July 31, 1969 (media performance) and August 1
(official opening night).

    Box: Oversize, 12¾" x 12¾". Front: Orange RCA Victor logo at lower right. Title is in white, 6" x
6" box with orange and pink print at upper right. International Hotel logo at upper right. Black-
and-white Elvis photo, same as first used on *From Memphis to Vegas / From Vegas to
Memphis*. Back: Black, no printing.

    Box Contents: *Elvis (NBC-TV Special)* RCA Victor LPM-4088 and *From Elvis in Memphis* LSP-
4155 (both are rigid discs, with orange labels); nine-page press release – a summary of Elvis'
life and career – page one of which is on RCA Victor Records Public Affairs letterhead; RCA
Victor 36-page, full-color, 1969 *Elvis' Records & Tapes* catalog (with pink, red and white cover);
RCA 1969 Elvis pocket calender with a color photo of Elvis in his gold suit on one side (calender
on reverse); color 8" x 10" Elvis photo, signed "Sincerely, Elvis Presley" (back announces Elvis'
International Hotel engagement. This photo first appeared as a bonus with the *From Elvis in
Memphis* LP); and two black-and-white, glossy 8" x 10" Elvis photos with blank backs (shots
from the NBC-TV Special). Included with box but not actually packaged inside it: a single page,
reading: "Dear Friend, Enclosed is a special promotion package with our compliments.
Sincerely, Elvis & the Colonel." Has two black-and-white Elvis photos, one at upper left and one
at upper right. Box only: $1,500 to $2,000. Complete set: $2,000 to $2,500.
    Top 1,000 ranking: 213

International Hotel, Las Vegas Nevada, Presents Elvis • Elvis Presley
(RCA Victor) 1969   **$2,500**
    Known as the "V.I.P. Box," this is the same as the other International Hotel boxes (1969 &
1970), except does *not* have printed, white 6" x 6" box with International Hotel logo and
engagement dates. Reportedly made without a date so it could be used for any performance or
promotion. Box only: $2,000 to $2,500.
    Top 1,000 ranking: 214

Speedway • Elvis Presley (RCA Victor LPM-3989).. 1968   **$2,100**
    Monaural LP. Soundtrack. This is the only standard catalog RCA Victor Presley release with a
solo track by another artist (*Your Groovy Self* by Nancy Sinatra). Cover: Front: Nipper logo at
top center, number at lower left. Seven color Elvis photos. Back: 12 color Elvis photos. Insert: a
color 8" x 10" Elvis (circa 1962) photo, signed "Sincerely, Elvis Presley" (back lists other RCA
Victor Elvis records). Shrink Sticker: red and white, reads: "Special Bonus, for a limited time
only, full color photo of Elvis." Disc alone: $800 to $1,000. Disc, cover, insert and sticker: $1,700
to $2,100.
    Top 1,000 ranking: 222

Milkcow Blues Boogie/You're a Heartbreaker • Elvis Presley (With Scotty and Bill)
(Sun 215) 1955   **$2,000**
    78 rpm. Near-mint price range: $1,000 to $2,000.
    Top 1,000 ranking: 283

Milkcow Blues Boogie/You're a Heartbreaker • Elvis Presley (With Scotty and Bill)
(Sun 215) 1955   **$2,000**
    45 rpm. Near-mint price range: $1,000 to $2,000.
    Top 1,000 ranking: 284

Elvis' Gold Records, Volume 4 • Elvis Presley (RCA Victor LPM-3921) 1968 $2,000

Monaural LP. Black label, "Monaural" at bottom. Cover: Front: RCA Victor logo at upper right and number at lower left. Has color photo of Elvis in front of a gold record. Back: Pictures five other Elvis LPs. Disc alone: $750 to $1,000. Disc and cover: $1,500 to $2,000.

Top 1,000 ranking: 363

International Hotel, Las Vegas Nevada, Presents Elvis 1970 • Elvis Presley (RCA Victor) 1970 $2,000

Specially prepared, complimentary gift box given to invited guests at the Showroom Internationale on January 26, 1970 (Elvis' opening night).

Box: Oversize, 12¾" x 12¾". Front: Orange RCA Victor logo at lower right. Title is in white, 6" x 6" box with orange and pink print at upper right. International Hotel logo at upper right. Black-and-white Elvis photo, same as first used on *From Memphis to Vegas / From Vegas to Memphis*. Back: Black, no printing.

Box Contents: *From Memphis to Vegas/From Vegas to Memphis* LSP-6020 (orange label, rigid disc LP) and an orange label 45 rpm of *Kentucky Rain/My Little Friend*, with picture sleeve; nine-page press release – a summary of Elvis' life and career – page one of which is on RCA Victor Records Public Affairs letterhead; RCA Victor, full-color, spiral-bound 1970 *Elvis' Records & Tapes* catalog (with red, white and black cover); RCA Victor 1970 Elvis pocket calender with a black-and-white photo of Elvis in leather suit, from '68 TV Special, on one side; black-and-white, 8" x 10" Elvis photo, signed "Thanks, Elvis" (back announces Elvis' International Hotel engagement "January 26th thru February 23rd"); 16-page photo booklet, color front and back covers, black-and-white photos inside (Elvis photo on front is identical to the one on the picture sleeve for *Suspicious Minds/You'll Think of Me*); four-page, complimentary dinner menu, with color front and back covers, black, red and white print inside (Elvis photo on front is identical to the one on the picture sleeve for *Suspicious Minds/You'll Think of Me*). Box only: $1,100 to $1,300. Complete set: $1,500 to $2,000.

Top 1,000 ranking: 368

Elvis Presley • Elvis Presley (RCA Victor EPA-747) 1956 $1,800

Temporary paper envelope/sleeve. Used until standard EP covers were available. Paper stock is white, with dark blue print. Cover actually reads "Blue Suede Shoes by Elvis Presley" with the other three tracks listed below in smaller type. Counterfeits exist. (Disc value, $20 to $30, is not included.) Price range for sleeve only: $1,000 to $1,800.

Top 1,000 ranking: 377

Surrender/Lonely Man • Elvis Presley (With Jordanaires) (RCA Victor 37-7850) 1961 $1,700

Compact 33 single with picture sleeve. First of five mono singles in this somewhat experimental and ultimately failed series. Compact 33s are seven-inch discs with a quarter-inch, LP-size, hole. Picture sleeve alone is $800 to $1,000. Price range for both: $1,300 to $1,700.

Top 1,000 ranking: 382

That's All Right/Blue Moon of Kentucky • Elvis Presley (With Scotty and Bill) (Sun 209) 1954 $1,600

78 rpm. Near-mint price range: $1,400 to $1,600.

Top 1,000 ranking: 383

TV Guide Presents Elvis Presley • Elvis Presley (RCA Victor GB-MW-8705) 1956 $1,600

EP with two inserts; no cover. Blue or white label. Single-sided, four-track, open-end interview. Promotional issue only. Inserts: "Suggested continuity," a pink, four-page suggested interview script; and a gray card which provides background on the interview and pictures the September 8-14, 1956 issue of *TV Guide* with Elvis on the cover. Counterfeits exist. Disc: $1,000 to $1,200. Each insert: $150 to $200. Price range for disc and both inserts: $1,400 to $1,600.

Top 1,000 ranking: 384

Jailhouse Rock/Treat Me Nice • Elvis Presley (RCA Victor 47-7035) 1957 $1,600

MGM special press preview theater ticket/sleeve. Sent wrapped around the standard *Jailhouse Rock* picture sleeve ($50 to $75), with a 45 rpm ($30 to $40) inside. Promotional issue only, distributed only to media film reviewers. Counterfeits exist. Price range for package with ticket but without stub attached: $500 to $750. Price range for package with ticket and stub still attached: $1,400 to $1,600.

Top 1,000 ranking: 387

Good Rockin' Tonight/I Don't Care If the Sun Don't Shine • Elvis Presley (With Scotty and Bill) (Sun 210) 1954 $1,500

78 rpm. Near-mint price range: $1,000 to $1,500.

Top 1,000 ranking: 416

That's All Right/Blue Moon of Kentucky • Elvis Presley (With Scotty and Bill)
(Sun 209) 1954   **$1,500**
  45 rpm. Near-mint price range: $1,000 to $1,500.
  Top 1,000 ranking: 417

Mystery Train/I Forgot to Remember to Forget • Elvis Presley
(RCA Victor 47-6357) 1955   **$1,500**
  Picture sleeve. The 45 rpm single is on the white "Record Prevue" label. One of a series of
  promotional "This Is His Life" issues, made for many different RCA Victor artists. Though not
  numbered, this is the first picture sleeve of any type issued with an Elvis record. Unfortunately,
  the "life story" is somewhat fabricated. 45 rpm single without picture sleeve is $300 to $400.
  Price range for both: $1,000 to $1,500.
  Top 1,000 ranking: 422

Surrender/Lonely Man • Elvis Presley (With Jordanaires)
(RCA Victor 68-7850) 1961   **$1,500**
  Stereo compact 33 single. Not issued with a picture sleeve. Near-mint price range: $1,000 to
  $1,500.
  Top 1,000 ranking: 461

Special Christmas Programming • Elvis Presley (RCA Victor 5697) 1967   **$1,500**
  Monaural LP. Identification number used since no selection number is shown. Promotional issue
  only for radio stations to air December 3, 1967. Insert: Script sheet with running times and
  program information ($50 to $100). Near-mint price range: $1,000 to $1,500.
  Top 1,000 ranking: 476

Good Rockin' Tonight/I Don't Care If the Sun Don't Shine • Elvis Presley
(With Scotty and Bill) (Sun 210) 1954   **$1,400**
  45 rpm. Near-mint price range: $1,000 to $1,400.
  Top 1,000 ranking: 487

Baby Let's Play House/I'm Left, You're Right, She's Gone • Elvis Presley
(With Scotty and Bill) (Sun 217) 1955   **$1,200**
  78 rpm. Near-mint price range: $800 to $1,200.
  Top 1,000 ranking: 515

RCA Radio Victrola Division Spots • Elvis Presley (RCA Victor 0401) 1956   **$1,200**
  Monaural LP. Maroon label, silver print. Single-sided disc with four 50-second radio commercials
  for RCA's Victrolas, as well as for the bonus SPD-22 *Elvis Presley (2 EPs)* and SPD-23 *Elvis
  Presley (3 EPs)*. Elvis is the announcer on all of the spots, which also include excerpts of songs
  from the two SPD extended plays. Issued only to radio stations running the spots. Near-mint
  price range: $800 to $1,200.
  Top 1,000 ranking: 518

Special Easter Programming Kit • Elvis Presley (RCA Victor 0651 & 0652) .. 1966   **$1,200**
  Gold Standard picture sleeve-mailer and two 45 rpm promo singles, *Joshua Fit the Battle/Known
  Only to Him* and *Milky White Way/Swing Down Sweet Chariot* in their sleeves and an Easter
  greeting card from Elvis. Has a black-and-white Elvis photo on front. Picture sleeve-mailer alone
  is $800 to $1,000. Price range for the complete kit: $800 to $1,200.
  Top 1,000 ranking: 550

Baby Let's Play House/I'm Left, You're Right, She's Gone • Elvis Presley
(With Scotty and Bill) (Sun 217) 1955   **$1,100**
  45 rpm. Near-mint price range: $800 to $1,100.
  Top 1,000 ranking: 558

Mystery Train/I Forgot to Remember to Forget • Elvis Presley (With Scotty and Bill)
(Sun 223) 1955   **$1,000**
  78 rpm. Near-mint price range: $750 to $1,000.
  Top 1,000 ranking: 620

Girls! Girls! Girls! Advance (Coming Soon) Theatre Lobby Spot/Girls! Girls! Girls!
(Now Playing) Theatre Lobby Spot • Elvis Presley
(Paramount Pictures SP-2017) 1962   **$1,000**
  45 rpm. Promotional issue to theaters for lobby play in advance of and during the run of *Girls!
  Girls! Girls!* film. Label does not identify Elvis as the singer. Near-mint price range: $750 to
  $1,000.
  Top 1,000 ranking: 708

Elvis: Aloha from Hawaii Via Satellite • Elvis Presley
(RCA Victor VPSX-6089) 1973   **$1,000**
Two quadraphonic LPs. Reddish-orange label. Cover: Front: Has two white stickers, listing contents and playing times (contents not printed on covers). There is no Saturn-shaped contents sticker, nor is there a QuadraDisc sticker. On this issue, stickers were on shrink wrap. Front has die-cut (5 ½" diameter) hole which allows inner sleeve to show. Double pocket cover. Promotional issue only. Near-mint price range: $750 to $1,000.
Top 1,000 ranking: 742

Mystery Train/I Forgot to Remember to Forget • Elvis Presley (With Scotty and Bill)
(Sun 223) 1955   **$900**
45 rpm. Near-mint price range: $700 to $900.
Top 1,000 ranking: 754

Old Shep/blank • Elvis Presley (RCA Victor CR-15) 1956   **$800**
45 rpm single-sided disc. White label, promotional issue only. Near-mint price range: $600 to $800.
Top 1,000 ranking: 773

The Real Elvis • Elvis Presley (RCA Victor EPA-5120)................... 1959   **$800**
EP and cover. Maroon label. Reissue of EPA-940. Disc alone: $625 to $725. Disc and cover: $600 to $800.
Top 1,000 ranking: 778

Surrender/Lonely Man • Elvis Presley (With Jordanaires)
(RCA Victor 61-7850).. 1961   **$800**
45 rpm. Living stereo. Near-mint price range: $600 to $800.
Top 1,000 ranking: 783

Elvis • Elvis Presley (RCA Victor LPM-1382) 1956   **$750**
Monaural LP. Black label, "Long Play" at bottom. Mistakenly pressed with an alternative take of *Old Shep*, not available on any other authorized U.S. vinyl release. Any copy with a "15S" or "17S" matrix on side 2 (matrix on side 1 is irrelevant) is likely to have the alternative; however, playing the track is the way to be certain. May also appear on some "19S" pressings; however, price applies to any pressing with the alternative take, regardless of identification number. Alternative is different throughout, instrumentally and vocally – especially Elvis' phrasing – but here are two lyric variations. Words in all upper case are exclusive to the alternative take (which can now be heard on the 1992 CD boxed set *Elvis – The King of Rock 'N' Roll, the Complete '50s Masters*): 1) "As the years fast did roll, Old Shep he grew old AND his eyes were fast growing dim." 2) "He came to my side and he looked up at me, and HE laid his old head on my knee." Price would apply to any other pressing with the alternative take, regardless of identification number. LP alone: $500 to $600. LP and cover: $500 to $750.
Top 1,000 ranking: 847

It's Now Or Never/A Mess of Blues • Elvis Presley (With Jordanaires)
(RCA Victor 47-7777).. 1960   **$750**
45 rpm. Made, mistakenly, with the piano track on *It's Now Or Never* missing. Near-mint price range: $500 to $750.
Top 1,000 ranking: 887

Special Palm Sunday Programming • Elvis Presley (RCA
Victor SP-33-461)... 1967   **$750**
Monaural LP. White label, black print. Reads: "Complete half-hour radio program with spot announcements and selections from the RCA Victor album *How Great Thou Art* (LPM/LSP-3758." Promotional issue only. Insert: Cue sheet with running times and program information. LP alone: $600 to $650. LP and insert: $500 to $750.
Top 1,000 ranking: 934

My Boy/Loving Arms • Elvis Presley (RCA Victor 2458EX) 1974   **$750**
45 rpm. Gray label. Includes paper, titles, single-sheet insert. Couples two songs not issued back-to-back in the U.S. Manufactured in the U.S. for distribution overseas. Near-mint price range: $500 to $750.
Top 1,000 ranking: 938

Peace in the Valley • Elvis Presley (RCA Victor EPA-5121) 1959   **$700**
EP and cover. Maroon label. Reissue of EPA-4054. Disc alone: $575 to $650. Disc and cover: $500 to $700.
Top 1,000 ranking: 961

Date with Elvis • Elvis Presley (RCA Victor LPM-2011) 1959 $700

Monaural LP. Black label, "Long Play" at bottom. Cover: Gatefold, though record pocket is the front instead of back panel and the pocket opening is at top rather than right side (as with most gatefold covers). Front: RCA Victor logo and number at upper right. Contents printed on a red sticker with white lettering, applied to front. No titles are printed on cover itself. Back is an "Elvis 1960" calendar, with March 24 circled in red. Banner: Aluminum foil wraparound banner, proclaiming this LP as one of 24 Alcoa Wrap "New Golden Age of Sound Albums," and announcing a Beautiful Hair Breck New Golden Age of Sound Preview LP. Makes no reference to this specific LP or to Elvis. In fact, a banner from any of the 24 Golden Age of Sound Albums could be used with *A Date with Elvis*. Banner alone: $200 to $300. Cover alone: $250 to $300. Disc, cover and banner: $500 to $700.
Top 1,000 ranking: 962

Are You Lonesome Tonight/I Gotta Know • Elvis Presley (With Jordanaires) (RCA Victor 61-7810)... 1960 $650

45 rpm. Living stereo. Near-mint price range: $500 to $650.
Top 1,000 ranking: 994

PRE-TEENS

What Makes Me Love You Like I Do/Pass It On • Pre-Teens (With Shytan Five) (J&S 1756) 1956 $1,000

45 rpm. Near-mint price range: $750 to $1,000.
Top 1,000 ranking: 632

PRETENDERS

Blue and Lonely/Daddy Needs Baby • Pretenders (Featuring Jimmy Jones with Rhythm Accompaniment) (Central 2605)... 1958 $2,000

45 rpm. Near-mint price range: $1,000 to $2,000.
Top 1,000 ranking: 315

PRISONAIRES

What'll You Do Next/There Is Love in You • Prisonaires ("Confined to Tennessee State Prison Nashville, Tennessee") (Sun 207) 1954 $5,000

45 rpm. Near-mint price range: $4,000 to $5,000.
Top 1,000 ranking: 49

Just Walkin' in the Rain/Baby Please • Prisonaires ("Confined to Tennessee State Prison Nashville, Tennessee") (Sun 186) 1953 $3,500

45 rpm. Red vinyl. Near-mint price range: $2,500 to $3,500.
Top 1,000 ranking: 99

PRYOR, Snooky

Crosstown Blues/I Want You for Myself • Snooky Pryor (Parrot 807)............ 1953 $1,500

45 rpm. Red vinyl. Near-mint price range: $1,000 to $1,500.
Top 1,000 ranking: 408

PUBLIO & VALIANTS

Image of Love/? • Publio & Valiants (Menard 6252) .... ? $750

45 rpm. Near-mint price range: $500 to $750.
Top 1,000 ranking: 944

PULLENS, Vern

Bop Crazy Baby/It's My Life • Vern Pullens (Spade 1927)............................. 1956 $750

45 rpm. Near-mint price range: $500 to $750.
Top 1,000 ranking: 848

PYRAMIDERS

Don't Ever Leave Me/How It Feels • Pyramiders (Scott 1205)....................... 1958 $750

45 rpm. Near-mint price range: $500 to $750.
Top 1,000 ranking: 864

PYRAMIDS

Someday/Bow Wow • Pyramids (With Fletcher Smith's Band)
(C Note 108)... 1955 $3,000
   45 rpm. Near-mint price range: $2,000 to $3,000.
   Top 1,000 ranking: 139
Someday/Bow Wow • Pyramids (With Fletcher Smith's Band)
(Hollywood 1047) 1955 $1,000
   45 rpm. Near-mint price range: $750 to $1,000.
   Top 1,000 ranking: 621
Someday/Bow Wow • Pyramids (With Fletcher Smith's Band)
(C Note 108)... 1955 $750
   78 rpm. Near-mint price range: $500 to $750.
   Top 1,000 ranking: 837

QUARTER NOTES

Baby/Hold Me Darling • Quarter Notes (Little Star 112)................................. 1962 $2,000
   45 rpm. Near-mint price range: $1,000 to $2,000.
   Top 1,000 ranking: 347

QUILLS

Whose Love, But Yours/Goin' to the Moon • Quills (Casino 106) 1959 $2,000
   45 rpm. Near-mint price range: $1,000 to $2,000.
   Top 1,000 ranking: 330

QUINTONES

Just a Little Loving/The Lonely Telephone • Quintones (Jordan 1601) 1956 $1,000
   78 rpm. Near-mint price range: $750 to $1,000.
   Top 1,000 ranking: 633

RAMISTELLA, Johnny

Little Girl/Two By Two • Johnny Ramistella (Suede 1401)............................. 1958 $650
   45 rpm. Ramistella became popular when he adopted the stage name: Johnny Rivers. Near-
   mint price range: $2,000 to $3,000.
   Top 1,000 ranking: 984

RAVENS

Count Every Star/I'm Gonna Paper My Walls with Your Love • Ravens
(National 9111)... 1950 $3,000
   45 rpm. Near-mint price range: $2,000 to $3,000.
   Top 1,000 ranking: 105
You Don't Have to Drop a Heart to Break It/Midnight Blues • Ravens
(Columbia 39112)... 1951 $2,000
   45 rpm. Near-mint price range: $1,500 to $2,000.
   Top 1,000 ranking: 232
You're Always in My Dreams/Gotta Find My Baby • Ravens
(Columbia 39194)... 1951 $2,000
   45 rpm. Near-mint price range: $1,500 to $2,000.
   Top 1,000 ranking: 233
You Foolish Thing/Honey, I Don't Want You • Ravens (Columbia 39408)..... 1951 $2,000
   45 rpm. Near-mint price range: $1,500 to $2,000.
   Top 1,000 ranking: 234
Time Takes Care of Everything/Don't Look Now • Ravens
(Columbia 1-903) 1950 $1,500
   Compact 33 single. Near-mint price range: $1,000 to $1,500.
   Top 1,000 ranking: 393
I'm So Crazy for Love/My Baby's Gone • Ravens (Columbia 1-925) 1950 $1,500
   Compact 33 single. Near-mint price range: $1,000 to $1,500.
   Top 1,000 ranking: 394

Four Great Voices • Ravens (Rendition 104) 1952 $1,000
    EP. Near-mint price range: $750 to $1,000.
    Top 1,000 ranking: 577
The Ravens Featuring Jimmy Ricks • Ravens (Featuring Jimmy Ricks)
  (King 310) 1954 $1,000
    EP. Near-mint price range: $750 to $1,000.
    Top 1,000 ranking: 609
Whiffenpoof Song/I Get All My Lovin' on a Saturday Night • Ravens
  (Okeh 6825) 1951 $750
    45 rpm. Near-mint price range: $500 to $750.
    Top 1,000 ranking: 804
Everything But You/That Old Gang of Mine • Ravens (Okeh 6843) 1951 $750
    45 rpm. Near-mint price range: $500 to $750.
    Top 1,000 ranking: 805

RAY DOTS

I Need Someone/Lu La • Ray Dots (Vibro 1651) 1956 $1500
    45 rpm. Near-mint price range: $1,000 to $1,500.
    Top 1,000 ranking: 430

REBELS

In the Park/In My Heart • Rebels (Kings-X 3362) 1959 $1,000
    45 rpm. Near-mint price range: $750 to $1,000.
    Top 1,000 ranking: 674

REED, Lula

Blue and Moody • Lula Reed (King 604) 1959 $750
    LP. Credits "Lula" Reed; however, some other releases show her as "Lulu" Reed. Near-mint
    price range: $500 to $750.
    Top 1,000 ranking: 873

REEVES, Jim

Jim Reeves Sings • Jim Reeves (Abbott 5001) 1956 $1,200
    LP. Near-mint price range: $800 to $1,200.
    Top 1,000 ranking: 519

RELF, Bobby, & Laurels

Yours Alone/Farewell • Bobby Relf & Laurels (Flair 1063)............................. 1955 $1,500
    45 rpm. Near-mint price range: $1,000 to $1,500.
    Top 1,000 ranking: 423

RE-VELS

My Lost Love/Love My Baby • Re-Vels Quartet (Atlas 1035) 1954 $5,000
    45 rpm. Near-mint price range: $4,000 to $5,000.
    Top 1,000 ranking: 50
So in Love/It Happened to Me • Re-Vels (With Gene Kutch & Butch Ballard
  Orchestra) (Teen 122)... 1956 $650
    45 rpm. Near-mint price range: $500 to $650.
    Top 1,000 ranking: 981

RHYTHM ACES

I Wonder Why/Get Lost • Rhythm Aces (Vee-Jay 124) 1954 $2,000
    45 rpm. Red vinyl. Near-mint price range: $1,000 to $2,000.
    Top 1,000 ranking: 274
Whisper to Me/Olly, Olly, Atsen Free • Rhythm Aces (Vee-Jay 138)............. 1955 $2,000
    45 rpm. Red vinyl. Near-mint price range: $1,000 to $2,000.
    Top 1,000 ranking: 285

RHYTHM CADETS
Dearest Doryce/Rocking Jimmy • Rhythm Cadets (Featuring George Singleton)
(Vesta 501/502) 1957 $2,000
    45 rpm. Near-mint price range: $1,500 to $2,000.
    Top 1,000 ranking: 302

RICH, Charlie
Lonely Weekends • Charlie Rich (Phillips International 1970) 1960 $800
    LP. Near-mint price range: $600 to $800.
    Top 1,000 ranking: 780

RICE, Eldon
Don't Let Love Break Your Heart/Our Love Won't Die • Eldon Rice
(El Rio 413) 1961 $750
    45 rpm. Near-mint price range: $500 to $750.
    Top 1,000 ranking: 898

RIGHTEOUS BROTHERS
Ebb Tide/For Sentimental Reasons (I Love You) • Righteous Brothers
(Philles 130) 1965 $1,500
    45 rpm. Custom label. Has Phil Spector's picture on the label. Promotional issue only. Near-mint
    price range: $1,000 to $1,500.
    Top 1,000 ranking: 473

RIP-CHORDS
I Love You the Most/Let's Do the Razzle Dazzle • Rip-Chords (Abco 105) ... 1956 $2,000
    45 rpm. Red vinyl. Near-mint price range: $1,000 to $2,000.
    Top 1,000 ranking: 296

RIPLEY COTTON CHOPPERS
Silver Bells/Blues Waltz • Ripley Cotton Choppers (Sun 190) 1953 $2,000
    78 rpm. Near-mint price range: $1,000 to $2,000.
    Top 1,000 ranking: 256

RISING STORM
Calm Before ... The Rising Storm • Rising Storm (Remnant 3571) 1969 $1,500
    LP. Near-mint price range: $1,000 to $1,500.
    Top 1,000 ranking: 479

ROANE, Johnny
Drag Strip Baby/Wasted Past • Johnny Roane (Wagon 1004) .... ? $700
    45 rpm. Near-mint price range: $500 to $700.
    Top 1,000 ranking: 969

ROBBINS, Marty
Rock'n Roll'n Robbins • Marty Robbins (Columbia 2601) 1956 $750
    10-inch LP. Near-mint price range: $500 to $750.
    Top 1,000 ranking: 849

ROBERTS, Lynn, & Phantoms
I'll Be Around/Miss You Tonite • Lynn Roberts & Phantoms (Oriole 101) 1954 $1,500
    45 rpm. Red vinyl. Near-mint price range: $1,000 to $1,500.
    Top 1,000 ranking: 418
I'll Be Around/Miss You Tonite • Lynn Roberts & Phantoms (Oriole 101) 1954 $750
    45 rpm. Black vinyl. Near-mint price range: $500 to $750.
    Top 1,000 ranking: 828

ROBINS
Rock 'N' Roll with the Robins • Robins (Whippet 703) 1958 $750
    LP. Near-mint price range: $500 to $750.
    Top 1,000 ranking: 865

ROCKERS

Tell Me Why/Count Every Star • Rockers (With Emmet Carter Combo)
(Carter 3029)... 1955 $2,000
45 rpm. Black vinyl. Any on red vinyl are bootlegs. Near-mint price range: $1,000 to $2,000.
Top 1,000 ranking: 286

ROCKETEERS

My Reckless Heart/They Turned the Party Out Down at Bessie's
House • Rocketeers (M.J.C. 501) 1955 $2,000
45 rpm. Near-mint price range: $1,000 to $2,000.
Top 1,000 ranking: 287

Foolish One/Gonna Feed My Baby • Rocketeers (Herald 415) 1953 $750
45 rpm. Red vinyl. Near-mint price range: $500 to $750.
Top 1,000 ranking: 817

ROCKETTES

I Can't Forget/Love Nobody • Rockettes (Parrot 789).................................. 1953 $2,000
45 rpm. Near-mint price range: $1,500 to $2,000.
Top 1,000 ranking: 257

ROCKIN' CONTINENTALS

The 309/2-3-4 • Rockin' Continentals (Casino 1007)................................... 1962 $900
45 rpm. Near-mint price range: $600 to $900.
Top 1,000 ranking: 757

RODGERS, Jimmie

Cowhand's Last Ride/Blue Yodel #12 • Jimmie Rodgers (Victor 18-6000).... 1933 $2,500
78 rpm picture disc. Near-mint price range: $1,500 to $2,500.
Top 1,000 ranking: 177

ROLLETTES

An Understanding/I'm Trying to Make You Love Me • Rollettes
(Melker 103) 1960 $2,000
45 rpm. Near-mint price range: $1,000 to $2,000.
Top 1,000 ranking: 340

ROLLING STONES

Street Fighting Man/No Expectations • Rolling Stones (London 909)............ 1968 $10,000
Picture sleeve. Approximately a dozen copies are known to exist. Near-mint price range: $5,000
to $10,000.
Top 1,000 ranking: 23

Stoned/I Wanna Be Your Man • Rolling Stones (London 9641) 1964 $4,000
45 rpm. Commercial issue. Near-mint price range: $3,000 to $4,000.
Top 1,000 ranking: 95

Stoned/I Wanna Be Your Man • Rolling Stones (London 9641) 1964 $2,000
45 rpm. Promotional issue. Near-mint price range: $1,000 to $2,000.
Top 1,000 ranking: 358

Beast of Burden/When the Whip Comes Down • Rolling Stones (Rolling
Stones 19309)... 1978 $2,000
Picture sleeve. Near-mint price range: $1,000 to $2,000.
Top 1,000 ranking: 372

The Rolling Stones • Rolling Stones (London 3375)...................................... 1964 $1,000
Monaural LP. White label. Promotional issue only. Near-mint price range: $750 to $1,000.
Top 1,000 ranking: 729

The Promotional Album • Rolling Stones (London RSD1) .... ? $1,000
LP. Near-mint price range: $750 to $1,000.
Top 1,000 ranking: 750

Heart of Stone/What a Shame • Rolling Stones (London 9725) 1965 $650
Picture sleeve. Near-mint price range: $500 to $650.
Top 1,000 ranking: 999

ROMAN, Net
Tears from My Eyes/This Is the Night • Net Roman (Sahara 102)................ 1963 $1,500
    45 rpm. Less valuable if credited to "Nap" Roman. Near-mint price range: $1,000 to $1,500.
    Top 1,000 ranking: 469

ROMAN, Nap [Net]
Tears from My Eyes/This Is the Night • Nap [Net] Roman (Sahara 102) 1963 $1,000
    45 rpm. More valuable if credited to "Net" Roman. Near-mint price range: $750 to $1,000.
    Top 1,000 ranking: 717

ROSS, Johnny
My Dreams Have Gone/That's What You Mean to Me • Johnny Ross (With A&R
    Man Chuck "Tequila" Rio) (Corvette 1006) 1958 $2,000
    45 rpm. Near-mint price range: $1,000 to $2,000.
    Top 1,000 ranking: 316

"SINGING" ROULETTES
Hasten Jason/Wouldn't Be Going Steady • The "Singing" Roulettes
    (Scepter 1204) 1959 $750
    45 rpm. Near-mint price range: $500 to $750.
    Top 1,000 ranking: 874

ROYAL BOYS
Darling Angel/Lover's Bells • Royal Boys (Tropelco 1007) 1960 $3,000
    45 rpm. Near-mint price range: $2,000 to $3,000.
    Top 1,000 ranking: 165

ROYAL DEMONS
Trembling Hand/Kiss Kiss • Royal Demons (Pek 8101)................................ 1961 $750
    45 rpm. Near-mint price range: $500 to $750.
    Top 1,000 ranking: 899

ROYAL-FIVE
Over the Rainbow/? • Royal-Five (P&L 317)... 1966 $750
    45 rpm. Near-mint price range: $500 to $750.
    Top 1,000 ranking: 931

ROYALS
If You Love Me/Dreams of You • Royals (Okeh 6832)................................... 1951 $750
    45 rpm. Near-mint price range: $500 to $750.
    Top 1,000 ranking: 806

ROYALS
Every Beat of My Heart/All Night Long • Royals (Federal 12064)................. 1952 $3,500
    45 rpm. Blue vinyl. *All Night Long* features blues star Wynonie Harris. Near-mint price range:
    $2,500 to $3,500.
    Top 1,000 ranking: 97
Starting from Tonight/I Know I Love You So • Royals (Federal 12077) 1952 $2,000
    45 rpm. Near-mint price range: $1,000 to $2,000.
    Top 1,000 ranking: 242
Moonrise/Fifth Street Blues • Royals (Federal 12088).................................. 1952 $2,000
    45 rpm. Near-mint price range: $1,000 to $2,000.
    Top 1,000 ranking: 243
A Love in My Heart/I'll Never Let Her Go • Royals (Federal 12098) 1952 $1,000
    45 rpm. Near-mint price range: $750 to $1,000.
    Top 1,000 ranking: 578
The Shrine of St. Cecilia/I Feel So Blue • Royals (Federal 12121)................ 1953 $1,000
    45 rpm. Near-mint price range: $750 to $1,000.
    Top 1,000 ranking: 592

Every Beat of My Heart/All Night Long • Royals (Federal 12064).................. 1952 $750
     45 rpm. Black vinyl. *All Night Long* features blues star Wynonie Harris. Near-mint price range:
     $500 to $750.
     Top 1,000 ranking: 810

SANDERS, Bobby
You've Forgotten Me/Maybe I'm Wrong • Bobby Sanders (Kent 382) 1962 $750
     45 rpm. Near-mint price range: $500 to $750.`
     Top 1,000 ranking: 906

SAVOY, Jules
Would You/Tutti Frutti Man • Jules Savoy (Singing Discovery of Hesperia Inn,
     Hesperia, Calif.) & Chromatics (Real 1320) 1957 $750
     45 rpm. Near-mint price range: $500 to $750.
     Top 1,000 ranking: 856

SAWYER, Henry, & Jupiters
It Takes Two/I Want • Henry Sawyer & Jupiters (With Music by Mike Tam) (Planet
     X 9621) 1957 $2,500
     45 rpm. Three known copies. Near-mint price range: $1,500 to $2,500.
     Top 1,000 ranking: 196

SCOTT, Lee, & Windsors
My Gloria/Cool Seabreeze • Lee Scott & Windsors (Back Beat 506) 1958 $4,000
     45 rpm. One known copy. Probably on promo only as no commercial copies are yet known to
     exist. Near-mint price range: $3,000 to $4,000.
     Top 1,000 ranking: 91

SCOTT, Seaphus, & Five Masqueraders
Summer Sunrise/Nature's Beauty • Seaphus Scott & Five Masqueraders
     (With Billy Gale Orchestra) (Joyce 303)... 1958 $750
     45 rpm. Near-mint price range: $500 to $750.
     Top 1,000 ranking: 866

SEARCH PARTY
Montgomery's Chapel • Search Party 1969 $2,500
     LP. Approximately a dozen made by this San Francisco band. Neither label name nor selection
     number used. Near-mint price range: $1,500 to $2,500.
     Top 1,000 ranking: 215

SERENADERS
M-a-y-b-e-l-l/Ain't Goin' to Cry No More • Serenaders (Swing Time 347) 1954 $1,200
     45 rpm. Near-mint price range: $800 to $1,200.
     Top 1,000 ranking: 509
I'll Cry Tomorrow/If Your Heart Says Yes • Serenaders (Motown 1046)........ 1963 $1,000
     45 rpm. Near-mint price range: $750 to $1,000.
     Top 1,000 ranking: 718

SHAGGS
Wink • Shaggs (MCM 6311)... 1967 $2,000
     LP. Near-mint price range: $1,500 to $2,000.
     Top 1,000 ranking: 361

SHAGGS
Philosophy of the World • Shaggs (Third World 3001)................................... 1972 $1,500
     LP. Reportedly 2,000 made. Near-mint price range: $1,000 to $1,500.
     Top 1,000 ranking: 485

SHANNON, Del
Runaway • Del Shannon (Big Top 1303) 1961 $650
     Stereo LP. Near-mint price range: $500 to $650.
     Top 1,000 ranking: 995

SHANTONES
Come to Me/Little Girl • Shantones (With Orchestra) (Trilyte 5001) 1956 $2,000

45 rpm. Approximately three copies known. Near-mint price range: $1,000 to $2,000.

Top 1,000 ranking: 297

SHANTONS
Lucille/To Be in Love with You • Shantons (With Billy Mure & Orchestra)

(Jay-Mar 241).. 1959 $750

45 rpm. Identification number shown since no selection number is used. Near-mint price range:

$500 to $750.

Top 1,000 ranking: 875

SHAW, John, & Dell-O's
Why Did You Leave Me/Why Does It Have to Be • John Shaw & Dell-O's

(With Billy Cooke & Orchestra) (U-C 5002).. 1958 $2,500

45 rpm. Near-mint price range: $1,500 to $2,500.

Top 1,000 ranking: 198

SHA-WEEZ
No One to Love Me/Early Sunday Morning • Sha-Weez (Aladdin 3170) 1952 $3,000

45 rpm. Near-mint price range: $2,000 to $3,000.

Top 1,000 ranking: 114

SHEIKS
Give Me Another Chance/Baby Don't You Cry • Sheiks (Ef-N-De 1000) 1955 $1,500

45 rpm. Near-mint price range: $1,000 to $1,500.

Top 1,000 ranking: 424

SHEKERYK, Pete, & Delua-Tones
Believe in Me/Little Baby • Pete Shekeryk & Delua-Tones (Ukey 101)................ ? $750

45 rpm. Near-mint price range: $500 to $750.

Top 1,000 ranking: 945

SHIELDS
You Told a Lie/Barnyard Dance • Shields (Continental 4072) 1961 $1,000

45 rpm. Near-mint price range: $750 to $1,000.

Top 1,000 ranking: 696

SHOWCASES
This Love Was Real/Anna, My Love • Showcases (Galaxy 732)................... 1964 $1,000

45 rpm. Near-mint price range: $750 to $1,000.

Top 1,000 ranking: 730

SIGGERS, Ruben, & His Fabulous Kool Kats
Those Love me Blues/Pretty Pretty Baby • Ruben Siggers & His Fabulous Kool

Kats (Vocal by Ephraim Siggers) (Spinks 600) 1957 $750

45 rpm. Near-mint price range: $500 to $750.

Top 1,000 ranking: 857

SILHOUETTES
Evelyn/Never Will Part • Silhouettes (With Dave McRae Orchestra)

(Junior 400) 1959 $1,500

45 rpm. Near-mint price range: $1,000 to $1,500.

Top 1,000 ranking: 451

SIMIELE, Ernie, & Eratics
Special Girl/? • Ernie Simiele & Eratics (Kind A Round 11765) .... ? $650

45 rpm. Also shows "RB 105." It's not clear which is the correct selection number. Near-mint

price range: $500 to $650.

Top 1,000 ranking: 1000

SINATRA, Frank

A Special Message to You from Frank Sinatra • Frank Sinatra (Reprise)...... 1961 $1,000
  45 rpm. Single-sided disc, made as a Reprise sales and promotional tool. No selection number
  used. Two different pressings exist. Near-mint price range: $750 to $1,000.
  Top 1,000 ranking: 697
From the Bottom of My Heart/Melancholy Mood • Frank Sinatra
(Brunswick 8443) 1939 $750
  78 rpm. Credited to "Harry James & His Orchestra," but is the first recording by Frank Sinatra.
  Near-mint price range: $500 to $750.
  Top 1,000 ranking: 799

SINCERES

Please Don't Cheat On Me/If You Should Leave Me • Sinceres
(Richie 545).. 1961 $650
  45 rpm. No mention of Roulette distribution on label. Near-mint price range: $500 to $650.
  Top 1,000 ranking: 996

SINGLETON, Jimmy, & Royal Satins

Each Passing Day/Sally • Jimmy Singleton & Royal Satins (With Hi-Fis) (Devere
006)... 1960 $1,000
  45 rpm. Near-mint price range: $750 to $1,000.
  Top 1,000 ranking: 688

SIPES, Leonard, & Rhythm Oakies

Campus Boogie/Too Beautiful to Cry • Leonard Sipes & Rhythm Oakies
(Morgan 106).. ? $800
  78 rpm. Near-mint price range: $400 to $800.
  Top 1,000 ranking: 798

SMACK

Smack • Smack (Audio House).. 1967 $2,000
  LP. Reportedly 200 made. No selection number used. Near-mint price range: $1,500 to $2,000.
  Top 1,000 ranking: 362

SMOTHERS, Smokey

Backporch Blues • Smokey Smothers (King 779)... 1962 $800
  Monaural LP. Near-mint price range: $600 to $800.
  Top 1,000 ranking: 787

SOF-TONES

Oh Why/? • Sof-Tones (Ceebee 1062) 1957 $4,000
  45 rpm. Approximately two copies known. Near-mint price range: $3,000 to $4,000.
  Top 1,000 ranking: 88

SOLITAIRES

Please Remember My Heart/South of the Border • Solitaires
(Old Town 1006/1007) 1954 $3,000
  45 rpm. Red vinyl. Near-mint price range: $2,000 to $3,000.
  Top 1,000 ranking: 134
Blue Valentine/Wonder Why • Solitaires (Old Town 1000) 1954 $2,000
  45 rpm. Red vinyl. Near-mint price range: $1,000 to $2,000.
  Top 1,000 ranking: 275
Chances I've Taken/Lonely • Solitaires (Old Town 1008).............................. 1954 $1,200
  45 rpm. Red vinyl. Near-mint price range: $900 to $1,200.
  Top 1,000 ranking: 510

SONICS

Marlene/? • Sonics (Gaiety 114) 1959 $1,500
  45 rpm. Near-mint price range: $1,000 to $1,500.
  Top 1,000 ranking: 452

Once in a Lifetime/It Ain't True • Sonics (X-Tra 107) 1958 $1,000
     45 rpm. Near-mint price range: $750 to $1,000.
     Top 1,000 ranking: 660

SPANIELS

Baby It's You/Bounce • Spaniels (Vee-Jay 101) 1953 $5,000
     45 rpm. Red vinyl. Near-mint price range: $4,000 to $5,000.
     Top 1,000 ranking: 46

Baby It's You/Bounce • Spaniels (Chance 1141)... 1953 $2,000
     45 rpm. Red vinyl. Near-mint price range: $1,000 to $2,000.
     Top 1,000 ranking: 258

Do-Wah/Don'cha Go • Spaniels (Vee-Jay 131) 1955 $2,000
     45 rpm. Red vinyl. Near-mint price range: $1,000 to $2,000.
     Top 1,000 ranking: 288

Baby It's You/Bounce • Spaniels (Vee-Jay 101) 1953 $1,000
     45 rpm. Black vinyl. Maroon label. Near-mint price range: $750 to $1,000.
     Top 1,000 ranking: 593

Bells Ring Out/House Cleaning • Spaniels (Vee-Jay 103) 1953 $750
     45 rpm. Red vinyl. Near-mint price range: $500 to $750.
     Top 1,000 ranking: 818

Play It Cool/Let's Make Up • Spaniels (Vee-Jay 116) 1954 $750
     45 rpm. Red vinyl. Near-mint price range: $500 to $750.
     Top 1,000 ranking: 829

SPARTANS

Faith, Hope and Charity/Lost • Spartans (Banjo Bill and His Rhythm Kings)
   (Capri 7201) 1954 $2,000
     45 rpm. Near-mint price range: $1,000 to $2,000.
     Top 1,000 ranking: 276

SPIDERS

Why Don't You Love Me/Hitchhike • Spiders (Mascot 112) 1965 $1,000
     45 rpm. Near-mint price range: $750 to $1,000.
     Top 1,000 ranking: 732

SPINNERS

In My Diary/At Sundown • Spinners (Motown 1155) 1969 $1,000
     45 rpm. Near-mint price range: $750 to $1,000.
     Top 1,000 ranking: 737

Marvella/My Love and Your Love • Spinners (Rhythm 125) 1958 $750
     45 rpm. Near-mint price range: $500 to $750.
     Top 1,000 ranking: 867

SPIRALS

Forever and a Day/Please Be My Love • Spirals (Admiral 912/913).............. 1961 $1,000
     45 rpm. Just two or three known copies. Near-mint price range: $750 to $1,000.
     Top 1,000 ranking: 698

Baby You Just Wait/? • Spirals (Indigo 500) 1960 $700
     45 rpm. Near-mint price range: $500 to $700.
     Top 1,000 ranking: 964

SPIRES, Big Boy, & His Trio

About to Lose My Mind/Which One Do I Love • Big Boy Spires & His Trio
   (With John Lee Henley) (Chance 1137)... 1953 $5,000
     45 rpm. Red vinyl. Near-mint price range: $4,000 to $5,000.
     Top 1,000 ranking: 47

SPORTTONES

So Sincere/In My Dreams • Sporttones (With Rhythm Acc.) (Munich 101).... 1959 $1,500
     45 rpm. Near-mint price range: $1,000 to $1,500.
     Top 1,000 ranking: 453

SPRINGSTEEN, Bruce
Born to Run • Bruce Springsteen (Columbia 33795) 1975   **$1,000**
> LP. Promotional issue. With script/title cover. Near-mint price range: $750 to $1,000.
> *Top 1,000 ranking: 744*

SQUIRES
The Sultan/Aurora • Squires (V Records 109) 1963   **$1,100**
> 45 rpm. Instrumental tracks recorded at CKRC (Winnipeg, Manitoba) radio's studio. Features Neil Young on guitar. Near-mint price range: $800 to $1,100.
> *Top 1,000 ranking: 560*

A Dream Come True/Lucy Lou • Squires (Kicks 1) 1954   **$1,000**
> 45 rpm. Near-mint price range: $750 to $1,000.
> *Top 1,000 ranking: 610*

STARLARKS
Fountain of Love/Send Me a Picture Baby • Starlarks (Elm 001) 1957   **$2,500**
> 45 rpm. Near-mint price range: $1,500 to $2,500.
> *Top 1,000 ranking: 197*

STARLIGHTERS
Until You Return/Whomp Whomp • Starlighters (Suncoast 1001) 1958   **$1,000**
> 45 rpm. Near-mint price range: $750 to $1,000.
> *Top 1,000 ranking: 661*

STARLINERS
Live at Papa Joe's • Starliners (Lejac 1001) 1960s   **$1,500**
> LP. Near-mint price range: $1,000 to $1,500.
> *Top 1,000 ranking: 481*

STARLITERS
Arline/Sweet Su • Starliters with Jonesy's Combo (Combo 73) 1955   **$750**
> 45 rpm. Near-mint price range: $500 to $750.
> *Top 1,000 ranking: 838*

STEPHENSON, N.A.
Boogie-Woogie Country Girl/Pins and Needles • N.A. Stephenson
(Westwood 201) 1959   **$700**
> 45 rpm. Near-mint price range: $500 to $700.
> *Top 1,000 ranking: 963*

STEREOS
Echo in My Heart/Tick Tack Toe • Stereos (Columbia 42626)........................ 1962   **$750**
> 45 rpm. Near-mint price range: $500 to $750.
> *Top 1,000 ranking: 907*

STEWART, Danny (Sly)
Long Time Alone/I'm Just a Fool • Danny (Sly) Stewart (Luke 1008) 1961   **$750**
> 45 rpm. Reissued on G&S as by Sylvester Stewart. Near-mint price range: $500 to $750.
> *Top 1,000 ranking: 900*

STEWART, Franklin
That Long Black Train/I'm Not Going to Cry • Franklin Stewart (Lu 501)....... 1957   **$1,000**
> 45 rpm. Near-mint price range: $750 to $1,000.
> *Top 1,000 ranking: 643*

STICK LEG'S
The Wedding/Flying Twist • Stick Leg's (sic) (With Butchering Persian's)
(Hard-Times 3002) 1962   **$750**
> 45 rpm. Near-mint price range: $500 to $750.
> *Top 1,000 ranking: 908*

STRONG, Barrett
Let's Rock/? • Barrett Strong (Tamla 54022) 1960 $1,200
　　45 rpm. Near-mint price range: $800 to $1,200.
　　Top 1,000 ranking: 536

SULTANS
Don't Be Angry/Blues at Dawn • Sultans (Jubilee 5077) 1952   　$750
　　45 rpm. Near-mint price range: $500 to $750.
　　Top 1,000 ranking: 811

SUNBEAMS
Please Say You'll Be Mine/You've Got to Rock n' Roll • Sunbeams
　　(Acme 719) 1957 $2,000
　　45 rpm. Near-mint price range: $1,500 to $2,000.
　　Top 1,000 ranking: 303

SUPREMES
Nobody Can Love You/Snap, Crackle and Pop • Supremes (Mark 129) 1958 $1,500
　　45 rpm. Near-mint price range: $1,000 to $1,500.
　　Top 1,000 ranking: 443
I Love You/Patricia • Supremes (Sara 1032) 1961 $1,500
　　45 rpm. Also released as by the Supremes 4. Near-mint price range: $1,000 to $1,500.
　　Top 1,000 ranking: 462

SUPREMES 4 [SUPREMES]
I Love You/Patricia • Supremes 4 (Sara 1032) 1961   　$800
　　45 rpm. Also released as by the Supremes. Near-mint price range: $600 to $800.
　　Top 1,000 ranking: 784

SUPREMES
I Want a Guy/Never Again • Supremes (Motown 1008) 1961 $1,000
　　45 rpm. Same number is also used on a Contours disc. Near-mint price range: $750 to $1,000.
　　Top 1,000 ranking: 699
Meet the Supremes • Supremes (Motown 606) 1963   　$750
　　LP. Front cover pictures each member sitting on a chair. Near-mint price range: $500 to $750.
　　Top 1,000 ranking: 922

SURFARIS
Surfer Joe/Wipe-Out • Surfaris (DFS 11/12) 1963 $1,000
　　45 rpm. Near-mint price range: $750 to $1,000.
　　Top 1,000 ranking: 719

SWALLOWS
My Baby/Good Time Girls • Swallows (After Hours 104) 1954 $4,000
　　45 rpm. Near-mint price range: $3,000 to $4,000.
　　Top 1,000 ranking: 82
Eternally/It Ain't the Meat, It's the Motion • Swallows (King 4501) 1951 $3,000
　　45 rpm. Blue or green vinyl. Near-mint price range: $2,000 to $3,000.
　　Top 1,000 ranking: 111
Tell Me Why/Roll Roll Pretty Baby • Swallows (King 4515) 1951 $3,000
　　45 rpm. Blue or green vinyl. Near-mint price range: $2,000 to $3,000.
　　Top 1,000 ranking: 112
Will You Be Mine/Dearest • Swallows (King 4458) 1951 $2,000
　　45 rpm. Near-mint price range: $1,500 to $2,000.
　　Top 1,000 ranking: 235
Tell Me Why/Roll Roll Pretty Baby • Swallows (King 4515) 1951 $1,200
　　45 rpm. Black vinyl. Near-mint price range: $800 to $1,200.
　　Top 1,000 ranking: 497
Eternally/It Ain't the Meat, It's the Motion • Swallows (King 4501) 1951   　$800
　　45 rpm. Black vinyl. Near-mint price range: $600 to $800.
　　Top 1,000 ranking: 765

SWANS

My True Love/No More • Swans (Rainbow 233).. 1953 $2,000
45 rpm. Red vinyl. Near-mint price range: $1,000 to $2,000.
Top 1,000 ranking: 259

Believe in Me/In the Morning • Swans (Steamboat 101)............................... 1957 $2,000
45 rpm. Near-mint price range: $1,500 to $2,000.
Top 1,000 ranking: 304

I'll Forever Love You/Mr. Cool Breeze • Swans (Fortune 822) 1955 $1,000
45 rpm. Near-mint price range: $750 to $1,000.
Top 1,000 ranking: 622

TABS

Oops/My Girl Is Gone • Tabs (Noble 720) 1959 $2,000
45 rpm. Near-mint price range: $1,000 to $2,000.
Top 1,000 ranking: 331

TAYLOR, Bill, & Smokey Jo

Split Personality/Lonely Sweetheart • Bill Taylor & Smokey Jo (Flip 502) 1955 $700
45 rpm. Near-mint price range: $500 to $700.
Top 1,000 ranking: 954

TEASERS

How Could You Hurt Me So/I Was a Fool to Let You Go • Teasers
(Checker 800) 1954 $1,200
45 rpm. Red Vinyl. Near-mint price range: $800 to $1,200.
Top 1,000 ranking: 511

TEDDY BEARS

The Teddy Bears Sing • Teddy Bears (Imperial 12010) 1959 $650
Stereo LP. Near-mint price range: $500 to $650.
Top 1,000 ranking: 988

TEENAGE MOONLIGHTERS

Sorry, Sorry/I Want to Cry • Teenage Moonlighters (Mark 134)..................... 1959 $3,000
45 rpm. Near-mint price range: $2,000 to $3,000.
Top 1,000 ranking: 160

TEEN KINGS

Ooby Dooby/Trying to Get to You • Teen Kings (Je-wel 101)........................ 1956 $2,500
45 rpm. May read "Vocal Roy Oribson," instead of "Orbison," on some labels. Beware since
some counterfeits exist that are difficult to identify. Consult an expert if in doubt. Near-mint price
range: $2,000 to $2,500.
Top 1,000 ranking: 192

TEEN-KINGS

Tell Me If You Know/That's a Teenage Love • Teen-Kings (Bee 1115)......... 1959 $3,000
45 rpm. Black vinyl. (Red vinyl disc is a 1996 reissue). Near-mint price range: $2,000 to $3,000.
Top 1,000 ranking: 161

TEENTONES

Love Is a Vow/Walkie Talkie Baby • Teentones (Featuring Arnold Malone with
Larry Luple Orchestra) (Rego 1004) 1958 $1,500
45 rpm. Near-mint price range: $1,000 to $1,500.
Top 1,000 ranking: 444

TEJUNS

Girl/Nobody Knows • Tejuns (100-Proof 144)... ? $750
45 rpm. Near-mint price range: $500 to $750.
Top 1,000 ranking: 946

TEMPOS
Promise Me/Never Let Me Go • Tempos (Rhythm 121)................................... 1958 $1,000
    45 rpm. Near-mint price range: $750 to $1,000.
    Top 1,000 ranking: 662

TENDER TONES
Just for a Little While/I Love You So • Tender Tones (Ducky 713)................ 1959 $1,500
    45 rpm. Near-mint price range: $1,000 to $1,500.
    Top 1,000 ranking: 454

THIRTEENTH FLOOR ELEVATORS
Easter Everywhere • Thirteenth Floor Elevators (International Artists 5)....... 1967 $750
    LP. Monaural. Does NOT have "Masterfonics" stamped in the vinyl trail-off. Near-mint price
    range: $500 to $750.
    Top 1,000 ranking: 935

THORNE, Roscoe
Peddler of Dreams/Dolores • Roscoe Thorne (Atlas 1033)........................... 1953 $3,000
    45 rpm. Near-mint price range: $2,000 to $3,000.
    Top 1,000 ranking: 123

THOSE FOUR ELDORADOS
A Lonely Boy/Go! Little Susie • Those Four Eldorados (Academy 8138) 1958 $1,500
    45 rpm. Near-mint price range: $1,000 to $1,500.
    Top 1,000 ranking: 445

THRASHERS
Jeannie/Forever My Love • Thrashers with Joe Ruffin Band
    (Mason's 178-062) 1957 $1,200
    45 rpm. Black vinyl. Reads: "Mason's Recording Co. 1630 Amsterdam Ave. N.Y.C." Red vinyl
    copies are 1961 reissues. Near-mint price range: $900 to $1,200.
    Top 1,000 ranking: 523

TIATT, Lynn, & Comets
Dad Is Home/Vilma's Jump-Up • Lynn Tiatt & Comets (Pussy Cat 1).................. ? $1,200
    45 rpm. Near-mint price range: $800 to $1,200.
    Top 1,000 ranking: 557

TONY & RAINDROPS
My Heart Cried/Tina • Tony & Raindrops (Crosley 340) 1961 $1,000
    45 rpm. Near-mint price range: $750 to $1,000.
    Top 1,000 ranking: 700

TOUCH
Street Suite • Touch (Mainline 2001) 1969 $1,500
    LP. Reportedly 100 made. Near-mint price range: $1,000 to $1,500.
    Top 1,000 ranking: 480

TRINIDADS
Don't Say Goodbye/On My Happy Way • Trinidads (Formal 1005) 1959 $4,000
    45 rpm. Near-mint price range: $3,000 to $4,000.
    Top 1,000 ranking: 92

TRU-TONES
Tears in My Eyes/Magic • Tru-Tones (Chart 634)... 1956 $650
    45 rpm. Near-mint price range: $500 to $650.
    Top 1,000 ranking: 982

TURNER, Baby Face
Blue Serenade/Gonna Let You Go • Baby Face Turner (Vocal Ray Agee) (Modern 882) 1952 $1,500
 45 rpm. Near-mint price range: $1,000 to $1,500.
 Top 1,000 ranking: 401

TURNER, Ike & Tina
River Deep – Mountain High • Ike & Tina Turner (Philles 4011) 1966 $15,000
 Monaural LP. Covers for a U.S. pressing on Philles are not known to exist. British pressings [London/Philles SHU-8298] do exist with covers. Near-mint price range: $10,000 to $15,000.
 Top 1,000 ranking: 9

TWILIGHTERS
Please Tell Me You're Mine/Wondering • Twilighters (With Frank Motley [Dual Trumpeter] & His Crew) (Marshall 702) 1953 $3,000
 45 rpm. Dark red vinyl. (Lighter red vinyl is a $300 to $400 reissue.) Near-mint price range: $2,500 to $3,000.
 Top 1,000 ranking: 124
Let There Be Love/Money Talks • Twilighters (Cholly 712) 1958 $2,000
 45 rpm. Near-mint price range: $1,000 to $2,000.
 Top 1,000 ranking: 317
How Many Times/Water Water • Twilighters (J-V-B 83) 1957 $1,000
 45 rpm. Near-mint price range: $750 to $1,000.
 Top 1,000 ranking: 644

UNEEKS
Look at Me (Vocal)/Look at Me (Instrumental) • Uneeks (Featuring Tiny Valentine) (Toledo 1501) 1960 $750
 45 rpm. Group is actually the Uniques (on Gone). Near-mint price range: $500 to $750.
 Top 1,000 ranking: 888

UNKNOWNS
One More Chance/You and Me • Unknowns (X-Tra 102) 1957 $1,000
 45 rpm. Near-mint price range: $750 to $1,000.
 Top 1,000 ranking: 645

VADEN, Clark, & Crescents
You Can Make It If You Try/? • Clark Vaden & Crescents (Dolly 5578) 1961 $1,000
 45 rpm. Identification number shown since no selection number is used. Near-mint price range: $750 to $1,000.
 Top 1,000 ranking: 701

VALAIRES
Launie, My Love/Which One Will It Be • Valaires (Willett 114) 1959 $1,000
 45 rpm. Near-mint price range: $750 to $1,000.
 Top 1,000 ranking: 675

VALENTINE, Leo, & Lyrics
Baby Doll/Please Don't Leave Me This Way • Leo Valentine & Lyrics (Skylight 201) 1962 $750
 45 rpm. Near-mint price range: $500 to $750.
 Top 1,000 ranking: 909

VALENTINES
Tonight Kathleen/Summer Love • Valentines (Old Town 1009) 1954 $1,000
 45 rpm. Near-mint price range: $750 to $1,000.
 Top 1,000 ranking: 611

VALIANTS
Wedding Bells/Velma • Valiants (Speck 1001) 1959 $3,000
    45 rpm. Near-mint price range: $2,000 to $3,000.
    Top 1,000 ranking: 162

VALQUINS
My Dear/Falling Star • Valquins (Gaity 161/162) 1959 $2,500
    45 rpm. Gold vinyl. Five known copies. Near-mint price range: $1,500 to $2,500.
    Top 1,000 ranking: 199
My Dear/Falling Star • Valquins (Gaity 161/162) 1959 $750
    45 rpm. Black vinyl. Near-mint price range: $500 to $750.
    Top 1,000 ranking: 876

VALS
Song of a Lover/Compensation Blues • Vals (Unique Laboratories/Theron) . 1961 $2,000
    45 rpm. Near-mint price range: $1,000 to $2,000.
    Top 1,000 ranking: 342

VAN BROTHERS
Servant of Love/Sweet Marie • Van Brothers (Poor Boy 111) 1960 $750
    45 rpm. Near-mint price range: $500 to $750.
    Top 1,000 ranking: 889

VARIOUS ARTISTS
Caine Mutiny • Various Artists (RCA Victor 1013)... 1954 $10,000
    Monaural LP. Soundtrack. Recalled immediately after being made, with very few copies making
    their way into circulation. Has original music and dialogue from the film, including the entire court
    martial scene. Near-mint price range: $7,500 to $10,000.
    Top 1,000 ranking: 17
Phil Spector Spectacular • Various Artists (Philles 100) 1960s $7,500
    LP. Promotional issue only. With letter signed by Phil Spector. Near-mint price range: $5,000 to
    $7,500.
    Top 1,000 ranking: 30
Phil Spector Spectacular • Various Artists (Philles 100) 1960s $6,000
    LP. Promotional issue only. Without the letter from Phil Spector. Near-mint price range: $4,000
    to $6,000.
    Top 1,000 ranking: 39
PRO-12 (RCA Victor Promotion Disc) • Various Artists (RCA
    Victor PRO-12)... 1956 $3,000
    EP. White label, black print. Promotional issue only. Cover: Paper sleeve. Custom made for
    WOHO radio, Toledo, Ohio. Front: Reads: "WOHO (1470 KC) Featuring RCA Victor." RCA
    Victor logo and number at upper right. Back is blank. We are uncertain as to how and why this
    item was offered. EP alone: $750 to $1,000. EP and sleeve: $2,000 to $3,000.
    Top 1,000 ranking: 143
Party After Hours • Various Artists (Aladdin 703)... 1956 $3,000
    10-inch monaural LP. Red vinyl. Near-mint price range: $2,000 to $3,000.
    Top 1,000 ranking: 144
Jamboree! • Various Artists (Warner Bros) 1957 $3,000
    Monaural LP. Soundtrack. No selection number used. Promotional issue only. Front cover is a
    slick pasted on generic, unprinted cardboard cover. Notes on back are printed right on the
    cardboard (no slick used on back). Original covers have a smooth surface. Front cover photos
    have gray-green background hue. Trail-off area on disc has "Jam 1," & "Jam 2" stamped (not
    etched) in vinyl. Label is light yellow. Warner "shield" logo has parallel lines as background, all
    with sharp, distinct lettering.
    Top 1,000 ranking: 151
Dealers' Prevue • Various Artists (RCA Victor SDS-7-2) 1957 $3,000
    EP. White label. Promotional issue only. Paper envelope used to mail SDS-7-2F: Front: Black
    and white Elvis photo. Reads: "Elvis Presley at His Greatest." The only selection number shown
    on the mailer is 47/20-7000 (for 45 and 78 rpm singles of *(Let Me Be Your) Teddy Bear / Loving
    You.* Disc alone: $800 to $1,000. Mailer alone: $1,500 to $2,000. Set: $2,000 to $3,000.
    Top 1,000 ranking: 152

Dealers' Prevue • Various Artists (RCA Victor SDS-57-39) 1957 $3,000
EP. Includes paper envelope/sleeve. Promotional issue only. Contains edited versions of songs
listed. Disc alone: $800 to $1,000. Mailer alone: $1,500 to $2,000. Both: $2,000 to $3,000.
Top 1,000 ranking: 153

RCA Victor Family Record Center • Various Artists (RCA Victor PR-121)...... 1962 $2,000
EP. Promotional issue only. Not issued with special cover. Near-mint price range: $1,000 to
$2,000.
Top 1,000 ranking: 348

Robert W. Sarnoff – 25 Years of RCA Leadership • Various Artists (RCA
 Victor RWS-0001) 1973 $2,000
Stereo LP. Orange label. Dynaflex vinyl. In-house promotional issue only. Approximately 50
made as souvenirs for RCA' Robert Sarnoff's retirement party. Includes excerpts of music
released during his years with the company. Near-mint price range: $1,500 to $2,000.
Top 1,000 ranking: 369

(1957) March of Dimes Galaxy of Stars (Discs for Dimes) • Various Artists
 (N.F.I.P. GM-8M-0653/0654) 1956 $1,600
Monaural LP. White and blue-green label. 16" transcription with 20 entertainers, including Elvis
Presley, speaking on behalf of the 1957 March of Dimes campaign. Issued only to radio stations.
Promotional issue only. Insert: 16 pages of dee jay announcements. LP alone: $1,350 to $1,500.
LP and insert: $1,400 to $1,600.
Top 1,000 ranking: 385

(1957) March of Dimes Galaxy of Stars (Disc Jockey Interviews) • Various Artists
 (N.F.I.P. GM-8M-0657/0658) 1956 $1,600
Monaural LP. White and blue-green label. 16" transcription with six vocal acts, including Elvis
Presley, providing an open-end interview on behalf of the 1957 March of Dimes campaign, and
introducing one of their songs. Issued only to radio stations. Inserts: Cover letter to Station
Managers on National Foundation for Infantile Paralysis (N.F.I.P.) letterhead, listing of National
Committee and State Chairmen, five-page script for the open-end interview with Elvis Presley;
five, five-page scripts for the open-end interviews with the other stars on this disc. LP alone:
$1,350 to $1,500. LP and inserts: $1,400 to $1,600.
Top 1,000 ranking: 386

SP-33-4 • Various Artists (RCA Victor SP-33-4) 1956 $1,500
Untitled promotional LP. Not issued with a special cover. Near-mint price range: $1,000 to
$1,500.
Top 1,000 ranking: 431

SPA 7-61 • Various Artists (RCA Victor SPA 7-61) 1957 $1,500
Untitled promotional sampler EP. Not issued with special cover. Near-mint price range: $1,000
to $1,500.
Top 1,000 ranking: 436

SP-33-10P • Various Artists (RCA Victor SP-33-10P) 1958 $1,200
Untitled promotional LP. Not issued with special cover. Near-mint price range: $800 to $1,200.
Top 1,000 ranking: 529

SPD-15 • Various Artists (RCA Victor SPD-15) 1955 $1,000
Set of 10 black label or gray label (juke box edition) extended plays. Both are dog on top. Has
one Elvis Presley EP, numbered 599-9089, representing sides 7 and 14 of 20. Box and inserts
are yet to be verified. Near-mint price range: $750 to $1,000.
Top 1,000 ranking: 623

Great Country and Western Hits • Various Artists (RCA Victor SPD-26)....... 1956 $1,000
10-EP boxed set. Includes insert/separator sheets. Near-mint price range: $750 to $1,000.
Top 1,000 ranking: 634

Party After Hours • Various Artists (Aladdin 703)........................... 1956 $1,000
10-inch monaural LP. Black vinyl. Near-mint price range: $750 to $1,000.
Top 1,000 ranking: 635

RCA Victor August 1959 Sampler • Various Artists (RCA Victor SP-33-27) .. 1959 $1,000
LP. Promotional issue only. Not issued with special cover. All songs except *Blue Moon of
Kentucky* (Elvis Presley) are true stereo. Near-mint price range: $750 to $1,000.
Top 1,000 ranking: 676

Your Favorite Singing Groups • Various Artists (Hull 1002)........................... 1963 $1,000
Monaural LP. Near-mint price range: $750 to $1,000.
Top 1,000 ranking: 720

Xanadu • Various Artists (MCA 10384)... 1980 $1,000
> LP. Soundtrack. Picture disc. Promotional issue only. Reportedly only 52 made. Near-mint price
> range: $750 to $1,000.
> *Top 1,000 ranking: 746*

RCA Victor February Sampler 59-7 • Various Artists (RCA Victor/
Camden SP-33-59-7)... 1959 $800
> Monaural LP. Promotional issue only. Not issued with special cover. Has RCA Victor black label
> on one side and RCA Victor Camden label on side 2, thus sampling tunes from LPs on both
> labels. Near-mint price range: $600 to $800.
> *Top 1,000 ranking: 779*

Who's Afraid of the Big Bad Wolf • Various Artists (RCA
Victor 224/225/226)..1930s $750
> Three, six-inch, 78 rpm black and white picture discs. Near-mint price range: $500 to $750.
> *Top 1,000 ranking: 800*

The Capitol Story • Various Artists (Capitol 197/198) 1954 $750
> EP. A Capitol promotional release. Sleeve says "The Capitol Story," but disc reads "The Capitol
> Record." 100 copies made. Near-mint price range: $500 to $750.
> *Top 1,000 ranking: 830*

Rock, Rock, Rock • Various Artists (Roost) 1958 $750
> Monaural LP. No selection number used. 20 tracks credited to seven different lables: Atlantic,
> Chess, Coral, Gee, MGM, Roost and Vik. Promotional issue only. Near-mint price range: $500
> to $750.
> *Top 1,000 ranking: 868*

RCA Victor October Christmas Sampler 59-40-41 • Various Artists (RCA
Victor SPS-33-54) 1959 $750
> LP. Promotional issue only. Not issued with special cover. All songs except Elvis' *Blue
> Christmas* and *Have Yourself a Merry Little Christmas* (Gisele MacKenzie) are true stereo.
> Near-mint price range: $500 to $750.
> *Top 1,000 ranking: 877*

RCA Victor November / December Sampler 59-44 Thru 59-47 • Various Artists
(RCA Victor SPS-33-57) 1959 $750
> LP. Promotional issue only. Not issued with special cover. Near-mint price range: $500 to $750.
> *Top 1,000 ranking: 878*

Bunch of Goodies • Various Artists (Chess 1441) 1959 $750
> LP. Multi-color vinyl – promotional issue only. Near-mint price range: $500 to $750.
> *Top 1,000 ranking: 879*

Go, Johnny, Go! • Various Artists 1959 $750
> Monaural LP. Neither label name nor selection number shown. Promotional issue only. Near-
> mint price range: $500 -$750.
> *Top 1,000 ranking: 880*

Love Those Goodies • Various Artists (Checker 2973).................................. 1959 $750
> Monaural LP. Multi-color vinyl – promotional issue only. Cover photo pictures same two models
> as also seen on *Oldies in Hi-Fi*. Near-mint price range: $500 to $750.
> *Top 1,000 ranking: 881*

Oldies in Hi Fi • Various Artists (Chess 1439).. 1959 $750
> Monaural LP. Multi-color vinyl – promotional issue only. Cover photo pictures same two models
> as also seen on *Love Those Goodies*. Near-mint price range: $500 to $750.
> *Top 1,000 ranking: 882*

RCA Victor October 1960 Popular Stereo Sampler • Various Artists (RCA
Victor SPS-33-96) 1960 $750
> Stereo LP. Promotional issue only. Not issued with special cover. Near-mint price range: $500 to
> $750.
> *Top 1,000 ranking: 890*

RCA Victor October '61 Pop Sampler • Various Artists (RCA
Victor SPS-33-141) 1961 $750
> Stereo LP. Promotional issue only. Not issued with special cover. Near-mint price range: $500 to
> $750.
> *Top 1,000 ranking: 901*

RCA Victor December '62 Pop Sampler • Various Artists (RCA
Victor SPS-33-191) 1962 $750
> LP. Promotional issue only. Not issued with special cover. Near-mint price range: $500 to $750.
> *Top 1,000 ranking: 910*

RCA Victor December '63 Pop Sampler • Various Artists (RCA
  Victor SPS-33-247) 1963 $750
  LP. Promotional issue only. Not issued with special cover. All tracks except *Anytime* (Eddie
  Fisher) are stereo. Near-mint price range: $500 to $750.
  Top 1,000 ranking: 923

RCA Victor September '63 Pop Sampler • Various Artists (RCA
  Victor SPS-33-219) 1963 $750
  LP. Promotional issue only. Not issued with special cover. Near-mint price range: $500 to $750.
  Top 1,000 ranking: 924

RCA Victor April '64 Pop Sampler • Various Artists (RCA
  Victor SPS-33-272) 1964 $750
  LP. Promotional issue only. Not issued with special cover. All tracks except *Saeta* (Carlos
  Montoya) are stereo. Near-mint price range: $500 to $750.
  Top 1,000 ranking: 928

RCA Victor April '65 Pop Sampler • Various Artists (RCA
  Victor SPS-33-331) 1965 $750
  LP. Promotional issue only. Not issued with special cover. All tracks except *Chapines* (Juan
  Serrano) are stereo. Near-mint price range: $500 to $750.
  Top 1,000 ranking: 929

RCA Victor August '65 Pop Sampler • Various Artists (RCA
  Victor SPS-33-347) 1965 $750
  LP. Promotional issue only. Not issued with special cover. All tracks except *Your Cheatin' Heart*
  (Elvis Presley) are stereo. Near-mint price range: $500 to $750.
  Top 1,000 ranking: 930

RCA Victor April '66 Pop Sampler • Various Artists (RCA
  Victor SPS-33-403) 1966 $750
  Stereo LP. Promotional issue only. Not issued with special cover. Near-mint price range: $500 to
  $750.
  Top 1,000 ranking: 932

VELOURS

Romeo/What You Do to Me • Velours (With Sammy Lowe Orchestra)
  (Onyx 508) 1957 $1,000
  45 rpm. Near-mint price range: $750 to $1,000.
  Top 1,000 ranking: 646

VEL-TONES

Broken Heart/Please Say You'll Be True • Vel-Tones (Vel 9178) 1958 $2,000
  45 rpm. Near-mint price range: $1,000 to $2,000.
  Top 1,000 ranking: 318

VELVET SOUNDS & COSMOPOLITES

Sing a Song of Christmas Cheer/Hanging Up My Christmas Stocking (Christmas
  Mambo) • Velvet Sounds & Cosmopolites (Cosmopolitan 530/531) 1953 $2,000
  45 rpm. Near-mint price range: $1,000 to $2,000.
  Top 1,000 ranking: 260

VELVET UNDERGROUND & NICO

All Tomorrow's Parties/I'll Be Your Mirror • Velvet Underground & Nico
  (Verve 10427) 1966 $5,200
  Picture sleeve and blue label 45 rpm. Produced by Andy Warhol. Sleeve may be a promotional
  issue only. Near-mint price range for sleeve alone: $4,800 to $5,000. Record and sleeve: $4,900
  to $5,200. For promo label disc, deduct $150 to $250.
  Top 1,000 ranking: 40

VELVETEERS

Tell Me You're Mine/Boo Wacka Boo • Velveteers (Spitfire 15) 1956 $2,000
  45 rpm. Near-mint price range: $1,000 to $2,000.
  Top 1,000 ranking: 298

VENDORS
Where All Lovers Meet/That's All Right • Vendors (Victorio 128)................... 1963 $1,000
    45 rpm. Actually a 1962 Invictors' issue [TPE 8221] but with the Victorio/Vendors label on top.
    Near-mint price range: $750 to $1,000.
    Top 1,000 ranking: 721

VENTURES
Walk Don't Run/Home • Ventures (Blue Horizon 101).................................... 1960 $750
    45 rpm. Reportedly 300 made. Near-mint price range: $500 to $750.
    Top 1,000 ranking: 891

VERNEE, Yvonne
Just Like You Did Me/? • Yvonne Vernee (Sonbert 5842)............................1960s $750
    45 rpm. Near-mint price range: $500 to $750.
    Top 1,000 ranking: 937

VIBES
Stop Torturing Me/Stop Jibing Baby • Vibes (Formerly the Vibranaires)
    (Chariot 105) 1954 $3,000
    45 rpm. "Jibing" is a label misprint; "Jiving." Near-mint price range: $2,000 to $3,000.
    Top 1,000 ranking: 135

VIBRANAIRES
Doll Face/Ooh, I Feel So Good • Vibranaires (Chariot 103) 1954 $5,000
    45 rpm. Near-mint price range: $4,000 to $5,000.
    Top 1,000 ranking: 51
Doll Face/Ooh, I Feel So Good • Vibranaires (After Hours 103).................... 1954 $4,000
    45 rpm. Red vinyl. Near-mint price range: $3,000 to $4,000.
    Top 1,000 ranking: 83

VICE-ROYS
My Heart/I Need Your Love So Bad • Vice-Roys (With Mike Metko Combo)
    (Ramco 3715) 1962 $2,000
    45 rpm. Near-mint price range: $1,000 to $2,000.
    Top 1,000 ranking: 349

VICTORIANS
I Guess You're Satisfied/Don't Break My Heart Again • Victorians
    (Specialty 411) 1950 $2,500
    45 rpm. Near-mint price range: $1,500 to $2,500.
    Top 1,000 ranking: 181

VIDELS
I Wish/Blow Winds Blow • Videls (Early 702)... 1960 $2,000
    45 rpm. Near-mint price range: $1,000 to $2,000.
    Top 1,000 ranking: 341

VINCENT, Gene
Right Now/Night Is So Lonely • Gene Vincent (Capitol 4237)....................... 1960 $1,000
    Picture sleeve. Near-mint price range: $750 to $1,000.
    Top 1,000 ranking: 689

VIOLINAIRES
Another Soldier Gone/Joy in the Beulah Land • Violinaires
    (Drummond 4000) 1953 $2,000
    45 rpm. Group name is misspelled on label as: "Voilinaires." Reportedly the same group as the
    Gales, on J-V-B and Mel-O. Near-mint price range: $1,000 to $2,000.
    Top 1,000 ranking: 261

VISCOUNTS
Wandering/? • Viscounts (Star-Fax 1002)..1950s $650
    45 rpm. Near-mint price range: $500 to $650.
    Top 1,000 ranking: 991

VISIONS
It's You I Love/? • Visions (R&R 3002) 1960 $1,200
    45 rpm. Near-mint price range: $800 to $1,200.
    Top 1,000 ranking: 537

VOLTONES
If She Should Call/Don't Monkey with a Donkey • Voltones (Dynamic 108) .. 1959 $1,500
    45 rpm. Near-mint price range: $1,000 to $1,500.
    Top 1,000 ranking: 455

WALT, PERCY & TRACERS
Wishing/My Money • Walt, Percy & Tracers (Three Rivers).................................. ? $1,000
    45 rpm. No selection number used. Reissued as by the Roberson Brothers. Near-mint price
    range: $750 to $1,000.
    Top 1,000 ranking: 751

WARD, Billy, & Dominoes
Billy Ward and His Dominoes • Billy Ward & Dominoes (Federal 295-94) 1954 $10,000
    10-inch LP. Near-mint price range: $7,500 to $10,000.
    Top 1,000 ranking: 18
Billy Ward and His Dominoes • Billy Ward & Dominoes (Federal 548) 1957 $1,500
    LP. Near-mint price range: $1,000 to $1,500.
    Top 1,000 ranking: 437
Clyde McPhatter with Billy Ward & Dominoes • Billy Ward & Dominoes with Clyde
    McPhatter (Federal 559) 1957 $1,500
    LP. Near-mint price range: $1,000 to $1,500.
    Top 1,000 ranking: 438

WEE WILLIE & MELLODIERS
When/? • Wee Willie & Mellodiers (Wow 110) .... ? $750
    45 rpm. Near-mint price range: $500 to $750.
    Top 1,000 ranking: 947

WHIPS
Pleadin' Heart/She Done Me Wrong • Whips (Flair 1025) 1954 $750
    45 rpm. Near-mint price range: $500 to $750.
    Top 1,000 ranking: 831

WHISPERS
Are You Sorry/We're Getting Married • Whispers (Gotham 312) 1955 $750
    45 rpm. Near-mint price range: $500 to $750.
    Top 1,000 ranking: 839

WHITMAN, Slim
America's Favorite Folk Artist • Slim Whitman (Imperial 3004) 1954 $650
    10-inch LP. Colored vinyl. Near-mint price range: $500 to $650.
    Top 1,000 ranking: 974

WIGFALL, William, & Lyrics
Come Back/Got to Get Along • William Wigfall & Lyrics (Skylight 202) 1962 $1,000
    45 rpm. Near-mint price range: $750 to $1,000.
    Top 1,000 ranking: 709

WILD COUNTRY
Wild Country • Wild Country (LSI 0275).. 1970 $1,000
LP. Near-mint price range: $750 to $1,000.
Top 1,000 ranking: 740

WILLIAMS, Andy, & Cavaliers
You Must Be Born Again/? • Andy Williams & Cavaliers (Our 305) 1957 $2,000
45 rpm. Near-mint price range: $1,500 to $2,000.
Top 1,000 ranking: 305

WILLIAMS, Ben E.
Nay-Oy-Gwor/Mamie Wong • Ben E. Williams (With Steps Four and
Del-Reys) (Riff 6102) 1961 $1,500
45 rpm. Near-mint price range: $1,000 to $1,500.
Top 1,000 ranking: 463

WILLIS, Rollie, & Contenders
Whenever I Get Lonely/That's the Way • Rollie Willis & Contenders (With
Matadors) (Saxony 1001).. 1962 $750
45 rpm. Near-mint price range: $500 to $750.
Top 1,000 ranking: 911

WILSON, Frank
Do I Love You/Sweeter As the Days Go By • Frank Wilson (Soul 35019)..... 1966 $10,000
45 rpm. Near-mint price range: $7,500 to $10,000.
Top 1,000 ranking: 22

WISDOMS
Two Hearts Make One Love/Lost in Dreams • Wisdoms (Gaity 169/170) 1959 $1,000
45 rpm. Near-mint price range: $750 to $1,000.
Top 1,000 ranking: 677

WOODS, Bennie, & Five Dukes
I Cross My Fingers/Wheel Baby Wheel • Bennie Woods & Five Dukes
(Atlas 1040)... 1954 $750
45 rpm. Near-mint price range: $500 to $750.
Top 1,000 ranking: 832

WOODSON, Johnny, & Crescendos
Dreamer from My Heart/All That's Good • Johnny Woodson & Crescendos
(Spry 108) 1957 $1,200
45 rpm. Near-mint price range: $800 to $1,200.
Top 1,000 ranking: 524

WRENS
Love's Something That's Made for Two/Beggin' for Love • Wrens
(Rama 53) 1954 $1,000
45 rpm. Near-mint price range: $750 to $1,000.
Top 1,000 ranking: 612
I Won't Come to Your Wedding/What Makes You Do • Wrens (Rama 184) .. 1955 $750
45 rpm. Near-mint price range: $500 to $750.
Top 1,000 ranking: 840

WRIGHT, Little Cholly
Eternally/I Believe • Little Cholly Wright (Cholly 7093).................................... 1956 $1,500
45 rpm. One source indicates *I Believe* as being credited to the Nu-Tones. Near-mint price
range: $1,000 to $1,500.
Top 1,000 ranking: 432

YA HO WA 13

Principles of the Children • Ya Ho Wa 13 (Higher Key) 1978 $800
    LP. Selection number not known. Near-mint price range: $600 to $800.
     Top 1,000 ranking: 795

I'm Gonna Take You Home • Ya Ho Wa 13 (Higher Key 3309) 1975 $750
    LP. Near-mint price range: $500 to $750.
     Top 1,000 ranking: 939

YOAKAM, Dwight

Guitars, Cadillacs, Etc, Etc. • Dwight Yoakam (Oak 2356) 1984 $750
    Six-track LP. 1986 Reissue (Reprise 25372) adds four tracks. Near-mint price range: $500 to
    $750.
     Top 1,000 ranking: 940

MORE LATE ADDITIONS

741.

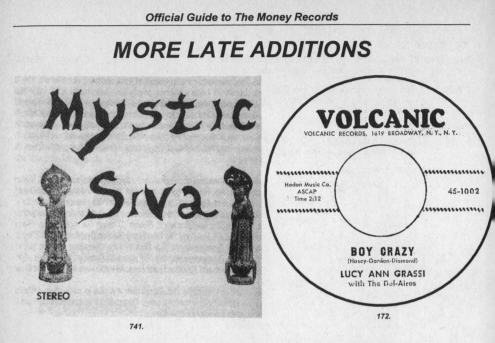

172.

593.

485.

310

Qualifying Titles
That Didn't Make the Cut

   Upon discovering that $650 would be the value of record No. 1,000 on the list, we also found there were enough $650 records to expand the list by another 20 or so titles.
   To break the tie, we supplied several of our advisers with all of the $650 titles, asking each person to rank them in order by value.
   The top 30 made the cut and hold positions 970 through 1,000.
   Since the remaining 21 certainly deserve honorable mention, they are listed here.

☐ I'm Just a Fool in Love/Hold Me Squeeze Me • Orioles
   (Jubilee 5061) 1951 $650
        45 rpm. Near-mint price range: $500 to $650.
        Members: Sonny Til; Alex Sharp; George Nelson; John Reed; Tom Gaither.
☐ Forget Me Not/What Will I Tell My Heart • Balladiers (Aladdin 3123)........1952 $650
        78 rpm. We have yet to confirm the existence of this disc on 45 rpm. Near-mint
        price range: $500 to $650.
☐ Trust in Me/Shrimp Boats • Orioles (Jubilee 5074)....................................1952 $650
        45 rpm. Near-mint price range: $500 to $650.
        Members: Sonny Til; Alex Sharp; George Nelson; John Reed; Tom Gaither.
☐ It's Over Because We're Through/Waiting • Orioles (Jubilee 5082)...........1952 $650
        45 rpm. Near-mint price range: $500 to $650.
        Members: Sonny Til; Alex Sharp; George Nelson; John Reed; Tom Gaither.
☐ Baby, Be There/You Made Me Cry • Kings (Featuring Bobby Hall)
   (Jax 316)...1953 $650
        45 rpm. Red vinyl. Near-mint price range: $500 to $650.
        Members: Robert Hall; Richard Holcomb; Adolphus Holcomb; Gil Wilkes.
☐ Set My Heart Free/I Wanna Love • Arthur Lee Maye & Crowns
   (Modern 944) 1954 $650
        45 rpm. Near-mint price range: $500 to $650.
        Members: Arthur Lee Maye; Richard Berry; Charles Colbert; Joe Moore; Johnny Coleman.
☐ Deep in My Heart for You/And I Need You • Pyramids
   (Federal 12233) 1955 $650
        45 rpm. White bio label. Promotional issue only. Near-mint price range: $500
        to $650.
        Members: Sidney Correia; Joe Dandy; Melvin White; Kenneth Perdue; Lionel Cobbs; Tom Williams.
☐ Please Forgive Me, Don't Forget Me/Let's Make It Real • Dave
   Bryan & Choraltones (Speck 103)..1956 $650
        45 rpm. Near-mint price range: $500 to $650.
☐ Now You're Gone/Did It • Laddins (Central 2602) 1957 $650
        45 rpm. Black label. Near-mint price range: $500 to $650.
        Members: David Coleman; Ernest Gordy; Bob Jeffers; Earl Marcus; John Marcus.

☐ Elvis' Christmas Album • Elvis Presley (RCA Victor LOC-1035)...............1957 $650

    📷 Monaural LP. Black vinyl. Black label, "Long Play" at bottom. Includes gold "gift giving" sticker, originally attached to plastic bag/cover. Near-mint price range: $500 to $650.

      Side 1: *Santa Claus Is Back in Town; White Christmas; Here Comes Santa Claus; I'll Be Home for Christmas; Blue Christmas; Santa Bring My Baby Back (To Me).*

      Side 2: *Oh Little Town of Bethlehem; Silent Night; (There'll Be) Peace in the Valley (For Me); I Believe; Take My Hand, Precious Lord; It Is No Secret (What God Can Do).*

☐ Your Souvenir/Taking a Chance on You • Willis Sanders & Embers

    (Jvpiter 213)...1957 $650

      45 rpm. From Jupiter Record Co., though label mistakenly reads "Jvpiter." Near-mint price range: $500 to $650.

☐ It's Now Or Never/A Mess of Blues • Elvis Presley (With Jordanaires)

    (RCA Victor 61-7777)...1960 $650

      45 rpm. Living stereo. Near-mint price range: $500 to $650.

☐ The Crystals Twist Uptown • Crystals (Philles 4000)...................1962 $650

      Stereo LP. Near-mint price range: $500 to $650.
      Members: Barbara Alston; Lala Brooks; Dee Dee Kennibrew; Patricia Wright; Mary Thomas.

      Side 1: *Uptown; Another Country – Another World; Frankenstein Twist; Oh Yeah, Maybe Baby; Please Hurt Me.*

      Side 2: *There's No Other (Like My Baby); On Broadway; What a Nice Way to Turn Seventeen; No One Ever Tells You; Gee Whiz, Look at His Eyes (Twist); I Love You Eddie.*

☐ She Loves You/I'll Get You • Beatles (Swan 4152) 1963 $650

      45 rpm. Glossy white label with red print. Words "Don't Drop Out" are not on the label. Uses boldface type style. Song titles do not have quotation marks. Known counterfeits have no machine stampings in the trail-off area of the vinyl; their label print is not sharp and type is broken. Their vinyl quality is substandard and has pitting and pot marks. Near-mint price range: $500 to $650.

      Members: John Lennon; Paul McCartney; Geroge Harrison; Ringo Starr.

☐ I'll Get You/Blank • Beatles (Swan 4152)....................................1964 $650

      45 rpm. Single-sided promotional issue. Glossy white label with thin black print reads: "Promotional copy not for sale." Intended to plug the B-side of *She Loves You.* B-side has blank white label and silent grooves. Near-mint price range: $500 to $650.

      Members: John Lennon; Paul McCartney; Geroge Harrison; Ringo Starr.

☐ Yetti-men • Yetti-Men / Uppa-Trio (Lak 4348)...........................1964 $650

      LP. Each group has one side of the LP. 150 copies pressed. Near-mint price range: $500 to $650.

☐ Frank Sinatra Reads from Gunga Din • Frank Sinatra (Reprise 45)..........1966 $650

    📷 45 rpm. Promotional issue only. Near-mint price range: $500 to $650.

☐ Penny Lane/Strawberry Fields Forever • Beatles (Capitol 5810)...............1967 $650

      45 rpm. Promotional issue. Light green label reads: "Promotion record not for sale." Does not have the trumpet solo at the end of *Penny Lane.* Near-mint price range: $500 to $650.

☐ The Many Sides of Jerry Raye Featuring Fenwyck • Jerry Raye
Featuring Fenwyck (De Ville 101) 1967 $650

   📷 LP. Red vinyl. Near-mint price range: $500 to $650.
     Members: Jerry Raye; Pat Robinson; Pat Maroshek; Keith Knighter.

☐ Hickory Wind • Hickory Wind (Gigantic)....................................1969 $650

   📷 LP. Reportedly 100 made. Selection number not known. Near-mint price
   range: $500 to $650.
     Members: Mike McGuyer; Alan Jones; Bob Strehl.

☐ Rockin' Rocket/? • Jimmy Nelis (ToJon 101) ....? $650

   45 rpm. Near-mint price range: $500 to $650.

E1

E18

EXPERIMENTAL PRESSINGS

☐ 1. Moody Blue • Elvis Presley (RCA Victor AFL 1-2428) 1977   **$7,500**

📷 Stereo LP. Picture disc. Has "Collector's Series" *Hound Dog/Don't Be Cruel* picture sleeve for 45 rpm on gold vinyl disc. Reportedly no more than two exist using this combination. Not intended for sale or distribution. Near-mint price range: $7,000 to $7,500.

Side A: *Unchained Melody; If You Love Me (Let Me Know); Little Darlin'; He'll Have to Go; Let Me Be There.*

Side B: *Way Down; Pledging My Love; Moody Blue; She Thinks I Still Care; It's Easy for You.*

☐ 2. Can't Buy Me Love/You Can't Do That • Beatles (Capitol PB-5150) 1964   **$6,000**

45 rpm. Yellow vinyl. Experimental pressing only. Reportedly a plant worker made about 10 copies, some of which may also be black and yellow vinyl. Not authorized by Capitol. Near-mint price range: $4,000 to $6,000.

☐ 3. Can't Buy Me Love/You Can't Do That • Beatles (Capitol PB-5150) 1964   **$3,500**

45 rpm. Yellow vinyl. Experimental pressing only. Reportedly a plant worker made about 10 copies, some of which may also be all yellow vinyl. Not authorized by Capitol. Near-mint price range: $2,500 to $3,500.

☐ 4. Moody Blue • Elvis Presley (RCA Victor AFL 1-2428) 1977   **$3,500**

📷 Stereo LP. Picture disc. Includes discs with the following art imbedded: 1. Eight assorted, circular photos of Elvis holding a guitar, on both sides. 2. Eight assorted, circular photos of Elvis holding a guitar, on one side; Elvis photo on reverse. Both, sometimes referred to as "dancing" Elvis discs, are experimental items. Neither were intended for sale or distribution. Near-mint price range: $3,000 to $3,500.

Side A: *Unchained Melody; If You Love Me (Let Me Know); Little Darlin'; He'll Have to Go; Let Me Be There.*

Side B: *Way Down; Pledging My Love; Moody Blue; She Thinks I Still Care; It's Easy for You.*

☐ 5. Elvis Today • Elvis Presley (RCA Victor AFL 1-1039) 1978   **$3,500**

Stereo LP. Picture disc. Includes discs with the following art imbedded: 1. Eight assorted, circular photos of Elvis holding a guitar, on both sides. 2. Eight assorted, circular photos of Elvis holding a guitar, on one side; Elvis photo on reverse. Both, sometimes referred to as "dancing" Elvis discs, are experimental items. Neither were intended for sale or distribution. Near-mint price range: $3,000 to $3,500.

☐ 6. Moody Blue • Elvis Presley (RCA Victor AFL 1-2428) 1977   **$3,000**

Stereo LP. Picture disc. Includes discs with the following art imbedded: 1. *Aloha from Hawaii via Satellite* inner sleeves. 2. *Elvis – A Legendary Performer, Vol. 3* picture disc photos. 3. *Aloha from Hawaii via Satellite* on one side; Crystal Gayle on reverse. 4. Colonel Parker in a Santa suit on one side; seven Christmas party photos on reverse. All were experimental or sample pressings of some sort. None of these were intended for sale or distribution. Near-mint price range: $2,500 to $3,000.

Side A: *Unchained Melody; If You Love Me (Let Me Know); Little Darlin'; He'll Have to Go; Let Me Be There.*

Side B: *Way Down; Pledging My Love; Moody Blue; She Thinks I Still Care; It's Easy for You.*

☐ 7. Moody Blue/She Thinks I Still Care • Elvis Presley (RCA Victor JB-10857) 1977   **$3,000**

45 rpm. Black label, dog near top. Colored vinyl experimental production singles done in red, white, gold, blue, and green. Price is for any of the five colors. Not intended for distribution. Near-mint price range: $2,000 to $3,000.

☐ 8. Elvis As Recorded at Madison Square Garden ● Elvis Presley (RCA Victor
   AFL1-4776).. 1978 $3,000
   Stereo LP. Picture disc. Pictures artwork from *Aloha from Hawaii via Satellite* inner sleeves.
   Experimental pressing. Probably only a handful, or less, made. Not intended for sale or
   distribution. Near-mint price range for each: $2,000 to $3,000. (A set of all five recently sold
   for $15,000.)
   Side 1: *Introduction: Also Sprach Zarathustra; That's All Right; Proud Mary; Never Been to Spain;*
   You Don't Have to Say You Love Me; You've Lost That Lovin' Feelin'; Polk Salad Annie;
   Love Me; All Shook Up; Heartbreak Hotel; Medley:Teddy Bear/Don't Be Cruel; Love Me
   Tender.
   Side 2: *The Impossible Dream; Introductions by Elvis; Hound Dog; Suspicious Minds; For the*
   Good Times; American Trilogy; Funny How Time Slips Away; I Can't Stop Loving You;
   Can't Help Falling in Love; Closing Riff.

☐ 9. Legendary Performer (Volume 1) ● Elvis Presley (RCA
   Victor CPL1-0341).. 1978 $2,500
   Monaural LP. Picture disc, with artwork from *How Great Thou Art As Sung By Elvis* (LSP-
   3758). Side 2 is blank. Experimental pressing. Probably only a handful, or less, made. Not
   intended for sale or distribution. Near-mint price range: $1,500 to $2,500.
   Side 1: *That's All Right; I Love You Because (Unreleased Version); Heartbreak Hotel; Don't Be*
   Cruel; Love Me (Unreleased Live Version); Trying to Get to You (Unreleased Live
   Version).
   Side 2: *Love Me Tender; (There'll Be) Peace in the Valley (For Me); (Now and Then There's) A*
   Fool Such As I; Tonight's All Right for Love; Are You Lonesome Tonight (Unreleased Live
   Version); Can't Help Falling in Love.

☐ 10. Legendary Performer (Volume 1) ● Elvis Presley (RCA
   Victor CPL1-0341).. 1978 $2,500
   Monaural LP. Picture disc, with artwork from *Elvis Presley* (LPM-1254). Side 2 is blank.
   Experimental pressing. Probably only a handful, or less, made. Not intended for sale or
   distribution. Near-mint price range: $1,500 to $2,500.
   Side 1: *That's All Right; I Love You Because (Unreleased Version); Heartbreak Hotel; Don't Be*
   Cruel; Love Me (Unreleased Live Version); Trying to Get to You (Unreleased Live
   Version).
   Side 2: *Love Me Tender; (There'll Be) Peace in the Valley (For Me); (Now and Then There's) A*
   Fool Such As I; Tonight's All Right for Love; Are You Lonesome Tonight (Unreleased Live
   Version); Can't Help Falling in Love.

☐ 11. Legendary Performer (Volume 1) ● Elvis Presley (RCA
   Victor CPL1-0341).. 1978 $2,500
   Monaural LP. Picture disc, with artwork from *Elvis* (LPM-1382). Side 2 is blank. Experimental
   pressing. Probably only a handful, or less, made. Not intended for sale or distribution. Near-
   mint price range: $1,500 to $2,500.
   Side 1: *That's All Right; I Love You Because (Unreleased Version); Heartbreak Hotel; Don't Be*
   Cruel; Love Me (Unreleased Live Version); Trying to Get to You (Unreleased Live
   Version).
   Side 2: *Love Me Tender; (There'll Be) Peace in the Valley (For Me); (Now and Then There's) A*
   Fool Such As I; Tonight's All Right for Love; Are You Lonesome Tonight (Unreleased Live
   Version); Can't Help Falling in Love.

☐ 12. Legendary Performer (Volume 1) ● Elvis Presley (RCA
   Victor CPL1-0341).. 1978 $2,500
   Monaural LP. Picture disc, with artwork from *Elvis Now* (LSP-4671). Side 2 is blank.
   Experimental pressing. Probably only a handful, or less, made. Not intended for sale or
   distribution. Near-mint price range: $1,500 to $2,500.
   Side 1: *That's All Right; I Love You Because (Unreleased Version); Heartbreak Hotel; Don't Be*
   Cruel; Love Me (Unreleased Live Version); Trying to Get to You (Unreleased Live
   Version).
   Side 2: *Love Me Tender; (There'll Be) Peace in the Valley (For Me); (Now and Then There's) A*
   Fool Such As I; Tonight's All Right for Love; Are You Lonesome Tonight (Unreleased Live
   Version); Can't Help Falling in Love.

☐ 13. Legendary Performer (Volume 1) • Elvis Presley (RCA
Victor CPL1-0341) 1978 $2,500
Monaural LP. Picture disc, with artwork from *Elvis' Golden Records, Vol. 3* (LSP-2765). Side
2 is blank. Experimental pressing. Probably only a handful, or less, made. Not intended for
sale or distribution. Near-mint price range: $1,500 to $2,500.
> Side 1: *That's All Right; I Love You Because (Unreleased Version); Heartbreak Hotel; Don't Be
> Cruel; Love Me (Unreleased Live Version); Trying to Get to You (Unreleased Live
> Version).*
>
> Side 2: *Love Me Tender; (There'll Be) Peace in the Valley (For Me); (Now and Then There's) A
> Fool Such As I; Tonight's All Right for Love; Are You Lonesome Tonight (Unreleased Live
> Version); Can't Help Falling in Love.*

☐ 14. Legendary Performer (Volume 1) • Elvis Presley (RCA
Victor CPL1-0341) 1978 $2,500
Monaural LP. Picture disc, with artwork from *On Stage: February 1970* on one side; *Elvis'
Golden Records* on reverse. Experimental pressing. Probably only a handful, or less, made.
Not intended for sale or distribution. Near-mint price range: $1,500 to $2,500.
> Side 1: *That's All Right; I Love You Because (Unreleased Version); Heartbreak Hotel; Don't Be
> Cruel; Love Me (Unreleased Live Version); Trying to Get to You (Unreleased Live
> Version).*
>
> Side 2: *Love Me Tender; (There'll Be) Peace in the Valley (For Me); (Now and Then There's) A
> Fool Such As I; Tonight's All Right for Love; Are You Lonesome Tonight (Unreleased Live
> Version); Can't Help Falling in Love.*

☐ 15. Legendary Performer (Volume 1) • Elvis Presley (RCA
Victor CPL1-0341) 1978 $2,500
Monaural LP. Picture disc, with artwork from *Welcome to My World* (APL1-2274).
Experimental pressing. Side 2 is blank. Probably only a handful, or less, made. Not intended
for sale or distribution. Near-mint price range: $1,500 to $2,500.
> Side 1: *That's All Right; I Love You Because (Unreleased Version); Heartbreak Hotel; Don't Be
> Cruel; Love Me (Unreleased Live Version); Trying to Get to You (Unreleased Live
> Version).*
>
> Side 2: *Love Me Tender; (There'll Be) Peace in the Valley (For Me); (Now and Then There's) A
> Fool Such As I; Tonight's All Right for Love; Are You Lonesome Tonight (Unreleased Live
> Version); Can't Help Falling in Love.*

☐ 16. Legendary Performer (Volume 1) • Elvis Presley (RCA
Victor CPL1-0341) 1978 $2,500
Monaural LP. Clear vinyl. Experimental pressing. Probably only a handful, or less, made. Not
intended for sale or distribution. Near-mint price range: $1,500 to $2,500.
> Side 1: *That's All Right; I Love You Because (Unreleased Version); Heartbreak Hotel; Don't Be
> Cruel; Love Me (Unreleased Live Version); Trying to Get to You (Unreleased Live
> Version).*
>
> Side 2: *Love Me Tender; (There'll Be) Peace in the Valley (For Me); (Now and Then There's) A
> Fool Such As I; Tonight's All Right for Love; Are You Lonesome Tonight (Unreleased Live
> Version); Can't Help Falling in Love.*

☐ 17. Moody Blue • Elvis Presley (RCA Victor AFL 1-2428) 1977 $2,000
Stereo LP. Colored vinyl – any color other than blue or black. Includes, but not limited to:
white, red, green, yellow, gold, as well as combinations of colors. All were experimental
pressings. None were intended for sale or distribution. Near-mint price range: $1,800 to
$2,000.
> Side A: *Unchained Melody; If You Love Me (Let Me Know); Little Darlin'; He'll Have to Go; Let Me
> Be There.*
>
> Side B: *Way Down; Pledging My Love; Moody Blue; She Thinks I Still Care; It's Easy for You.*

☐ 18. Big Hits, High Tide & Green Grass • Rolling Stones
(London 9134) 1969 $1,500
📷 Stereo LP. Picture disc. Some have photo of the group Ten Years After on one side. All
have music from *Thru the Past Darkly*. Experimental pressing. Near-mint price range:
$1,000 to $1,500.
Members: Mick Jagger; Keith Richards; Bill Wyman; Brian Jones.

☐ 19. Kissin' Cousins • Elvis Presley (RCA Victor LSP-2894)...................... 1977 **$1,500**
Stereo LP. Black label, dog near top. Blue vinyl. Experimental pressing only, not intended for sale or distribution. Near-mint price range: $1,000 to $1,500.
Side 1: *Kissin' Cousins (No. 2); Smokey Mountain Boy; There's Gold in the Mountains; One Boy, Two Little Girls; Catchin' on Fast; Tender Feeling.*
Side 2: *Anyone (Could Fall in Love with You); Barefoot Ballad; Once Is Enough; Kissin' Cousins; Echoes of Love; (It's a) Long Lonely Highway.*

☐ 20. Elvis As Recorded at Madison Square Garden • Elvis Presley (RCA Victor
AFL1-4776)... 1978 **$1,500**
Stereo LP. Clear vinyl. Experimental pressing. Probably only a handful, or less, made. Not intended for sale or distribution. Near-mint price range: $1,000 to $1,500.
Side 1: *Introduction: Also Sprach Zarathustra; That's All Right; Proud Mary; Never Been to Spain; You Don't Have to Say You Love Me; You've Lost That Lovin' Feelin'; Polk Salad Annie; Love Me; All Shook Up; Heartbreak Hotel; Medley:Teddy Bear/Don't Be Cruel; Love Me Tender.*
Side 2: *The Impossible Dream; Introductions by Elvis; Hound Dog; Suspicious Minds; For the Good Times; American Trilogy; Funny How Time Slips Away; I Can't Stop Loving You; Can't Help Falling in Love; Closing Riff.*

☐ 21. Jurassic Park • Various Artists (MCA/BMG) 1993 **$1,200**
Stereo LP. Soundtrack. Picture disc. No selection number used. Made in very small quantity for in-house use. Near-mint price range: $800 to $1,200.

☐ 22. Let's Be Friends • Elvis Presley (Pickwick/Camden CAS-2408)......... 1977 **$1,000**
Stereo LP. Gold vinyl. Experimental pressing, not intended for sale of distribution. Near-mint price range: $750 to $1,000.
Side 1: *Stay Away, Joe; If I'm a Fool (For Loving You); Let's Be Friends. Let's Forget About the Stars; Mama.*
Side 2: *I'll Be There (If You Ever Want Me); Almost; Change of Habit; Have a Happy.*

☐ 23. Let's Be Friends • Elvis Presley (Pickwick/Camden CAS-2408)......... 1977 **$1,000**
Stereo LP. Multi-color, or *splash* vinyl. Experimental pressing, not intended for sale of distribution. Near-mint price range: $750 to $1,000.
Side 1: *Stay Away, Joe; If I'm a Fool (For Loving You); Let's Be Friends. Let's Forget About the Stars; Mama.*
Side 2: *I'll Be There (If You Ever Want Me); Almost; Change of Habit; Have a Happy.*

☐ 24. Moody Blue • Elvis Presley (RCA Victor AFL 1-2428)....................... 1977 **$1,000**
📷 Stereo LP. Picture disc. Includes discs with the following art imbedded: 1. Collage of photos of the Outlaws Band. 2. Album art for an Alice Cooper LP. 3. Collage of assorted band members. 4. Picture of Joan Baez on one side; Rhythm Aces on reverse. All were experimental or sample pressings of some sort. None of these were intended for sale or distribution. Near-mint price range: $750 to $1,000.
Side A: *Unchained Melody; If You Love Me (Let Me Know); Little Darlin'; He'll Have to Go; Let Me Be There.*
Side B: *Way Down; Pledging My Love; Moody Blue; She Thinks I Still Care; It's Easy for You.*

☐ 25. Legendary Performer (Volume 3) • Elvis Presley (RCA
Victor CPL1-3078)... 1978 **$1,000**
Stereo LP. Picture disc. Pictures cassettes cover artwork from Neil Sedaka and John Denver tapes. Experimental pressing. Probably only a handful, or less, made. Not intended for sale or distribution. Near-mint price range: $750 to $1,000.
Side 1: *That's All Right; I Love You Because (Unreleased Version); Heartbreak Hotel; Don't Be Cruel; Love Me (Unreleased Live Version); Trying to Get to You (Unreleased Live Version).*
Side 2: *Love Me Tender; (There'll Be) Peace in the Valley (For Me); (Now and Then There's) A Fool Such As I; Tonight's All Right for Love; Are You Lonesome Tonight (Unreleased Live Version); Can't Help Falling in Love.*

☐ 26. Elvis As Recorded at Madison Square Garden • Elvis Presley (RCA Victor
AFL1-4776)... 1978   **$1,000**

Stereo LP. Picture disc. Pictures John Denver on one side; Joan Baez on reverse.
Experimental pressing. Probably only a handful, or less, made. Not intended for sale or
distribution. Near-mint price range: $750 to $1,000.

Side 1: *Introduction: Also Sprach Zarathustra; That's All Right; Proud Mary; Never Been to Spain;*
You Don't Have to Say You Love Me; You've Lost That Lovin' Feelin'; Polk Salad Annie;
Love Me; All Shook Up; Heartbreak Hotel; Medley:Teddy Bear/Don't Be Cruel; Love Me
Tender.

Side 2: *The Impossible Dream; Introductions by Elvis; Hound Dog; Suspicious Minds; For the*
Good Times; American Trilogy; Funny How Time Slips Away; I Can't Stop Loving You;
Can't Help Falling in Love; Closing Riff.

☐ 27. Elvis As Recorded at Madison Square Garden • Elvis Presley (RCA Victor
AFL1-4776)... 1978   **$1,000**

Stereo LP. Picture disc. Pictures cover artwork from a Barry Manilow album. Experimental
pressing. Probably only a handful, or less, made. Not intended for sale or distribution. Near-
mint price range: $750 to $1,000.

Side 1: *Introduction: Also Sprach Zarathustra; That's All Right; Proud Mary; Never Been to Spain;*
You Don't Have to Say You Love Me; You've Lost That Lovin' Feelin'; Polk Salad Annie;
Love Me; All Shook Up; Heartbreak Hotel; Medley:Teddy Bear/Don't Be Cruel; Love Me
Tender.

Side 2: *The Impossible Dream; Introductions by Elvis; Hound Dog; Suspicious Minds; For the*
Good Times; American Trilogy; Funny How Time Slips Away; I Can't Stop Loving You;
Can't Help Falling in Love; Closing Riff.

☐ 28. Blondes Have More Fun • Rod Stewart (RCA/Warner Bros. 3276).... 1979   **$1,000**

📷 Stereo LP. Picture disc. Pictures Rod Stewart and a woman on one side; Elvis Presley
(from NBC-TV Special) on reverse. Experimental pressing. Perhaps only one made. Not
intended for sale or distribution. Near-mint price range: $500 to $1,000.

E4

E28

E24

BUYERS & SELLERS DIRECTORY

The pages in every Official Price Guide Buyers-Sellers Directory are packed with personal and business ads, certain to appeal to anyone with an interest in music collecting – whether you're buying or selling.

When using the Directory to search for someone who may possibly be a buyer for your records, first please read "What to Expect When Selling Your Records to a Dealer," found in the Introduction.

The Buyers-Sellers Directory is an excellent and inexpensive way to locate those elusive discs you've been seeking for your collection. For over 22 years, the results of advertising in the Osborne books have proven to be tremendous. We are especially proud of our high rate of repeat advertisers, one that far surpasses industry standards.

Look the ads over carefully. You might just find the dealer or contact you've been wanting to assist you in building your collection. When responding, be sure to say you saw their ad in this publication.

You can advertise in the next *Official Price Guide to Records,* or any of the other books in our series. Simply contact our office and ask for complete details.

Osborne Enterprises
Box 255
Port Townsend WA 98368
Phone: (360) 385-1200 — Fax: (360) 385-6572
www.jerryosborne.com — e-mail: jpo@mail.com

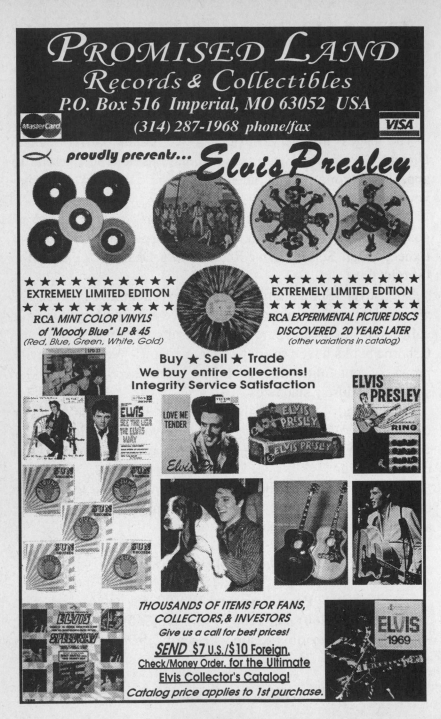
322

329

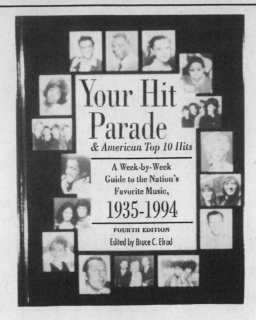

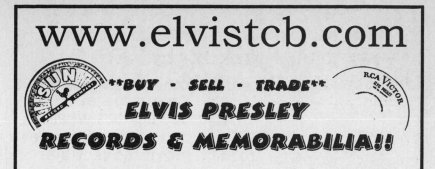

334

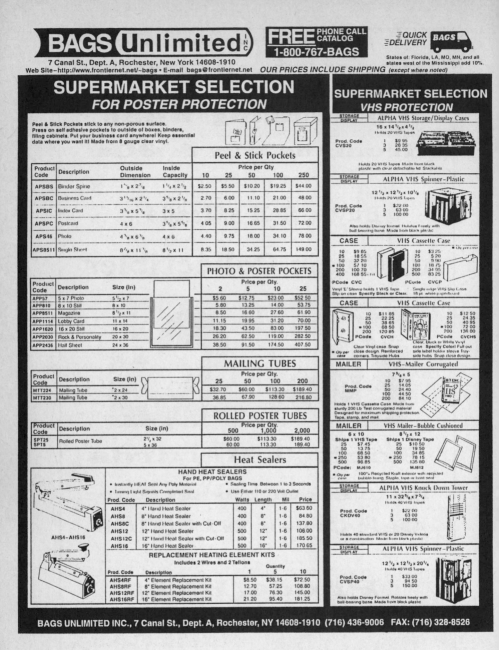

BAGS Unlimited INC

FREE PHONE CALL CATALOG
1-800-767-BAGS

QUICK DELIVERY

7 Canal St., Dept. A, Rochester, New York 14608-1910
Web Site–http://www.frontiernet.net/~bags • E-mail bags@frontiernet.net

States of: Florida, LA, MO, MN, and all states west of the Mississippi add 10%.

OUR PRICES INCLUDE SHIPPING (except where noted)

SUPERMARKET SELECTION
FOR POSTER PROTECTION

Peel & Stick Pockets stick to any non-porous surface. Press on self adhesive pockets to outside of boxes, binders, filing cabinets. Put your business card anywhere! Keep essential data where you want it! Made from 8 gauge clear vinyl.

Peel & Stick Pockets

Product Code	Description	Outside Dimension	Inside Capacity	Price per Qty 10	25	50	100	250
APSBS	Binder Spine	1 5/8 x 2 7/8	1 1/4 x 2 1/2	$2.50	$5.50	$10.20	$19.25	$44.00
APSBC	Business Card	3 11/16 x 2 1/4	3 5/8 x 2 1/8	2.70	6.00	11.10	21.00	48.00
APSIC	Index Card	3 3/8 x 5 3/8	3 x 5	3.70	8.25	15.25	28.85	66.00
APSPC	Postcard	4 x 6	3 5/8 x 5 5/8	4.05	9.00	16.65	31.50	72.00
APS46	Photo	4 3/8 x 6 3/8	4 x 6	4.40	9.75	18.00	34.10	78.00
APS8511	Single Sheet	8 7/8 x 11 3/8	8 1/2 x 11	8.35	18.50	34.25	64.75	149.00

PHOTO & POSTER POCKETS

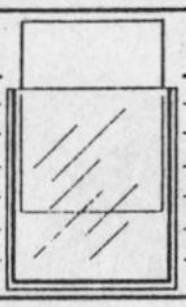

Product Code	Description	Size (in)	Price per Qty. 2	5	10	25
APP57	5 x 7 Photo	5 1/2 x 7	$5.60	$12.75	$23.00	$52.50
APP810	8 x 10 Still	8 x 10	5.80	13.25	14.00	53.75
APP8511	Magazine	8 1/2 x 11	8.50	16.60	27.60	61.90
APP1114	Lobby Card	11 x 14	11.15	19.95	31.20	70.00
APP1620	16 x 20 Still	16 x 20	18.30	43.50	83.00	197.50
APP2030	Rock & Personality	20 x 30	26.20	62.50	119.00	282.50
APP2436	Half Sheet	24 x 36	38.50	91.50	174.50	407.50

MAILING TUBES

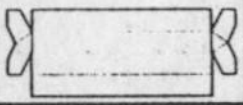

Product Code	Description	Size (in)	Price per Qty. 25	50	100	200
MTT224	Mailing Tube	*2 x 24	$32.70	$60.00	$113.30	$189.40
MTT230	Mailing Tube	*2 x 30	36.85	67.90	128.60	216.80

ROLLED POSTER TUBES

Product Code	Description	Size (in)	Price per Qty. 500	1,000	2,000
SPT25	Rolled Poster Tube	2 1/2 x 32	$60.00	$113.30	$189.40
SPT5		5 x 36	60.00	113.30	189.40

Heat Sealers

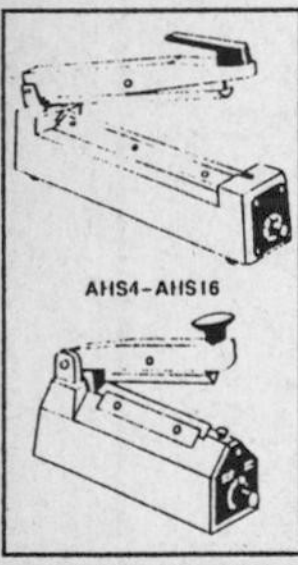
AHS4–AHS16

HAND HEAT SEALERS
For PE, PP/POLY BAGS

- Instantly HEAT Seal Any Poly Material
- Timing Light Signals Completed Seal
- Sealing Time Between 1 to 3 Seconds
- Use Either 110 or 220 Volt Outlet

Prod. Code	Description	Watts	Length	Mil	Price
AHS4	4" Hand Heat Sealer	400	4"	1-6	$63.60
AHS8	8" Hand Heat Sealer	400	8"	1-6	84.80
AHS8C	8" Hand Heat Sealer with Cut-Off	400	8"	1-6	137.80
AHS12	12" Hand Heat Sealer	500	12"	1-6	106.00
AHS12C	12" Hand Heat Sealer with Cut-Off	500	12"	1-6	185.50
AHS16	16" Hand Heat Sealer	500	16"	1-6	170.65

REPLACEMENT HEATING ELEMENT KITS
Includes 2 Wires and 2 Teflons

Prod. Code	Description	Quantity 1	5	10
AHS4RF	4" Element Replacement Kit	$8.50	$38.15	$72.50
AHS8RF	8" Element Replacement Kit	12.70	57.25	108.80
AHS12RF	12" Element Replacement Kit	17.00	76.30	145.00
AHS16RF	16" Element Replacement Kit	21.20	95.40	181.25

SUPERMARKET SELECTION
VHS PROTECTION

STORAGE / DISPLAY — ALPHA VHS Storage/Display Cases

16 x 14 1/2 x 4 1/2
Holds 20 VHS Tapes

Prod. Code	Qty	Price
CVS20	1	$9.95
	3	28.35
	5	45.00

Holds 20 VHS Tapes. Made from black plastic with clear detachable lid. Stackable.

STORAGE / DISPLAY — ALPHA VHS Spinner–Plastic

12 1/2 x 12 1/2 x 10 1/8
Holds 20 VHS Tapes

Prod. Code	Qty	Price
CVSP20	1	$22.00
	3	63.00
	5	100.00

Also holds Disney format. Rotates freely with ball bearing base. Made from black plastic.

CASE — VHS Cassette Case

Qty	PCode CVC
10	$9.85
25	18.55
50	32.20
■ 100	57.10
200	100.70
400	168.55

Vinyl 'E' Sleeve holds 1 VHS Tape. Slip on case. **Specify Black or Clear.**

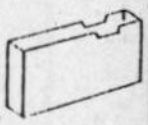

Qty	PCode CVCP
10	$3.25
25	5.20
50	9.90
100	18.75
200	34.95
500	83.25

Single edge VHS Slip Case. 18 pt. white paperboard.

■ Qty per case

CASE — VHS Cassette Case

Qty	PCode CVCH
10	$11.85
25	22.25
50	38.65
■ 100	68.50
200	120.85

Clear Vinyl case. Snap close design. Reinforced corners. Trayside Hubs.

Qty	PCode CVCHS
10	$12.50
25	24.35
50	40.95
■ 100	72.00
200	136.00

Clear, Black or White Vinyl case. **Specify Color!** Full out side label holder sleeve. Tray-side hubs. Snap close design.

■ *Qty per case*

MAILER — VHS–Mailer Corrugated

7 5/8 x 5

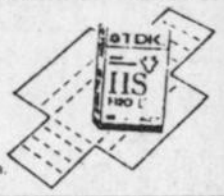

Prod. Code	Qty	Price
MMP	10	$7.95
	25	14.05
	50	24.40
	100	44.50
	200	84.10

Holds 1 VHS Cassette Case. Made from sturdy 200 Lb Test corrugated material. Designed for maximum shipping protection. Tape, stamp, and mail.

MAILER — VHS Mailer–Bubble Cushioned

6 x 10 Ships 1 VHS Tape		8 1/2 x 12 Ships 1 Disney Tape	
25	$7.45	25	$10.50
50	13.75	50	19.50
100	68.50	100	34.85
■ 250	53.80	■ 250	78.15
500	96.85	500	135.80
PCode:	MJ610		MJ812

■ *Qty per case*

100% Recycled Kraft exterior with recycled bubble lining. Staple, tape or heat seal.

STORAGE / DISPLAY — ALPHA VHS Knock Down Tower

11 x 32 5/8 x 7 3/4
Holds 40 VHS Tapes

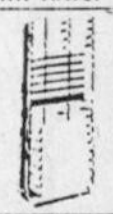

Prod. Code	Qty	Price
CKDV40	1	$22.00
	3	63.00
	5	100.00

Holds 40 standard VHS or 20 Disney Videos or a combination. Made from black plastic.

STORAGE / DISPLAY — ALPHA VHS Spinner–Plastic

12 1/2 x 12 1/2 x 20 1/4
Holds 40 VHS Tapes

Prod. Code	Qty	Price
CVSP40	1	$33.00
	3	94.50
	5	150.00

Also holds Disney Format. Rotates freely with ball-bearing base. Made from black plastic.

BAGS UNLIMITED INC., 7 Canal St., Dept. A, Rochester, NY 14608-1910 (716) 436-9006 FAX: (716) 328-8526

D & J
RECORDS

212 E. Main St.
Carnegie, PA. 15106
(10 Minutes From Pittsburgh)

OVER 1 MILLION 45'S IN STOCK

Music From the 40's To the 90's
On 45's-LP's-CD's & Cassettes
35 Years In The Music Business
We Buy Collections

412-279-8888

Fax 412-279-5538

The NIGHT SHADOWS

To serious record collectors, The Night Shadows were the grand patriarchs of garage bands. Through their music and appearance, the group became a microcosm of contemporary culture from the innocent times of late 1950's through the social, political and sexual revolution of the 1960's. Volume 1 (1959-1964) features their earliest recordings and includes the ribald classics "The Garbage Man" and "The Hot Dog Man" plus a 16-pg booklet loaded with info and pics.

Volume 2 chronicles the years (1964-1967) that the group hit the charts with Little Phil as their front man. Includes two ribald tunes too risqué for airplay, their radio hits and several unreleased tracks that were recently discovered. Includes a 20-pg booklet loaded with info & pics. (Final volume of the trilogy, Volume 3: The Psychedelic Era 1967-1969, will be released in Spring 1998)   www.hottrax.com

Volume 1: The Rhythm & Blues Period 1959-1964
$11.95 + 3.00 S&H

Volume 2: The Little Phil Era 1964-1967
$11.95 + 3.00 S&H

To order: Send $11.95 for each CD+ $3.00 S&H for each shipment to:
Hottrax Records, 1957 Kilburn Drive, N.E., Atlanta, GA 30324

PRO  AUDIO/VIDEO

TAPES • SUPPLIES • SERVICE

BASF 5 Series Normal Bias		BASF 8 Series Super Chrome	
Item #	Price	Item #	Price
5C-10	0.59	8C-10	0.85
5C-15	0.60	8C-15	0.86
5C-20	0.62	8C-20	0.91
5C-25	0.63	8C-25	0.95
5C-30	0.65	8C-30	0.99
5C-40	0.68	8C-40	1.04
5C-45	0.71	8C-45	1.10
5C-60	0.77	8C-60	1.18
5C-75	0.85	8C-75	1.30
5C-90	0.95	8C-90	1.42
5C-105	1.03	8C-100	1.52
5C-122	1.28	We sell this premium tape in Shape™ Mark X shells only.	

CASSETTE DISCOUNT
50-99 10% • 100-499 12% • 500+ 15%
Cases and labels sold separately.

TO PLACE YOUR ORDER, CALL (414) 425-6967

Serving Home, Studio, Karaoke, and Broadcast with World Class BASF Recording Tape and Supplies.

524 Raynor Ave. Franksville, WI 53126-9764

http://www.nconnect.net/~polkasnd/proaudio

339

ABOUT THE AUTHOR

An avid collector of records for nearly 40 years, Jerry Osborne has also worked full-time as an author of record price guides and reference books since 1975.

In the 23 years since work began on his first *Record Collector's Price Guide*, the number of Jerry's published works on music now includes 62 books and 152 periodicals. As busy as ever, he continues to produce several titles per year.

Among other music-related ventures, Jerry has, since 1986, written the popular, weekly newspaper feature, *Mr. Music*. This entertaining and informative nationally syndicated column answers readers' questions about music and records.

The rest of Osborne's past is also saturated with music. Upon graduation from high school, he began a 14-year career in radio and television (1962–1976) as an announcer, or dee jay.

Over the years, Jerry founded and published three collectors news and marketplace magazines: *Record Digest* and *Music World* and the still-popular *DISCoveries*. In the mid-'80s, he began publication of *The Osborne Report*, a monthly newsletter covering new releases.

Osborne's influence and involvement in record collecting has been chronicled in virtually every major magazine and newspaper in the country: *Reader's Digest, The Wall Street Journal, USA Today, People Magazine, Esquire, Oui, National Enquirer, Money, Changing Times, Photoplay, High Fidelity, Billboard, Cash Box, Music City News, Collectibles, Kiplinger's, Woman's Day* and *Rolling Stone* —just to name a few.

Jerry has been a frequent guest on many major radio and TV talk shows, discussing the record collecting hobby. Among these are: "Good Morning America," the "Today Show" "The Nashville Network," "Backstage Live" and far too many local and regional shows to enumerate.

He worked in the mid-'80s as a technical advisor and consultant for the critically acclaimed ABC-TV nostalgic news-magazine program, "Our World," and has served as a consultant for HBO, and CBS-TV's "West 57th Street."

Clearly, no one person has been more responsible—directly or indirectly—for the amazing growth of the music collecting hobby.

THIS BOOK IS #1 ON THE CHARTS!

Now that vinyl records are no longer being produced, record collecting is hotter than ever, and *The Official Price Guide to Records*, written by *the* expert, Jerry Osborne, is a hit!

• Lists every charted hit from 1926 to the superstars of today, including jazz, country, rhythm and blues, and soul

• Clearly indexed by artist and group for fast, easy access

• Invaluable tips on buying, selling, grading, and caring for your collectible records

• Fully illustrated, with a solid-gold, eight-page color insert

HOUSE OF COLLECTIBLES
Serving Collectors for More Than Thirty-Five Years

ORDER FORM

☐ YES. Please send me *The Official Price Guide to Records*, 0-676-60051-4. My price direct from the publisher is just $24.00 plus $3.00 shipping and handling. If not satisfied, I may return this book at the end of 30 days for a prompt refund.

Name_____

Address_____

City_____State_____ Zip Code_____

☐ Check enclosed for $_____* (payable to House of Collectibles).
☐ Charge my
    ☐ VISA   ☐ MasterCard   ☐ American Express   ☐ Discover

_____ _____ _____
   Credit Card Number   *Expiration Date*   *Signature (required)*

* Please add applicable sales tax.

HOUSE OF COLLECTIBLES
P.O. Box 3580 • Wallingford, CT 06494

Allow at least 4 weeks for delivery   Dept. E51-001

HOUSE OF COLLECTIBLES

THE OFFICIAL® IDENTIFICATION AND PRICE GUIDES TO

ACTION FIGURES
1st edition
Stuart W. Wells III & Jim Main
676-60080-8 $19.95

AMERICAN INDIAN ARROW-
HEADS
1st edition
John L. Stivers
876-37913-7 $17.50

ANTIQUE AND MODERN
FIREARMS
8th edition
Robert H. Balderson
876-37907-2 $17.00

ANTIQUE AND MODERN
TEDDY BEARS
1st edition
Kim Brewer & Carol-Lynn
Rossel Waugh
876-37792-4 $12.00

ANTIQUE CLOCKS
3rd edition
876-37513-1 $12.00

ANTIQUE JEWELRY (ID)
6th edition
Arthur Guy Kaplan
876-37759-2 $21.00

ANTIQUES AND COL-
LECTIBLES
15th edition
Eric Alberta & Art Maier
876-37960-9 $15.00

ARTIFACTS OF ANCIENT
CIVILIZATIONS
1st edition
Alex G. Malloy
676-60079-4 $19.95

ARTS AND CRAFTS
The Early Modernist
Movement in American
Decorative Arts, 1894–
1923 (ID) 2nd edition
Bruce Johnson
876-37879-3 $12.95

AUTOMOBILIA
1st edition
David K. Bausch
676-60030-1 $19.95

THE BEATLES
Records and Memorabilia
1st edition
Perry Cox & Joe Lindsay,
with an
introduction by Jerry Osborne
876-37940-4 $15.00

BEER CANS
5th Edition
Bill Mugrage
876-37873-4 $12.50

BOTTLES
12th edition
Jim Megura
676-60009-3 $17.00

CIVIL WAR COLLECTIBLES
1st edition
Richard Friz
876-37951-X $17.00

COLLECTIBLE TOYS (ID),
5th edition
Richard Friz
876-37803-3 $15.00

COLLECTOR CARS
8th edition
Robert H. Balderson
676-60024-7 $17.00

COLLECTOR HANDGUNS
5th edition
Robert H. Balderson
676-60038-7 $17.00

COLLECTOR KNIVES
11th edition
C. Houston Price
876-37973-0 $17.00

COLLECTOR PLATES
6th edition
Rinker Enterprises
876-37968-4 $17.00

COMPACT DISCS
1st edition
Jerry Osborne
876-37923-4 $15.00

COUNTRY MUSIC RECORDS
1st edition
Jerry Osborne
676-60004-2 $15.00

DINNERWARE OF THE 20TH
CENTURY: THE TOP 500
PATTERNS
1st edition
Harry L. Rinker
676-60085-9 $29.95

ELVIS PRESLEY RECORDS
AND
MEMORABILIA
1st edition
Jerry Osborne
676-37939-0 $14.00

FINE ART
2nd edition
Rosemary and Michael
McKittrick
876-37909-9 $20.00

FRANK SINATRA RECORDS
AND CDs
1st edition
Vito R. Marino and Anthony
C. Furfero
876-37903-X $12.00

GLASSWARE
1st edition
Mark Pickvet
876-37953-6 $15.00

HARRY L. RINKER COL-
LECTIBLES
1st edition
Harry L. Rinker
676-60106-5 $18.95

MOVIE/TV SOUNDTRACKS
AND ORIGINAL CAST
ALBUMS
2nd edition
Jerry Osborne
676-60044-1 $15.00

OLD BOOKS
2nd edition
Marie Tedford and
Pat Goudey
676-60041-7 $17.00

ORIENTAL RUGS
2nd edition
Joyce C. Ware
676-60023-9 $15.00

POSTCARDS (ID)
1st edition
Diane Allmen
876-37802-5 $9.95

POTTERY AND PORCELAIN
8th edition
Harvey Duke
876-37893-9 $15.00

RECORDS
12th edition
Jerry Osborne
676-60051-4 $24.00

ROCK AND ROLL—MAGA-
ZINES, POSTERS, AND
MEMORABILIA (ID), 1st edi-
tion
David K. Henkel
876-37851-3 $12.50

SILVERWARE OF THE 20TH
CENTURY: THE TOP 250
PATTERNS
1st edition
Harry L. Rinker
676-60086-7 $24.95

STAR TREK COLLECTIBLES
4th edition
Sue Cornwell & Mike Kott
876-37994-3 $19.95

STAR WARS COLLECTIBLES
4th edition
Sue Cornwell & Mike Kott
876-37995-1 $19.95

STEMWARE OF THE 20TH
CENTURY: THE TOP 200
PATTERNS
1st edition
Harry L. Rinker
676-60084-0 $24.95

WATCHES
10th edition
Cooksey Shugart &
Tom Engle
876-37808-4 $18.00

R.L. WILSON GUN
COLLECTING
1st edition
R.L. Wilson
676-60122-7 $19.95

BECKETT GREAT SPORTS HEROES

TROY AIKMAN
676-60035-2
$15.00

WAYNE GRETZKY
676-60032-8
$15.00

ANFERNEE HARDAWAY
676-60033-6
$15.00

MICHAEL JORDAN
876-37878-X
$15.00

DAN MARINO
676-60034-4
$15.00

JOE MONTANA
876-37981-1
$15.00

SHAQUILLE O'NEAL
876-37980-3
$15.00

FRANK THOMAS
676-60029-8
$15.00

More listings and order form on following page